Dorchester Remembers the Great War

Could their mother have clasped their hands,
The sons she knew so well.
Or kissed their brow when death was near
And whispered 'my sons farewell'.
I seem to see their dear sweet faces
Through a mist of anxious tears.
But a mother's part is a broken heart
And a burden of lonely tears.
We miss you, for we loved you,
As memories we recall.
The parting with our dear ones
Was the saddest day of all.

Epitaph to John Hare and Edmund Lamb
by their mother Lavinia Hare
Dorset County Chronicle
11 Sept 1919

Drawing by K. Bartolmay, a German prisoner, showing prisoners relaxing at the POW camp, Poundbury. Entitled 'Evening from the sparrow's view'. (Source: Dorset History Centre.)

Dorchester Remembers the Great War

Brian Bates

Roving
Press

© 2012 Brian Bates

Published by Roving Press Ltd
4 Southover Cottages, Frampton, Dorset, DT2 9NQ, UK
Tel: +44 (0)1300 321531
www.rovingpress.co.uk

First published 2012 by Roving Press Ltd

ISBN: 978-1-906651-169

British Library Cataloguing in Publication Data
A catalogue record for this book is available from the British Library

Cover design by Tim Musk
All photos by the author unless stated otherwise.

Front cover photo: *Dorchester recruits to Kitchener's New Army being escorted to the Depot Barracks by pipers of the Scottish Fusiliers in August 1914. (From the private collection of Mr S. Poulter.)*
Back cover photos: (Top) *Colliton House in use as a VAD hospital. (Source: The Keep Military Museum.)* (Bottom right) *'The Keep', Dorchester, entrance to the Depot Barracks. (Source: The Keep Military Museum.)*

Set in 11/13 pt by Beamreach Printing (www.beamreachuk.co.uk)
Printed and bound by Beamreach Printing (www.beamreachuk.co.uk)

Contents

This book is dedicated to my wife Beth

Foreword

I was delighted to be asked to write the Foreword to this book. In the years I have known Brian, I have come to recognise him as an energetic and tenacious champion in the interests of Dorchester's military history. He has spent many years researching, and the picture he now paints is through his hard work, his talks and photos of servicemen and women, his interest in the names on the Cenotaph and the memorials around the town, looking at those who lost their lives in the Great War. I have visited the Cenotaph every year without fail on Armistice Day, and in 1965 there were only three wreaths laid; last year there were 37. One of my first speeches as councillor was about the proposed moving of the Cenotaph to The Keep, which I opposed. I wish Brian the best of luck with the book and am sure it will be a good read for many people.

Leslie Phillips, MBE

(Courtesy of the Dorset Echo.)

Note from the Publisher

Leslie came to Dorchester from the East End of London in 1936, when his father was employed to build the new county offices. He schooled in Dorchester, left school at 13 and became an apprentice blacksmith and farrier. He was called up for National Service on a three year engagement with the Household Cavalry, Royal Horse Guards, Knightsbridge, but returned to Dorchester intent on fulfilling his lifelong ambition of becoming Mayor of Casterbridge. He was elected Mayor no less than four times during his 46-year-long career in the council. In 2000 he retired as a farrier, and after his retirement as Mayor in 2011 was granted the Honorary Freedom of the Town.

Preface

On Remembrance Sunday 2005 I stood before Dorchester's main war memorial where just a few minutes previously several hundred people had gathered, with representatives of numerous organisations, civic dignitaries and clergy. Now the service was over, the prayers had been said, the wreaths laid and the Last Post played. The crowed had dispersed, except for two or three lingerers who, like me, were standing before the list of names of those who had died in the Great War. As my eyes passed down the list, noting the various Forces in which they had served, I wondered just who all these people were. Occasionally a surname was repeated, raising the question as to how they were related, if at all. What were the circumstances of their deaths? Were they killed in battle or did they die of illness? Where did they die? I recognised a few names that might have been members of well-known local families but by far the majority were not familiar to me. Then and there, I decided to find out more about them, and those on Dorchester's other memorials, for surely each person named must have a story to tell.

The usual avenues of WWI military and genealogical sources produced what I expected. The men and one woman named on Dorchester's memorials came from all walks of life and included every rank, from Colonel to Private. There were several familial relationships; brothers, fathers, sons, uncles, nephews and cousins. Local newspapers and books were a good source of material, and descendants of the families provided me with invaluable information and made available family treasures.

As the body of the work began to build the nature of the project took on new meaning for me. What started off as an objective collection of facts became a crusade to make their stories known. As one tragic narrative added to another, a picture of individual and collective sacrifice emerged. On many occasions I came across a death that for those concerned seemed particularly saddening, thinking that surely this was the worst case I would encounter, only to find another that dug deeper into the layers of personal despair for the families involved.

My hope is that those who spend time looking at Dorchester's Great War memorials on future Remembrance Sundays, having read this book may see more than just a name on a list and understand better the sacrifices that were made.

Brian Bates

Acknowledgements

I would like to thank the many people who helped me produce this book. My wife Doreen has not only had to put up with me droning on incessantly about 'my soldiers' but also advised me on the text and often prompted my memory. Thanks also to my daughters, Joanne for proofreading the work and Sophie for her encouragement. Karen Tynan kindly applied her analytical mind and solved many of the genealogical conundrums thrown up in my research and Keith Parsons has been very generous with his resources. Special thanks go to my grandson Jacob who helped me take some of the photographs. I am indebted to the staff of the Dorset History Centre, Dorset County Museum and the Keep Military Museum for their assistance with my research and allowing me to use photographs from their collections.

The stories contained in the book would not have been so rich in personal detail had it not been for a very special group of people. The descendants of many of those who appear on Dorchester's memorials have been generous with their time and provided personal photographs and memorabilia for the book. I am delighted to say that some have also become friends.

Julie and Tim of Roving Press not only are thoroughly professional but also have led me through the minefield of grammar and style needed to produce a published book. I do not hesitate in recommending them to any budding author.

Notes to Help the Reader

In telling nearly 300 different stories within the single context of the Great War I am aware that there is bound to be some repetition, which I have tried to keep to a minimum by cross-referencing where possible and using footnotes. For example, if three men were killed in the same battle I have only given details of the conflict in which they died in the first case and referred the reader back to this in the other two cases.

The casualties appear in chronological order, except where members of the same family are involved or where it better facilitates the story. To help put the individual stories into the wider context I have included, at the beginning of each year, a short summary of the main battles and operations.

Appendix 1 shows how the British Army was organised at the time, with special reference to the Dorsetshire Regiment. Some readers will find it useful to refer to this before embarking on the main body of the book, as it explains some of the military terms used. Appendix 2 gives the locations of former place names in Dorchester. Where a street or road is mentioned in the text without further qualification as to its whereabouts, the reader can assume that it is, or was, within the town. As for villages in the surrounding areas, I have indicated where they are in relation to Dorchester.

Abbreviations

2 Lt	Second Lieutenant	Lt-Col	Lieutenant Colonel
ASC	Army Service Corps	Lt-Cmdr	Lieutenant Commander
Bde	Brigade	Maj.	Major
BEF	British Expeditionary Force	Maj. Gen.	Major General
Btn	Battalion	MEF	Mesopotamian Expeditionary Force
Bty	Battery		
Capt.	Captain	MGC	Machine Gun Corps
CEF	Canadian Expeditionary Force	MM	Military Medal
C/Sgt	Colour Sergeant	MO	Medical Officer
Col	Colonel	NA	National Archives
CO	Commanding Officer	NCO	Non-Commissioned Officer
Coy	Company	OR	Other Ranks
Cpl	Corporal	OTC	Officer Training Corps
CQMS	Company Quartermaster Sergeant	Pte	Private
		QMS	Quartermaster Sergeant
CSM	Company Sergeant Major	RAMC	Royal Army Medical Corps
CWGC	Commonwealth War Graves Commission	RFA	Royal Field Artillery
		RFC	Royal Flying Corps
DCM	Distinguished Conduct Medal	RGA	Royal Garrison Artillery
DSO	Distinguished Service Order	Rgt	Regiment
DHC	Dorset History Centre	RHA	Royal Horse Artillery
Gen.	General	RMLI	Royal Marine Light Infantry
Gnr	Gunner	RNAS	Royal Naval Air Service
GWR	Great Western Railway	RSM	Regimental Sergeant Major
HE	High Explosive	SDGW	Soldiers Died in the Great War database
HMHS	His/Her Majesty's Hospital Ship		
		Sgt	Sergeant
IAOR	Indian Army Officer Reserve	SR	Service Record
L/Sgt	Lance Sergeant	S/Sgt	Staff Sergeant
LSWR	London and South Western Railway	TMB	Trench Mortar Battery
		VAD	Voluntary Aid Detachment
Lt	Lieutenant	WD	War Diary

Edwardian Dorchester

A visitor to the town of Dorchester at the dawn of the Edwardian era would have found a thriving community with an abundance of businesses and services typical of a county town. At the centre of an agricultural area, it was the needs of the farmer that regulated its heartbeat. Dorchester had been an important wool centre since the 16th century and still held sheep markets and wool sales, organised by local auctioneers Henry Duke and T. Ensor and Son. Market day was particularly busy, when the carriers brought merchandise on their carts from the surrounding farms and villages, impeded by sheep slowly making their way through country lanes to auction. Candlemas Fair, when traditionally each February agricultural workers entered the county town to find employment, was still held in the High Street.

Although predominantly an agricultural town, Dorchester did have its share of industry. Lott and Walne, iron founders, and Eddison's Steam Plough Works had embraced the technologies brought by the industrial revolution, but the demands for their products were largely driven by agriculture, the former producing ploughs, harrows and water pumps, the latter hiring out steam ploughs and traction engines and road rollers. It might be said that the town's largest employer, Eldridge, Pope & Co., also catered to the requirements of those who worked on the land and many others besides, by brewing beer at its brewery on Weymouth Avenue.

However, Dorchester's status as the county town did not depend on agriculture or commerce alone. It was also the centre for most of the county-wide judicial and administrative services. For centuries it had been the home of the Assize Courts and as a consequence also had the County Gaol. The Board of Guardians and the county medical services, including the County Hospital, were also located in the town, and when Dorset County Council was established under the 1889 Local Government Act, Dorchester naturally became its home.

When the railway arrived it brought tourists who were keen to see the world of Thomas Hardy's novels, something that Durnovarians were not slow to exploit. Visitors were particularly taken by the town's shops, including the ones that sold agricultural implements of every kind. With the mechanisation of agriculture and subsequent depression in farming came a national migration from the countryside to the towns, which was reflected in an increase in Dorchester's population during the last two decades of the 19th century. The 1881 census gave a population for the town of 7,576, which rose to 9,548 by 1901, an increase of approximately 25%. This compares with an increase of just over 5% in the next 20 years, up to 1921. The town's response to this influx of newcomers was to increase the housing stock. New terraces like South Walks' Terrace and Brownden Terrace sprung up and St Helen's Road and Duke's Avenue were among the new roads built. At the end of the century a major development was started on the western side of town with Victoria Park Estate.[1] In addition, fine villas and large houses were built in Cornwall Road and Queen's Avenue to house the better-off.

Socially, Dorchester was a microcosm of English society, where everyone knew their place. Top of the pack were families such as the Aclands, whilst Alfred Pope, Douglas

Cornhill, circa 1908.

Marrable and George Andrews [2] were typical of the more successful business and professional classes. Beneath them were owners of small enterprises, from shop owners to decorators – the emerging middle classes. One type of resident Dorchester had perhaps more so than many towns was that of retired military families, like the Chadwicks, Tweedies and Hoskins [3], who had settled in the town.

At the bottom of the social strata were the poor, many of them agricultural labourers working on farms surrounding the town. It has become a cliché in Dorchester and not one without foundation that the poorest folk lived in Mill Street, Fordington. Despite Rev. Henry Moule's [4] attempts to sweep away the slums of the area, they remained and people were still living in insanitary and overcrowded conditions up until the 1950s. As was often the case in such poor areas, informal social structures were strong. This was particularly so in Fordington which, not so long ago, had been a parish quite separate from Dorchester and still held on to its individuality. There are people alive today who remember the rival youth gangs of Fordington and Dorchester. Fordington even had its own mayor. The Swan Inn was a popular pub at the bottom of Mill Street and on occasions drunks leaving the pub fell into the nearby River Frome; thereafter they were elected 'Mayor of Fordington' and wore a chain of office until it passed to the next person to get a soaking. Communities like Mill Street came into their own during the War, with neighbours offering emotional and practical help.

With a population of over 9,000, Dorchester had a variety of shops and businesses. High East Street was the primary shopping thoroughfare, not South Street as is the case today. All manner of shops could be found there. Arthur Angell made and sold boots at no. 8 and Henry Bailey offered the latest men's fashions at no. 40. It was the home of the County Stores and where butchers Frederick Greening and T.R. Higgins hung meat and game outside their shops. To help residents of the newly built houses furnish their homes, curtains could be bought in Harry Gould's drapers at no. 13 and Hannah and Holland of 8 Cornhill offered fashionable furniture, While businesses like these catered for the basic comforts of life, others looked to the new opportunities for recreation. Tilley and Son at the

High East Street, circa 1905, showing Channon's, which made parts for gun carriages during the War and where Reg Dabinett worked. On the right is Wood's furnishers and undertakers, which officiated at many of the military funerals in the town. (From the private postcard collection of Michael Russell, OPC for Dorchester & Fordington. © Mr M. Russell FIPD.)

bottom of South Street catered for those participating in the popular pastime of cycling, offering lessons as part of the service. At the other end of town, with premises at 6 High East St, Edward Channon and Sons were building and selling another new innovation, the motor car, soon to take over from the horse and cart on Dorchester's streets.

The military influence

The Depot Barracks, home of the county regiment, and the adjacent Royal Artillery Barracks were located on the western side of Dorchester, just a few hundred yards from the town centre. Consequently, there were always soldiers to be seen in the streets. They attended services at Holy Trinity, the garrison church, frequented local pubs (the Old Ship Inn in High West Street was a favourite) and added to the economy of the town by using the local shops. Many a soldier fell for the charms of a local girl and married her, some with more haste than others. The sound of the Army was ever present, be it the bugle sounding reveille each morning or the clip-clop of horses' hooves as an artillery battery moved through the town. The sound of a military band was often heard, be it in the Borough Gardens on a Sunday afternoon, at a 'smoking concert' in the Corn Exchange or just marching through the streets.

Such a strong military presence begs the question were Dorchester boys more likely to join up when war came than others? Dorchester lads were certainly exposed to the Army at a very early age. Both the Boys' School in Colliton Street and the Grammar School in South Street had their own military corps, although to underline the difference in status between the two the latter only trained prospective officers, while lads at Colliton Street were destined to fill the lines of Other Ranks.[5] The Colliton Street corps had its own bugle band and a photograph shows some as young as 8 or 9 in military uniform,

Dorchester infantry barracks, home of the Dorsetshire Rgt. Out of picture on the right was the gymnasium, now part of the postal sorting office. The double-ended gable building with porch was the officers' quarters and the next single gable belonged to the house of the RSM. The low building in the right-hand corner was the stores. The long building facing the camera is the Little Keep. The building to the left in the corner was the Sergeant's Mess and the long building on the left, going out of picture, was the barrack block. (Source: Dorset County Museum.)

carrying imitation rifles. Opportunities for boys to get a taste of army discipline were not confined to school. In the days before television and radio, youth organisations like the Boys' Brigade and Church Lads' Brigade were popular and had religion and discipline as their cornerstones. The Boys' Brigade taught army drill and marched with their bands through the town in army-style uniforms, whilst the Church Lad's Brigade was organised on military lines, having diocesan regiments, battalions and companies.

Dorchester Boys' School military corps, 1915. (Source: Dorset County Museum.)

When it came to work there were lots of opportunities for school-leavers. Local shops were mainly staffed by male shop assistants who started their careers as errand boys, delivering goods around the town by hand cart or bicycle. With the Army always looking for new recruits, an errand boy's journey might well have been interrupted by someone like Sgt Winzar, one of the Dorset Regiment's recruiting officers, telling him that he was just the type of young fellow the Army needed and why not become a part-time Territorial soldier. Lots of local men like the Membury brothers and Joseph Green did just that. [6] The Territorial and Reserve Forces Act of 1907 transferred the functions of Volunteer and Yeomanry units to a new force, the Territorial Army. Men enlisted for a maximum of 4 years and, as well as drill in the local drill hall, were required to attend an annual camp. Should the need arise the force could be mobilised but the men could not be forced to serve abroad. However, when in 1914 they were asked to do so, over 70% agreed.

Dorset Volunteers marching down High West Street. (Source: The Keep Military Museum.)

A less tangible but no less powerful pressure on men to join the Forces was the spirit of the era. It was the age of the British Empire and with empire came patriotism and a feeling of invincibility. Dorchester folk had demonstrated their patriotism when their men returned from fighting in South Africa. They were feted and the town welcomed them by building two triumphal arches, one for the regular regiment and another for the local rifle volunteers. They were also honoured by being granted the Freedom of the Borough.

So, when the call to arms came in August 1914 many Dorchester young men were prepared. They had both the skills and inclination to fight. If we add to that the excitement of the hustle and bustle in town when War was declared and the fact that some boys had fathers or brothers already in the county regiment or friends from military families, then the pressure to enlist must have been great. Many did, and never returned.

Durnovarians welcome the Rifle Volunteers on their return from the Boer War by erecting a triumphal arch at the bottom of South Street. (Source: The Keep Military Museum.)

---

[1] Roads on the estate all had some connection with the Queen, several being named after her children. During the War there was a proposal to change the names of Coburg Road and Dagmar Road, as they had German connotations.

[2] See Percy Pope, Douglas Marrable and Charles Andrews.

[3] See Frederick Chadwick, Arthur Caruthers-Little and Charles Hoskins.

[4] Henry Moule (1801–1880), vicar of Fordington in 1829, fought for improved sanitary conditions, not just in Fordington but in towns and villages in general. He was also the inventor of the earth closet.

[5] Soldiers who were not officers.

[6] See William Membury and Thomas Green.

The War Comes to Dorchester

If the pages of the *County Chronicle*, published on 30 July 1914, less than a week before the declaration of war, are anything to go by the people of Dorchester were sleeping safely in their beds, with little indication that war was around the corner. It was business as usual. Much of the harvest had already been gathered and in celebration the County Hospital was holding its annual harvest festival. Mr Hawkins, gardener to Denzil Hughes-Onslow [1], had just taken second prize in the Dorchester and District Gardeners' Association sweet pea competition, unaware that within a year his employer would lay dead in France, a German bullet in his head. In the newspaper's advertising columns Mr Fred Dabinett, decorator and paper hanger, announced that he was now starting up his own business in the town and 'hoped by careful attention and good craftsmanship to merit public support' [2]. Wheeler's photographers, at the Van Dyok Studio, Weymouth, advertised its services with little inkling that the demand for its portraits was about to escalate, as enlisted men sat for their obligatory photograph in military uniform before going off to the Front. Fred Dabinett's two sons Bertie and Reginald were to have their photographs taken together in India while serving with the Dorsets, but only one of them would return home.

It was also that time of the year when the Grammar School held its prize-giving. On 27 July the headmaster stood up and gave his annual speech. He praised, in particular, two members of staff, Mr Gordon-Davies and Mr Palmer, for their work with the Officers' Training Corps and reiterated his view that the OTC had a high educational value in its influence on the general character, demeanour and methodological habits of the boys. He

On the right is Dorchester Grammar School adjoining Napper's Mite almshouse. Next to that is Thurman's ironmongers, where William Dean worked. (From the private postcard collection of Michael Russell, OPC for Dorchester & Fordington. © Mr M. Russell FIPD.)

was particularly pleased that it had received a good report following a recent inspection from an officer of the War Office. In July 1917 the headmaster once again gave his annual address but this time it had a different tone. In addition to the usual plaudits to scholars and staff it contained the roll of honour of 20 former pupils who had died in the War.

When the next issue of the *Chronicle* was published, on 6 August, 2 days after Britain entered the conflict, the Dorchester pages were dominated by war matters, signalling the whirlwind that was to radically affect all aspects of life in the county town. Six months later the *newspaper* was able to comment that, 'The War has changed our habits along with our mood. Instead of a round on the golf links, a spin with the motor cycling club, a trip to Bournemouth or Weymouth, afternoons are now devoted to sterner stuff, defence of the Motherland.'[3]

Being a garrison town meant that there was always something of a military flavour going on in Dorchester. On 6 July 1914 the men of the 3rd Dorsets assembled at the Depot Barracks before going to their annual training camp on Salisbury Plain, the Dorchester Coy commanded by Capt. H. Duke and Lt G. Symonds, both prominent men in the town. A couple of weeks later a meeting of the Territorial Association, held in Dorchester under the chairmanship of Lt-Col Mount Batten, was informed that the strength of the county force stood at 1,795, but no mention was made of the impending conflict.

The most immediate effect of the War came on the very first day. Hundreds of new recruits, as well as existing regular soldiers, could be seen making their way to and from the Depot Barracks, and 'Debonair and active recruiting sergeants, flaunting their alluring ribbons' [4] were abroad in the town, stopping any likely candidates for military service. The *Chronicle* described Dorchester as being like 'a leagured town in the bustle, excitement, and the many and varied uniforms seen in the throng, hurrying to and fro'.[5] Members

William Loveless (see page 70) working in the Soldiers' Home and Institute, North Square, Christmas 1909. (Source: Mrs P. Collins.)

of the Reserve of Officers hurried to the Depot to learn of their new duties and Reservists were reporting to the Barracks to be clothed and armed. One batch of five officers and 100 NCOs and men left by train from Dorchester West Station, on their way to Belfast to join the 1st Dorsets, while others had shorter journeys to training camps in the county or other parts of the country. The continual movement of troops in the town and the need to billet them continued throughout the War and, of course, brought with it its own problems and opportunities for the town's inhabitants.

Drunkenness has always been a particular problem for garrison towns and Dorchester was no exception. Now, with an even greater military presence, finding ways of keeping the soldiers sober and amused became a priority. The Soldiers' Home and Institute in North Square [6] had been opened in 1885 and provided an alternative to the public house, as a place where soldiers could relax. It had a coffee bar, reading room, library, bathrooms, and a recreation and smoking room. The soldiers' spiritual needs were met by gospel or temperance meetings, which were held nearly every night in the mission rooms. This type of facility was extended when, in 1916, the Dorchester Federation of the Church of England Temperance Society established a tea and games room in the Town Hall.

The temperance movement in Dorchester was very active, through organisations like the Temperance Society and the Band of Hope. They taught children like Leonard Thompson [7] about the virtues of being teetotal and the War provided the perfect opportunity for them to further their cause. Russia had banned the drinking of vodka and France the consumption of absinthe among their troops and although prohibition was not introduced here, pub opening hours were reduced. On the back of that, the licensed victuallers of Dorchester agreed not to sell alcohol to soldiers after 9 pm. Not that this act of patriotism prevented two Australians appearing before the local magistrates in December 1915 for being drunk, disorderly and incapable. Alcohol may also have contributed to an event that took place around the town pump in July 1915. A young preacher was holding forth when he was approached by two Canadian soldiers who suggested that he would look better in khaki. There ensued an excitable debate that attracted quite a crowd and had to be broken up by the local bobby. One very serious case that came before the Bench concerned a Lance Corporal of the Montgomeryshire Yeomanry and a Dorchester widow. They were accused of running a house of ill-repute at Courtney Villa, All Saints' Road, which in itself might not have raised too high an eyebrow in a military town. However, the case had a much darker side because the woman's 14-year-old daughter was living on the premises where prostitution was alleged to be taking place. The case was referred to the next assizes.

Considering that thousands of servicemen passed through the town in the four and a half years of the War, generally speaking there were no serious incidents. This was partly achieved by the town and military working together to keep the troops amused. Civil as well as military concerts were held regularly and Harry Pouncy gave regular magic lantern shows, often on the progress of the War. The Picturedrome cinema in Durngate Street was always popular. In August 1914, Mr Charles, the owner, was showing a number of comic pictures to packed houses, but the main feature was a film of the recent boxing contest between French boxer Georges Carpentier and the American Edward 'Gunboat' Smith, for the 'White Hope' heavyweight championship of the world. [8] In July 1915 customers were treated to a film depicting the life of a sailor in the Royal Naval Division.

One consequence of the War that was to change temporarily the face of the town and increase its population considerably appeared on 10 August, 1914. Viewed by a crowd of hundreds, a group of 18 Germans stepped from a train at Dorchester West railway station as prisoners of war. This contingent was shortly followed by a larger consignment a few days later, all of whom were accommodated in the vacated family accommodation block at the artillery barracks. These 'Teutonic folk,' [9] as the *Chronicle* called them, were met by the people of Dorchester with a mixture of curiosity, amusement and foreboding. The initial group were not military personnel but unfortunate merchant seamen who happened to be in British ports at the wrong time and civilians who had been interned. Further prisoners arrived at regular intervals throughout the War and soon the need for a purpose-built prison camp was recognised. Consequently, a wooden hutted camp was built at Poundbury, on the north-western edge of town, which at its peak in 1919 accommodated over 4,000 men, equal to two-fifths of Dorchester's population. The town authorities realised that in the prisoners they had a potential source of labour and soon Germans and Austrians could be seen sweeping the streets and maintaining the Walks. One prominent townsman was quick to spot an opportunity when he heard that one of the new residents was a landscape gardener and commandeered him to redesign his garden.

German prisoners being escorted from Dorchester South railway station.
(Source: Dorset County Museum.)

Some of the local girls were particularly curious about the new intake of males to the town, much to the disgust of one resident who felt compelled to write to the *Chronicle* to request 'the feather-brained daughters of Eve who congregate about the Dorchester barracks when the German prisoners are marching out for their daily walk to remember that they are Englishwomen'. [10] There was the occasional scare. For instance, one night, two shots rang out from the direction of the camp, signalling in people's minds an escape. It turned out that the reason for the firing was that the newly installed, state-of-the-art lighting which illuminated the prison area had failed and two of the sentries had given the appropriate response for such an event. There were a number of escapes from the camp, the most famous of which was that of Otto Kohn who hid in a match-box packing case measuring 3×2×2 ft. This was placed with the luggage of a number of older prisoners who were being repatriated to Hamburg, via Tilbury Docks, and it was there that Otto's luck ran out. Some stevedores, while loading the ship, rolled the case along the wharf and the packing broke. Out of the end of it popped the 6-ft-plus body of the German, who was promptly returned to Dorchester with the packing case.

The population of the town was increased further when, on 7 November 1914, a VAD Hospital was established at Colliton House, the home of Denzil Hughes-Onslow. [11] The commandant was a Miss Winifred Marsdon, daughter of the rector of Moreton, and Maj. Burrough-Cosens was the Medical Officer in Charge. Opening with just 18 beds, by April 1917 this had risen to 200, most of which were accommodated in marquees erected in Colliton Park. The largest single intake of wounded came on 1 May 1917, when 145 men were taken off the hospital train, some of whom had to be accommodated temporarily in the Freemasons' Hall in Prince's Street. Mr John Acland of Woolaston House also set up a Red Cross hospital in Durngate Street at the junction with Church Street, directly opposite his house. His wife became the matron.

It was not long before the patriotic folk of Dorchester were rallying to help the hospitals and all manner of other good causes. Motorists joined the Dorset Motor Volunteers and provided vehicles to convey the wounded from the railway stations to the hospitals, and numerous concerts and dances were organised to raise funds. But, the most tangible support came from gifts from individuals, the *Chronicle's* pages regularly listing the names of donors. In February 1915 Mrs Acland thanked members of the Dorset Poultry Fanciers Association for their donations of cash and acknowledged contributions from other local people, which included magazines from Mrs Lock of Fordington Dairy, butter from Mrs Kingman, fruit and cigarettes from Mrs Thomas, and crockery from Hannah and Holland. Meanwhile Mrs Methuen [12], whose son was a Lt-Cdr in the Royal Navy and who died of typhoid in 1918, was busy collecting mufflers and mittens for sailors.

The generosity of Durnovarians, displayed throughout the War, also included support to national appeals. In August 1918 four charity days were held in the town and at the beginning of the War, in response to an appeal from the Prince of Wales, the Mayor of Dorchester organised local collections towards the National Relief Fund [13], which had been set up to help families suffering financially because of the absence of their wage earner. Then there was the National Egg Collection, which did just what its title suggested. Communities were asked to collect eggs for despatch to France, where they were fed to

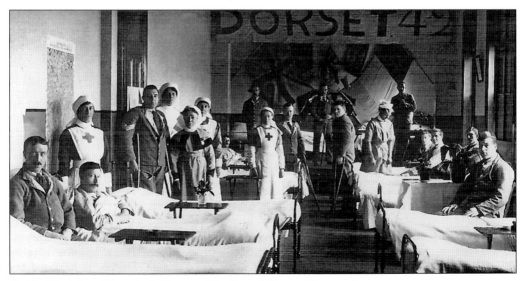

Inside Mr Acland's hospital. (Source: The Keep Military Museum.)

Patients and nurses standing outside bell tents that were extension wards to Colliton House (see back cover). Those shown appear to have been sited where the county library building now stands. (Source: The Keep Military Museum.)

the sick and wounded. The aim was to collect a million per week. Another call came from Mrs Winwood [14] and the Needlework Guild who, at the behest of Queen Mary, asked its members to provide garments for the poor '... in this time of anxiety'. [15] Youngsters were also asked to do their bit. Following an announcement by Lord Baden-Powell, the 2nd Dorchester Scout Troop began recruiting lads over the age of 12 for duties helping the military. Employers were asked to give every assistance by releasing boys in the Empire's hour of need.

All sections of Dorchester society were asked to make sacrifices. While housewives were donating eggs, in January 1915 sporting gentlemen were asked to send in their field glasses for use by the Army. One of the most difficult sacrifices brought about by the unpleasant exigencies of war fell on those persons who owned horses. The demand for horses was so huge that they were unceremoniously commandeered from local farms and businesses, without regard to the needs of harvesting, and there were even cases reported of animals being separated from their carts in the streets of the town. The *Chronicle* reported that, 'no respect of persons was shown by the authorities in making good the equine shortage and the pick of the stables of many gentlemen in the neighbourhood had to be yielded to urgent military necessity'. [16]

When it came to supporting servicemen the Dorset Rgt naturally had a special place in the hearts of Durnovarians. A Comforts Fund was created for troops serving at the Front and when, in 1916, Kut in Mesopotamia fell, with the subsequent taking prisoner of 370 officers and men of the 2nd Dorsets, Col Lord Ellenborough set up a fund to provide for the men whilst they were in the hands of the Turks. Dorchester took the lead by organising a 'Kut Day', which took place on 26 July 1916 and was followed quickly by Weymouth and Bridport. During the year a sum of just over £1,600 was raised, which was used to send food and postal orders to the captives. After the War those local soldiers who returned were treated to a special dinner at the Corn Exchange and monies that were left over were distributed to local hospitals.

During the early days of the War one major concern of the local authorities was that the population might panic. It was not long before stories were circulating around the town about spies and espionage and the Chief Constable felt moved to issue a statement to the effect that there was no truth in the many rumours circulating that foreign agents were trying to poison or pollute the water supply or destroy property. Despite his assurances the vigilant people of Dorchester remained alert and in one case a man was accused of signalling to a German prisoner by shining a light, but the case was dismissed. The War inevitably brought with it greater regulation. Fear of enemy air attack led to the town's lights being turned off, just one of the many inconveniences the people had to endure. Travellers were asked to avoid using trains because they were needed to ferry troops, and if their journey was absolutely necessary to take as little luggage as possible as every inch of space was required.

On the economic front there were also concerns about people panicking. On 27 August 1914 the *Chronicle* carried a notice from Mayor Allen telling the townsfolk that 'There is not the slightest reason for panic. Full arrangements are being made to meet the situation. Do not store goods or create an artificial scarcity to the hurt of others. Remember that it is an act of mean and greedy selfish cowards.' [17] On the other side of the coin, an anonymous customer wrote to the *Chronicle* highlighting the dangers of some shopkeepers making unfair profits from the War, but adding that the majority of the retail classes in the county would scorn the idea of taking advantage in such a time of crisis. Another correspondent wrote protesting against the general increase of prices being charged in Dorchester for staple articles of food, compared to the rest of the county. Relationships between retailers and customers remained strained and rising prices were not the only cause. Despite

This group of Dorchester folk in fancy dress pose whilst collecting money for the relief of troops besieged and then captured at Kut-al-Amara. They cleverly advertise their task by changing the spelling of the words. (From a postcard by Furbear of Dorchester.)

Dorchester Town winning football team 1911, with Reginald Dabinett (see page 180) right front row. Matches were cancelled for the period of the War. (Source: Mrs J. Caddy.)

rationing there was clearly a feeling in some quarters that not all customers were being treated equally. On 24 January 1917 the County Stores published an advertisement which contained the following statement: 'A lot of lies are going around by agitators and pacifists that the richer folk are getting more than their fair share. Our experience is that richer folk do not get proportionately as much as poorer folk.'

Given the extraordinary circumstances brought about by the War, anything that smelt of unpatriotic sentiment was jumped on. On 11 January 1917, for instance, the secretary of the local golf course at Came Down was required to publish a statement in the *Chronicle* pointing out that of the 33 caddies working there before the War, 21 had joined the Colours, and that those employed at present were small boys living near the links. He was also at pains to mention that not one of the members was a 'shirker' and that the club provided recreation for officers on leave or recovering from wounds. Golf was not the only local sport affected by the War. Cricket matches were cancelled, as were football fixtures, partly because players were enlisted and stadiums were requisitioned by the military.

It is well known that the Great War served as a catalyst for changing the role of women in society. Before the War nearly all shop assistants in Dorchester were male, so there was some excitement when they were replaced by women. This was especially so when it was found that the Post Office was employing female letter-carriers and sorters. Then, there was plenty of voluntary work for women to do to aid the war effort, be it knitting socks for soldiers, collecting eggs or helping to sell war bonds. Nationally, the most visible face of women working for the War was in the munitions factories, of which Dorchester had none. However, Channon's did make parts for gun carriages and was one of the first local firms to employ women, ending up with an almost exclusively female workforce. But, of course, the majority of women, especially those who had been left to bring up large families on their own, did not work and their role has tended to be overlooked. As I researched this book and uncovered one tragedy after another, I came to realise that these women were every bit heroes as the men at the Front. Gilbert Nobbs was a soldier of the Great War who wrote an account of his experiences and his words concerning the women left at home poignantly sum up their plight:

> 'The fighting man looks upon his share of the war with a light heart. Events come too rapidly upon him to feel depressed. He does not feel the gnawing hunger of the lonely wait; the emptiness of the world when the parting is over; the empty chair at the table, and the rooms made cheerless by his absence. There is no one to describe the terrors of the morning casualty list; the hourly expectation and frozen fear of the telegraph boy's "rat tat", bringing some dreadful news. There are no crowds to cheer her; no flags or trumpets to rouse her enthusiasm and occupy her thoughts. No constant activity, thrilling excitement, desperate encounter. Hers is a silent patriotism. She is the true hero of the war. And in hundreds of thousands of homes throughout the empire, her silent deeds, her wonderful fortitude, are making the womanhood of Britain a history which medals will not reward, nor scars display.' [18]

Some women of Dorchester did, of course, receive medals – those of their dead husbands and sons – and they certainly bore emotional scars, though they were not always visible. At the end of the conflict it was the mothers and widows who were left to count the cost. Some left Dorchester to rebuild their lives elsewhere, but the majority remained in the town and did the best they could to bring up what was left of their families.

---

[1] See Denzil Hughes-Onslow.
[2] *Chronicle* 23/07/1914. See also Reginald Dabinett.
[3] *Chronicle* 4/3/1915.
[4] *Chronicle* 15/7/1915.
[5] Ibid.
[6] The Soldiers' Home was situated opposite the town's Covered Market on a site currently occupied by a tyre-fitting company.
[7] See Leonard Thompson.
[8] Carpentier beat Smith at Olympia, on 16 July.
[9] *Chronicle* 30/8/1914.
[10] *Chronicle* 22/4/1915.
[11] See Denzil Hughes-Onslow.
[12] See Paul Methuen.
[13] The Prince of Wales' National Relief Fund was set up to raise funds to help the dependants of service personnel who were suffering because of the War.
[14] See Thomas Winwood.
[15] *Chronicle* 13/8/1914.
[16] *Chronicle* 6/8/1914.
[17] *Chronicle* 27/8/1914.
[18] Nobbs, 1917.

The Memorials

After the War had ended with the Armistice on Monday 11 November 1918, the question arose as to what to do with the bodies of those killed. Some were buried in graves on the battlefield, others in mass graves and some in local cemeteries. The problems facing the British Government were complex. Firstly, many of the bodies could not be identified and so could not be claimed by loved ones. Three bodies might be found together but with only one identity disc. Secondly, there was the sheer cost of transporting the remains at a time of austerity. One option was for families to pay to have remains returned, but it was felt that this was unfair to those who could not afford the costs involved. In the end, the Government decided that everyone should be treated equally, regardless of rank or class, and that those who fell should remain where they were. For the families and loved ones the War had finished but their grieving had not and part of that process was the need for some kind of recognition of their loss. This feeling was not confined to individuals; communities like Dorchester also felt the desire to have some tangible, permanent record of the sacrifice made. As a consequence of these factors, memorials of different types began to spring up in nearly every town and village throughout the land.

Dorchester Cenotaph

Dorchester's main war memorial was never officially called a cenotaph, but most locals call it by that name. In the text I have used the name to differentiate it from the town's other memorials. It has to be said that it did not have an easy birth. The idea of creating something that would be a memorial to the sacrifice made by the people of the town was first discussed publically at a meeting at the Corn Exchange on 14 March 1919, when the mayor said that they had a duty to erect some memorial to 'the gallant Dorchester men who had so nobly sacrificed their lives for King and Country'.[1] There was no paucity of ideas forthcoming at the meeting; Mrs Logan suggested a swimming pool for children and Mr Kibbey a workingman's institute. Other suggestions included a rest home for soldiers and sailors, the endowment of scholarships for the sons of working-class men and a convalescent home for children. Then, Maj. Cosens appealed, saying, 'Don't for goodness sake talk about a hall for the working man, or also something for the babies, or washhouses for one section of the population.' [2] In his opinion no particular section of the community should be singled out and that what was required was something that reminded posterity of the sacrifice made. Presented with such a diversity of suggestions, it was decided to appoint a committee of 24 persons to deal with the matter. Accordingly, they went away to deliberate and reported back to another public meeting on 2 June.

Not surprisingly, with so many members the committee could not agree on a single proposal and instead presented both a minority and a majority report. The majority report proposed a monument located at the junction of South Street and Trinity Street, outside Ernest Tilley's cycle shop, and in addition the erection of a memorial institute and victory

Mourners around the Cenotaph on 24 May 1921. Hersella Loveless (wearing a white blouse), wife of William Loveless (see page 70), is standing front row right centre with her two children. (Source: Mrs P. Collins.)

hall, providing the money to pay for it could be found. The minority report agreed with the idea of the memorial but not its siting and did not consider that funds could be raised for the memorial hall. Matters got a little personal at the meeting between Cosens, who was clearly against the idea of erecting a hall, and a supporter of the idea. Cosens asked the man whether his 'class' would be willing to make financial contributions, in reply to which the man said that his class had always been generous when it came to giving money to good causes. It took a woman, Mrs Logan, to step in and tell them to stop squabbling and get on with the business in hand. The meeting finally decided to defer the item until public subscriptions showed what funds might be available for the memorial hall.

Things came to an impasse at that point and any idea of a memorial might have been mothballed forever had it not been for the Dorchester Comrades of the Great War who, in January 1920, wrote to the town council and asked for the scheme to be resuscitated. The matter was duly resurrected and it was finally agreed that a monument should be built on its present position at the corner of South Street and South Walks. Even at this late stage alternative proposals were still being sent in, including an interesting one from John Acland, consisting of an arch gate to be placed in the Borough Gardens.

When it came to the design for the monument the council looked to Sir Edwin Lutyens, the designer of the Cenotaph in Whitehall, and wrote asking if the design was copyrighted. His office replied that it was but they were sure that he would not object to it being copied, providing he supervised the work. The expenses of employing such a renowned architect were too much for the council so, instead, they sought estimates from local firms for the design, carving and erection of a monument. The winning tender was that of Algernon Grassby, monumental mason, of Maumbury Way, at a cost of £400. To accommodate the

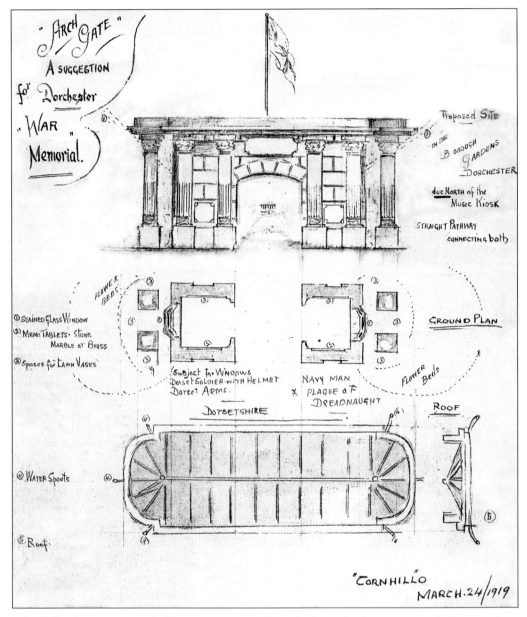

John Acland's never erected alternative memorial, with classical columns, stained-glass windows and flower vases. (Source: Dorset History Centre.)

structure some of the chestnut trees in the Walks had to be removed and the kerb realigned. Made of Portland whitbed stone, the monument is 15 ft high and weighs 17 tons. Both back and front are decorated by relief panels, with a carved laurel leaf and crusader's sword, with the dates 1914–1918 on a scroll. Attached to the front of the memorial are bronze plaques bearing the names of the fallen. These were made by Robert Membury at the Model Brass Foundry in Colliton Street. [3] I have been told that the trowel Algernon Grassby used to complete the work is buried within the stonework.

The process of collecting names was done through public advertisement, with notices inserted in newspapers and posters appearing around the town. Letters were also sent to local churches asking if they had any nominations for inclusion. Except for a couple of complaints concerning omissions, everyone seemed happy with the 239 names listed. The list includes 16 sets of brothers, three cases where both father and son died, one uncle and nephew and two cousins. It also includes one woman, Constance Hodges.

At the forefront of the multitude gathered before the Cenotaph on the day of unveiling, 24 May 1921, were the mourners. The remainder of the congregation included local dignitaries, Red Cross nurses, representatives of the Dorset Rgt and RFA, the Girl Guides, Boys' Brigade and Church Lads' Brigade, as well as a contingent of the Grammar School OTC. An approach had been made to the Prince of Wales, through the Deputy Lieutenant of the county, requesting him to do the unveiling, but as he was not available the job fell to the Right Hon. Lord Ellenborough, who had served with the 2nd Dorsets in the Boer War and had worked tirelessly in the recent conflict. After the singing of several hymns, addresses by local clergy and a reminder to all about the sacrifice that had been made, the Last Post was played and Dorchester's Great War dead were finally put to rest.

St George's Church, Fordington

The St George's memorial is inside the church and consists of a white marble plaque mounted on a black marble background. The plaque records 65 names of members of the parish who died, two of whom seem to have been added at a later date. Another seven names were added to the black background. The memorial lists four sets of brothers.

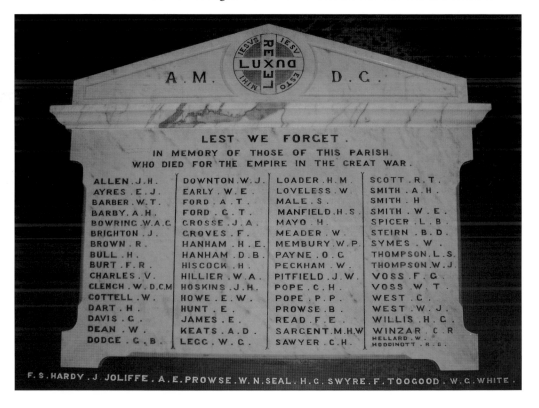

Holy Trinity Church, High West Street

Holy Trinity is now used as a Catholic church but at the time of the Great War it was Church of England. The memorial is fixed to the outside of the south wall of the building and consists of a rectangular plaque carved with an angel carrying a flag in one hand and a sheaf of corn in the other, representing the bread of life. The memorial records 38 names and includes four sets of brothers and one father and son. It was erected to 'The glory of God and in proud memory of these members of our church and parish who died for us in the Great War'.

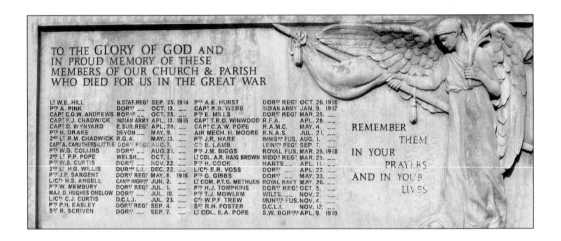

TO THE GLORY OF GOD AND IN PROUD MEMORY OF THESE MEMBERS OF OUR CHURCH & PARISH WHO DIED FOR US IN THE GREAT WAR

LT W.E. HILL	N.STAF.REGT	SEP. 25. 1914	PTE A.E. HURST	DORST REGT	OCT. 26. 1916
PTE A. PINK	DORST	OCT. 13.	CAPT R.B. WEBB	INDIAN ARMY	JAN. 9. 1917
CAPT C.G.W. ANDREWS	BORDR	OCT. 25.	PTE E. MILLS	DORST REGT	MAR. 25.
CAPT E.J. CHADWICK	INDIAN ARMY	APL. 13. 1915	CAPT T.R.O. WINWOOD	R.F.A.	APL. 28.
CAPT D. WYNYARD	E.SUR.REGT	APL. 20.	CAPT C.A.W. POPE	R.A.M.C.	MAY. 4.
PTE H. DRAKE	DEVON	MAY. 9.	AIR MECH. H. MOORE	R.N.A.S.	JUL. 21.
2ND LT R.M. CHADWICK	R.G.A.	MAY. 13.	PTE J.R. HARE	INNISKg FUS.	AUG. 1.
CAPT A. CARUTHERS-LITTLE	DORS REGT	AUG. 7.	CL E. LAMB	LEINSTR REGT	SEP. 7.
PTE W.G. COLLINS	DORST	AUG. 21.	PTE J.M. BIGGS	ROYAL FUS.	MAR. 25. 1918
2ND LT P.P. POPE	WELSH	OCT. 1.	LT COL. A.R. HAIG BROWN	MIDDX REGT	MAR. 25.
PTE W.S. CURTIS	DORST	NOV. 22.	PTE H. COOK	HANTS	APL. 11.
2ND LT H.G. WILLIS	DURHM L.I.	DEC. 22.	L/CPL E.R. VOSS	DORST	APL. 27.
PTE J.F. SARGENT	DORST REGT	MAY. 8. 1916	PTE G. GIBBS	DORST	MAY. 23.
L/CPL H.S. ANGELL	CANDN HIGHRs	JUN. 2.	LT COM. P.T.G. METHUEN	ROYAL NAVY	MAY. 26.
PTE W. MEMBURY	DORST REGT	JUL. 1.	PTE H.J. TOMPKINS	DORST REGT	OCT. 5.
MAJ. D. HUGHES ONSLOW	DORST	JUL. 10.	PTE T.J. MOWLEM	WILTS.	NOV. 2.
L/CPL C.J. CURTIS	D.C.L.I.	JUL. 23.	CPL W.P.F. TREW	MUNSTR FUS.	NOV. 4.
PTE P.H. EASLEY	DORST REGT	SEP. 4.	SGT R.H. FOSTER	D.C.L.I.	NOV. 12.
SGT R. SCRIVEN	DORST	SEP. 7.	LT COL. E.A. POPE	S.W. BORDRS	APL. 9. 1919

REMEMBER
THEM
IN YOUR
PRAYERS
AND IN YOUR
LIVES

St Peter's Church, High West Street

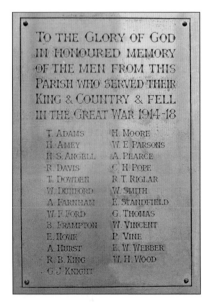

TO THE GLORY OF GOD IN HONOURED MEMORY OF THE MEN FROM THIS PARISH WHO SERVED THEIR KING & COUNTRY & FELL IN THE GREAT WAR 1914-18

T. ADAMS	H. MOORE
H. AMEY	W. E. PARSONS
H. S. ANGELL	A. PEARCE
R. DAVIS	C. H. POPE
T. DOWDEN	R. T. RIGLAR
W. DUTFORD	W. SMITH
A. FARNHAM	E. STANDFIELD
W. F. FORD	G. THOMAS
B. FRAMPTON	W. VINCENT
E. HOWE	P. VINE
A. HURST	E. W. WEBBER
R. B. KING	W. H. WOOD
G. J. KNIGHT	

St Peter's has three memorials. The one outside the front of the church, which was dedicated on 20 December 1920, comprises a cross on an elongated, octagonal pillar sitting on a plinth. The names of 24 fallen are commemorated on bronze plaques and include three sets of brothers. A memorial inside the church, which consists of a framed plaque of different names, honours 25 'men of the parish'. The final memorial, erected by the Dorchester Branch of the Salisbury Diocesan Guild of Bellringers, lists nine campanologists, one of whom, William Painter, came from Dorchester.

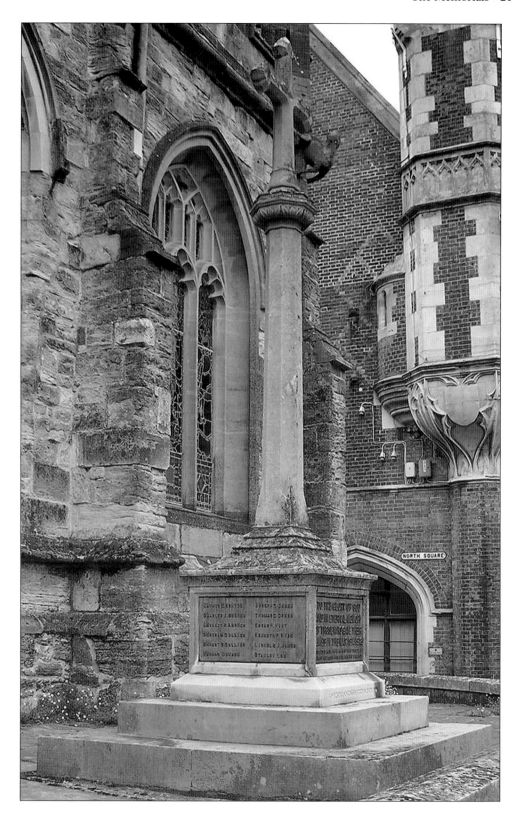

Post Office Memorial, Trinity Street

The Post Office memorial consists of a small rectangular marble plaque carved with black lettering. The designer's name was added to the bottom right-hand corner, no less than the town's own Thomas Hardy. It is located high up on the wall and commemorates 11 men of the district postal service who gave their lives during the Great War.

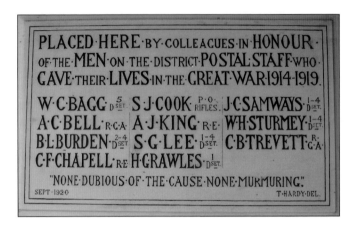

Other churches

Curiously, All Saints' Church in High East Street has no dedicated war memorial and the only clue to those of the parish who perished in the Great War lies in a scrapbook containing extracts cut out from church magazines. None of the non-conformist churches has memorials.

Weymouth Avenue Cemetery

Weymouth Avenue Cemetery on the southern outskirts of town contains the graves of nineteen men who either died in Dorchester or whose bodies were brought home from elsewhere in the UK.

Fordington Cemetery

The cemetery attached to St George's Church has thirty two Great War graves, but very few of them have connections with Dorchester other than the fact that they died in the town – mostly in one of the town's hospitals after being wounded or taken ill.

German War Memorial, Fordington Cemetery

There cannot be many towns that have a Great War memorial dedicated to the enemy. Dorchester's is located at the eastern end of Fordington Cemetery, built into a grassy bank, and commemorates the 45 Germans who were buried here. It was erected at the end of the War and depicts a German soldier in uniform, kneeling with bowed head, holding a rifle. The inscription underneath reads 'Hier Ruhen Deutsche krieger in fremder erde doch unvergessen' (Here lie German soldiers in a foreign land but not forgotten).

Drawing of the German War Memorial in Fordington Cemetery made by K. Bartolmay, a German prisoner. (Source: Dorset History Centre.)

The first prisoner to die was Bernhard Schneider, whose funeral set the pattern for others that followed. The time chosen was early morning, to avoid the traffic. A funeral service was held at the prison camp by Rev. Stratton Holmes, pastor of the local Congregational Church, who not only spoke German but also was considered acceptable by the mainly Lutheran prisoners. Despite the early start of 6.30 am the crowds turned out and two policemen led the procession through town to clear the way. The Bobbies were followed by an officer of the National Reserve who led the firing party, which consisted of seven files of rifle-bearers with arms reversed. This preceded the Prison Guard brass band. Then came the coffin, draped in the German flag, lying on a gun carriage with field gun, the whole drawn by horses. On each side of the coffin were three bearers, consisting of the deceased's comrades. Behind them was a contingent of about 50 more prisoners, accompanied by members of the prison guard. Finally came an open carriage full of wreaths, some from

British officers and men, others from the dead man's comrades. The whole spectacle must have been impressive and one wonders what the good folk of Dorchester made of it. One Fordington woman made her views known when she said, 'I only hope that in Germany they treat our men as well and pay as much respect to those who die'. [4]

The memorial bears no names and the Roll of Honour below is taken from cemetery records. There is little information about the men who were interred, but we do know that two died of appendicitis, one of whom was Emil Drygalla, one of gas poisoning and another of carbolic poisoning. One man was shot while trying to escape. On the night of 16 May 1919 Rupert Gilder of the Royal Rifle Brigade was sergeant of the guard at the camp. At about 12.45 am he was startled by two shots and immediately raised the alarm with his officer. The two men ran to where the shots came from and found two sentries, who when asked why the shots had been fired replied that a prisoner had attempted to escape. The man lying fatally wounded in the barbed wire was Franz Radgowski, a 20-year-old Pole who was found to have a pair of wire cutters on his person. Franz was taken to the camp hospital but soon died. At the inquest the jury were satisfied that the proper warnings had been given and the guards were exonerated.

What strikes one, looking at the list below, are the dates of the deaths. Up until September 1918 there were only 12 fatalities at the camp, but after that the number escalates to 18 for the remainder of 1918 and 15 in 1919. Most of these were doubtlessly caused by the flu epidemic which also killed some of the guards at the camp. The bodies of those interred in Fordington Cemetery were later exhumed and buried in the Cannock Chase war cemetery, Staffordshire. [5]

German Roll of Honour

Name	Date died	Age
Bernhard Schneider	28/08/1915	25
Wilhelm Braun	06/12/1915	26
Emil Drygalla	10/03/1916	28
Alfred Hammel	11/03/1916	19
Georg Meissner	27/10/1916	34
Michail Reitinger	13/11/1916	31
Johann Holste	18/03/1917	20
Karl Becker	07/04/1917	33
Adolf Mally	25/04/1917	32
Johann Fischer	14/06/1917	22
Hermann Waitkowski	01/11/1917	31
Johann Kaltenberger	23/12/1917	41
Wilhelm Schmelger	25/09/1918	29
Herman Hofmann	17/10/1918	30
Karl Melzmacher	26/10/1918	27
Paul Shotta	27/10/1918	25
Edward Wannemacher	27/10/1918	29
Wilhelm Germann	27/10/1918	32
Karl Graseduck	28/10/1918	34

Wilhelm Willms	30/10/1918	20
Alfred Konrad	02/11/1918	31
Karl Joos	02/11/1918	23
Hermann Rindefusse	04/11/1918	22
Lorenz Clauson	06/11/1918	28
Karl Heinz	09/11/1918	28
Peter Kemmer	09/11/1918	37
Hugo Kampe	10/11/1918	37
Karl Nimmler	11/11/1918	27
Emanual Prudio	23/11/1918	29
Alfred Borse	24/11/1918	34
Josef Kohler	01/01/1919	36
Ernst Zimmermann	01/01/1919	27
Wilhelm Zimmermann	07/02/1919	31
Marten Dingenthal	28/02/1919	20
Heinrich Nollhoff	15/03/1919	40
Victor Giera	17/03/1919	29
Johann Schigulla	18/03/1919	24
Peter Schauss	18/03/1919	28
Paul Schwarz	28/03/1919	22
Franz Radgowski	17/05/1919	20
Frederick Kronenmeyer	13/06/1919	20
Adalbert Petzolor	31/08/1919	22
Paul Boettcher	23/10/1919	21
Jakob Oeffler	25/10/1919	36
Robert Fischer	29/10/1919	20

[1] *Chronicle* 20/3/1919.
[2] Ibid.
[3] See William Membury.
[4] *Chronicle* 2/9/1915.
[5] Some local people believe that the remains were sent back to Germany and as there is no definitive list it is difficult to establish how many of the 5,000 buried in Cannock Chase came from Dorchester.

1914
The Battle Front

France and Belgium

Mons, 23 August

The BEF landed in France on 14 August under the command of Sir John French, intent on moving up the Belgian coast to meet the French army at Charleroi. However, before reaching its destination some cavalry units of the German 1st Army were encountered and, realising the enemy was at hand, French decided to stop and attack. By the next day he had changed his mind and ordered his five divisions to take up defensive positions near the Mons Canal, deploying two infantry corps commanded by Generals Smith-Dorrien and Haig along a 40-km front.

Doubtless with the words of the Kaiser in mind to 'Walk over General French's contemptible little army', commander of the German forces, Gen. von Kluck, determined to make a frontal assault on the BEF on 23 August. The BEF was vastly outnumbered – 70,000 troops against 160,000 and 300 guns against 600 – but, despite the overwhelming advantage, the German offensive began disastrously against the withering rifle fire of the British Tommies, who had been trained to shoot at 15 rounds per minute. Such was the ferocity of the fire that the German General assumed that machine guns were being used. Checked in their footsteps, the Germans waited for reinforcements and resumed the attack in the evening. By now it was clear to French just how large the enemy's forces were and he ordered a retreat.

Le Cateau, 26 August

The retreating British troops were exhausted, having little food and less sleep, under constant harassment from their pursuers. On 25 August they were near Le Cateau when their commander Smith-Dorrien decided to stop and fight the next day, against the orders of his commander. The battle opened with a German barrage that continued until noon, followed by an infantry assault. Again, it was the fire power of the Tommie that allowed the British to make a strategic withdrawal in the afternoon. British casualties were nearly 8,000 men.

Battle of the Marne, 6–12 September

During the first month of the War the German forces had a series of victories and the Allies were forced back in the direction of Paris. It appeared that, as the British and French forces retreated to the area of the River Marne, Paris would be taken. In accordance with the Schlieffen Plan the Germans were advancing rapidly into France and the French capital was almost within their grasp. However, Gen. Joffre, the French Commander-in Chief, had other ideas and decided to make a counterattack. Supported by the British, on the morning of 6 September 150,000 French troops attacked the German right flank. The Germans manoeuvred to meet the French and in doing so opened up a gap in their line into which the BEF and members of the French 5th Army poured. However, by 9 September the Germans had almost made a breakthrough and might have done so, had it not been for a fleet of 600 Paris taxis that brought French reserves into the line. On the same day the Germans began to retreat, but the Allied forces' pursuit was leisurely and the German Armies dug in north of the River Aisne; stalemate and trench warfare that so typified the Great War was born at this moment. At the end of the battle one thing was clear – the Germans' hope of a swift completion of the War would not be realised.

First Battle of the Aisne, 13–28 September

The German 1st and 2nd Armies, joined by the 7th, were located on a plateau overlooking the River Aisne, an excellent vantage point. Despite this, a full frontal attack was launched by the French and British, both of whom crossed the river and started to make their way up the slopes, though they were unable to make any great advance. By 18 September the attacks had lessened considerably and on the 28th they ceased.

Antwerp

While the French and British were fighting in France, the Belgians were engaged in a fighting retreat in their own country. After capturing the fortified cities of Liege and Namur the Germans were advancing on Antwerp. Five divisions under the command of Gen. von Boseler were given the job of taking the city and on 28 September the assault began. This caused considerable concern to the British government because Antwerp's capture could threaten the Channel ports and even Britain itself. As a result they agreed to send a division of troops to aid the Belgians and then, in response to a plea from the Belgian government, sent another 6,000 troops of the Royal Naval Division. The latter arrived at Antwerp too late – on 6 October, the day after the Germans broke the city's defences and it seemed that their capture was inevitable. Rather than capitulating, they crossed over the border into the Netherlands, which was neutral, and were interned for the rest of the War.

Back in France the adversaries realised that a breakthrough was not possible and there followed a series of battles that were part of what has become known as the 'race to the sea'. This consisted of each side moving north and west, trying to outmanoeuvre each other, ending inconclusively on the North Sea coast. In the south the main battles were those of La Bassée (10 Oct–2 Nov), Messines (12 Oct–2 Nov) and Armentières (13 Oct–2 Nov), whilst in the north the First Battle of Ypres was fought.

First Battle of Ypres, 20 October–22 November

The Allies were at Nieuport, near Ypres, and were joined by the remains of the BEF in their retreat from Antwerp, arriving by 19 October. The British forces held a line of trenches 35 miles long at the middle of a salient.[1] Facing them were the forces of Gen. von

Falkenhayn, whose offensive began on 20 October in an attempt to break through to the ports of Calais and Boulogne. In the first phase of the fighting the Belgians neutralised the German advance by flooding the low-level land between them. Attacks on the British part of the line began on 31 October and after heavy fighting the BEF managed to hold the line. Fighting around Ypres continued until late November, when the effects of winter halted further actions. Falkenhayn had failed to achieve his breakthrough and the casualties on both were horrendous. Between 14 October and 30 November the BEF incurred over 58,000 casualties and Britain's professional Army had all but been killed off.

Mesopotamia

Basra, 5–21 November

The British government was concerned that neutral Turkey might have territorial designs in Mesopotamia should it join the War and also recognised the importance of controlling the oil pipeline at Abadan. When the Turks did join the conflict on 4 November, the British lost no time in dealing with the Turkish-held city of Basra. Dismissing the light resistance at Abadan and repelling an attack by 400 Turks Brig.-Gen. Delamain launched a full-scale attack on Basra on the 19th. Finding fighting conditions against the first line of defences difficult, because of deep mud caused by heavy rain, it was not until British artillery was brought into play that the Turkish defenders fled. The next day the city was evacuated and the British entered it on the 21st. As a result, oil supplies in the Middle East were secured.

The War at Sea

Heligoland Bight, 28 August

This engagement between the British and German fleets was the first naval battle of the Great War. The action was part of the plan to attack German patrols off the northwest coast of Germany and in it the First Battle Cruiser Squadron outgunned several of the enemy's ships which retreated under the cover of mist.

---

[1] A part of a military front, line or fortification that projects outwards into enemy-held territory or towards the enemy.

1914
Roll of Honour

Sgt William Charles Cake – aged 23
1st Btn Dorsetshire Rgt – 8323
Cenotaph

On entering Dorchester from Sherborne or Yeovil the first public house the thirsty traveller came across was the Old Compasses [1], sited at the bottom of The Grove at the junction with Miller's Close. The building remains but its use has long gone. At the beginning of the 20th century the landlord was Albert Legg, who also managed to run a butcher's business at the same time. Albert and his wife Clara produced eleven children, the eldest daughter being Elsie who, after leaving school, got a job as a dressmaker. It may well have been around 1911 that she met a young soldier of the Dorsets who was stationed at the Depot Barracks in the spring of that year.

The soldier, Cpl William Cake, son of Henry and Alice, was born at Owermoigne, a village 7 miles southeast of Dorchester, but moved as a child with his family to live near Salisbury. When he was 18 he decided to give up his job as an engine cleaner and embarked on an army career. He enlisted in the Dorsets at Devises on 2 April 1907 and went to the 1st Btn. Within 18 months he had been promoted to lance corporal and in October 1910 gained his second stripe. Just before the outbreak of war the 1st Btn was serving in Northern Ireland, and it was there that William married Elsie, on 7 January 1914.

The couple had just 7 months together before William left for France, disembarking on 16 August with the rank of sergeant, and he was soon in action. The 1st Btn started the advance towards Mons and on 23 August contact was made with the enemy. The following day William was killed in action, along with another Dorchester man, Bandsman William Teversham.

Elsie was living with her family in Dorchester when she received the news of her husband's death but that was not the end of the story. The following April she was sent a Princess Mary gift box [2] which was intended for her husband and one cannot but wonder whether her feelings were those of pride or anguish when it arrived. For 7 years Elsie waited to hear what had happened to her husband's body. Then, in November 1921, a glimmer of hope appeared when the Imperial War Graves Commission [3] informed the Infantry Record Office that they had received a batch of personal effects of British soldiers, including some belonging to William. His consisted of two French coins, a brooch and a damaged watch. On receiving them Elsie immediately wrote back asking where the broken watch had been found, for surely William would have been buried in the vicinity. The anguish of not knowing where he was laid to rest is evident from the letter she wrote: 'I am very anxious to visit his grave, which the War Graves cannot find yet. So if you could let me know I would be very grateful to you'. There followed a series of correspondence between the various authorities and Elsie, the result of which was inconclusive. The last letter, dated 5 May 1922, informed her that no further information had yet been found. Even today there are some doubts about what happened to William. There is a gravestone for him in Hautrage Military Cemetery near Mons which bears the inscription, 'Believed to be buried in this cemetery'.

[1] The name was subsequently changed to the New Compasses.
[2] The Princess Mary gift box was a brass embossed box sent to servicemen at Christmas 1914. All of them contained a Christmas card and a picture of the princess but the other contents varied. For soldiers who smoked it contained a pipe and an ounce of tobacco, or 20 cigarettes and a tinder lighter. Non-smokers and boys received a packet of sweets, a propelling pencil and a khaki writing case.
[3] Now the Commonwealth War Graves Commission.

Bandsman William Ralph Teversham – aged 28
1st Btn Dorsetshire Rgt – 6414

Sgt Percy Thomas Teversham – aged 29
2/7th Btn West Yorkshire Rgt – 9693

Both are remembered on the Cenotaph

William, Percy, Lionel and Sam Teversham were brothers who had grown up with the Army. Their father George was a colour sergeant with the 3rd Btn Dorsets and the boys spent part of their childhood living among soldiers in the married quarters at the Depot Barracks, with their mother Kezia, while their father was away with the Rgt. In the infantry barracks some families lived in part of the Little Keep, but most were accommodated in a block behind. When George retired the family moved to 23 Mountain Ash Terr., a stone's throw from the barracks, and he got a job as Caretaker with the Dorchester Rifle Club. Kezia died in 1901 and George remarried a girl 26 years his junior.

Given their background there was perhaps greater enthusiasm, or even pressure, for the Teversham brothers to join the War. Lionel, the youngest son, joined the RFA and Percy enlisted in the West Yorkshire Rgt, while William and Sam followed their father into the Dorsets.

William, who was born in 1886, was employed as a draper's errand boy and became, with William Cake, the first of the Dorchester men to become a casualty. He was killed in action on 24 August during the Battle of Mons and is remembered on the La Ferte-Sous-Jouarre Memorial, Seine et Marne, France. Percy, who was a year older than William, served with the 2/7th Btn, West Yorkshires which did not go to France until January 1917. Percy was killed on 1 November 1917 and is commemorated on the Arras Memorial.

Unfortunately, the War had not finished with the Teversham family. Brother Lionel enlisted in August 1914 and was discharged as unfit for duty on 13 May 1915 due to gas poisoning and shellshock. Despite Kezia's untimely death she was, at least, spared the tragedies that befell her family.

Pte Henry George Rawles – aged 31
1st Btn Dorsetshire Rgt – 6494
Post Office Memorial

SDGW lists a soldier named Henry George Rawles. Born at Chalbury, Wimborne, he enlisted in the 1st Dorsets in Dorchester and was killed in action on 9 September 1914. Unfortunately, the database does not give his residence at the time of enlistment. The most likely candidate is Henry, son of Henry and Emily, who married Grace Battrick in Wareham in 1910. In the 1911 census he and Grace were living in Salisbury and he was employed as a railway porter, so his association with the Dorset postal service probably came afterwards.

At the time Henry died the 1st Dorsets were in retreat with the rest of the BEF and had reached the River Marne. On 9 September, the day of his death, three of the battalion's companies were detailed to attack a feature called Hill 189, half a mile south of Montreuil in Seine-Marne, where the Germans were entrenching. Two of the three began to advance without artillery or machine gun support. Their path lay over open stubble fields and, exposed to the enemy's heavy machine guns hidden in woods on their flanks, their venture was doomed to failure and they had to stop. Meanwhile, 3rd Coy made good progress through a wood, but they too were unsupported and became involved in heavy fighting. The Dorsets lay in exposed positions across the battlefield and with bullets whizzing over their heads had to remain there until they could retire after dark.

The Dorsets' riflemen had brought heavy fire onto Hill 189 and when the position was later taken, 47 dead Germans were found there, nearly all shot through the head. The Dorsets lost three officers and seven OR, 31 were wounded and four missing. Henry was among those killed. He is buried in Montreuil-aux-Lions British Cemetery.

Pte Edwin John Ayres – aged 29
1st Btn Dorsetshire Rgt - 7167
Cenotaph and St George's

In 1902, 19-year-old Beatrice Catley married Thomas Parrott, a soldier in the Dorsets, in Dorchester, where their first two children were born. A third child was born in Gosport and then Thomas was posted to India, accompanied by Beatrice and the children. In India two further sons were added before tragedy struck. Thomas died in 1910, leaving Beatrice a widow with five children in a country thousands of miles from home. Fortunately, help was at hand in the name of Edwin Ayres, a private in the same battalion as Thomas. Beatrice and he were married in Madras on 14 November 1910 and when they eventually returned to Dorchester went to live at 11 Olga Rd. Alas, Beatrice was soon to lose a second husband and the children a second father.

Edwin Ayres was born in Greenwich to Frederick, an engine stoker, and Hannah, a laundress, and became a regular soldier with the Dorsets. In 1914, he was fighting with C Coy of the 1st Btn and died of wounds on 10 September. There is no information about when he was wounded but he may have been one of the 43 casualties following the fighting on the Marne, 2 days before his death. He is buried in Montreuil-Aux-Lions British Cemetery.

L/Cpl Frederick James Ansell – aged 34
2nd Btn Sussex Rgt – L5928
Cenotaph

One thing that connects the village of Angmering in West Sussex and the town of Dorchester is a name on their respective war memorials – that of Frederick James Ansell, the son of Walter, an agricultural labourer, and Mary, of Angmering. Frederick was born in 1880 and after leaving school and working for some time as a labourer, he became a professional soldier when he joined the Royal Sussex Rgt. We do not know how he met his wife, Edith Stevens from Melbury Osmond, but they married on 9 December 1908 in Holy Trinity Church, Karachi, India, where Frederick was serving with the 2nd Btn. We still find them in Karachi in 1911 now with the addition of a daughter, Freda.

The 2nd Btn returned to the UK in time to train and prepare before joining the BEF, with which Frederick landed in France on 24 August. He died of his wounds on 11 September inflicted during the Battle of the Marne and his grave can be found, together with those of five of his comrades from the same battalion, in Priez Communal Cemetery, south of Soissons. Back in England, Edith received the news of her husband's death at 19 Sydney Terrace in St Martin's Road.

Lt Walter Edward Hill – aged 22
3rd Btn North Staffordshire Rgt
Holy Trinity

Now a suburb of Dorchester, the former parish of Fordington once almost surrounded the town. The area outside the western part of the Roman walls was known as West Fordington and had its own school, now the Arts Centre, and its own church, Christchurch. It was built for the soldiers in the adjacent artillery barracks by the Rev Henry Moule, with income generated by a successful book he wrote entitled *Barrack Sermons*.

In 1889 Canon Charles Rowland Hill arrived in Dorchester from Evershot with his wife Ellen to take up the vacant incumbency at Christchurch, which he occupied for 5 years before obtaining a post at Lyme Regis. Then, in 1899, he returned to the county town as Rector of Holy Trinity Church. He seems to have

(Source: www.ww1photos.com.)

been a very energetic man, making improvements to the fabric of the building and fully involved in the community. He and Ellen lived in Holy Trinity Rectory which, with the largest garden in Dorchester, was situated in Prince's Street and regularly hosted garden parties and fetes.

On 6 September 1892 Ellen gave birth to Walter, their only child, who at the age of 10 was sent to the notoriously uncomfortable and spartan Durnford Preparatory School, Langton Matravers. [1] Each morning Walter was required to make his way down the cliffs with the other boys and bathe in the sea off Dancing Ledge. After spending 3 years at Durnford, as did Damer Wynyard [2], Walter completed his education at Winchester College where he played cricket for his house. In 1911 he obtained a commission in the 3rd Btn, North Staffordshire Rgt and on mobilisation joined the 1st Btn in Ireland.

Walter became frustrated at what seemed to him to be an inordinately long time on home duty whilst the rest of the BEF was already fighting in France. However, when he did eventually set foot on French soil his war turned out to be a very short one. His battalion disembarked on 13 September and the next week was spent getting to the Front, partly on the march and partly by train. Finally Walter saw action in the Battle of the Aisne, but on 25 September his life was taken when he was shot by a sniper. His Batman, a Pte Barnes, seeing that his officer had been hit, put his own life in danger trying to recover his body, but, alas, Walter had been mortally wounded. Pte Barnes was Mentioned in Despatches for his gallantry and received a silver plate from Walter's mother, as a thank you.

After her son's death, Ellen, who had been widowed in 1911, published a book of her son's letters, prefixed by an appreciation of Walter's character by a close friend. This, together with his letters, suggests that Walter, who was never physically strong, had a difficult passage from childhood to adulthood, but, when war broke out, life for him changed: 'doubts, hesitations, and difficulties faded away like mist before the sun, and he felt deep down in his heart that success lay in his grasp'. [3] Alas, his grasp fell short. Walter is buried in Soupir Cemetery, Aisne, and is commemorated on the Durnford School Memorial.

---

[1] Thomas Pellatt, Headmaster of Durnford School, insisted on the boys starting their day by swimming in the sea off Dancing Ledge. He later had a salt-water swimming pool blasted out of the rocks. One of the most famous of the school's pupils was Ian Fleming.

[2] See Damer Wynyard.

[3] Cotton, 1924.

Pte Frederick Robert Burt – aged 26
1st Btn Dorsetshire Rgt
Cenotaph and St George's

The *Chronicle* reports listing the casualties of the Dorsets involved in the fighting that took place along the Canal d'Aire, between Bethune and La Bassée, in October 1914 gave the townsfolk of Dorchester the first indication that this was a war that was going to strike at the heart of their community. On one day, Ptes Burt, Pink, Sharpe and Watts and L/Cpl Collier, all of the 1st Btn Dorsets, were killed.

The major part of the 1st Btn which embarked with the BEF to France in August 1914 consisted of existing and former full-time professional soldiers, many of whom had fought in South Africa or served in the outposts of the British Empire. On 13 October the 1st Btn was involved in a battle at Pont Fixe, the result of which was described by Lt-Col A.L. Ramsome: 'Well supplied with reinforcements, and fortunate perhaps, in not suffering very heavy casualties … the battalion was at full strength and its fighting spirit excellent. No one would dream that in the short space of five days it would be reduced, in what was perhaps its severest ordeal in the whole war, to a mere skeleton ….' [1] The casualty figures for the 5 days' fighting make grim reading: 18 killed, 288 missing and 129 wounded. Some days later a burial party discovered an additional 130 killed.

John Burt joined the 2nd Btn Dorsets in 1903 and was followed by his younger brother Frederick, who enlisted on 4 October 1907. The siblings were two of eight children belonging to John, an agricultural labourer, and Sarah, of Fordington. Frederick was born in 1887 at 43 Mill St and after serving 8 years with the 1st Btn he was transferred to the Army Reserve. At the outbreak of war he was mobilised and rejoined his old battalion in Northern Ireland. On 14 August Frederick and his comrades boarded the *Anthony* which took them to Le Havre and the battlefields of France.

On 13 October, at about midday, B Coy, of which Frederick was a member, had to be withdrawn from the front line because of overwhelming opposition and it may well have been during this manoeuvre that he went missing. His death was later confirmed. He is commemorated on the Le Touret Memorial, Pas-de-Calais, and his medals were sent to his mother at 18 Short's Lane, off Mill Street.

[1] Regimental history.

Pte Arthur Pink – aged 25
1st Btn Dorsetshire Rgt – 8099
Cenotaph and Holy Trinity

Arthur Pink, who was born in Emsworth, Hampshire, was a regular soldier with the Dorsets and in 1911 was serving with the 1st Btn at Alma Barracks, Blackdown. Presumably he met his wife-to-be, Nellie Aplin, when he was stationed in Dorchester. Nellie was the daughter of George Aplin, a house painter in the town, and the couple married in the early summer of 1913, a little over a year before Arthur died. He was killed on 13 October and his name joined those of his fellow Durnovarians on the Le Touret Memorial. [1]

[1] See Frederick Burt for a description of the fighting in which Arthur was killed.

L/Cpl Horace Austin Collier – aged 20
1st Btn Dorsetshire Rgt – 9411
Cenotaph

Another regular soldier, Horace Collier was born in Cerne Abbas, the son of a miller and baker, William and Emily. At the age of 17 Horace decided to throw in his job as a farm labourer and join the Army. In January 1912 he took the King's Shilling by joining the Special Army Reserve of the Somerset Light Infantry and then transferred to the Dorset Rgt 5 months later. Serving with the 1st Btn Horace appears to have been a good soldier; the only misdemeanour that appears on his Conduct Sheet is an occasion when, during an inspection, he was found to have a dirty rifle. His good behaviour was rewarded in April 1914 when he was promoted to lance corporal.

As Horace prepared to go to war his thoughts naturally turned to home and in particular to one special person in his life. Just before he embarked for France he wrote the following two letters to his dear 'Birdie', which show him to be religious, patriotic and obviously in love. The letters were found in a bible after the War and although there is no indication of the identity of the recipient, the most likely candidate is Eliza Jane Amey, who also lived in Cerne Abbas and was 3 years younger than Horace. The first letter, addressed from Victoria Barracks, Belfast, was written some time between 4 and 13 August 1914:

Dear Birdie,

Well dear, I suppose it is all settled for us to go to war, but I go with a good heart, knowing that I have left someone behind who will pray and think of me. Now Bird I don't want you to upset yourself because I shall fight with a good heart knowing that my country's subjects' lives are at stake. The only thing that is making me feel a bit down is the thought of leaving my relations and you without seeing you, but never mind when I come back, if ever I do, I will take great care to make up for lost time. I don't think you need to write until I let you know if we are in a settled place. I think this is all this time.

I remain yours till death,
H. Collier
God Bless You

Horace's second letter was written on the 13th, the day a church service was held for the 1st Btn in Belfast Cathedral and the day before their embarkation for France:

Dear Birdie,

Just a few lines before we leave Belfast. We are leaving tomorrow morning so we will go to Aldershot and from there to the Front. Well Dear, cheer up it won't be many years before we are back again to dear old England and home to see you. Keep a brave heart the same as I am trusting to God to bring us safe back again. We have just come back from the Cathedral, I was almost crying, when I left some lady came up to me crying and shook hands with me and said God Bless you that done it. Well Bird my love, when you write again don't forget to put the address on front page you will see there. Give my best respects to Mr & Mrs Amey also all the family and may God keep you all in health and strength while this terrible war is on. Well darling I can't write any more now. Good-bye and God bless you.

I remain your ever loving sweetheart,
Horace [1]

Alas, Horace did not return to his beloved 'Birdie'. He was killed in action on 13 October 1914 and is commemorated on the Le Touret Memorial. His service record contains a touching letter which his mother wrote to the military authorities after receiving his 1914 Star. In it she thanks them for sending the medal, 'which you so kindly sent me and which I shall always prize and keep in memory of my dear boy'. Horace's brother Thomas lived in Dorchester and it was probably he who ensured that his name was added to Dorchester's Roll of Honour. Horace's name also appears on the memorial of St Mary's Church, Cerne Abbas.

---

[1] SR.

Pte Herbert James Watts – aged 27
1st Btn Dorsetshire Rgt – 7979
Cenotaph

The 1901 census shows Emma Watts and her family living at 17 Olga Rd, Victoria Park, but her husband James was absent from the household, possibly because he was away fighting in South Africa. A professional soldier and 14 years Emma's senior, he was born in Madras, suggesting that his father may also have been in the Army. James must have spent a considerable amount of his career in Dorchester because the births of four of his children were registered in the town.

Ten years later, the 1911 census indicates that another member of the family was absent on military duties, this time son Herbert, who was stationed at Blackdown Barracks, Camberley, with the 1st Dorsets. By then James had retired and was working as a golf caddie, presumably at Came Down golf course, and would have known John Sargent, who also worked there [1]. The 1911 census also shows that just around the corner from the Watts family lived Rhoda Tizard, who was staying with her brother. Rhoda and Herbert met and married at Christmas 1913. Sadly, the marriage turned out to be a very short one because Herbert was killed in action on 13 October 1914, along with Frederick Burt, Horace Collier and Arthur Pink. [2] He is commemorated on the Le Touret Memorial. After the War Rhoda remarried and moved to Miller's Close.

------

[1]See John Sargent.
[2] See Frederick Burt for details on the fighting of 13 October.

Pte Frank John Sharpe – aged 31
1st Btn Dorsetshire Rgt – 7135
Cenotaph and St Peter's[1]

Frank Sharpe was not a Dorchester man but was born in Yeovil, in June 1883, the son of George, a labourer, and Annie. Before joining the 1st Btn Dorsets, on 6 February 1904, he served in the Reserve Btn of the Somerset Light Infantry. Frank's first overseas posting with the Dorsets was to India where he stayed for 4 years. In July 1908 he went down with an attack of bronchitis caused by asthma and was sent to the seaside town of Poonamalle in the district of Tamil Nadu for a change of air. The treatment was obviously ineffectual as he was sent back to England in November, where he spent a month in the Royal Victoria Military Hospital, Netley, Hampshire, before being discharged from the Army. We do not know how Frank met Laura James of Dorchester, but he was living with her family at 25 Holloway Rd prior to their marriage, on 17 February 1912 at St George's Church. The marriage was quickly followed by the birth of their first child Thora, that August.

Frank's health does not seem to have deteriorated and may have improved, because he rejoined his old battalion and went off to France with them in August 1914, a month after his second child, William, was born. On the day of Frank's death, 13 October 1914, he was fighting with C Coy, which suffered from German skulduggery. Frank's was the first of the 1st Btn's companies to be attacked by the enemy out of Givenchy. From reports of the officers and men who were in the trenches at the time, about 250 Germans suddenly appeared to their right and were mistaken as French cavalry. As soon as the error was recognised orders were given to open fire and fix bayonets. The men continued to advance slowly, with either hand or both hands in the air, suggesting they were surrendering. Firing ceased and some of the Dorsets got out of the trench and went towards the oncoming hoard, at which point the Germans closed rapidly on the left flanks of the trench and enfiladed [2] it. Unfortunately, the trench was narrow and deep, so the men of C Coy could not get out to make a charge. Instead, they held on as best they could and were then ordered to withdraw. Frank was reported missing and Laura had to wait until February 1916 until he was officially declared dead. He is commemorated on the Le Touret Memorial.

[1] On the memorial at St Peter's Church his name is spelled Sharp.
[2] Enfilade – to direct gunfire along a line from end to end.

Pte Arthur Lincoln Hornsby – aged 32
1st Btn Royal Warwickshire Rgt – 7752
Cenotaph

(Source: Mrs V. Green.)

Like Frank Sharpe, Arthur Hornsby was not a native of Dorchester but, as his name suggests, was born in the city of Lincoln, on 18 September 1882. He was the son of Richard and Elizabeth and sometime in the 1880s the family moved to Birmingham, where Richard worked as a master watch-maker. Their son Arthur joined the Royal Warwickshire Rgt as a drummer at the age of 18 and served with the 2nd Btn, and it is quite likely that he was one of the many soldiers who were stationed in Dorchester and took a fancy to a local lass. The girl on this occasion was Ada Woolvin, the daughter of Daniel Woolvin who, like Arthur, had been in the Army. Daniel and his wife Helen lived in Charles Street [1] with their family, but when Arthur and Ada were married Ada was living with her grandparents at 47 High West St. Arthur, who had returned to Dorchester for the marriage, was staying with Ada's aunt at 16 Sydney Terr. The couple were married in Dorchester Registry Office on 5 March 1908 and their daughter Muriel entered the world a year later, followed by Regina in 1911 and then Cecil, who was born 5 months before his father's death.

On the outbreak of hostilities Arthur rejoined his old regiment and disembarked to France with the 1st Btn on 22 August 1914, but soon after he was severely wounded and sent back to England for treatment. Unfortunately, he did not see his homeland again but died at sea on 16 October during his return to the UK. He is buried in St James' Cemetery, Dover.

[1] The houses in Charles Street, which were situated behind the shops on the east side of South Street, were demolished and replaced by a car park in the 1970s. There was considerable local opposition when the residents had to move out.

Pte Bertie Prowse – aged 31
1st Btn Dorsetshire Rgt – 6104
Cenotaph and St George's

Following the tragic events of 12 and 13 October 1914 [1], what was left of the 1st Btn Dorsets were, on 22 October, digging trenches on a new line near Violaines, Pas-de-Calais. In the vicinity the Cheshire Rgt had working parties out doing the same, when the Germans launched a surprise attack and took their position, forcing them to retreat. It was a particularly murky morning and no one in the Dorsets knew what was happening. Consequently, Lt Woodhouse was sent out to find the Cheshires when, suddenly, he heard loud cheering on his right and as he pressed forward, he encountered several of the Cheshires retiring. The enemy who were following were now able to take up position to bring fire down onto the Dorsets' who were forced to abandon their half-completed trenches. The situation was grave and by the end of the day the 1st Btn had sustained 134 casualties, including 101 missing men.

(Left) Bertie and Elizabeth, with their children Hilda and Thomas. (Right) Bertie's personal effects, which were returned to Elizabeth. They include the Princess Mary gift box, given to troops at Christmas, Bertie's pipe and his cap badge. His medals comprise the 1914–15 Star, the British War Medal and the Victory Medal, known affectionately as Pip, Squeak and Wilfred. (Source: Mr L.B. Sprules.)

Included among the dead that day was Bertie Prowse, a native of Dorchester. He was born in 1883 and in 1891 he was living with his parents Charles, a railway labourer, and Annie, at Coal Yard Cottage in King Street. In 1904 Bertie married Elizabeth Godden and 7 years later they were living at 1 Lester Square. Bertie was now employed as a carter with a coal merchant and his wife, who had found work doing laundry, had given birth to two children, Hilda and Thomas.

As soon as war was declared Bertie joined the Dorset's and went with them to France in the August. After his death his belongings, which consisted of his pipe and cap badge, were returned to Elizabeth, and later she also received the Princess Mary gift box which would have been sent to Bertie for Christmas. Elizabeth remarried in 1919 and ran a sweet shop at 3 Holloway Rd. There she displayed her former husband's belongings on the wall. Bertie is commemorated on the Le Touret Memorial.

[1] See Frederick Burt.

Capt. John Henry Strode Batten – aged 38
1st Btn King's Liverpool Rgt
Thomas Hardye School Roll of Honour

The Hamlet of Up Cerne is hidden away in the Dorset countryside between Cerne Abbas and Minterne Parva. The Manor House was built around 1601 and the 1891 census shows that it was then occupied by John Mount Batten and his wife Margaret, their six children, a governess and seven servants. John had retired from the Army as a lieutenant colonel and was now one of the principal landowners in the area. He was also active in public life, serving in several posts, including Deputy Lieutenant of the county, High Sheriff, Justice of the Peace and Alderman of the County Council. His regiment had been the King's Liverpool, in which he had served for 42 years, commanding the 3rd Btn during the Boer War. After his retirement he kept up his connection with the military through the Dorset Territorial Association.

(Source: www.ww1photos.com.)

The eldest son of the family, John Henry Strode, was born in December 1875 and educated at Dorchester Grammar and Rossall schools, before going on to Trinity Hall, Cambridge. After obtaining an arts degree he was gazetted to his father's old regiment on 20 May 1899 and promoted to 2 Lt in 1901 and captain in 1909. Like his father, John served in the Boer War where he was employed with the Mounted Infantry and later as a Supply Officer. He took part in operations in Natal, Orange Free State and Transvaal, and in actions at Reitfontein and Lombard's Kop. He was also part of the British contingent that was besieged at Ladysmith and was involved in the fighting on 6 March 1900 when the Boers attempted to storm the British defences. For his service in Africa he was awarded the Queen's Medal with two clasps [1] and the King's Medal with two clasps. After returning home John married in 1908 Alberta Kavanagh, the daughter of a London doctor, and in the same year was elected to the Dorset Bench.

On the outbreak of war in Europe, Capt. Batten disembarked in France on 12 August 1914 with the first BEF, and it was not long before he was making a name for himself. On 20 September the 1st Btn King's Liverpool was engaged in the Battle of the Aisne and facing a critical situation. John's actions were described by his brigadier: 'On a particular occasion, quite regardless of himself, he encouraged and steadied the men on the right of his battalion and of the brigade when very heavily attacked, and when the situation at that point was critical. It was owing to his very gallant conduct on that occasion that the portion of the line held its own.' Another officer, Col Stevenson, added, 'He saved the whole line on 20 September just by his grit. Nothing would move him from the line he had to take up when Kyrke Smith and others were wounded.' [2] Further testimony to his actions was given by a Lieut. P.C. Snatt who wrote, 'I owe him a debt I can never repay. If it had not been for his work on 20 Sept I should now be a prisoner … and it was Strode who saved the line.' [3] For his gallantry John was mentioned in Despatches [4] 6 days before his death. At 9.15 am on 25 October 1914 John left his trench to confer with his CO but he got no more than 20 yards before a sniper shot him through the heart. Col Stevenson wrote, 'He was killed outright crossing a small gap in a hedge by some men hidden in a house about 500 yards away … we buried him that night beside the Colonel in an orchard close to a farm outside the village where he was shot.' [5]

A report of John's death appeared in the *London Times* on the same date, 4 November, as that of Capt. Charles Andrews. [6] Locally, the *Chronicle* carried two reports on John's death commenting that 'his amiability and character and love of his native county, endeared him to the employees on his father's estate, and very great regret at the death of this gallant officer is felt by the villagers, with whom he was deservedly popular'. [7] John is commemorated on the Menin Gate Memorial near Ypres.

---

[1] Clasps were attached to the medal ribbon and although sometimes having very specific names they represented wider areas of operation. For example, the Defence of Ladysmith was awarded to any troops in Natal north of and including Estcourt, and included those who were present at the Battles of Skion Kop and Colenso.

[2] *Chronicle* 19/11/1914.

[3] De Ruvigny, 1922.

[4] *London Gazette* 19/10/1914.

[5] De Ruvigny, 1922.

[6] See Charles Andrews.

[7] *Chronicle* 5/11/1914.

Capt. Charles George William Andrews – aged 36
2nd Btn Border Rgt
Cenotaph, Holy Trinity, Thomas Hardye School Roll of Honour

On the northeast wall inside All Saints' Church is a memorial consisting of an oblong plaque of white marble dedicated to Charles George William Andrews. Charles was born in Dorchester on 16 May 1878, only son of George and Catherine. The family lived at 10 Trinity St and George had but a short walk each morning to his place of work, through Antelope Passage to the offices of the well-established firm of solicitors Andrews, Son and Huxtable at 6 South St. As a diversion from the law his father was involved with the Dorsetshire Rgt of Volunteers as a lieutenant with the 1st Btn, later promoted to major. He may well have expected his son to follow him into the law profession, but after completing his education at Dorchester Grammar School Charles decided to join the Border Rgt, and was commissioned 2 Lt on 5 February 1896, 4 years after his father's death.

Charles saw action in the Boer War, including operations in Cape Colony where he was wounded, Orange Free State and Transvaal, as well as taking part in the relief of Ladysmith. On his return to England he was awarded the Queen's South Africa Medal with four clasps and the King's Medal with two clasps. [1] In 1905 he married Diana Norrington, the daughter of a Plymouth chemical manufacturer, and their son George was born on 1 July 1910. In the years between the Boer War and the Great War Charles held various posts with the Volunteer and Territorial units of the regiment and was promoted to captain on 13 April 1910. In the 1911 census the family was living at Headley in Hampshire, with three servants.

In October 1914 the 2nd Btn Border Rgt was camped at Lyndhurst, Hampshire, where their Adjutant, Capt. Charles Andrews, was busy preparing the regiment for embarkation for France, as part of the BEF. Orders came on the 4th to march to Southampton where they boarded the ships *Turkoman* and *Minneapolis* to cross the Channel. However, when the battalion landed in Zeebrügge it was evident that they were not going to reinforce the BEF in northern France. Instead an urgent request for help was received from the Belgian government to prevent Antwerp falling into German hands, but events happened so quickly that the city had to be evacuated on 7 October. What was intended to be an offensive battle for the British became a desperate defence of the Channel ports. After moving to Ghent, the 2nd Btn was sent to dig trenches and hold the line near the village of Kruisek. Charles and comrades were in a vulnerable position, unable to leave their trenches during daytime because the position was overlooked by German artillery. On 26 October, the Germans launched an attack at 9.00 am and took the Borderers' front line trenches and it was probably during this attack that Charles was killed, along with four other officers and 25 OR.[2] His body was not recovered and he is commemorated on the Menin Gate Memorial.

Back home, Charles' death was reported in the *London Times* and the *Chronicle* and Diana was left to deal with her grief. Their son George Lewis, nicknamed 'Geordie', took up the military baton his father left behind by entering the Army, ending up as Assistant Commandant of the Royal Military Academy, Sandhurst. Diana remarried, to Sir Richard Gambier-Parry who led the Communications Section of MI6 during World War II.

[1] See John Roberts, footnote 4.

[2] The CWGC and *Times* newspaper gave the date of Charles' death as the 28th, but the field diary records no casualties on that date. The memorial in All Saints shows the 26th.

Pte Percy Hand – aged 43
7th Btn Yorkshire Rgt – 36965
Fordington Cemetery

Percy was one of nine children born to John and Mary Ann Hand of Stourbridge, Worcestershire, and before joining the 7th Service Btn Yorkshire Rgt he was employed as a painter in Derby. The 7th had been formed on 16 September 1914 as part of Kitchener's Army and was training at Worgret Camp near Wareham when Percy was taken ill. He was admitted to the County Hospital in Dorchester but died of lobar pneumonia, on 30 October 1914. Because he did not serve abroad he was not entitled to the usual war medals.

Sapper Alfred John King – aged 24
26th Field Coy, Royal Engineers
Post Office Memorial

Alfred King was born in West Knighton, the eldest son of Henry and Christine who ran the post office and stationers in the village of Winfrith. He was killed in action on 1 November while serving with the 26th Field Coy, RE at the first Battle of Ypres and is remembered on the Menin Gate Memorial.

Pte William Meader – aged 37
1st Btn Dorsetshire Rgt – 3/7404
Cenotaph and St George's

William Meader, who was born in Fordington, had a plumbing business that employed two boys. In the 1880s he and his wife Mary moved to Trinity Street with their two daughters and only son William, who was born in 1877. By 1891 the Meaders had again moved, this time to the intriguingly named Cuckold's Row at the bottom end of Holloway Road, where, in the 1901 census, 48 families were recorded. The name disappeared when it was incorporated into Holloway Road. When William Junior left school he worked as a plumber's assistant, presumably with his father's firm, and in 1898 he married Ellen Austin. Their first child Dorothy was born in 1899 and four more children were added, after which Ellen sadly died in 1913.

During their marriage William had been an army volunteer and, despite having the responsibility of five motherless children between the ages of 6 and 15, wanted to do his bit for his country. So in 1914 he enlisted in the Dorsets and after spending some time in

Weymouth with the 3rd Btn disembarked in France on 23 October to join the depleted 1st Btn. The battalion war diary shows that the day of 16 November 1914 started quietly for William and his fellow soldiers, who were fighting around Ploegsteert Wood, situated southwest of Commines and nicknamed Plugstreet Wood by British troops. By the end of the day William and four other men were dead and two others wounded after part of his company had been buried alive after some shelling of the area. Back in Dorchester five children were now orphans. His name was added to the Menin Gate Memorial.

Pte Rupert Cuthbert Phelps – aged 26
2nd Btn Dorsetshire Rgt – 8675
Cenotaph

Among the names of Dorset Rgt casualties listed in the *Chronicle* on 21 January 1915 was that of Rupert Phelps. Rupert was the third son of a large Dorchester family, his mother Kate giving birth to 11 children. His father James was a provisions merchant and the family was affluent enough to employ a couple of servants in their home at 4 North Square. By 1911 James had become an invalid and the family had moved to 4 Friary Lane, just round the corner. The young man, who presented himself to Cpl Butler at the recruiting office in Dorchester on 13 January 1909, was hardly the picture of a fighting man. At almost 20 years old, Rupert was just 5 ft 2½ in tall and weighed 7.5 st. He gave his occupation as a tailor and expressed a wish to join the Royal Irish Rgt. However, in the unique way the Army worked, his request was duly considered and dismissed and he was put instead into the 2nd Btn Dorsets.

Before 1914, Rupert spent most of his 5½ years in the Army in India, where he seems to have kept his nose clean, his Conduct Sheet showing that he was only disciplined on one occasion, when he was confined to barracks for 3 days for wearing the wrong belt on parade. He was not so fortunate when it came to his health. Like so many soldiers who found themselves in an alien environment, Rupert suffered from endemic illnesses and diseases. In 1910 he caught dysentery and 2 years later spent a week in hospital in Poona after being bitten by a sand fly. This was followed by a more serious ailment, relating to his lymph gland, which resulted in another stay in hospital of nearly 3 months. Despite these debilitating illnesses and his small physique Rupert appears to have been quite an athlete. One of the treasures of the Military Museum in Dorchester is a silver cup which bears an inscription showing that he won a marathon race, and among the personal effects that were returned to his mother after his death were four sports medals.

After some speculation about its destination, the 2nd Btn finally set sail on 18 October 1914 from Bombay to the Persian Gulf on the Troopship *Varela*. On arrival Rupert spent an unpleasant week cooped up on ship, where he and his colleagues suffered from the heat, exacerbated by a shortage of water. On 5 November Britain declared war on Turkey and the Allies started their advance. Initially, there was little resistance until 14 November when about 3,000 Turks were engaged at Saihan and eventually overcome. The next objective was Basra, but before that it was necessary to dispose of the Turkish fighting forces that had withdrawn to Sahil. For this battle Rupert was required to march across the desert carrying his rifle and greatcoat, cooked rations for 24 hours and 200 rounds of ammunition, a heavy load in the best of circumstances, but to make things worse a sudden rainstorm slowed progress considerably. The Turkish defences at Sahil were well organised and it was not long before the Dorsets came under fire as the battle ensued on the 17th. Advance was difficult, over flat open ground, but eventually the Allies won the day, with the Dorsets contributing more than their fair share of the 500 British casualties. Rupert was one of the 23 Dorsets killed, with another 150 wounded. He is buried in Basra War Cemetery.

Pte John Samuel Swinnerton – aged 32
8th Btn South Staffordshire Rgt – 13310
Fordington Cemetery

At 2.30 pm on 20 November 1914 an inquest was opened into the death of Pte John Swinnerton of the South Staffordshire Rgt. John, who before the War lived in Walsall, Staffordshire, with his wife and three children, had only been in the Army 11 weeks when an unfortunate sequence of events led to his death. On the Friday previous to the inquest he turned out for afternoon parade at Lulworth Camp and complained of a sore throat. He was sent to the camp hospital where he was told that if he bathed it in cold water it would be alright, but on the Sunday matters were worse and, after seeing the MO again, he was told that he had abscesses but that nothing could be done until they had burst. A lance corporal George Swingler told the inquest that on the Monday night they had a terrible time with him, 'as it seemed at every moment as if he would choke'. [1]

John returned to the camp hospital, only to be told by the medical orderlies that they could not summon the doctor because they did not know which tent he was sleeping in, and when eventually an ambulance was called for from Wareham Camp it did not arrive, and it was not until the next day that John was taken to Dorchester Hospital by private car. Dr Collard, acting house surgeon there, described how he observed, on John's arrival, that the swelling under his jaw, which he believed to be caused by a decaying tooth, stretched from one ear to the other and after consulting with the dental surgeon it was agreed to remove the offending tooth under anaesthetic. Then, seeing that the patient was turning blue and breathing badly, the doctor placed John on the floor and tried to resuscitate him, but in vain.

The post-mortem report said that the patient, who was in a weakened state because he had been unable to eat, had died of suffocation, but the Coroner was quick to point out that his death had been exacerbated by a series of blunders. He thought it extraordinary that the medical orderlies did not know which tent the doctor slept in, and that a camp comprising over 4,000 men did not have its own ambulance. He also expressed his surprise that the tooth was not extracted days earlier at the camp and added, 'There was difficulty enough in getting men for the army, and it was a pity that any should be lost in such a way as this'. [2] The reason given by the Army doctor for the tardiness in recognising the seriousness of the case was that they did not consider it urgent because 'in the camp there are many false alarms'. [3]

---

[1] *Chronicle* 26/11/1914.
[2] Ibid.
[3] Ibid.

Telegraphist William Thomas Vincent – aged 19
HMS Bulwark, RN – J/12355
Cenotaph, St Peter's, Thomas Hardye School Roll of Honour

Someone taking a stroll on Southend-on-Sea pier in the early morning of 26 November 1914 would have been very alarmed when the structure beneath their feet started shaking. The cause was an explosion that sent one of His Majesty's battleships, *HMS Bulwark,* to the bottom of the sea. Of the crew of 750 only 14 sailors survived, two of whom subsequently died. The ship had been anchored in the Thames Estuary just off Sheerness and had a full complement of men on board. One of the survivors, Sgt John Albert Budd, RM, was finishing his breakfast on the portside second mess deck when he saw a sudden flash aft. He turned and then the deck seemed to open up under him and he fell down. He recalled coming to the surface of the water and saw that the *Bulwark* had disappeared. He was rescued from the water but suffered a fractured leg and burns. There was great speculation about what caused the explosion. Initially, some thought the ship had been hit by a torpedo or had been the victim of a saboteur. However, expert witnesses at the subsequent inquest contended that the explosion was ignited by some internal cause and, although denied by the Admiralty, there were suspicions that cordite and ammunition had been stored in the corridors between the gun turrets.

Several Dorset men, including two from Burton Bradstock, perished in the disaster and Dorchester also paid a price. William Vincent, who lived at 44 Icen Way, eldest son of William, a blacksmith, and Ellen, attended Thomas Hardye School and then he worked as a clerk in the town. On his 18th birthday he signed on with the Royal Navy for 12 years and joined the training ship *HMS Impregnable,* and afterwards transferred to *HMS Britannia* before joining the *Bulwark* as a Telegraphist, 8 days before his death. The 19-year-old's body was never found after the sinking. His name appears on the Portsmouth Naval Memorial.

William was well known among the congregation of All Saints' Church and the following notice appeared in the December newsletter: 'From our parish we have lost William Vincent, an old choirboy and member of the Rectory Bible Class. He used to attend this often when at home for Sunday leave. He leaves behind him the memory of a sound Christian character, and a very promising life suddenly cut off. His is the first name to be recorded on the War's Roll of Honour for our parish'. [1]

---

[1] Dorchester All Saints Parish Magazine, 1883–1932

Pte William John Benjafield – aged 19
1st Btn, Dorsetshire Rgt – 6755

Pte Frederick Arthur Benjafield – aged 21
51st Field Bakery ASC – S/4/042273

Both are remembered on the Cenotaph

At the lower end of Monmouth Road there is a terrace of nine houses and although their address now forms part of Monmouth Road a plaque on the wall states that they were once known as Railway Terrace. Built in 1889 by the LSWR there were originally ten houses, but number one has since been extended into the Baker's Arms public house. In 1901 this house was both the home and place from which Thomas Benjafield, baker, ran his business, and if you go into the pub today you can still see the bread ovens he used. William and Frederick were the youngest of Thomas and his wife Elizabeth's three sons and in 1911 they were both gainfully employed, Frederick as a baker and William as a cook with a steam plough team. [1]

In January 1913 William joined the Dorsets as a Reservist and his introduction to military life was not without incident. A month after enlistment he was admitted to hospital with scabies and then got himself into trouble early in 1914 when he absented himself from camp. He obviously had a good reason for being absent because in the 'Punishment awarded' column of his service record is written, 'Case Explained'. William went into active service on 24 October 1914 and joined the 1st Btn in France. Following the battle of Armentières, the Dorsets were operating in an area about 7 miles south of Ypres. It was a quiet period for the troops, but even in quiet periods soldiers succumbed to enemy snipers or shellfire. William was killed on 3 December while the battalion was being relieved in the trenches by the Norfolks. He is buried in R.E. Farm Cemetery, Wytschaete, Belgium. The news of his death was received by his parents at their new address at 4 Colliton St.

Given his profession, it was no surprise when Frederick Benjafield enlisted into the ASC to bake bread for the troops. Before the War he worked for Buglar's and Son, bakers at 1 Prince's St, and then moved to Winton in Bournemouth, where he met and became engaged to a Miss Squires of Corfe Mullen. His army record shows that he enlisted on 12 January 1915 and after attending the Military Workshop in Aldershot, where he had to prove his competence, he was posted to the 51st Field Bakery at the port of Alexandria, as a Third Hand Baker.

On 6 July 1915 Fred and some of his friends were bathing in Dock Q of the port, which was not surprising when one considers how hot and uncomfortable it must have been for them working with bread ovens at the height of an Egyptian summer. What happened next was described in a deposition read at the inquest into Frederick's death. 'Pte Drummond heard the cry for help. He turned round to see what was wrong and all he could see were ten fingers disappearing under the water. He shouted to Barnett to come, then he dived but it was too late, when he came up he learned that it was his friend Frederick Benjafield that was down. By this time Barnett had dived but he too was unsuccessful. There were several other soldiers and a sailor and they all tried their best for about an hour. He gave up hope of getting Benjafield that night. He went down so sudden that no one got a chance of getting near him. How he came to be out of his depth no one knows.'[2]

Frederick's body was not recovered until the following afternoon and the verdict of the enquiry was that he met his death by drowning, most probably as the result of a sudden attack of cramp. In addition to being sent Frederick's personal belongings and medals, his parents received a letter from his CO which read, 'I feel it my duty to pay tribute to your son's sterling qualities. While under my command he led a clean upright life, and although circumstances were often trying, he never failed to perform all his duties in a thoroughly satisfactory manner. His loss we deeply deplore, and feel we have lost a good comrade.' [3] Frederick was buried on 8 July at Alexandria (Chatby) Military and War Memorial Cemetery.

[1] See Frederick Toogood.

[2] Inquest into the death of Pte Frederick Arthur Benjafield, held on 12/7/1915 at H.B.M
Provincial Court, Alexandria – SR.

[3] *Chronicle* 15/7/1915.

1 Railway Terrace, home of the Benjafield family, was later extended and is now the Baker's Arms public house. The bread ovens used by Thomas Benjafield can be seen inside.

1915
The Battle Front

France and Belgium

Neuve Chapelle, 10–13 March

Neuve Chapelle is a village that lies midway between Bethune and Lille, south of Ypres. It witnessed an offensive by Sir John French's forces, which would go on to put pressure on the Germans at Lille. The attack, led by Haig's First Army, commenced on 10 March and following a 35-minute barrage, the village was captured in just 4 hours. The German response was to bring up reserve troops and launch a counterattack on the 12th. The British held on but were unable to take their next objective, the village of Aubers.

Second Ypres, 22 April–25 May

The second Ypres offensive consisted of a number of battles around the Ypres Salient, where the British line, which followed the course of the canal, bulged around the town of Ypres and was the only major offensive by the Germans in 1915. The battle consisted of four distinct operations and has become infamous for the introduction of chlorine gas as a weapon on the Western Front. [1] On 22 April, 5,700 canisters of gas were released against 4 miles of the Allied line near Gravenstafel. The receiving men, French and British Territorials, fled and were followed by German troops advancing warily through the green mist. The German commanders, who had underestimated the effect of their new weapon, did not have adequate reserves to exploit the situation and consequently the assault was stopped by a counter-offensive. Two days later the Battle of St Julian took place, where further gas was released, this time against Canadian forces. The Germans made ground and after fierce fighting took the village of St Julien. Subsequent attempts by the British Brigades to retake the village failed with terrible loss of life.

Between 1 and 3 May the Allies withdrew nearer to Ypres and fighting renewed on the 8th at Frenzenberg Ridge, continuing until the 13th. On 24 May the Battle of Bellewaarde commenced and at the end of 2 days' fighting the British had lost another 1,000 yd of ground. Ballewaarde was the last action of the 2nd Ypres and the Germans gave up on the idea of capturing the town, deciding to destroy it by artillery fire instead. Casualties during the offensive are estimated as 69,000 Allied and 35,000 German.

Aubers Ridge, 9–10 May

Haig's 1st Army attack on the strengthened German lines around Neuve Chapelle was a total failure. The British artillery failed to destroy the German lines and their machine guns reaped their harvest when the British troops left their trenches.

Festubert, 15–27 May

The Battle of Festubert was fought by British, Canadian and Indian troops, so as to tie up German forces that might be transferred to Arras, where the French were fighting. After a 4-day bombardment, mostly Indian troops captured the enemy front line and the Germans retreated to a position just outside Festubert. A further assault was made by the Canadians on the 18th and more between the 20th and the 24th, until eventually the village was captured. The offensive ceased on the 27th; the Allies had gained 1 km at the cost of 16,000 casualties.

The summer of 1915 was characterised by static warfare and there was no major change to the situation. Casualties numbered about 300 per day, from shelling and sniper fire.

Loos, 25 September–18 October

The Battle of Loos, which was part of a combined Anglo-French attack against the German Fifth Army between Arras and La Bassée, was the first time that the British used chlorine gas. It was also the first time that most of the newly recruited Kitchener's Army saw battle. Back in Britain rumours were circulating about a 'big push' in the offing. British gas was emitted at 5.50 am on the 25th, in less than ideal wind conditions, and 2,632 British troops suffered the consequences. An hour later the attack began, the infantry having varying degrees of success along the 20-mile line. The southern section did well on the first day and captured Loos, but the need for supplies and re-enforcements brought it to a standstill. In the north I Corps had not been so effective but did manage to get a foothold on the Hohenzollern Redoubt. The inability to provide reserves meant that the British enterprise was doomed and after several more days of sporadic fighting they were forced to retire. Another attack was launched on the 13th with further heavy losses. During the battle British casualties amounted to 50,000.

Gallipoli

The ill-fated land forces' attempt to occupy the Gallipoli peninsular and consequently control the Dardanelles Strait was originally planned as a purely naval affair. The first attacks were made by British and French ships between 19 and 25 February but their bombardment was unable to overcome the Turkish defences, as were further attempts a week later and in March. It was clear that what was required was an assault by land forces. On 25 April, 18,000 French colonial troops and 75,000 men under British command, mainly untried Australians and New Zealanders, made the landings at Helles and on the coast near Gabe Tepe, which became known as Anzac Cove. Despite heavy casualties two precarious beachheads were established. Optimistically, Sir Ian Hamilton, the regional commander, then decided to head towards Krithia, but attempts made in April, May and June were all repulsed by the defending Turks. Back home, the awful realisation of the futility of the exercise was realised and Winston Churchill resigned from his post of First Lord of the Admiralty over the matter.

Despite the desperate situation it was agreed to send more troops into the mêlée and this time make a three-pronged attack, with the main emphasis at Suvla Bay. The landings at Suvla were initially successful, but by 10 August the general assault lost momentum through a combination of command confusion and indecision, difficult terrain and strongly held Turkish positions, leaving the troops in a terrible situation.

Back in London and Paris, the whole enterprise was losing credibility and Hamilton was replaced by Sir Charles Munro, who recommended a withdrawal. After much prevarication the British Government agreed, on 7 December, that the peninsular should be evacuated. The last troops left on 9 January 1916. Approximately 480,000 Allied troops had been involved in the operation, of which 252,000 became casualties.

Mesopotamia

Battle of Shaiba, 13–14 April

Following the Allied capture of Basra and the town of Qurna in December 1914 the Turkish forces had been pushed up the River Tigris to Ruta, where they established a line. Their leader, Col Subshi Bey, planned an April offensive at Shaiba and Qurna, the main assault to take place at Shaiba. On the 13th an attack by Turkish cavalry was dispersed and the troops retired to a wood, which the British took on the 14th, incurring heavy casualties.

Battle of Nasiriyeh, 24 July

The British continued to harass the Turks, despite being badly equipped and desperately short of medical supplies. Consequently, it was decided to attack the Turkish supply base at Nasiriyeh. A force of about 5,000 attacked the garrison there on 24 July and with the help of a gunboat on the river took the town, the Turkish defenders retreating to Kut.

Battle of Ctesiphon, 22–25 November

Following a string of successes culminating in the capture of Kut in September, the British Command now had its eye on Baghdad. The next objective on the road to capturing that city was Ctesiphon, where their good fortune deserted them. The Turkish lines there were two deep and straddled the River Tigris. Gen. Sir Charles Townsend decided to attack on one side of the river only, with about 11,000 Anglo-Indian troops. The following day the Turkish forces made a strategic withdrawal, believing that enemy re-enforcements were coming, but when they realised their mistake they halted. Hearing of the Turks' change of strategy and with casualties of 40%, Hamilton ordered a withdrawal to Kut.

Siege of Kut-al-Amara, began 7 December

The Siege of Kut and the subsequent surrender of British troops, followed by their march to imprisonment, has gone down as one of the greatest disasters in British military history.

The Turkish forces arrived at Kut on 7 December and after trying unsuccessfully to breach the British defences on three occasions elected to besiege the town. The siege continued into 1916.

Salonika

In October 1915, a combined British/French force was sent to Salonika, Greece, the objective being to help the Serbs in their fight against the Bulgarians. The plan came to nothing, as the former had already been beaten before the force was ready to go into action. However, it was decided to leave the troops there for further operations.

---

[1] Chlorine gas had previously been used by the Germans on the Eastern Front.

1915
Roll of Honour

Pte Richard Brown – aged 38
8th Reserve Bty, RFA – 88690
Cenotaph and St George's

There is little left now of the former Dorchester Artillery Barracks. What buildings survived its demolition and subsequent building of the Grove Industrial Estate stand out as solid redbrick structures, among the myriad of industrial boxes. Standing among them today, it is difficult to imagine that in spring 1901 the area housed 183 officers, gunners and drivers of the RFA, with their families and any number of horses. One of the drivers there was soldier Richard Brown from South Shields. At the other end of Dorchester, living at 8 Pound Lane, was a young lady by the name of Ada Voss. The two met and married at St George's Church on 14 April 1903 and soon after their first child John was born. By then Richard had already left the Army and gone into the Reserve. The family remained in the town, living at 29 Holloway Rd, where Richard found employment as a labourer and Ada went on to have another five children.

After War started, Richard disembarked with the RFA on 26 September 1914 as a Driver, then changed rank to Gunner and fought in the Battle of Mons. He was serving with the 8th Reserve Bty when he was sent back to Britain and admitted to the Red Cross Hospital at Hazelwood, Ryde, on the Isle of Wight. Richard had a particularly unpleasant death from encephalitis caused by the ingestion of the eggs of a tapeworm, probably through drinking infected water. The symptoms of his illness were such that he was transferred to the Carisbrooke Lunatic Asylum, where he died on 3 January 1915, aged 38, and was buried in the local cemetery. As if the death of her husband was not enough for Ada to endure, later in the War two of her brothers, Frederick and William, also perished. [1]

---

[1] See Frederick Voss and William Voss.

Rifleman Austin Joseph Damen – aged 40
2nd Btn King's Royal Rifle Corps
Thomas Hardye School Roll of Honour

The Damen family was a well-established firm of Dorchester corn and grain merchants and Austin's grandfather, Robert, was made mayor of the town in 1871. After Robert's death the family business passed to his son John who lived with his wife Teresa and their family in Prince's Street. In 1874 Teresa gave birth to a son, Austin, but sadly she died when he was only three, leaving John to bring up their four children. Austin attended Dorchester Grammar School and sometime after migrated to South Africa. He returned in August 1914 and enlisted in the King's Royal Rifle Corps in London, joining the 2nd Btn in France on 23 November 1914.

The 2nd Btn war diary states that the trenches occupied by Austin and his fellow soldiers in January 1915 were not pleasant; the men's feet were constantly wet and their rifles jammed because of the mud. On 9 January the CO received orders that next they were to attack the German positions they had unsuccessfully attempted to capture a few days earlier. The assault commenced at 2 pm after an artillery bombardment and was initially successful, but the trenches could not be held and the British troops had to retire to their own lines. The number of casualties was given as approximately 40 wounded and 20 dead, one of the latter being Austin. He is buried in Caudry British Cemetery, Nord, France.

Cpl Ernest William Howe – aged 25
1st Btn Dorsetshire Rgt – 3/5395
Cenotaph, St Peter's and St George's

Anyone walking along High East Street could easily miss the narrow passageway between Nos 44 and 45 despite the ornate archway adorning its entrance. Step inside and the row of small cottages it contains evokes a picture of the past. They have the address of Greening's Court and living at No. 1 at the time of her husband's death in 1915 was Lilian Howe and her newly born son. The child's father, Ernest, was born in the USA (Jersey) and around 1900 moved with his parents to Dorchester, the place of his father Reuben's birth. At the age of 12 Ernest was living at 9 Friary Lane and probably attended Dorchester Boy's School in Colliton Street.

When Ernest and Lilian married they went to live at 1 Mill Bank, Fordington, near Ernest's parents and grandparents, both of whom were then living in Mill Street. Later they moved to 1 Greening's Court. Ernest worked for some years for James Hallot, who ran the Borough Fish Supply in Greyhound Yard at the top end of South Street, and was a 'well known and popular young fellow'. [1]

Ernest was a Reservist and consequently called up the outbreak of war. He enlisted in the 3rd Dorsets at Lodmoor Camp, Weymouth, and later formed one of a reinforcing draft for the 1st Btn. The war diary for 11 January 1915 shows that the 1st Dorsets were near Wulverghem in Belgium and the day was quiet, except for the fact that D Coy was shelled by a light gun. This was possibly the cause of Ernest's death. He is buried at R.E. Farm Cemetery.

---

[1] *Chronicle* 8/2/1915.

Pte George Lacey – aged 22
8th Btn South Staffordshire Rgt – 14098
Fordington Cemetery

George Lacey died on 14 January 1915 in the County Hospital, whilst encamped at Bovington with the South Staffordshire Rgt. His funeral took place 4 days later at Fordington Cemetery. George was the son of George and Edith and before enlisting he was employed as a solicitor's clerk in Birmingham, the city of his birth.

Pte Frank Adams – aged 16
3rd Btn Dorsetshire Rgt – (3)7737
Cenotaph

Charles and Ada Adams married in 1896 and in 1901 were living with their son Frank and daughter Dorothy at 28 High St, Fordington. Unfortunately Ada died in 1909 and Frank and his sister were taken under the wing of William and Ellen Holley of 6 Salisbury Terr. The death of his wife was not the only tragedy in Charles' life.

On 31 August 1914, young Frank appeared before the recruiting sergeant in Dorchester to enrol with the Dorsets. As part of the attestation process [1] he was required to answer a number of questions, including one about his age, which he gave as 19 years 2 months. The figure standing before him, weighing just 7 st 12 lb and measuring only 5 ft 2 in in height, might have put some doubt in the sergeant's mind about Frank's true age but, nevertheless, he was recruited into the 3rd Btn.

As a Special Reserve Btn the role of the 3rd Dorsets during the Great War was to raise and train drafts of soldiers for the Front. As part of their training the men were required to guard important strategic places and installations and whilst the majority of the 3rd Btn marched off in early August from the Depot Barracks to Wyke Regis, the company that Frank joined was destined for Upton Camp, Ringstead, with the job of, among other things, guarding Weymouth waterworks.

Five months after Frank joined his company the following headline appeared in the *Chronicle*: 'Fatal accident at Upton Camp'. [2] The report that followed was of an inquest that had taken place into the circumstances of Frank's death. Through the graphic testimony of several witnesses a tragedy unfolded. Two days before the day of the inquest, which was held on 21 January, Frank and his fellow recruits returned to their barracks after a day of musketry training, using blank bullets. The inquest jury heard from Pte Harry Belcombe that at about 8.30 pm he was getting into bed and saw Frank and his good friend Stevens larking about with a rifle. He said to Stevens, 'You had better put that rifle down, or something will happen', to which Stevens answered, 'Alright'. What Harry did not see was Stevens pick up a bullet and load it into the rifle, which he then pointed at Frank and pulled the trigger. His friend immediately fell to the ground. Sgt Maj. Searle, who was in the canteen when the incident occurred, was immediately summoned to the hut where he found the young private lying unconscious, his heart beating feebly. He asked Stevens if he had shot Frank, to which he replied, 'Yes, quite by accident, having picked up a live cartridge instead of a dummy one'. The dozen or so men present confirmed that Frank and Stevens were good friends and the shooting had been a complete accident. Dr T.A. Walker told the inquest that when he arrived on the scene Frank was quite dead. The bullet had entered the centre of his left breast and struck the spine, breaking three or four ribs before passing out of the body. Stevens took the accident badly, was admitted to hospital the same night and was assessed to be too ill to attend the inquest to give evidence.

At the inquest his father informed the Coroner that his son had celebrated his 16th birthday a month before his death. [3] In answer to a question from the Coroner, Sgt Maj. Searle said that according to the official papers Frank was 19 and that his real age did not concern the Army. The section on Frank's service record showing his age is very telling. The handwritten age of 19 years 2 months has clearly overwritten a previous entry that suspiciously looks like the figure 16.

The funeral cortege must have made an impressive sight. Frank's coffin was borne on a gun carriage from the Hampshire RFA Bty and was draped in a Union Jack upon which were laid his cap and badge. Present was the full regimental band, which played as the procession wound its way through the streets of Weymouth to

Extract from Frank's service record, clearly showing that his age had been altered. Note his height and weight. (Image reproduced by kind permission of Ancestry.com Operations Inc.)

Melcombe Regis Cemetery, accompanied by a large body of Dorsets with arms reversed. On arrival at the cemetery Frank's body was lowered into a grave to the sound of the Last Post played on the bugle, followed by three sharp rifle volleys. Ironically, the coffin bore the inscription 'Frank Adams, died 19th January 1915, aged 19 years'.

[1] The attestation form is a statement of facts about the recruit that he declares to be true when he enlists.
[2] *Chronicle* 21/1/1915.
[3] At the time the minimum age for recruitment into the Army was 18 for home service and 19 for service abroad.

Able Seaman Alexander Henry Barby – aged 25
HM Submarine E10, RN
Cenotaph and St George's

The young bride standing before the alter of St George's on Saturday 4 December 1914 was blissfully unaware that the events of family life that most of us experience over several decades would, for her, be condensed into less than 4 months. After the ceremony Rev Bartelot noted in the register that the bride was Elizabeth Alice Bartlett, aged 24, of 45 Dukes

Ave, and the groom was Alexander Barby, a sailor from Wicken in Northamptonshire. On 11 April 1915 the vicar was again officiating before Elizabeth, this time at the baptism of her son Alexander but, on this occasion, one of the principal actors in the ceremony was missing. Written into that part of the register giving the father's occupation is the following: 'The father was a seaman RN, drowned in submarine'. As if that were not enough, Elizabeth was soon back in St George's Church mourning the death of baby Alexander who survived just 25 days.

On 4 December 1907, the day of his 18th birthday, Alexander had signed up with the Royal Navy for 12 years as a Boy Sailor. After training at the shore establishment *HMS Ganges II* at Shotley and serving on several ships, including the battleship *HMS Bulwark* and the cruiser *King George V*, he transferred in October 1913 to one of the newest arms of the Navy, the submarine service. After 10 months' training at *HMS Dolphin*, the submarine training establishment at Gosport, Alexander was sent to *HMS Maidstone*, a submarine depot ship anchored at Harwich, from which the navy were using *E-Class* submarines as part of the blockade of German ships.

On 18 January 1915, *HMS E10*, with Alexander and 29 other crew members on board, left Harwich for operations NNW of the German island of Heligoland, and at 7.50 pm on the 21st the submarine parted company with her sister vessel *E5*. That was the last that was heard of the *E10* and her fate remained a mystery until the year 2002, when a team of divers found her wreckage in 42 m of water. They reported that the vessel was fairly intact, but that the starboard ballast tank had been badly holed, strongly suggesting that it had hit a mine. They also said that the torpedo tubes had been emptied and the hatches were open, suggesting a possible escape attempt by Alexander and his fellow crew. Alexander is commemorated on the Portsmouth Naval Memorial.

Pte James Lugg – aged 49
Dorset National Reserve
Fordington Cemetery

On Christmas Day 1914 James Lugg, one of the National Reserve guarding the prisoners at Poundbury Camp, complained of feeling ill and was admitted to the Red Cross Hospital in Durngate Street. He was attended by doctors Walker and Gowering [1] but despite rallying for a time he had a relapse and died of heart trouble on 25 January. Once again, there followed an impressive military funeral, which the *Chronicle* described to its readers in detail. His body was taken to the mortuary at the County Hospital and on the day of his funeral, 26 January, no less than 160 members of the Dorset and Cornwall National Reserve were lined up waiting to accompany his body on its journey to Fordington Church. The procession took the longer route down High West Street to London Road, to avoid the possibility of the horses slipping on the steep gradient of Fordington High Street.

The son of Catherine Lugg, James came from Bere Regis where he worked as a butcher's lad, probably for Joseph Kellaway, the village butcher. At the age of 21 he enlisted in the Army, serving with the Transport Corps for 12 years, and during that period he married Mary Ann Turner in Farnham, Surrey, possibly while he was posted at Aldershot. After his discharge from the Army James took Mary back to Dorset where they lived in Wool and had five children. At the time of his death they were living at Littlemoor, a suburb of Weymouth.

---

[1] Dr Benjamin Gowering of 49 High West Street.

Pte George Hayes Topper – aged 22
10th Btn Nottinghamshire and Derbyshire Rgt – 20556
Fordington Cemetery

George Topper was serving with the Sherwood Foresters at Wool when he died in the County Hospital, on 26 January 1915. He was born in Cadnor, Derbyshire, the son of Phillip, who was a tailor, and Ellen. His father died when he was just a year old and his mother remarried to James Brown, a coal miner. George's mother then died before he reached the age of 14. He did not serve abroad before his death.

Pte Arthur William Hellard – aged 26
2nd Btn Dorsetshire Rgt – 9298
Cenotaph

About half way up Fordington High Street the road forks to the left into Holloway Road, which then leads to King's Road. In the 19th century the High Street end of this thoroughfare was known as Holloway Row and in 1891 it boasted two pubs and a grocers. Among the families living there were the Hellards: Walter, who described himself as a plumber/painter, his wife Emma and their three children, including baby Arthur who had been born the previous year. When it was time for Arthur's education he doubtless attended the local infants' school, a few doors away, run by Miss Langdon. Arthur eventually got a job as a groom and then, at the age of 21, joined the Army. He signed up with the Dorsets and after spending a short while in Belfast was attached to the 2nd Btn in India. It appears that he did not settle easily into the Unit, as his conduct sheet shows that he was charged with three offences between September and November 1913, twice for not being presentable on parade, for which he was confined to barracks, and once for being drunk, for which he was admonished. He also visited the MO with a dose of gonorrhoea.

On the night of 11 April 1915 Arthur slept at his battle station, in a trench which formed part of the British defences at Shaiba in Mesopotamia. Cavalry patrols had already warned of an enemy attack and at 5 am the next morning the order came for the Dorsets to stand to. At 10 am Arthur's company was sent to defend a position around a building which had been used as a kiln and, whilst the Turkish attack was repulsed, Arthur received wounds from which he died the following day. He is buried in Basra War Cemetery.

Capt. Frederick James Chadwick – aged 32
104th Wellesley's Rifles

2 Lt Richard Markham Chadwick – aged 20
11th Siege Bty, RGA

Both are remembered on the Cenotaph and at All Saints'

Amy Torkington's father was the Rector of Tarrant Crawford church and as a child her family, along with eight servants, lived in 'Crawford', a large house in the village of Spetisbury in North Dorset. In 1882, at the age of 27, she married Edward Chadwick, an officer in the 33rd Duke of Wellington's West Riding Rgt and twice her age. Eleven years later, Edward had retired from the Army with the rank of colonel, Amy had given birth to six children and the family was living in 'Nappers', a house in Chetnole near Sherborne.

Frederick Chadwick.

The imposing row of villas that run along Cornwall Road in Dorchester were built around the turn of the century. 'Westfield' on the corner of Cornwall Road and Albert Road was a 15-roomed house that the Chadwicks moved into sometime in the early 1900s. [1] Compared to most Dorchester folk Amy Chadwick had a comfortable life, but fate was about to shatter her world by the death of her husband and two sons within the space of 4 months.

Frederick, Amy's eldest son, was born on 31 August 1883 and was destined to follow a military career. After completing his education at Connaught House, Weymouth, and Cheltenham College, he entered the Royal Military Academy at Sandhurst and on 19 August 1903 he was commissioned 2 Lt and attached to the 59th Rgt of Foot, before joining the Indian Army in 1904. He Served in Poona with the 104th Wellesley's Rifles, was promoted to lieutenant in November 1905 and, after taking part in the Mekran (gun running) Expedition, [2] made captain in August 1912. In 1915 Frederick was in Mesopotamia alongside the 2nd Btn of his home regiment, the Dorsets, and it was while fighting with them at the Battle of Shaiba on the 13 April that he was wounded while leading a machine gun section and later died.

The previous February the *Times* in India published Despatches in which Frederick was mentioned for his gallantry and recommended for reward. His body lies in Basra War Cemetery and he is also commemorated in St Peter's Church, Chetnole. Amy Chadwick was still grieving the death of her husband, who died at home on 1 February 1915, when she heard the news that her eldest son had been killed. She received the customary letter from the King and Queen, not knowing that in a month's time she would receive another, in respect of her youngest son.

Richard Chadwick, who was 11 years younger than Frederick, was also educated at Connaught House and then went on to Wellington School, before attending the Royal Military Academy at Woolwich, which specialised in training officers for the Royal Artillery and Royal Engineers. At the age of 19 he was commissioned 2 Lt and joined the 10th Coy,

RGA at Spike Island, Ireland. When war came Richard disembarked in France on 21 April 1915 with the 11th Siege Bty.

Before improvements to ground-to-air communications, artillery targets were mainly pinpointed by officers in advanced observation points and the information sent back to the guns. It was a lonely job and also very dangerous. If their position became known to the enemy the observers became sitting ducks for enemy artillery fire or the sniper's bullet. The CO of Richard's battery recorded the circumstances of his young lieutenant's death in his field diary, when he wrote: 'Touret – 12/5/15 – 5.30 pm. 2 Lt Chadwick RM was struck by portions of an HE shell which burst in observing station, and fatally injured. He was carried to Bethune and attended in hospital but died the same night.' [3] He was interred in Bethune Town Cemetery, Pas-de-Calais, the following day.

Richard Chadwick.
(Source: Wellington College, Berkshire.)

---

[1] 'Westfield' was later used as a Catholic school for girls, run by nuns. It was then demolished and replaced by an ugly office block.

[2] Gun running in the Persian Gulf was a continual problem for the British Army in India.

[3] WD.

Cpl Charles Joseph Hoskins – aged 25
2nd Btn Dorsetshire Rgt – 7546
Cenotaph

Capt. Joseph Hoskins – aged 50
4th Btn Dorsetshire Rgt
Cenotaph and St George's

The day after Arthur Hellard's death, 14 April 1915 was the one chosen for the Allies to advance on the new Turkish positions in Mesopotamia. The movement started at 9.15 am but by midday the 2nd Dorsets were finding it difficult to push on, due to the advantage of the enemy's position and the heavy rifle fire coming in their direction. To make matters worse Bandsman Cpl Charles Hoskins and comrades were lying in the open, the sun beating down on their backs and with hardly any water. Most of the troops had received very little sleep due to the need to be constantly alert. An officer summed up the situation: 'I don't think I remember being so unutterably weary, or having such a raging unquenchable thirst. None of us could face a meal, our throats and mouths were so parched.' [1] Eventually, the Turkish forces were overcome but casualties among the Dorsets, who had played a prominent part in the fighting, were high. Among those killed was Charles Hoskins, who, like his fellow Durnovarians Arthur Hellard and Frederick Chadwick, was buried in Basra War Cemetery.

Charles was the son of the well-known and much-respected Dorset Rgt veteran Joseph Hoskins and his wife Ellen and was one of five brothers who served their country in the Great War, four in Mesopotamia and one in France. Their father's service record shows that he was the epitome of a soldier who had joined up as a young man and worked his way up through the ranks. He was born in North Allington, Bridport, in March 1868 and wasted no time in joining the Army at the age of 18 years 7 months, having already served as a Reservist. Initially he served with the 1st Btn and was appointed to lance corporal after just a year and then promoted to corporal a year later. In March 1890 he went to Egypt, where he was raised to the rank of sergeant and spent some time with the mounted infantry. After 5 years in the Middle-East Joseph's career path took him further away from the UK when, in September 1893, he was sent to India, where he married Ellen Neal on 24 March 1894 at Colaba, Bombay. Given that Joseph's eldest son Charles was born in 1891, presumably he was married previously, but I have been unable to trace a record of this. The year following his marriage another promotion came, this time to colour sergeant, which he retained throughout his service in India. Joseph spent 5½ years in the Subcontinent before returning to England with Ellen and their two sons. Back in Dorchester, Joseph was not one of the Dorsets that went off to the Boer War but instead remained at the Depot until 1907, when he became sergeant instructor of the Wareham Coy, a group of soldiers that would be amalgamated to form the 4th Btn (Territorials). By now, Joseph had been with the county regiment for 21 years and, in recognition of this, received Good Conduct and Long Service medals, to go with the Coronation Medal presented to him in 1902. The family lived in East Street, Wareham, for the next 7 years, then moved to Dorchester when Joseph was made RSM at the Depot and lived at 5 Aldhelm Villas in Damer's Road.

Joseph Hoskins. (Source: The Keep Military Museum.)

His departure from the ranks was a cause for celebration. At a gathering in the sergeant's mess, of which he was President, his fellow sergeants congratulated him on being granted a commission as lieutenant quartermaster and presented him with a gold half-hunter watch to commemorate his 30 years' association with the battalion.

The war brought another change of direction for Joseph when he went back to India, this time without his family. But he was soon to return, suffering from a bout of dysentery, and after recovering was posted to the Reserve Btn as captain in Northern Ireland. Joseph's illness had undermined his health and on hearing that her husband lay seriously ill in Ebrington Barracks, Londonderry, with emphysema Ellen immediately headed for Ireland with her daughter. Sadly, her journey was interrupted in London by a telegram to say that her husband had died. His life ended on 6 October 1918 and he is buried in Weymouth Avenue Cemetery.

Pte Frederick William Fickus – aged 37
1st Btn Dorsetshire Rgt – 3/7541

Lionel Frederick Fickus
Military service unknown

Both are celebrated on the Cenotaph

Frederick was born in Preston, Weymouth, and then the family moved to Godmanstone when his father Frederick, a retired naval signaller, got a job as an attendant at the County Lunatic Asylum at Herrison. In 1899 young Frederick married Mary White from Gloucestershire and they set up house at 13 Miller's Close, just a few doors away from his parents who had since moved to Dorchester and were residing at No. 25. After being employed by Mr Bryan Jones, a horse dealer on Fordington Green, Frederick started his own horse trading business working from the stables of Capt. Acland at Woolaston House, where his father was now working as a gardener. Mr Fickus Senior became well known in the town, especially after saving a young boy from drowning at 'Ten Hatches' above Grey's Bridge. [1, 2]

Frederick Junior's service record indicates that he had spent some time in the Dorsets before the War but the document showing the period of his service is damaged and the dates cannot be read. He re-enlisted in them in February 1915 and joined them at the Front, leaving behind his wife and three children, who were now living at 19 Miller's Close. [3]

Frederick's brother John was also serving with the 1st Btn Dorsets and on 16 April 1915 he was acting as stretcher bearer. The order came to go and pick up a man who had been

Mary Fickus's locket, showing Lionel (left) and Frederick (right). (Source: Mrs A. Jones.)

seriously wounded, probably during one of the raids on enemy trenches that the Dorsets were undertaking at that time. John went to where the man lay and found to his horror that the casualty with the severe head wound was his elder brother Frederick. His sibling never regained consciousness so he was unable to comfort him or say goodbye. Frederick died 2 hours later and John helped bury him in Woods Cemetery, Ypres.

Lionel, the eldest son of Frederick and Mary, was born in 1900 and also appears on the town's Cenotaph. However, there is very little information about him. The memorial states that he served with the Staffordshire Yeomanry but he does not appear on their Roll of Honour. A photograph of him and his father, both in uniform, are contained in a locket, which presumably Mary wore, and the badge on his cap looks more like that of the Dorset Yeomanry. There is no Medal Roll Card for Lionel, suggesting that he never served abroad, but neither does his death seem to have been registered in England. The family story is that Lionel lied about his age when he enlisted and even used a different name, perhaps his mother's maiden name of White. Further, his mother contended that he died in France in 1917 and his body was never found. There is some possible evidence for this on the back of a photograph attributed to him, which states that the sitter was killed in France in 1917. It is, unfortunately, one of those cases where the researcher has to draw a blank. Frederick's brother John, who reached the rank of sergeant, was sent home wounded in 1918 and survived the war.

[1] *Chronicle* 10/8/1916.

[2] The River Frome just above Grey's Bridge and to the east of the town was dammed and a swimming pool was built there around the turn of the century. It was closed in the early 1960s following a national epidemic of polio. The remains of it can still be seen.

[3] The houses in Miller's Close have long gone and it is now part of the Grove Trading Estate.

German prisoners enjoying the open-air swimming pool below Ten Hatches, Grey's Bridge, on the River Frome. (Source: The Keep Military Museum.)

Capt. Damer Wynyard – aged 25
1st Btn East Surrey Rgt
Holy Trinity

(Source: www.ww1photos.com.)

Damer Wynyard was the sixth in direct succession from father to son to take up a military career. His grandfather, a general, and his uncle, a colonel, were both well-known veterans in Dorchester, as was another uncle, Col M. Wynyard, who was buried in Weymouth Avenue Cemetery in March 1915. His aunt, Miss Wynyard, also lived in the town at Clarence House, Clarence Road. His father Richard was a lieutenant colonel in the East Surrey Rgt and his mother Sophie was an American from Staten Island.

Damer was sent as a boarder to Durnford School, Langton Matravers [1], and then went on to Wellington and Sandhurst, where he rose to the rank of colour sergeant. On passing out from Sandhurst, in 1909, he joined his father's old regiment, the East Surreys, as a lieutenant and was posted to the 1st Btn, which formed part of the original Expeditionary Force to France. At the Battle of Mons Damer was wounded in the left arm which necessitated a return to the UK where, after recovering, he and Olive Wakeley, the daughter of an Irish judge, were married. Having already been wounded, one wonders what the young couple said to each other as they parted almost immediately after the wedding. Damer went back to France and it is unlikely that they ever saw each other again.

Hill 60 was the name given to a piece of high ground near the village of Zillebeke, Ypres, which before the War was known locally as 'Lover's Knoll,' a favourite meeting place for courting couples, but in 1915 it was a very different place. After the First Battle of Ypres it formed part of the front line with the Germans occupying the upper parts. The lower slopes were held by the French who were relieved by the British in early 1915. On 16 April the 1st East Surreys were resting in barracks when a warning arrived to be ready to support the 15th Brigade at Hill 60. They moved into the front trenches the next day, to be greeted by an intense artillery bombardment. Damer was killed on 20 April and the circumstances of his death were graphically described in the battalion war diary. 'A quiet time till 11 am then heavy shelling of the hill, communicating and support trenches commenced, with great effect, the Germans scoring many direct hits with heavy howitzers, trenches were blown in and many men killed and buried. During this time Capt. & Adjt Wynyard, seeing some men attending wounded men near a shelled spot, went towards them, moved the men along the trench away from the danger spot, attended the wounded himself and in doing so was blown to bits.' [2]

Olive replied to the letter that she had received on behalf of Their Majesties, thanking them for their sympathy at her husband's death and also for the information that he had been mentioned in Sir John French's Despatches for gallantry and distinguished service, but more important to her husband's memory perhaps were the comments made about him by Gen. Maude, [3] commanding the 14th Brigade at the time, when he wrote: 'He was not only an ideal Adjutant, but the type of a true soldier, modest, unassuming, brave and thorough in his work. The last time I saw him was the night I was hit, and I walked into his shelter in the trenches to have my wounds dressed by the MO of the East Surreys. I shall never forget his kind solicitude for me, and the last act as I was carried away on the stretcher was to place his own rug over me to keep me warm … He fell as a gallant soldier in the performance of his duty ….' [4] Damer's name is inscribed on the Menin Gate Memorial, and he is remembered on the Durnford and Wellington Schools' Rolls of Honour and on the Cattistock War Memorial.

On 12 July 1914 Damer had been appointed captain and acting adjutant of his battalion and his service record contains an interesting piece of correspondence concerning this. His father wrote a letter to the Secretary of the War Office, dated 24 June 1915 and addressed from the Navy and Military Club, Piccadilly, in which he points out that his son took over the duties of adjutant in an acting capacity from his return to his battalion until his death. He then adds, 'Like all good soldiers, my son's ambition was to be Adjutant of his battalion, and it would be a great satisfaction to his mother, his widow and myself if, without in any way affecting the position of Capt. Bowring (the holder of the appointment), we could see him Gazetted as such. This application is based purely on personal and sentimental grounds.' [5] It appears that the War Office did not acquiesce to the family's request.

[1] See Walter Hill.
[2] WD.
[3] Lt Gen. Sir Frederick Maude KCB, CMG, DSO.
[4] *Dorset Year Book* 1915/16.
[5] SR.

Pte Joseph Joel Boyce Bartholomew – aged 23
1st Canadian Btn Ontario Rgt – 6773
Cenotaph

In 1911 Joseph Bartholomew was living at 22 Maie Terr. Joseph was the eldest son of Robert Bartholomew, former professional soldier and now house painter, and his wife Emily. Joseph worked as an engine cleaner at the South Western Railway station and was an active member of the 2nd Dorchester Coy of the Boy's Brigade.

When he was 19, Joseph decided to migrate to Canada, where he found employment as a fireman with the Canadian Pacific Railway, and then became a farmer. However, when he landed on Canadian soil in August 1913 he had no inkling that he would be making a return journey to England in 14 months' time as part of the Canadian Expeditionary Force.

As a dominion still owing allegiance to the Crown, Canada immediately entered into the War, the Prime Minister Sir Wilfred Laurier declaring, 'It is our duty to let Great Britain know and to let the friends and foes of Great Britain know that there is in Canada but one mind and one heart and that all Canadians are behind the Mother Country'. [1] Like thousands of young Canadians Joseph rushed to defend the country of his birth and joined the 1st Canadian Infantry Btn (Western Ontario) sailing for England on the White Star liner *Laurentic*. He arrived in England on 21 October 1914 and after training at Salisbury headed for France. In April 1915 his battalion was part of the Canadian 1st Division, which was holding a line to the northwest of Ypres. Fighting during the second half of the month was characterised by Allied and German attacks and counterattacks, and on the 30th, the date of his death, Joseph and colleagues were trying to hold the front line under heavy artillery fire, and it is likely that he was killed by a German shell. He is commemorated on the Menin Gate Memorial.

[1] http://en.wikipedia.org/wiki/Military_history_of_Canada_during_World_War_I.

2 Lt John Henry Charles Roberts – aged 36
1st Btn Dorsetshire Rgt
Cenotaph [1]

John Roberts was one of three men who shared the doubtful privilege of being the first on Dorchester's memorials to die from the effects of what was described by an officer of the Dorset Rgt as 'the dirtiest trick that any British regiment has yet had to put up with'. [2] He was referring to the use of chlorine gas by the Germans.

Hill 60 was not a natural feature but made up of spoil from the adjacent railway. Sited about 3 miles southeast of Ypres it offered an elevated viewpoint in a flat landscape and was bitterly fought over, changing hands several times during the War, and on 29 April 1915 orders were received for the 1st Btn Dorsets to relieve the 2nd Cameron Highlanders, who were supporting the 1st Devons in defending the hilltop.

The 1 May began as a bright sunny day, with a slight south-easterly breeze and the enemy were unusually quiet. The first German gas attack against the French had concentrated the minds of the authorities on what was the best kind of protection against this new weapon. Makeshift respirators consisting of pieces of flannel and green gauze were issued and John was ordered to carry his at all times and wet it in the event of a gas cloud coming over. At 7.15 pm, following a severe bombardment of the hill, thick white clouds of gas were seen to shoot out of nozzles opposite the British trenches and the effects were immediate and devastating. As the breeze blew the cloud toward the Dorsets the men cowered in the bottom of the trenches, which was the worst thing they could do. Those who survived were the ones that took a chance by standing on the firing platform and raising their heads high. John was badly affected by the gas and admitted to the field ambulance station at 10 pm, where he subsequently died on the 5th. His body lies in the Bailleul Communal Cemetery, Nord, France. The casualty list for the battalion, following the attack makes grim reading; 53 men died and 206 others were admitted to the field ambulance station, many of whom succumbed later. In addition, 32 others crawled away to die a painful death and their bodies were located later. Only one man was killed and one wounded from shell fire or rifle fire.

John was born 1 August 1878 at Parandhur, India, where his father was serving as a sergeant with the East Yorkshire Rgt. The family moved to Dorchester when Sgt Roberts was made Superintendent of the Royal Artillery Hospital. After attending the Royal Hibernian Military School in Dublin John enlisted in the 2nd Dorsets at the age of 14. During the South African war he acted as orderly to Sir Charles Warren, commander of the 5th Division,[3] but was invalided home to the Depot Barracks in Dorchester where he remained until the outbreak of war. By then he was married with a family and living in family quarters within the confines of the barracks. Now demolished, the family quarters consisted of a block behind the Little Keep, a fine building that now provides the entrance to a modern development of flats. At the time there were two wives living there with the surname of Roberts and it seems most likely his spouse was Alice, whom he married in 1906. For his work in the Boer War John was awarded the Queen's Medal with two clasps, one for operations at Tugela Heights and another for the Relief of Ladysmith. [4] Such was John's experience that he was granted a commission in December 1914 and immediately made Adjutant of the 7th Btn Dorsets, based at Wyke Regis before being sent off to join the 1st Btn in March 1915.

[1] Wrongly shown as J.M.C. Roberts.
[2] Regimental history.
[3] Sir Charles Warren GCMG, KCB, FRS. Warren was a career soldier who also attempted to become an MP, but he is mostly known as the Metropolitan police commissioner who failed to capture Jack the Ripper.
[4] See John Batten, footnote 1.

Pte Alfred Thomas Ford – aged 29
1st Btn Dorsetshire Rgt – 3/8471
St George's

The second of Dorchester's trio of men to be killed by gas attacks on Hill 60 was Alfred Ford. Alfred was born in Piddlehinton in 1886 to Ellen and husband Henry, a shepherd working at Forston Farm, Charminster. In 1905 Alfred married Lilian Collins from Litton Cheney and in 1911 they were living at Milborne Wick near Sherborne with their two sons and a daughter. It is not known when they moved to Dorchester but in 1916 Lilian gave her address as 17 Holloway Rd.

Alfred enlisted in the Dorsets in September 1914 and joined the 1st Btn in Belgium at Ypres and saw action at the Battles of Armentières and the First Ypres. He officially took his last breath at 5.15 am on 4 May 1915 at No. 13 General Hospital, Boulogne, where he died. Lilian received the news of his death at 84 Mill St and this was to be the first of two blows she had to endure within 2 months, their youngest son Leslie dying in July of the same year. Alfred was buried in the Eastern Boulogne Cemetery. The gas attack at Hill 60 had cost the 1st Btn dearly. On 30 April the battalion had gone into the line over 800 strong and by 6 May it had been reduced to 173 all ranks.

L/Cpl Ernest Clarke [1] – aged 20
1st Btn Dorsetshire Rgt – 9653
Cenotaph and St Peter's

Like John Roberts,[2] Ernest Clarke died as a result of the gas attack on Hill 60 on 1/2 May 1915. The son of Robert, a coal carter, and Hannah Curtis, he was born in West Fordington and lived at 16 Frome Terr, a delightful row of cottages by the River Frome. Ernest was employed as a shop assistant when he joined the Dorsets in January 1914 at the age of 18, having been a Special Reservist. At Hill 60 he was wounded on 27 April before being one of the first to be affected by the poisonous cloud of chlorine. He died on 4 May and is commemorated on the Menin Gate Memorial, suggesting that his body was never found and that he may have been one of those men who crawled away from the battlefield to a slow death from asphyxiation.

[1] Ernest was born Francis Ernest Clarke.
[2] See John Roberts.

Pte George Bertram Dodge – aged 34
13 Btn London (Kensington) Rgt – 3173
Cenotaph

On 11 October 1917, the *Chronicle* informed its readers that Sgt Montague Dodge had been wounded and that his elder brother George had been missing for over 2 years. The fact that George had not been officially declared killed gave his mother some hope that her son might be a prisoner of war, but he did not return home. Instead his name can be found among the 11,447 others carved onto the Ploegsteert Memorial, Hainaut, Belgium.

George was not a local man but was brought up in Puddletown, 5 miles east of Dorchester, where his father worked as a gamekeeper to Col William Brymer on the Ilsington Estate. The Dorchester connection came when his father died and his mother Ellen moved to 3 Chestnut Villas. Having spent all his childhood in the countryside George went to London and found a job as a porter in the Metropol Hotel, St Martin in the Field. He then moved to Kensington where, after the start of War, he enlisted in the Kensington Btn of the London Rgt.

On 8 May 1915 the Kensingtons were preparing to attack enemy positions, their main objective being the capture of Delangre Farm, situated just outside the French village of Fromelles. At 2 am the following morning the attack commenced with an artillery barrage aimed at cutting the extensive German barbed wire defences and destroying their trenches. Then at 5.40 am, the barrage lifted, two mines were exploded under the German lines and George climbed out of his trench and headed towards the enemy just a hundred or so yards away. By 6.40 am the CO of the Kensingtons reported that whilst a footing had been gained in the German trenches, casualties had been very heavy. George was taking part in a desperate battle, with the Kensingtons running short of ammunition and suffering from withering machine gun and rifle fire from the farm, which had remained untouched by the British artillery. To make things worse, George and comrades were inadvertently being strafed by the machine guns of the East Riding Division. By mid-afternoon it was clear that no progress was going to be made and the order came to retire. When the tally of casualties for the assault was made the Kensingtons had 95 men killed, 109 wounded and 222 missing. George was counted among the latter.

Sapper Henry John Swyre [1] – aged 34
11th Field Coy, Royal Engineers – 13304
St George's

Henry Swyre was born in December 1881, the son of William, an iron moulder, and Sarah. It is quite likely that William worked for Lott and Walne's foundry, one of the major employers in the town with its premises at the bottom of Fordington High Street, not far from where he lived with his family at 53 Mill St. Their son Henry was a stonemason's labourer, but by the time he applied to join the Royal Engineers in January 1904, he had been working for 3 years as a bricklayer. The recruitment officer had no hesitation in recommending him for acceptance, describing him as strong and healthy and 'a likely looking man' [2] who, if he could not be a bricklayer, was willing to be a driver. After 7 years as a Regular, Henry went back to Civvy Street with a good conduct badge and a glowing reference, which stated that he was thoroughly trustworthy. As a Reservist he was back in uniform at the outbreak of War and went to France with the 11th Field Coy, Royal Engineers, but was only there for a short time, returning home in February 1915. Whilst home he married Harriet Hanham, a local girl from Colliton Street, but their time as husband and wife was cut short when he returned to the Front in April. They never saw each other again.

At the beginning of May 1915 Henry was helping with the many tasks allotted to a Sapper, like mending roads, filling in shell holes and repairing trenches, in preparation for an assault on the enemy at Ferme Du Bois, Festubert, Pas-de-Calais. The attack commenced at 11 pm on 15 May and two Sections of his unit had the job of accompanying the advancing troops to search for mines and 'surprises' (booby traps). The attack on the wood failed and the 11th Btn sustained 31 casualties, including Henry, who died on the 16th. His name is inscribed on the Arras Memorial.

---

[1] St George's memorial shows Henry G Swyre, which is incorrect.
[2] SR – Army form B.208.

Pte Reginald Bertie Hoddinott – aged 34
Portsmouth Btn Royal Naval Division, RMLI – PO/11024
Cenotaph and St George's

Reginald Hoddinott came from a large family. His mother Emily [1] gave birth to 11 children, 10 of whom survived into adulthood. Her husband John was a stoker in the Dorchester Gas Works which was sited on land between Icen Way and Salisbury Fields. On 22 November, 1880, Emily gave birth to her second son, Reginald, when the family was living in Mill Street and when he grew up he got a job as a porter in a wine store, before joining the Royal Marines at the age of 20. After his induction and training at the Royal Marine Depot at Deal, Reginald joined his first ship *HMS Camperdown*, a battleship of the line, where he spent a year manning the guns. His next posting sent him off to Malta, attached to the base ship *HMS Hibernia*, before returning to sea for 2 years on the cruiser *HMS Indefatigable*, and a further 2 years on another cruiser, the *Grafton*. After 12 years' service, Reginald was discharged with a good character into the Royal Fleet Reserve, which like the Territorial Army required him to attend a week's training camp once a year.

In 1913, Reginald married Dorothy Brownsea in Camberwell, London, where she was working as a laundry maid in a hospital, and they set up home in the Capital. As a member of the RFR Reginald had to be available should an emergency arise and, of course, it came in August 1914. If, however, Reginald thought he would be serving in ships again, he was mistaken.

At the beginning of the War the Navy found that it had 20–30,000 more men than it had jobs for on any warship, so it was decided to turn sailors into soldiers by establishing two Naval Brigades and a Royal Marines Brigade to fight on land. Reginald landed with the RM Brigade in Dunkirk in September 1914 as part of a force known collectively as the Royal Naval Division, which had orders to defend the port of Antwerp. In the rush to get fighting men to Belgium the majority of the RMB did not even have the basic equipment such as packs or water bottles, and some had antiquated rifles. In the subsequent withdrawal from Antwerp Reginald managed to get back to the UK and avoided being one of the unfortunate men who were forced to cross into Holland and were interned for the rest of the War. Following regrouping and training in the UK the Marines joined the ill-fated expedition to Gallipoli and it was there that Reginald was wounded on 14 May 1915. He was sent to one of the base hospitals at Alexandria in Egypt, where he died on 26 May. He is buried in Alexandria (Chatby) Military and War Memorial Cemetery. His parents received the news of their son's death at their new address, Fern Cottage, 34 Fordington Hill.

---

[1] Emily was also known as Maria.

Pte Jack Colenso – aged 21
9th Btn Duke of Cornwall's Light Infantry –
19502
Fordington Cemetery

Like many towns, Dorchester had its isolation hospital where those suffering from infectious diseases were treated. Dorchester's was situated well away from the town's population, in Herringston Road and it was there that Jack Colenso of the Duke of Cornwall's Light Infantry died on 2 June 1915 from cerebral meningitis. Jack was born in 1894 in Falmouth, the son of Stephen Colenso, who at one time in his career drove the stagecoach from Falmouth to Penzance, and Sophia. He was with the 9th Btn DCLI at Wareham Camp when he was taken ill.

(Source: Mr F. Colenso.)

Pte Henry Mark Loader – aged 36
2nd Btn Hampshire Rgt – 5506
Cenotaph and St George's

Compared to today, the roads of Edwardian Dorchester had few motor vehicles and the town was relatively quiet. One thing that did disturb the peace, however, was the rumble of one of Francis Eddison's steam traction engines making its way through the streets of the town. The Eddison Steam Plough Works was located in Fordington [1] and, with the brewery and Lott and Warne's foundry, was one of Dorchester's largest employers. One of its employees was Henry Loader, who worked as an assistant in the stores and lived with his wife Ada at 11 Shamrock Terr.

On 30 May 1915 Henry was in reserve trenches with the 2nd Hampshires, 2 miles southwest of Krithia, on the Gallipoli peninsula. Meanwhile, preparations were being completed for a general attack on Turkish lines by the 8th Bde, of which the Hampshires formed a part. The day chosen was 4 June, the time noon, following an artillery barrage. The battalion's first objective was the enemy's front line, which was to be taken by X and Y Companies, followed by W and Z, which would pass through the former and make an assault on the second line. As soon as the bombardment ceased the first of the Hampshires advanced and despite heavy enemy fire captured their objective. The supporting troops went through the leaders, as planned, and they too were successful. Any further advance was delayed because the regiments to the left of the Hampshires had been held up, but soon they were able to move forward again and it was reported that some of the advance troops had got to the fifth line of the enemy's defences. When the counterattack came it came in force and holding the advanced positions was untenable, and at 6 pm the Hampshires were ordered to fall back to an earlier secured line. Overall, the attack had been successful, gains had been made and prisoners taken, but losses to the 2nd Btn were high. Fifty-six Other Ranks were killed or missing and 95 were wounded out of a total force of 300. Henry was one of those killed in action and is remembered on the Helles Memorial.

---

[1] The Plough Works site was near the present Government Buildings in Prince of Wales Road.

Pte William Loveless – aged 33
1st Btn Border Rgt – 7588
Cenotaph and St George's

The name of Loveless is forever linked with the small village of Tolpuddle, situated to the east of Dorchester, through the fact that two brothers, James and George Loveless, were part of a group of agricultural labourers who were transported to Australia for forming a trade union. [1] Thirty or so years after the trial of the Tolpuddle Martyrs, another James Loveless was finding life difficult in the village, as an agricultural depression began to hit the countryside. The response of James and

(Source: Mrs P. Collins.)

his brother William was to look for work elsewhere. It may well be that they had heard of the great cotton mills of the North and their insatiable appetite for labour but, for whatever reason, they decided to head in that direction. The family story is that they walked until they reached Bolton in Lancashire, where they decided to settle. James did not end up working in a mill but instead became a police constable in March 1875. Interrupting his duty a year later he returned to Dorset to marry Fanny Pearce, a fellow Tolpuddler. After their marriage the couple returned to Bolton with a child and in 1881 Fanny gave birth to their second son William.

At the age of 19 William was working in one of the local cotton mills and 3 years later decided on a change of occupation and became a regular soldier. He enlisted in the Border Rgt at Manchester and after completing his basic training at the Depot in Carlisle was posted to the 1st Btn in Plymouth. At this point William's story becomes a little vague. As a regular soldier he would have enlisted for a minimum of 7 years and then gone into the Reserve. However, in his case it looks as if he may have left the Army prematurely. The evidence for this comes from the fact that when he married his cousin Hersella in 1908 his marriage certificate gave his employment as that of insurance agent. There is also a photograph of William working at the Soldiers' Home, North Square, [2] at Christmas time 1909. Hersella was the daughter of William's uncle Stephen Loveless and lived at 18 Duke's Ave. After their marriage the young couple lived with her parents until they moved into a house opposite, at No. 31.

Whatever the circumstances of William's previous military service, there is no doubt that he rejoined the Border Rgt in 1914 and went into the 2nd Btn, one of the last units to join the BEF in France. Soon afterwards he was wounded and on 5 November admitted to No. 4 General Hospital, Versailles, with a gunshot wound to the fingers sustained during fighting near Ypres. Then, the following March, William was again admitted to hospital with something far more serious, trench foot, caused by standing in water for long periods of time. After being admitted to the 3rd Canadian Field Ambulance at Sailly-Sur-La-Lys he was shipped home, and that proved to be the end of William's association with the 2nd Btn. After recovering sufficiently he rejoined the War and was posted to the 1st Btn which was engaged in the bitter

Hersella (third from left) with her parents and older sister Nellie outside their house in Duke's Avenue. (Source: Mrs P. Collins.)

fighting at Gallipoli. He embarked on the Orient line ship *SS Orsova* in early May 1915 and it was from this, whilst anchored off Plymouth, that William wrote a postcard to Hersella, saying that he was in the best of health. It appears that he also stopped off at Gibraltar, where he sent further postcards, including one to his young son, reminding him to be a good boy to his mother.

The 1st Btn had landed on X beach at Cape Helles on 25 April, and when William joined them around the end of May they were trying to capture the village of Krithia, from which the Turks were pouring down a rain of fire. On 6 June, the day of his death, the CO responded to requests from the Scots Guards and the Hampshire Rgt for re-enforcements. He sent one and a half companies and it is probable that William was one of those who went. He is commemorated on the Helles Memorial.

[1] They were charged with swearing an illegal oath.
[2] See photograph on page 8.

Pte Richard Neild – aged 30
12th Btn Manchester Rgt – 4305
Fordington Cemetery

The funeral procession that passed through the streets of Dorchester on 24 June 1915 was unusually quiet. The mourners were not accompanied by a military band, which was normal on such occasions, none being available in the town on that day. The body being escorted from the mortuary at the County Hospital to Fordington Cemetery was that of Richard Neild, a private in the 12th Btn Manchester Rgt. Richard was in hutments at Wool when he was discharged from the Army as being unfit and immediately admitted into Mrs Acland's Red Cross Hospital in Durngate Street where, 'in spite of every medical attention and careful nursing, he died' [1] on 21 June. His wife Mary and other relatives travelled down from Manchester for the funeral.

[1] *Chronicle* 1/7/1915.

Pte George Percy Stanley – aged 18
9th Btn Oxfordshire and Buckinghamshire Light Infantry – 17236
Fordington Cemetery

Just 3 days after the *Chronicle* reported the funeral of Richard Neild the body of another young soldier was being prepared for burial in the cemetery at Fordington. This time the man was George Stanley, a native of Birmingham, where he lived with his parents George and Annie. He served with the Ox and Bucks Light Infantry and died in the County Hospital on 4 July 1915.

Pte Harry Mayo – aged 53
Depot, Dorsetshire Rgt – 11668
St George's

The sign hanging outside 8/9 Holloway Rd declares it to be the 'Quaker Meeting House', but the design of the building betrays its previous use as the Eldridge Pope public house, the Union Arms. The area in which the building is situated was formerly known as Cuckolds Row, and in 1885 the licence of the hostelry was about to be transferred to a Mr Joseph Bush, who then decided that he could not find the necessary £43-12s-6d to buy the contents and furnishings. A regular customer of the pub, the chimney sweep Elias Mayo, overhearing the dilemma whilst supping a pint or two, declared, 'I'll buy it!' and that is just what he did, [1]the licence then remaining within the family until 1969. After his death his daughter Mary took over and living with her in 1911 was her brother Harry, aged 47 and single, who had served his apprenticeship as a blacksmith but was then working as a labourer.

On 17 September 1914 Harry presented himself to the Recruiting Officer at the Depot Barracks to enlist, declaring that he had already spent 21 years and 88 days with the 3rd Btn of the county regiment, as a Reservist. He was too old to fight and was therefore posted to the Depot Barracks. However, it was not long before he was discharged from the Army after being found to be physically unfit for service. The report of the Medical Board, dated June 1915, suggests that he was suffering from prostate cancer, from which he died on 4 July, 4 days after his discharge.

[1] Strange, 1995.

Capt. Arthur William Palling Caruthers-Little – aged 30
5th Btn Dorsetshire Rgt
Holy Trinity

Icen Way in Dorchester runs from High East Street, gradually rising until it reaches King's Road. The High East Street end of this thoroughfare is characterised by terraced cottages, but further along the nature of the housing changes and there are several fine detached and semi-detached houses. Living at No. 25 Calder in 1901 was John Tweedie, a colonel in the RFA.

John came from an eminent military family; his father, Capt. Michael Tweedie, fought alongside Wellington, one of his uncles was a major general and another Physician General to the East India Company. Among his brothers he could count a major general and a colonel, and completing the roll was his nephew, Admiral Sir Hugh Tweedie. When War was declared John was ineligible to fight because of his age but was determined to have some kind of role, be it on the Home Front. As well as taking on two honorary secretary jobs to the Sailors and Soldiers Families Association, and the Soldiers' Home, he was County Commandant of the Dorset Volunteers, and when conscription was introduced in 1916 he became the military representative on the Borough's Military Service Tribunal, which was established to hear and determine appeals for exemption from having to serve.

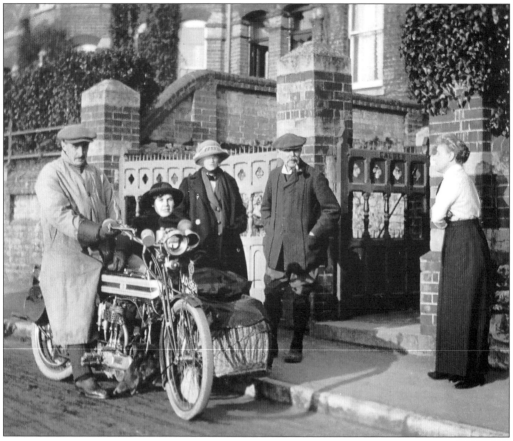

Arthur and Polly on their motorcycle, with Polly's father, mother and sister, outside their home in Icen Way. (Source: Mr R. Calcutt.)

On 10 May 1915, at Holy Trinity Church, John's youngest daughter Olive, who was called Polly within the family, married a captain of the Dorsets, Arthur Caruthers-Little, the son of Lt-Col John Caruthers-Little and his wife Jemima. The Little family lived in Pitchcome House near Stroud since it was built around 1740 and it is still occupied by them today. Arthur was born in 1884 and educated at Saugan School, Bournemouth, Sherborne Public School and Queen's College, Oxford. The family association with Dorchester came when he was commissioned from the Gloucestershire Militia into the 2nd Btn Dorsets at the age 23 and after serving with them in India was posted back to the Depot Barracks, where he stayed for some years. He joined the 5th Btn on its formation in October 1914 and was immediately made adjutant, followed quickly by promotion to captain. The battalion was not immediately sent overseas and so Arthur took the opportunity to marry Olive just before the orders for him to go abroad were received.

The 5th Btn were to form part of the re-enforcements for the MEF fighting in Gallipoli, and at the beginning of July 1915 Arthur set sail from Liverpool on the Cunard liner *Aquitania* with 7,000 other men. The plan was for the Dorsets to land at Suvla Bay, off of the Destroyer *Bulldog*, but things did not go well when the lighters [1] that were to take them ashore ran aground in 3 ft of water, requiring the men to wade to the beach. To make things worse the disembarkation was made under enemy fire. It was night when Arthur stepped ashore and he had the immediate task of gathering the scattered men together in the darkness. When the count of those present was made it was found that the battalion had incurred over 100 casualties during the landing. After establishing their position in very difficult conditions an order was given, on 4 August, to issue the men with enough rations for 3 days, the first indication that an operation was imminent.

On the 6th the Dorsets advanced on Hill 10, a strongly defended feature that had already defied capture by the

Arthur and Polly on their wedding day. (Source: Mr R. Calcutt.)

Northumberland Fusiliers, but this time, by the end of the day, it was in British hands. Lt-Col Hannay, the battalion commander, now decided to wait for further information before moving on but as nothing was forthcoming he decided to go back the next day accompanied by Arthur and find out for himself what was going on. What happened next was related to Polly in a letter from Hannay: 'I made up my mind to go back to see our General. We got back 100 yds or so walking apart on account of snipers who had been peppering us all morning, when we got into the target of one of these fiends and after nearly getting me he shot Arthur through the heart. He never spoke after he fell … Littler collected all Arthur's personal war kit next morning but he too fell victim to another sniper in the same place.'

The 'Littler' referred to above was Pte Charlie Littler, [2] a well-known Dorchester soldier who had been servant to several adjutants at the Depot Barracks before going to Gallipoli with Arthur. The account of his death in the *Chronicle* differs slightly from the one given by Hannay. According to the newspaper Littler ran to Arthur as soon as he was shot and was probably killed by the same sniper. Charlie left behind a widow and small child. Both men are commemorated on the Helles Memorial, which bears the names of more than 21,000 men. The regimental history of the Dorsets contains the following words which serve as Arthur's eulogy: 'His death was a great blow to the 5th. Always helpful and considerate, more apt to help than find fault, he had been a splendid Adjutant, efficient and painstaking, and the smooth running of the Battalion's "interior economy" was in no small measure his work. During the trying hours which had elapsed since landing he had shown himself cool and collected under fire and absolutely without regard for danger.' [3]

In the midst of the carnage in Gallipoli, where each soldier had survival in the front of his mind, one man took time to think of Arthur's wife and performed a touching act of kindness. Sgt Swain wrote the following letter to his own wife: 'This is just an extra line dear should you see Mrs Little, to give her this flower which was picked not two yards away from where poor Capt. Caruthers-Little fell. It was given to me by Sgt F Barrett D Coy signalling Sgt who was always talking with the Adjt, as he had been a signalling officer and they knew one another pretty well; it just shows how thoughtful he must have been towards the Adjt and Mrs Little to pick this flower ....' [4]

Polly with baby Kitty. (Source: Mr R. Calcutt.)

In April 1918 another wedding took place in Holy Trinity Church, where the congregation were enchanted by the young bridesmaid. Not yet 2 years old, Kitty Caruthers-Little wore a white muslin dress and carried a bouquet of forget-me-knots. She was the daughter of Arthur and Olive, who was pregnant when her husband was killed. Olive, who never married again, lived to celebrate her 100th birthday.

[1] Boats with shallow bottoms used on rivers for cargo.
[2] Pte Littler does not appear on any Dorchester war memorial.
[3] Atkinson, C.T. (1947) *History of the Fifth Battalion. The Dorsetshire Regiment 1914–1919.* Naval and Military Press, Uckfield.
[4] Letter undated provided by a relative.

Cpl William Joseph Brien – aged 29
5th Btn Dorsetshire Rgt
Cenotaph

Not long after Capt. Caruthers-Little's death a messenger arrived from HQ ordering the Dorsets to wait, as a further attack by the Division was being planned (see above). The target chosen was Kireetch Tepe Sirt, a ridge that rose 600 ft and commanded the surrounding area. The date and time chosen for the attack was 9 August at 6 am. Unfortunately, because of the early start, Cpl Brien was unable to hand water bottles to his men in C Coy because they had not been returned after refilling. Despite this the battalion started off and, after crossing several gullies and ridges, a halt was called while the remainder of the Brigade caught up. The situation was none too satisfactory; the Turks were not only increasing their fire but also pressing forward, the men were becoming exhausted in the blazing sun because of the lack of water, and William and comrades could neither advance nor retreat. Eventually, at about 4 pm, the Dorsets were ordered to retire with the rest of the British troops, William Brien's company providing covering fire. Whether or not he took part in the withdrawal we do not know, for it was on this day that he was killed in action along with 19 others of the 5th. He is commemorated on the Helles Memorial.

William had joined the 5th Dorsets in Dorchester on 28 August 1914, but he was not a native of the town. Born in Newcastle, Glamorganshire, it was there that the young coalminer married Beatrice Young in 1908. It is not clear whether Beatrice was a Dorchester lass, but sometime after May 1913 they came to settle in the town where their fourth child Bernard was born, at 18 High St, Fordington. William's time in the Army had not been without incident. Twice he was brought up on a charge, once for being missing on parade and once for gross neglect of duty, but despite these misdemeanours, he was obviously considered to be a good soldier because he retained his rank of corporal. The army encountered a completely different kind of problem with Pte Brien when it came to winding up his affairs. It was found that he was known not only by the name of Brien but also by that of Bryant and it took letters from his wife and his mother to convince the authorities that the man known as Bryant in Wales was the same as the one named Brien in Dorchester. Things were eventually cleared up and Beatrice received his medals, plaque and scroll. In 1919 she married a William Churchill and moved to No. 14 in High St, Fordington.

Chief Stoker William Nathaniel Seal – aged 36
HMS Lynx, RN – 285287
Cenotaph and St George's

William Seal, who came into the world in April 1879, was the seventh of eight children born to Josiah and Caroline Seal. Josiah was a navy veteran who, after his retirement, had taken up work as a labourer on a farm and in 1881 the family was living in Loud's Road. Aged 19, William followed his father by signing up with the Royal Navy as a stoker, and after training his first posting was to the new battleship *HMS Glory*, upon which he served for 5 years on the China Station. This was followed by shorter periods of time at shore bases in England and on various ships, including the battleship *HMS Erebus* and the Apollo Class Cruiser *HMS Indefatigable*. By 1905 William had risen to the rank of Stoker Petty Officer and after that mainly worked on Destroyer Tenders.

HMS Lynx was a *K. Class* Destroyer which William joined in March 1915 as Chief Stoker. On 9 August she was patrolling in the Moray Firth as part of the Grand Fleet located at Scapa Flow when, at about 6.15 am, she was hit by a mine under No. 1 boiler room, destroying the bridge, braking the ship's back and sending the fore part of the vessel to the bottom of the sea almost immediately, followed by the stern half 10 minutes later. Of the 89 persons on board 63 lost their lives, including William. He is remembered on the Portsmouth Naval Memorial and left behind a wife Elena, whom he married in 1910, and a child William, born in 1913.

**Capt. Gerald Robert O'Sullivan VC – aged 26
1st Btn Royal Inniskilling Fusiliers
Cenotaph**

There is no evidence to confirm that Gerald O'Sullivan, the only recipient of the Victoria Cross listed on the town's Great War memorials, ever visited the town. He was born in 1889 in Douglas, County Cork, Ireland, son of George O'Sullivan, a lieutenant colonel in the Argyll and Sutherland Highlanders, and Charlotte. Gerald was educated at a private school in Greenwich, which could list among its pupils a Prince of Siam, then went on to Wimbledon College and finally entered the Royal Military Academy, Sandhurst, in 1907. He was gazetted to 1st Btn Inniskilling Fusiliers as 2 Lt and went with them to Tientsin, China. There he witnessed the sacking of the Imperial Palace during the 1911 revolution, before moving on to Secunderbad, India, where the regiment remained during 1913 and 1914.

(Source: www.ww1photos.com.)

On 14 December 1914 Gerald left India and sailed to join the 29th Division which was destined to fight in Gallipoli and it was there that he received his award for conspicuous gallantry. The first of his two acts of bravery occurred on the evening of 18 June 1915, when trenches that were being improved by the Fusiliers were attacked and occupied by Turkish bombers. At 4.30 am Gerald led a party of about six men and drove the Turks away, saving a critical situation. As a result of his action he was wounded in the leg, evacuated to hospital in Egypt and recommended for a VC, but on that occasion it was declined.

After a rapid recovery Gerald returned to Gallipoli and in June he was again recommended for a VC, which this time was awarded. The citation reads: 'On the night of 1/2 July 1915 when it was essential that a portion of a trench which had been lost should be regained, Capt. O'Sullivan, although not belonging to the troops at this point, volunteered to lead a party of bomb throwers to effect the recapture. He advanced in the open under a very heavy fire, and in order to throw his bombs with greater effect, he got up on the parapet, where he was completely exposed to the fire of the enemy occupying the trench. He was finally wounded, but not before his inspiring example had led on his party to make further efforts, which resulted in the recapture of the trench.'

Gerald's death occurred during the same attack on Scimitar Hill in which Charles Budden was killed. The battalion war diary describes how the Inniskillings attacked on the afternoon of 21 August and seized the front line but had to fall back with heavy casualties. It then rallied within about 150 yd of the top of the hill and with troops of the Border Rgt and the South Wales Boarders made another charge, but it did not hit home, the enemy standing on the parapet of their trenches, firing from the hip and throwing hand grenades at the advancing men. Seemingly in a desperate situation Gerald then called upon about 50 men to join him in 'one more charge for the honour of the Old Regiment'. [1] He was never seen again and only one man of the group returned. He is commemorated on the Helles War Memorial and the Wimbledon College Memorial.

Gerald's mother Charlotte was living at Rowan House in Prince of Wales Road when she received news of her son's gallant deeds. But the very next day her joy was taken away when the official casualty lists were published, showing Gerald as missing. Charlotte does not appear to have had any particular reason for living in the town, although she did have some connection with the county as her daughter Maud was born in Sherborne.

[1] Information provided by the Inniskillings Museum.

CQMS Stephen Edward Orchard – aged 36
5th Btn Dorsetshire Rgt – 6614
Cenotaph

The 21st August 1915 was a black day for the people of Dorchester, although they were not aware of it until the casualty lists of men fighting in Gallipoli started to appear in the *Chronicle*. No less than eight of the men listed on the town's memorials died as a result of fighting on that day.

On the Gallipoli peninsular the 5th Dorset's failure to make ground at Suvla was a reflection of the whole British advance in the area, which had come to a standstill. Undeterred, Gen Sir Ian Hamilton determined on a fresh effort, supported by experienced troops brought round from Cape Helles and a dismounted yeomanry division from Egypt, which included the Dorset Yeomanry. The 5th Btn Dorsets were enjoying a short rest behind the lines at Lala Baba, and among C Coy the most popular man was doubtless CQMS Orchard who, after the recent shortages of water and food, ensured that his men got plenty of both. Their rest lasted just 36 hours before the battalion was sent forward and after some difficult fighting they halted at the ominously named 'Dead Man's House trenches'.

Preparations had by now been made for a renewed British attack on the high ground occupied by the Turks on Scimitar Hill, starting at 3 pm on 21 August. At the allotted hour the Dorsets advanced briskly towards the enemy trenches running between Aire Kayak and Susak Kayu and despite shrapnel fire took them with the bayonet. However, their jubilation did not last long when it was found that there was an even stronger force of Turks about 40 yards further on. The men continued their assault and may have taken the second trench had they not encountered heavy fire. Out of the confusion of the battle little accurate information is available about precisely what happened but from the accounts of the few men who returned it appears that the troops were enfiladed from both flanks. On returning to Lala Baba it was found that of the officers of the 5th who reached the Turkish trenches none returned. Casualties among the NCOs had been particularly heavy and Stephen was counted among those killed.

Stephen, who was a regular soldier and had been with the battalion since the beginning of the War, was born at Lytchett Matravers near Poole. He enlisted in the regiment in Dorchester, where his wife Agnes was living at 15 The Grove at the time of his death. He is commemorated on the Helles Memorial.

Pte Thomas George Green – aged 29
5th Btn Dorsetshire Rgt – 10367

Pte Joseph Samuel Green – aged 22
1/4th Btn Dorsetshire Rgt – 200430

Both are commemorated on the Cenotaph and St Peter's

Joseph Green. (Source: Mrs J. Pollard.)

In a family of eight children Thomas and Joseph Green were born just over a year apart. Their parents were Fred, who worked as an agricultural labourer and later as a coal porter, and Minnie. The boys were born in Mill Street, probably at No. 61 and by 1911 the family had moved to 60 Holloway Rd. Both the boys were working at that time, Thomas on a dairy farm and Joseph as a labourer in a flour mill.

Minnie Green with her family. Thomas is on the right and Joseph front left. Behind Joseph is a younger brother Frederick who died in 1905, aged 12. (Source: Mrs J. Pollard.)

We know that before the War Joseph was in the Dorset Territorials, as he was awarded a medal for his service, and it may well have been the case that Thomas also served with them. The brothers both enlisted in the Dorsets for the War but did not serve in the same battalions and were sent to different parts of the globe. Thomas served with the 5th Btn in Gallipoli and went missing during the ill-fated attack on the Turkish trenches between Aire Kayak and Susak Kuyu on 21 August 1915. His death was not formally acknowledged until May 1917. He is commemorated on the Helles War Memorial.

When news of the Armistice came Fred and Minnie Green must have had very mixed feelings. On the one hand, they had lost their dear son Thomas but at least Joseph had survived. Joseph had spent the majority of the War with the 1/4th Btn in India and Mesopotamia and some of the anxiety they felt about him was now tempered by the prospect of having him home. However, fate had a last card to deal to the Green family. In 1919 the ruler of Afghanistan, Amānullāh, attacked India by crossing the border and capturing the town of Bagh. Joseph was sent to fight there as part of a territorial force and, on completion of the short war, he was attached to the 2nd Dorsets. He died of disease on 19 August 1919, was buried in Peshawar and is remembered on the Delhi Memorial, India. His medals, which included the India service medal, with a clasp for the Afghan war, were sent to his parents at 12 Friary Lane, Dorchester.

A whimsical photograph of 'prospective' officers'. Thomas is second from the right, back row. (Source: Mrs J. Pollard.)

Pte Wilfred Charles Bagg – aged 18
5th Btn Dorsetshire Rgt – 10562
Post Office Memorial

Wilfred Bagg was the first Dorset postal worker to be killed in the Great War. He lived with his parents Walter and Mary Jane at Lestridge Cottage, Warmwell, where he worked as a postman. Walter joined the 5th Btn Dorsets on 1 September 1914 and went with them to Gallipoli in 1915. He was wounded on 21 August during the attack on Turkish trenches between Aire Kayak and Susak Kuyu, Suvla, then later on the same day he was reported missing. He is commemorated on the Helles War Memorial and the memorial at Holy Trinity Church, Warmwell.

Pte William George Collins – aged 27
5th Btn Dorsetshire Rgt – 10148
Cenotaph and Holy Trinity

Although born in Charminster, William Collins spent some of his early years living in Dorchester at 35 Grove Buildings, and when his father Giles, a veteran soldier, died in 1899 his death had a profound effect on the family. Two years after her husband's death, William's mother Elizabeth was living back in Charminster, in the house of Janet Burt, both declaring themselves to be paupers. Unable to look after her two sons Elizabeth had to commit William and his 7-year-old brother Thomas into Dorchester Workhouse [1] but by 1911 things had improved and the family was reunited. They moved into Dorchester, living at 9 Colliton St, and Elizabeth found employment as a charlady, whilst William worked as an agricultural labourer in Upwey. He later became a carman, the equivalent to today's white van driver.

William joined the Dorsets on 25 August 1914 and was posted to the 5th Btn, remaining in England until June 1915, when he went to Gallipoli. He was reported missing on 22 August after the attack on Turkish trenches between Aire Kayak and Susak Kuyu, but his death was not confirmed until the following June. He is commemorated on the Helles Memorial. His medals were sent to Elizabeth at her new address at 26 Colliton St.

[1] Dorchester Workhouse was located in Damer's Road, opposite the junction with Maud Road. The buildings are now offices.

Pte Charles Ernest Budden – aged 21
1/1st Queen's Own Dorset Yeomanry – 1016
Thomas Hardye School Roll of Honour

Today, Burngate Farm, West Lulworth, is a bed and breakfast establishment but in 1901 it was where Charles Budden lived with his family and three servants. Charles Junior was born in 1894 and, after completing his education at Dorchester Grammar School, helped his father on the farm. When the call of King and Country came Charles enlisted in the Dorset Yeomanry, which had been founded in 1794 as the Dorsetshire Rgt of Volunteer Yeomanry Cavalry in response to the threat of invasion during the Napoleonic Wars.

In 1915 the QODY were first deployed overseas in Egypt, before being sent as part of a larger dismounted force to Suvla in Gallipoli, where they arrived in August. On 21 August, it was intended that Charles and his fellow Yeomanry would be kept back in Reserve at Lala Baba, while the infantry, including 5th Dorsets, were to make the main attack on Scimitar Hill.

After the initial success of the infantry attack and then subsequent failure and withdrawal, described above, [1] it was decided to commit the Yeomanry regiments to their first battle, but delays meant that it would have to be a night attack. The QODY moved forward across an open plain under artillery fire, and as darkness came they attacked. Advancing through the burning bushes and scrub, ignited by artillery explosions, stepping over the dead, the Yeomanry started to ascend Scimitar Hill. Given the lie of the land and strength of Turkish positions, the subsequent charge was made more in hope than expectation, but despite the odds and rising casualties the QODY took the first line of trenches, only to be confronted by the Turk's main position further up. Regrouping, they attacked again and, despite many more men succumbing to enemy fire, got into the enemy's main position. But by now they were so weakened that they were unable to hold their gains and were ordered to withdraw to Chocolate Hill. It had been a terrible baptism for the Yeomanry, which lost all of its officers, except one. Charles was counted among the 119 OR that were killed or went missing, out of a total force of 301. He is commemorated on the Helles War Memorial.

[1] See Stephen Orchard.

Cpl Thomas Edward Yard – aged 23
5th Btn Dorsetshire Rgt – 105933

Sgt Charles James Yard – aged 22
119th Siege Bty, RGA – 39258

Both are commemorated on the Cenotaph

In an age of patriotism and a time of war the *Chronicle* took every opportunity to report on those families that it considered were making an exceptional contribution. The headline of an article published in May 1918 read 'Record of Seven Young Sons' and then went on to describe the Yard family as 'a sturdy patriotic Dorset family'. [1] Their sturdiness may have resulted from the fact that Thomas Yard and most of his sons worked on the land, some as shepherds and others as labourers. In 1901 Thomas, his wife Sarah and their nine children were living in Tolpuddle; then in 1908 tragedy struck when Sarah died aged 51. It was after this event that the family moved to Maiden Castle Farm, Dorchester. Of the six Yard sons and a son-in-law who served their country, four fought with the Royal Artillery, one (who was wounded and sent home) with the Devonshire Rgt and two with the Dorsets.

Thomas Yard was working as an attendant in the County Asylum at Charminster when on 3 September 1914 he enlisted in the 5th Btn Dorsets. By 1915 he had gained the rank of corporal. Thomas became another casualty in the fighting for the Turkish trenches at Suvla when he received a gunshot wound to the shoulder on 21 August. After having his wound dressed he boarded the troopship *Alaunia* to be taken to Mudros on the Greek island of Lemnos to be treated, but Thomas never set foot on land again because he died on the ship on 24 August. The only personal item of his that was returned to his parents was his identity disc. He is buried in East Mudros Military Cemetery, Lemnos.

Charles entered the Army 2 years before Thomas when he was just 17 and by the age of 22 he had risen to the rank of sergeant. He was serving with the 119th Siege Bty near Ypres when he was killed by fragments of an exploding shell on 3 May 1918. He is buried in the Gwalia Military Cemetery, West-Vlaanderen, Belgium.

---

[1] *Chronicle* 23/51918.

Pte Arthur William Holland – aged 23
5th Btn Dorsetshire Rgt – 10157
Cenotaph

The service record of Arthur Holland states that he was admitted into No. 17 General Hospital in Alexandria on 12 August 1915, dangerously ill with a gunshot wound to the neck which he sustained whilst fighting in Suvla. He succumbed to his wounds on 26 August. Born in Leatherhead, Surrey, in 1891 to John and Annie, before joining the Dorsets he was employed as a labourer. Arthur appears on the Cenotaph because his sister Annie married George Dunford of Dorchester and settled in the town at 33 The Grove. Arthur is buried in Alexandria (Chatby) Military Cemetery.

Pte William Thomas Voss – aged 21
10th Btn Cameronians (Scottish Rifles)

Pte Frederick George Voss – aged 22
6th Btn Dorsetshire Rgt

Both are commemorated on the Cenotaph and St George's

Every death in the Great War was, of course, a tragedy but the stories behind the names on Dorchester's memorials show that some families seem to have had grief piled upon grief. Such is the story of the Voss family of Holloway Road. Within the space of 17 years Elizabeth Voss lost her husband, her two eldest sons and a son-in-law. In 1891 Thomas and Elizabeth Voss were living in Mill Street with their four daughters and may have wondered if they were ever going to be blessed with sons. Blessed they were, when William came along, closely followed by Frederick the next year. The family then moved to 8 Pound Lane, so named because it was the site of the enclosure where, in former times, stray animals found wandering around the town were kept until the owner turned up to collect them, doubtless after paying the necessary release fee. Tragedy first hit the family when Thomas died in 1901 at the age of 46, a few months before his son Frank was born, and his wife was left to bring up the family. In January 1915 Elizabeth once more had to put on her mourning clothes when the husband of her daughter became a victim of the War [1] and she was probably still wearing them when the telegram boy knocked on the door to deliver the news of her son William's death.

William, who curiously served as William Boss, died on 25 September, the first day of the Battle of Loos, whilst fighting with the 10th Btn Cameronians. On that day his battalion, as part of the 15th Scottish Division, was given the task of capturing the town of Loos, which it did but then found itself pinned down on Hill 70. With the fear of a counterattack the advance came to a halt, the Cameronians having suffered heavy casualties. He is commemorated on the Loos, Memorial, Pas-de-Calais.

William's brother Frederick enlisted in the 6th Btn Dorsets and joined them in France in March 1916. The battalion was resting after being engaged in heavy fighting around Ypres and when he arrived there he could have been forgiven for thinking that perhaps the War was not as bad as he had heard. The men were able to bathe and there was an abundance of food, drink and entertainment. But the illusion was short lived, as Frederick went on to fight at Albert, Arras, Passchendaele and The Somme, all of which have become synonymous with some of the worst fighting of the War. He apparently remained unscathed until 22 February 1918, when he was shot in the back, probably near Cambrai. The wound was serious and he was returned to England where he entered St George's Hospital, Lambeth, for treatment. He died on 30 June and his body was returned to Dorchester for burial in Fordington Cemetery on 6 July.

---

[1] See Richard Brown.

Pte Peter James Bishop – aged 64
Depot, Dorsetshire Rgt
Fordington Cemetery

Like William Bussell, [1] Peter Bishop, commonly known as James, was an old soldier who wanted to do his bit for the War. He had begun his military career as a drummer in the Royal Fusiliers and went with the regiment to India. Afterwards he proceeded to South Africa where he joined the Cape Mounted Rifles, serving with them for 5 years before returning to England. Peter was born in Bridport and in 1877 married Eliza Wood from Weymouth, where they were living at the time of his death.

On the outbreak of War he was mobilised with the National Reserve and posted with the 3rd Dorsets to undertake military police duties at the Depot Barracks. Unfortunately, James suffered from rheumatism and was admitted to the County Hospital where he was treated by Dr Broadway. [2] In the meantime, his wife was staying with their nephew at 12 Duke's Ave. The treatment was almost complete and Peter was looking forward to returning home, but on 24 September 1915 he had a seizure and died suddenly. He was interred in Fordington Cemetery.

---

[1] See William Bussell.
[2] Dr Theodore B. Broadway of 5 Cornwall Rd.

Lt James Richard Anderton Rigby – aged 25
3rd Btn Princess of Wales Own Yorkshire Infantry
Thomas Hardye School Roll of Honour

After leaving Dorchester Grammar School James Rigby entered Emmanuel College Cambridge in 1909 and was later commissioned into the 3rd Btn Yorkshire Rgt in February 1914. He was promoted to lieutenant just before his attachment to the headquarters staff of the 2nd Btn in May 1915. At that time they were involved in the Battle of Festubert and in June fought at Givenchy, where the battalion incurred heavy casualties.

On the first day of the Battle of Loos the battalion attacked a crossroads on the northeast corner of the village of Hulluch and then went on to Cité St Elie. The following day James and his company were moving south when they were fired on by advancing German troops, forcing them to fall back into Breslau Trench, a former German communication trench, and it was here that the young lieutenant was killed, on 26 September.

Born 1880, James was the son of the Rev James Rigby, vicar of Sheriff Hutton in North Yorkshire, and in 1914 he married Sarah Gill-Anderton. Other than James' attendance at the Grammar School his family appears to have no obvious connection with Dorchester. His father may have worked in the county or James may simply have been a boarder at the school. His name appears on the Loos Memorial.

L/Cpl Alfred Joseph Meadway – aged 22
1/4th Btn Dorsetshire Rgt – 35048
Thomas Hardye School Roll of Honour

Alfred Meadway was another ex-pupil who was added to the Grammar School's Roll of Honour. Born in 1893 in Maiden Newton he was the only son of Alfred and Alice who ran the village butchers a couple of doors away from the Castle Inn in Beaminster Road. When he had completed his education Alfred went to work for his father and doubtless hoped to inherit the shop, as his father had done from his father.

Alfred joined the 1/4th Dorsets in India, where they had been acting as a garrison force, enabling the more experienced troops who had been stationed there before the War to join the fighting in France. Alfred died of wounds on 28 September and is commemorated on the Basra War Memorial, indicating that he was part of a force sent to Mesopotamia to reinforce the 2nd Btn.

2 Lt Percy Paris Pope – aged 33
1st Btn Welsh Rgt
Cenotaph, Holy Trinity and St George's

Capt. Charles Alfred Whiting Pope – aged 39
RAMC
Cenotaph and Holy Trinity

Lt-Col Edward Alexander Pope DSO – aged 43
3rd Btn Welsh Rgt
Cenotaph and Holy Trinity

The *Daily Mail* on New Year's Day 1916 published, among its usual war photographs, portraits of Alfred Pope, the Dorchester brewer, nine of his sons and a son-in-law, all of whom were serving in the Great War. The Dorset *Chronicle* also picked up on this phenomenon and came up with the patriotic headline 'Nine in the Line', adding that, 'we think that this really must be a record'. [1] In fact, Alfred had 11 sons who served their country, the nine mentioned above, plus one who was a sergeant in the National Volunteer Defence Corps and another a sub-lieutenant in the Royal Navy, who died of tuberculosis in 1901.

Pope's brewery was the biggest employer in Dorchester during the Edwardian period but its owner's first choice of profession as a young man was not that of brewing but a somewhat dryer subject, the law. After gaining his articles in Bath, Alfred came to Dorchester in 1868, where he joined fellow solicitor George Andrews, establishing the firm of Andrews and Pope. Then, in 1880 his career took a completely different path when he became a partner in the firm of Eldridge, Pope and Co., later becoming its chairman. Under Alfred's leadership the enterprise began to grow and he to prosper.

The Popes had two homes, one in Dorchester at South Court, South Walks Road, and another at Wrackleford, Stratton, about 3 miles northwest of the town. With economic and social success came public office and Alfred was twice elected Mayor and Chief Magistrate of Dorchester, and became Chairman of the Governors of the Grammar School, where he was educated as a boy with his contemporary Sir Frederick Treves. [2] Alfred was also active in military matters, joining the Somerset Rifle Volunteers while serving his articles in Bath and later enrolling as a captain in the Dorset National Reserve in 1909. In 1919 a book was published, with a foreword by Thomas Hardy, which is a history of the service given by the Popes entitled *A Short Summary of the Service and Sacrifice Rendered to the Empire in the Great War by One of the Many Patriotic Families of Wessex*. If patriotism were measured by sacrifice of human life then the Pope family certainly qualified, as Alfred and his wife Elizabeth lost three sons and a son-in-law as a result of the Great War.

Percy was the fifth child of Alfred and Elizabeth, whose second Christian name of Paris was suggested to his father by his godfather, the Rev Russell-Wright, when the two men were in that city at the time of the child's birth. His godfather was also responsible for the boy's early education at Purbeck College, Swanage, from whence he went to Twyford School, Reading, to prepare for entry into Winchester College. He became a pupil of Winchester in 1895 and then went on to New College, Oxford, in 1901, where he read modern languages. At one stage Percy considered a future in the church but instead went for the law and was called to the Bar in 1907, joining the Western Circuit.

The outbreak of hostilities in Europe found Percy taking a holiday in Paris but instead of returning home he decided to remain and see the War first-hand. When his thoughts finally turned to how he might play a part in things his first reaction was to help the French by joining the Foreign Legion and his parents had some cause for concern when they did not hear from him for over a month. He returned to England in October 1914 and joined the Inns of Court Officers' Training Corps for 5 months and was afterwards commissioned 2 Lt in the 3rd Btn Welsh Rgt, under the command of his elder brother Edward. Within 2 months Percy was attached to the 1st Btn and proceeded to the Western Front.

During the afternoon of 1 October 1915 the officer commanding the 1st Btn called together his officers and told them that orders had been received to take a trench called Little Willie, an extension of the Hohenzollern Redoubt near Loos, at the point of the bayonet, regardless of cost. The attack was to be made after dark and in complete silence. Percy's company was in the middle of the line and what happened next was related to Alfred Pope in a letter from his son's battalion commander Lt-Col Hoggen: 'The timing was perfect – precisely at 8.00 pm the 1st Welsh crept over the parapet like one man, officers in line with the men … so silently was the advance carried out that the regiment were within 100 yds of the enemy before being discovered. Then, from both flanks machine guns opened fire, and the whole length of the opposing trench opened fire … In 20 seconds, there were 250 men and a proportion of officers on the floor – the remainder were in the trench, bayoneting those in the trench and firing on the retreating Prussian Guards.' [3] Col Hoggen goes on to describe how after the initial success things began to deteriorate. The companies on the extreme left and right of Percy's had lost touch and the men in the trenches were running out of ammunition, and despite repeated requests for support little was forthcoming. The whole night and the next morning were spent in bombing battles between the opposing sides, the difference being that the Germans had an inexhaustible supply of ammunition but by 10 am the British troops had none. The Welsh fought on in a bitter struggle until 2.30 in the afternoon of 2 October, with the German bombers using the bayonet, and were eventually relieved by the 6th Welsh. Percy disappeared in the last rush of German bombers and it was hoped that he had been taken prisoner. It was not until August 1916 that his parents received official notification from the War Office that, 'The Army Council are regretfully constrained to conclude that 2 Lt Pope is dead, and that his death occurred on or since the 1st day of October, 1915'. [4] He is commemorated on the Loos Memorial.

In August 1917 a notice appeared in the *Parish Magazine* of St George's, Fordington, informing the parishioners that Percy had left a legacy to the church and his roller-top desk, 'to stand in the vestry of the said Church, for the use of the Vicar, for the time being, for ever'. This last part of the legacy was of some significance to the family as the Vicar of St George's was Percy's brother-in-law, the Rev R.G. Bartelot.

Charles Pope was the third son of Alfred and Elizabeth and like his brother Percy was initially educated at Twyford School but then went on to Charterhouse in common with five of his brothers. On leaving Charterhouse, Charles entered Trinity College where he

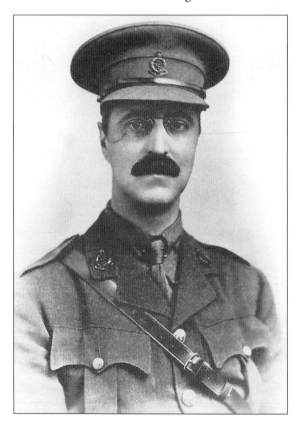

attained an MA and a Bachelor of Medicine degree. He chose medicine as a career and after training at St Bartholomew's Hospital held several appointments in England before taking up a post in Cape Town as a House Physician. On his return to the UK in 1907, Charles' life took two different directions. Firstly, in 1909 he married Marion Gravener of Avenue House, Dorchester, at St George's Church, Fordington, and secondly, he became a GP, first practising in Rugby and then St Leonard's-on-Sea, where he was when War was declared.

Charles did not join the conflict immediately but offered himself in 1915 and was passed for home service only. Given this, it must have been of considerable surprise to him when in 1917 he was ordered to Egypt and embarked on the troopship *Transylvania* with over 3,000 troops, hospital nurses and crew. Early in the morning of 4 May 1917 the ship left Marseilles and at 10 am, as she was sailing in the Mediterranean, the captain saw a small sailing craft change course. From behind it appeared a German submarine which fired a torpedo at the transporter, causing much damage when it hit but leaving the engines intact. The shore was about 8 miles away and the captain thought that he might be able to beach his vessel. Then, a quarter of an hour later, another torpedo struck the engine room and the ship sunk in about 50 minutes. Charles' fate was described by a fellow member of the RAMC: 'he was in charge of us on the *Transylvania* and was missing when we landed. He died as every British Officer likes to die – doing his duty, and went down with the ship whilst dressing the wounds of the poor fellows who were hit by the explosion. I happen to know this as I was working with him up to about 3 minutes before she sank, when he ordered me over the side. He was a good officer and we are all very sorry to lose him.' [5]

Despite the circumstances, the *Transylvania* did manage to get all of the nurses and most of the troops and crew to safety, and it was hoped that Charles would be among them, but after some months of anguish and enquiry his widow received news from the War Office that, 'his death has now been accepted for official purposes as having occurred'. [6] Charles is commemorated on the Savona Memorial, Italy, and a memorial service for him and Percy was held at Stratton Church, where a memorial bronze tablet was erected in their memory.

When the Armistice was signed Dorchester celebrated and the Pope family, whilst grieving for their two lost sons, must also have breathed a sigh of relief. But, tragically, the gods of War had not finished with them yet as their eldest son Edward was destined to die later in 1919. Born in Dorchester in 1875, Edward, known in the family as Alec, elected to go into the family brewing business, and like his father also ventured into civic life, when he was elected to the County Council for Dorchester East and in 1915 became a JP. However, it was in the Army that Edward was to find his true vocation.

Edward's introduction to the military came when at the age of 19 he obtained a commission as 2 Lt with the Dorset Militia. Three years later he was transferred to the 3rd Welsh Rgt as a captain and then in 1899, on the outbreak of the Boer War, sailed with his battalion on the troopship *Majestic*, landing at Cape Town on 26 February 1900. After a year at Yryburg near Mafeking, where Edward was responsible for the eastern and northern defences of the town and the gaol containing 170 Boer prisoners, he was made Provost

Marshal and given command of *Spitfire*, an armoured train, with the task of protecting troops repairing the line between De Aer and Kimberley. The train was involved in several skirmishes and seriously engaged with the Boers on 20 December 1900, when the stoker was killed and three of the crew wounded.

Edward commanded the train for 7 months but his service was cut short when he developed severe sciatica and had to be sent back to the UK. His return to Dorchester was something of an event. On his arrival he was met at the railway station by a large body of cheering men who proceeded to pull him in a carriage the 3 miles to Wrackleford, the procession headed by the Volunteer Band, and all this happening as church bells in the town pealed their welcome home. Later, in common with all of the Dorchester men who returned from the Boer War, he was awarded the Freedom of the Town. Edward never returned to South Africa but maintained his ties with the Army through the Special Reserve. His personal life took a major change when, in 1904, he married Sybil Briggs, the daughter of a lieutenant colonel and sister of a lieutenant general.

On 6 August 1914 Edward's old battalion was mobilised and he immediately joined up in Cardiff, where he was given the job of training those reservists and recruits who would replace the casualties of the original BEF. The following April he undertook the raising and training of a Bantam Btn, in which all of the men barring the officers and instructors were no taller than 5ft 3in. The 12th Service Btn South Wales Borders, as it was designated, was one of several Bantam units, mostly formed in heavy industrial areas like coal mining where restricted height was not synonymous with physical weakness. By November 1915 the Borderers were ready to join the other Welsh battalions forming the 119th Bde in France and in a report on the success of its formation the *South Wales Argus* gave a pen picture of Edward: 'Tall, finely built, a born leader, a stickler for discipline and efficiency, detesting all that smacks of slackness or denotes a slacker, he has instilled the soldierly spirit into those over whom he has command. He has won the respect and esteem of his officers and the admiration of his men …'. [7]

On 2 June 1916 the 12th Borderers arrived at Le Havre but did not take part in the Battle of the Somme. Their first serious encounter with the enemy came in April 1917 when the 12th captured the formidable defences of Fifteen Ravine, southwest of Cambrai. Meanwhile, Edward had been mentioned in Despatches in November 1916, and awarded the DSO in January 1917, for skilfully leading his battalion. Then, at the end of April he was forced to return home after being wounded and such was his health that subsequently he was passed fit for home service only, and with the new rank of substantive lieutenant colonel took command of his old 3rd Btn, firstly at Redcar and then after the War at Chatham. It was while at Chatham that he was admitted into Queen Alexandra's Hospital for Officers where he died on 9 April 1919 from 'disease contracted on active service'. [8]

The *Chronicle* [9] reported Edward's funeral, informing its readers that following a service in the Guards' Chapel his body was conveyed to Golder's Green Crematorium, where it was met off the train by the band of the 3rd Welsh and a 160-strong firing party, which must have created quite a bang when the volley was fired. At the same time, back in Dorchester, a memorial service was being held in Holy Trinity Church. Edward's remains were returned home the next day and placed in the family vault at Stratton. St Mary's Church contains various memorials to the Pope sons, but the most touching perhaps is a plaque fixed to the wall beneath a faded green and white flag bearing the Welsh red dragon. It explains that the flag was sent to Alfred Pope by Brig-Gen. Crozier, commander of the Welsh Rgt, who wrote, 'You are entitled to it by the laws of merit. It is the Flag of the 3rd Welsh, which flew at their Quarter Guard from August 4/14 to July 20/19, and must have been saluted daily at Retreat by your son, both at the very beginning of the War and in '17, '18 and '19 when he was in command: after he returned wounded, only to die at duty of his wounds sustained in April '17, near Gouzeaucourt.' Edward is also commemorated on memorials at Sherborne Abbey and St Aldhelm's Church, Weymouth, and appears on the Freemasons' Roll of Honour.

Flag of the 3rd Welsh in Stratton church.

[1] *Chronicle* 6/1/1916.

[2] Sir Frederick Treves, GCVO CH CB, surgeon to King Edward VII, benefactor of Joseph Merrick ('the Elephant Man').

[3] *Pope Book of Remembrance.*

[4] Ibid.

[5] Ibid.

[6] Ibid.

[7] Ibid.

[8] Ibid.

[9] *Chronicle* 17/4/1919.

Pte Barzillai Major – aged 61
3/4th Btn Duke of Cornwall's Light Infantry – 20277
Fordington Cemetery

Born at a time when Britain was engaged in another conflict, the Crimean War, Barzillai Major, who was the son of a Penzance tailor, joined the Royal Navy at the age of 19 and served for 19 years. He married Susan Wakefield in 1884 and after leaving the Navy had several jobs, including those of coastguard, mineral water cart driver and caretaker. Like James Bishop and William Bussell, he was not going to let his advanced years prevent him from helping his country at a time of need. So, when the War came along he enlisted in the 3/4th Btn Duke of Cornwall's Light Infantry, which had been established in 1915 as a depot training unit, and in October 1915 moved with the battalion from Bodmin to Dorset. He died on 2 October at the County Hospital of illness or as the result of an accident.

Sgt Charles Fraser Woolston – aged 20
6th Btn East Kent Rgt – 69
Thomas Hardye School Roll of Honour

On 24 April 1915 the *Chronicle* in an outburst of patriotic language reported on 'par nobile fratrum', [1] referring to two former Grammar School boys who had joined the War. The lads concerned were Arthur Woolston and his younger brother Charles, and the *Chronicle* chose them as an example to 'many who still hold back' from joining the War and congratulated them for their 'promptness and wholeheartedness'.

Charles Fraser Woolston's connection with Dorchester came through his grandfather William Woolston, who lived in the town in the 1860s, making and selling confectionary in his shop at 16 Cornhill. William's son Charles Walter Woolston attended the Grammar School and later went to live in London, where he worked as a mercantile clerk and then as an accountant with an engineering company. He married Elizabeth Bevan in 1886 and they lived in Bermondsey, where their sons Charles and Arthur were born. The name of Woolston returned to Dorchester when the two boys were sent to the Grammar School, and in 1911 Charles, aged 14, was boarding there with, among others, two brothers of Charles Budden. [2]

After school Charles took up farming, before enlisting in the 6th Btn East Kent Rgt (Buffs) in August 1914. As part of Kitchener's new Army, Charles, together with 26 officers and 866 OR, disembarked at Boulogne from *SS The Queen* on 1 June 1915 and after a short stay at a rest camp moved to Bailleul, were the raw recruits were taught the basics of fighting. They were toughened up with daily 8-mile route marches. This initiation lasted just 10 days before they were on the move again, to Armentières, where they were introduced to the trench and Charles, who had been promoted to corporal, and his fellow NCOs attended lectures on trench warfare. The men of the 6th Btn learned about life in the trenches at Ploegsteert Wood [3] and Despierre Farm but nothing could prepare them for the terrible events that would soon be upon them.

On 13 October the newly promoted Sgt Woolston sat in a trench waiting for the order to charge the German line running between Gun Trench and the Quarries, 3 miles to the north of Loos. The Battle of Loos had been raging for some 2½ weeks and Charles would have been only too aware that he was about to traverse the same ground that the regiment's 6th Btn had crossed on 26 September, sustaining 582 casualties, hardly a cheering thought for him and his section of machine gunners. At noon an artillery barrage opened up on the enemy's trenches and what happened next is described in the battalion's war diary: 'At about 2.00 pm all the smoke had cleared. At 2.15 pm the order was given to charge … The men were met with a terrific fire of machine guns on three sides while the Germans were lying on their parapets giving rapid fire. The three companies were practically wiped out.' The attack had lasted just a few minutes and the troops had travelled barely 100 yd. On their withdrawal it was found that there were 409 casualties, including Charles and two of his team. In a letter to his parents his Lieutenant said of him, 'He was in charge of one of our machine guns and was working it with great courage and coolness, when he was killed and two of his men with him. In Sgt Woolston I have lost a most valued NCO, one whom

I knew I could trust to carry out any enterprise, whatever the difficulties or dangers'. [4] He is remembered on the Loos Memorial. Back in England the Society of Dorset Men in London, of which his father was a member, drank a toast to him at one of their meetings.

Charles' brother Arthur survived the War and distinguished himself at Gallipoli, serving with the Armoured Car Section of the RNAS. On 22 July 1917 the *Chronicle* felt compelled to print a letter that had been sent to his father from Josiah Wedgewood MP, a lieutenant commander in the RNVR. In the letter referring to Arthur he wrote: 'I hardly knew him before we landed at Gallipoli, but you find out about a man pretty quickly when you share the same trench biscuit, and even blanket, and face both the same death. Fortunately he was smaller than I so they missed him. He was a man who never showed fear. He volunteered for every dangerous service, up night after night fighting, helping wounded, or digging. He was never too tired to do more. I mentioned him twice in my Despatches … he has naturally acquired the respect of the whole squadron, on which his modesty and cheerfulness had already made him beloved.' [5]

---

[1] A noble pair of brothers.
[2] See Charles Budden.
[3] Known by the soldiers as Plugstreet Wood.
[4] *Dorset Year Book* 1915/16.
[5] *Chronicle* 22/7/1915.

Pte George Albutt – aged 38
12th Btn Worcestershire Rgt – 20420
Fordington Cemetery

George Albutt was one of the soldiers who had no association with Dorchester but is buried in Fordington Cemetery. The son of David and Ann Albutt of Bromsgrove, he married his wife Elizabeth in 1899 and at the time of his death the family was living in Westfield Lane, Bromsgrove.

On the 28 December 1914 George enlisted in the 12th Btn Worcestershire Rgt, which arrived in Wareham for training in 1915. It was there that George was taken seriously ill and admitted to the County Hospital suffering from pleurisy and bronchopneumonia. He succumbed to his illnesses on 14 October 1915 and was buried with full military honours on the following Saturday afternoon. Elizabeth was left to bring up their 11 children.

Pioneer James Brighton – aged 40
4th Labour Btn Royal Engineers – 115373
Cenotaph and St George's

In the Great War the shovel was as important as the gun. Large movements of troops over a wide area and the requirement of ammunition and food to be continually supplied to the Front meant that roads, bridges, railways and canals all had to be built and maintained. These jobs were the lot of the men of the labour battalions and later the Labour Corps.

James Brighton had been a labourer before he enlisted in the Royal Engineers in August 1915. He arrived in France on 25 August but was there for less than a month before being admitted to the No. 2 Canadian General Hospital at Le Tréport near Dieppe, complaining of pains in the chest and continual coughing at night. He was diagnosed as having bronchitis, returned to the UK and treated at a hospital in Leicester, before going on to another in Eastbourne, where it was considered that he had recovered sufficiently to be discharged as fit for duty. James returned to his home in Dorchester but the joy of his wife and child was short lived because shortly after his arrival he was admitted into one of the military hospitals in the town and then transferred to the County Hospital. His wife was at his bedside when he died of acute pneumonia on 17 November. James was buried in Fordington Cemetery 3 days later.

James Brighton was a Londoner who worked on the railways as a plate layer. He married Mary Bridge in January 1905, a Dorchester girl, daughter of Samuel Bridge and Roseina, and after their marriage the young couple went to live with Mary's parents at 55 Mill St In the same year as their marriage Mary's sister Sarah Sprules died in childbirth and they took on the responsibility of bring up her child Robert. Eventually the young family set up their own home at 46a Holloway Rd. After James' death Mary wrote to the authorities enquiring about a pension for 'the child we have been looking after since he was 11 days old and kept him', adding, 'He is going on 11 [and] now he will want to be kept and clothed'. [1] She was granted a pension of 17/6d.

---

[1] SR.

Pte William Sidney Curtis – aged 23
1/4th Btn Dorsetshire Rgt – 2243 & 200611

L/Cpl Charles James Curtis – aged 19
1st Btn Duke of Cornwall's Light Infantry

Both are commemorated on the Cenotaph and Holy Trinity

William Curtis was used to taking orders from army officers. Before he joined the military he had been a servant to a Capt. Nicholson and his family at Mappercombe near Bridport and after returning to Dorchester, the town of his birth, he found a position as footman to Maj. Hughes-Onslow [1] at Colliton House and according to the *Chronicle* became a very popular lad around the town. [2] Like his employer William enlisted in the Dorsets, but unlike him he was not destined for France but instead went to India with the 1/4th Btn in October 1914. In 1915 he was one of 25 soldiers who volunteered to go to modern-day Iraq to re-enforce the 2nd Btn and took part in the Battle of Kut-al-Amara on 28 September, from which he emerged unscathed. Following that encounter the powers that be decided that an advance should be made towards Basra, but in order to do so the Turkish stronghold of Ctesiphon had to be dealt with first.

The night of 21 November was bitterly cold and William had neither blanket nor great-coat so got little sleep. He, along with the remainder of the battalion, were hiding behind the bank of a water-channel and when dawn came at about 6.30 am with it came a damp mist from the river to add to his discomfort. Climbing from his foxhole William and his fellow Dorsets advanced on the Turkish lines, the famous Arch of Ctesiphon clearly visible. After heavy fighting much of the enemy's front line and some of its second line had been captured and it seemed that the battle had been won, but in achieving their gains the attacking force had used up all its reserves, whereas the Turks had reserves in depth, which they began to bring up to develop a counterattack. The Dorsets found themselves in a very precarious position. With ammunition running out and the forces opposing them gathering strength they had no alternative but to fall back before being surrounded. One of the men who did not make it back to the British line was William. He had fought gallantly, for which he was mentioned in Despatches, but went missing. [3] Back in Dorchester, his parents, Thomas and Eliza Curtis of 5 Maud Rd, were informed that he was probably a prisoner. However, nothing more was heard of him and the official record states that he was killed on 22 November. He is remembered on the Basra Memorial.

William's younger brother Charles laid down his life for King and country at the tender age of 19. Formerly employed by Messrs Woods and Son's, Domestic Stores, 34 High East St, [4] the *Chronicle* described him as, 'one of a party of smart Dorchester lads who joined the Somerset Light Infantry shortly before the outbreak of war'. [5] William subsequently transferred to the DCLI and was killed on 23 July 1916, when the 1st Btn attacked High Wood as part of the Battle of the Somme. Charles was at one time a member of Holy Trinity choir and the Rev Bowden-Smith made the following reference to him: 'I have heard this morning that Cpl Charles Curtis has laid down his life in the cause of King and country. We may well believe that he died as he lived – a good soldier of Jesus Christ'. [6] Charles' name appears on the Thiepval Memorial, Somme, France.

[1] See Denzil Hughes-Onslow.
[2] *Chronicle* 13/4/1916.
[3] The *Chronicle* reported that he was awarded the DCM but I have found no record of it.
[4] Woods still have their premises at the same address.
[5] *Chronicle* 3/8/1916.
[6] Ibid.

2 Lt Henry George Willis – aged 27
2nd Btn Durham Light Infantry
Cenotaph and Holy Trinity

On Christmas Eve 1915 most of the good people of Dorchester, despite the curtain of war drawn over the town, were preparing for the celebrations of the next day. But for those who had lost loved ones the season had a void. For Annie Early it was a time of deep anxiety. Her daughter Louise was in France visiting her fiancé Henry Willis who had been wounded. But Annie's relationship with Henry was far more than that of prospective mother-in-law. It appears that Henry had a tragic past. Born on 20 December 1888 he was the son of Henry Willis but for some reason he did not know the name of his mother. In the 1901 census he and his sister Violet were inmates of the Dorchester Workhouse but no parents were present. Annie Early took on the young boy and probably his sister too, as her own children. [1] Henry went to Dorchester Boys' School and, if the *Chronicle* is to be believed, was a very popular boy in the town. At the age of 18 he decided on an army career and enlisted in the Royal Engineers for 3 years. He obviously enjoyed army life because a year later he extended his service to 7 years. His first 2 years were spent at home with the 39th Coy followed by 4 years in Jamaica with the 44th Coy. After attending a series of courses at Army school, Henry gained the qualification of machine mechanic, was promoted to sergeant on 29 July 1913 and then joined 2 Signal Squadron at Ludgershall, Wiltshire, before going off to France to fight in the War. The degree of Henry's local popularity is measured by the fact that his gaining a commission into the DLI in October 1915 was fully reported in the *Chronicle*. It was while he was serving with the 2nd Btn in trenches 1.5 miles east of Ypres that the young lieutenant was shot and severely wounded on 18 December.

Louise, who was informed of the seriousness of her fiancée's condition, caught the first train to Folkestone and crossed over to Boulogne where Henry was in hospital, only to hear on her arrival that he had passed away 3 days before Christmas. Henry was laid to rest in the Boulogne Eastern Cemetery. The journey that Louise made to be with Henry was indicative of their love, a love that had matured over time, and it is also shown in his letters to her. In them he refers to Zog, his nickname for her. In one letter he tries to reassure, when he writes, 'I rather fancy you are a little downhearted that's natural I suppose, yet you must cheer up Zog for remember that every cloud has the proverbial you know. Please don't look at the black side for I don't intend to be killed or anything nasty like that'. [2] He then tries to take her mind away from the possibilities ahead by telling her about the fact that he has just been given a new car, 'a new Sunbeam, absolutely a spanker'. One section of the letter suggests that he lost contact with the Early family, probably when he joined the Army. In it he says, 'I now look back and bless the day I was prompted to drop a card to 3, Harvey's Buildings. It was the best few minute's work I ever did. That minute's work gained me mother, sweetheart, friends, yes and position in business, home, oh well everything that a lone fellow requires. Above all Zoggie dear the most glorious little girl a man worried with'. Henry was obviously very serious about his love for Louise, his letter going on to detail how he wants to arrange for his pay to be sent home for her and her mother. In another letter, [3] sent a month before his death, he discusses the apparent delay in the post, something that must have caused great distress to both relatives back home and soldiers at the Front, for whilst the letters kept arriving everything was fine. On the day Henry died the letters did stop and Zoggie returned home to be with her mother and continue her job teaching at the Dorchester Girls' School. Her fiancée's personal effects, which included cigarette case, tube of morphia pills, a gold signet ring and wristwatch, were returned home for her to keep in his memory. On 15 June 1916 an entry appeared in the *London Gazette* stating that Henry had been mentioned in Despatches for gallantry.

[1] The *Chronicle* of 7/9/1916 has an interesting article, in which Henry's elder brother wishes it to be known that he is his next of kin, perhaps paving the way for a challenge to the Early family receiving Henry's pension.

[2] Letter dated 23/9/1914 – SR.

[3] Letter dated 18/11/1915 – SR.

1916
The Battle Front

France and Belgium

Vimy Ridge, 21 May

Operations during the spring of 1916 centred on Ypres. On 14 February the British lost and then regained their line at the Bluff and fighting took place at St Eloi, where the Germans had a salient. In contrast, the Vimy Ridge sector was quiet when the British relieved the French there but the policy of live and let live did not last for long. On 21 May the explosion of a mine under the British line was followed by the usual bombardment, signalling the attack by infantry. The German troops overran the 150 Division's front line and dug defensive positions. After several attempts to regain the ground the British command concluded that the large number of guns required to mount a major counterattack would be better used elsewhere and ceased operations. The guns were due to move to the Somme area.

Battles of the Somme, 1 July–18 November

Much emphasis has been placed on the events of the first day of the Somme with its 58,000 British casualties, but the whole operation lasted until November and consisted of a number of battles. It is not in the remit of this book to describe them in detail so they are listed below.

> Battle of Albert, 1–13 July; Battle of Bazentin, 14–17 July; Attack at Fromelles, 19 July; Attacks on High Wood, 20–25 July; Battle of Delville Wood, 15 July–3 Sept; Battle of Pozieres, 23 July–3 Sept; Battle of Guillemont, 3–6 Sept; Battle of Ginchy, 9 Sept; Battle of Flers-Courcelette, 15–22 Sept; Battle of Morval, 25–28 Sept; Battle of Thiepval, 26–28 Sept; Battle of Le Transloy, 1–18 Oct; Battle of the Ancre Heights, 1 Oct–11 Nov; Battle of the Ancre, 13–18 Nov.

Mesopotamia

Besieged at Kut the plea went out for the beleaguered men to be relieved. Accordingly, a relief force was put together, mainly made up of troops imported from India and in January it began its journey up the Tigris. The first obstacle was encountered at Sheikh Sa'ad where its way was blocked by 22,500 Turks. After two attempts to shift them failed another was launched on 9 January, only to find that the enemy had withdrawn. The engagement cost the British 4,000 casualties. There were four more encounters on the way to Kut, the battles of the Wadi (13 Jan), Hanna (21 Jan), Dujaila (7–9 Mar) and Kut (5–29 Apr), all of which led to heavy losses, before the venture was called off. In October the new leader of the British forces in Mesopotamia, Sir Frederick Maude, determined to make an attack on Kut, now in the hands of the Turks. On the night of 13/14 December 50,000 men started their advance but it was not until the following February that the British entered the town.

Palestine

On 3/4 August, a mixed force of Arabs and Turks, under German leadership, made a second attempt to gain control of the Suez Canal by attacking British forces at Romani. Although they initially captured part of the town, after British counterattacks they had to retreat, partly due to lack of water.

Salonika

The Salonika force spent the first months of the year establishing a position and then repulsed an attempt by Bulgarian forces to capture Greece, in July. In October, the British, reinforced by Serbian, Russian and Italian troops, advanced towards the Greek city of Serres. The campaign was successful and the force halted just a few miles from the city.

The war at sea

Battle of Jutland, 31 May–1 June

Jutland, the greatest and only major sea battle of the Great War, was fought at the end of May. Details of the battle are given in the story of Walter Smith.

1916
Roll of Honour

L/Cpl Walter George Clench DCM – aged 24
2nd Btn Dorsetshire Rgt – 9038
Cenotaph and St George's

Walter Clench was another Durnovarian who followed his father into the Dorsets. William Clench spent 12 years with the Colours and served in the East Indies and after his retirement he lived with his wife Alice and their family at 2 Tubbs Rd.

Walter enlisted in Dorchester on 23 January 1911, just before his 19th birthday, and was posted to the 2nd Btn in India. He generally kept his nose clean during his time in the Army and was considered to be sober, honest and hardworking. His conduct record shows that he was only punished on one occasion, when he was confined to barracks for 3 days for using obscene language in the barrack room. Like William Hellard, Walter also visited a house of ill-repute and paid the price by ending up in hospital in Poona for 45 days suffering from syphilis. He also spent his 23rd birthday in a hospital bed with colitis.

In November 1914 the 2nd Btn moved from India to Mesopotamia and following the hard-won Battle of Shaiba in April 1915, it was decided to continue the advance along the River Tigris towards Baghdad. Newly promoted to L/Cpl in B Coy, Walter found the river journey difficult, mainly because of the heat, and like many others entered hospital at Basra with heatstroke. After 9 days of rest and a light diet he returned to his comrades on their trek and by September Gen. Townsend's men had reached Sannaiyat where preparations were made to attack the town of Kut-al-Amara. The objective given to Walter's company on 28 September was to capture part of a Redoubt which formed a section of the extensive Turkish defences. At 9.30 am B Coy was ordered to advance and despite mounting casualties they pressed steadily forward, though their expenditure of ammunition was great and they were in danger of running out. Walter was one of the men who volunteered to go back and bring more, a dangerous task because the forward troops were barely 300 yd from the Redoubt. For this brave action he was awarded the DCM and his citation reads: 'When close to the enemy's trenches he chose to go back under heavy fire for ammunition and brought it up very rapidly.' [1] Thanks to men like Walter the Dorsets took their objective and Townsend's men took the town.

Sadly, Walter would never get to wear his gallantry medal. On 30 December 1915, 3 days after his 23rd birthday, he was dangerously wounded when a shell exploded in the hospital compound in Kut. He was treated for a compound fracture of the right thigh but to no avail, tetanus had set in and he died on 9 January 1916. His body lies in Kut War Cemetery. Back in Dorchester, Walter's mother received official news of her son's death in a letter signed by Lord Kitchener, in which he conveyed the sympathy of the King and Queen. This was followed by another 4 days later from the War Office telling her of her son's medal award. The *Chronicle*, reporting with no little irony on the events, expressed the view that, 'his bereaved mother has the satisfaction of knowing that his heroism did not go unrewarded, and that his life was nobly given for King and Country'.

[1] *Chronicle* 27/1/1916.
[2] Ibid.

Pte George Williams – aged 45
Royal Warwickshire Rgt – 20050
Fordington Cemetery

George Williams found himself in Dorchester as one of the men guarding the German prisoners at Poundbury. In the winter of 1915/16 he was admitted into the military hospital where he died of painful Bright's disease [1] on 4 February 1916. George came from Birmingham but was buried locally in Fordington. He left behind a widow and three children.

[1] A generic name for several diseases of the kidneys.

2 Lt Christopher John Fitch – aged 42
6th Btn Dorsetshire Rgt
Cenotaph

The 6th Btn Dorsets was born on 6 September 1914 in Dorchester and during the following fortnight over 1,000 volunteers passed through the square of the Dorchester barracks. Only 300 were native to the county; the remainder included 400 Londoners, 400 from Warwickshire and 70 Welsh miners. Few of their officers had seen active service and several, like Denzil Hughes-Onslow, came out of retirement. [1] Another soldier who came out of retirement was C/Sgt Christopher Fitch who, in helping to organise the battalion, was 'invaluable for his knowledge and cool-headed efficiency'. [2] Christopher had served in the Dorsets for no less than 21 years before being pensioned off in October 1912. He was a Londoner who originally joined the Northamptonshire Rgt on 10 October 1891 but was almost immediately transferred to the 1st Btn

(Source: The Keep Military Museum.)

Dorsets. After a period of home service he went to India with them and remained there for 13 years, helping to defend British interests. His own interests included fencing and he was also a keen musician.

In 1897 Christopher fought in what proved to be a difficult campaign for the 1st Dorsets on the North-West Frontier. The Dorsets were part of a force of about 40,000 troops sent into the Tirah region with the aim of establishing control over the Afridis and Orakzais tribesmen who had attacked British and Indian troops in the Khyber Pass and Samana Range. [3] The first objective of Lt-Gen. Sir William Lockhart, the British commander, was to get control of the Dargai Heights which, if held by tribesmen, would threaten the moveable column of men and animals. There were two separate battles to gain control of the Heights. The first scaling of the Heights, on 18 October, was completed without much trouble by the 3rd Gurkhas and King's Own Scottish Borderers but it was decided to abandon the mountain as the men did not have provisions for a prolonged stay. As soon as the Heights were abandoned the tribesmen reoccupied them in great numbers and the whole exercise had to be repeated, this time with an enemy that was in waiting. On the 20th the 2nd Gurkhas led the assault with the 1st Dorsets, who had been serving in southern India and were not used to mountain warfare. For the attacking troops the worst part of the climb up the Heights was an open area which had to be crossed with sharp-shooting tribesmen 200 yards above them. At 10 am the Dorsets gave covering fire as the Gurkhas dashed across, sustaining 71 casualties in 10 minutes.

Next it was the Dorset's turn. The first four companies had been giving covering fire and seen how ineffective it was against well-hidden tribesmen. E Coy was first to go and most of the leading section went down. A few got across, some reaching the halfway rocks. F and G Coys fared little better and only a few of the Dorsets reached the cover of the low cliff the other side of the space because each man that tried faced almost certain death. Ammunition was running low and the men could go neither forward nor back so it was with no little relief when the Gordon Highlanders swept past them and took the enemy position. The men of the 1st Btn who died are commemorated on a memorial in the Borough Gardens, Dorchester.

During a home leave from India Christopher had married Jessie Dunning on 13 March 1903 and having survived the Dargai Heights and the numerous tropical diseases that beset the soldier in India, he finally returned to England to be with his wife in December 1906, adorned by three sergeant's stripes. While Jessie was following him around the country with his battalion she gave birth to two of their three children in Portsmouth and when he was finally stationed at the regimental depot in Dorchester they lived at 1 Shirley Terr.

Christopher was not 2 years into his retirement on a colour sergeant's pay when Germany denied Belgium its neutrality and forced Britain into a war. Christopher's reaction was to re-enlist in the 6th Btn and it was not long before he was granted a commission. He was made one of the officers responsible for transport when the battalion went to France in July 1915 and moved into the area around the Ypres Salient. At a meeting with his commanding and fellow officers at 9 pm on 15 February 1916 Christopher could hardly have been full of enthusiasm as the plans for attacking a feature called the Bluff, situated on the Ypres-Comines Canal, were discussed. There would be no time for reconnaissance and there were no guides to take Christopher and his men into a night of pitch-black darkness. The subsequent attack was a failure, leaving over 100 men lying in the snow and 40 dead. Christopher was among the dead and is buried in Spoil Bank Cemetery, West-Vlaanderen, Belgium.

[1] See Denzil Hughes-Onslow.
[2] Regimental history.
[3] See Frederick Andrews.

Capt. John Thomas Allen – aged 40
RFA
Dorchester Cenotaph

Emily Holly moved to Dorchester from Yeovil sometime in the 1870's and lived with her parents in King Street, before settling down at 4 East Parade. After completing her education she gained employment as a dressmaker and in 1897, at the age of 21, married John Thomas Allen, a captain at the artillery barracks.

By the time John met Emily he had already had an esteemed military career and it might be said that service life ran though his veins. He was one of five sons who followed their father into the Army, while two more entered the Navy. One of his naval brothers was killed in the sinking of *HMS Hogue* in the North Sea by a German submarine. John's army career was a classic example of an officer who came up through the ranks. As a boy he became a trumpeter in the RFA, stationed at Woolwich, but he was later persuaded by his brother to transfer to T Bty, RHA, which at the time was stationed in Dorchester. During his 2-year stay in the town, such was his character that he soon made a host of friends and was actively involved in the Baptist Church and the Old Soldier's Home in North Square and married Emily. It was not long before their daughter Violet was born in 1898. John was then called away to fight in South Africa. He survived the Boer War but not before being invalided home owing to an injury received by being pinned beneath his horse after it had been killed. After recuperation he was transferred to the RGA stationed at Rangoon, as a sergeant instructor. This time Emily went with him and it was there that their eldest son Frederick was born.

On their return to England the family lived in Woolwich, the home of the Royal Artillery, where, after passing a Master Gunner's course with flying colours, John was promoted to the rank of lieutenant in the RFA, and with his commission came another move, this time to Athlone in Ireland. 1914 arrived and with it another promotion. Capt. Allen was now involved in organising the mobilisation of troops in the area, which lasted until January 1915 when orders came for him to embark for France, where he was to head an ammunition column.

On 25 September 1915 the Loos offensive began and as an overture to the attack John took part in the 4-day bombardment of the German lines, which involved the firing of 250,000 shells. Despite this massive show of firepower and the extensive use of chlorine gas the offensive was called off on 28 September as a failure. It was most probably his experiences in this battle that led to John being sent home in November suffering from a nervous breakdown. He had lost the use of his left arm and leg which a London specialist attributed to his nervous disorder. John returned to his family in Dorchester, Emily having moved back there to be near her parents, and he was treated by military doctors at the Depot Barracks. Hopes were entertained for his recovery and arrangements were made for him to go into a convalescent home, when he unexpectedly sustained a cerebral haemorrhage and died on 18 February at his sister-in-law's house at 41 Dukes Ave. Emily let it be known that she wanted her husband's funeral in Weymouth Avenue Cemetery to be a private affair. His coffin was carried to his grave by a glass-topped funeral car but absent from the funeral procession was the military band and escort of soldiers that normally accompanied military funerals in the town.

In the language typical of the time the *Chronicle* commented, 'Thus was another life given up for King and country, and the gallant officer has left behind a glorious record of what can be accomplished by grit and determination in rising from the ranks'. [1] Emily was awarded a pension of £75 a year and £20 per annum for each of her five children.

---

[1] *Chronicle* 24/2/1916.

Stoker Walter Thomas Barber – aged 19
RN – K/28978
Cenotaph and St George's

On the afternoon of 6 March 1916 those folk who lived in the vicinity of St George's Church, Fordington, heard, not for the first time nor the last, a mournful tune being played by a military band. On this occasion the reason for the music was the burial of a 19-year-old sailor, Walter Barber. The Barber family had lived in Mill Street for less than 5 years. Before that their life had been somewhat nomadic, living at Blandford, Shaftesbury, Mere in Somerset and Southwick in Wiltshire. The reason for the moves was Walter Senior's need to find work as an agricultural labourer, a sign that the age of the journeyman was not yet dead. It was in Southwick that Rose Barber gave birth to Walter Thomas on 18 January 1897 and after leaving school their son was also drawn towards agriculture, helping his father to operate a steam threshing machine as employees of the local steam plough works.

The 18-year-old Walter who arrived at the naval recruitment office on 8 November 1915 was 5 ft 5¾ in tall. He had brown hair and eyes and a healthy complexion. As to his demeanour, the *Chronicle* described him as 'genial and well set up as a sailor'. [1] After signing on for 12 years Walter reported to *HMS Victory II*, the onshore naval establishment at Crystal Palace in London, with the rating of Stoker Second Class. In less than 2 months he had been promoted to Stoker First Class and the following spring he returned home for a few days' leave. It was while he was home with his family that he caught a severe cold that necessitated the services of Dr Theodore Broadway. He was eventually admitted into the County Hospital but what started as a cold turned into acute pneumonia, from which he died on 3 March.

---

[1] *Chronicle* 9/3/1916.

2 Lt John Frederick Johnson – aged 20
6th Btn King's Own Royal Lancaster Rgt [1]
Thomas Hardye School Roll of Honour

John Johnson was another farmer's son who attended the Grammar School in Dorchester. He was born in 1895, the son of Frederick and Kate who farmed at Forston Grange, north of Dorchester. When John left school he too took up farming but of a very different kind. He sailed 6,000 miles to Brazil to grow coffee in the red soil of Dumont. Despite the distance involved, when War came he decided to return to England to defend his country and on 11 December 1914 enlisted in the Army, stating a preference to join one of the sportsman's battalions. He was duly signed up with the 24th Btn Royal Fusiliers which was one of the 'Pals' [2] battalions except, rather than being formed by geographical proximity like the Leeds and Accrington Pals, it was initially made up of men from the sporting world. John was posted to home duty until he gained a commission on 26 March 1915 and then transferred to the 9th Btn KORL Rgt, where he remained until he was attached to the 6th Btn, joining them at Portshead in Egypt.

The Lancasters sailed from Egypt to Mesopotamia in April 1916 to be part of the 13th Division, which was to make an attempt to relieve the British and Indian soldiers besieged in Kut. In its path were the heavily fortified Turkish positions at Sanniyat. It was decide to attack the enemy line there on 9 April after dark. Following previous heavy fighting Lt Johnson's company was the weakest in the battalion and was to be kept in reserve at the commencement of the attack, but he had other ideas. John's fate in the ensuing battle was described in a letter written to his mother by a Pte Colin Macfarlane: 'I am pleased to say I was Mr J F Johnson's servant and was in the charge with him when he died. On the night of 8/9 April we were ordered to make a charge. Your son's platoon was the weakest and was put into the second line. When he got to know of this he immediately volunteered to take the front line. While in the charge he received a wound in the body and tried to get on his feet again but received another one in the head. It was impossible to give help at the time but sorry to say we saw no more of him. I really must say he died a hero. I have been servant to him for some time. I always found him good and faithful – he was well liked by his platoon and deeply regret his fate.' [3] John's parent's must have held out some hope that their son had been captured and was held prisoner, especially when in the *Times* on 17 April he was reported missing and not killed. Any hope, however, vanished when they received a letter from another witness to their son's death, this time a Pte Peter Barnes who said, 'we were both in the attack on the San Yatt [Sanniyat] position where Mr Johnson was killed outright owing to a bullet passing through his head. I seen him fall so therefore I know for sure he is dead and not taken prisoner.' [4] Pte Barnes goes on to explain that very few men reached the Turkish trenches and those that did were lying in them wounded or dead. The attack was a complete failure with 1,807 casualties, and five Victoria Crosses were awarded for the fighting on that day. John is commemorated on the Basra Memorial.

---

[1] CWGC shows 9th Btn but the 9th did not serve in Mesopotamia.

[2] Pals battalions were units of the British Army recruited through special recruiting drives. The members came from specific groups and the men were told that they would serve

together, rather than be dispersed throughout the Army. Some, like the Accrington Pals, suffered terrible losses at the Battle of the Somme.

[3] Letter dated 14 May 1916 – SR.

[4] Letter dated 2 June 1917 – SR.

Pte Thomas Sturmey – aged 31
20th Btn Canadian Infantry (Central Ontario Rgt) – 57936
Cenotaph

Pte Walter Harry Sturmey – aged 22
1/4th Btn Dorsetshire Rgt – 1386 and 20007
Cenotaph and Post Office Memorial

The Sturmey family originated from Cerne Abbas but in the 1890s moved to Dorchester and lived in Maumbury Way. Mary Sturmey gave birth to six sons before her husband George, a bricklayer and plasterer, died in 1909. Added to that tragedy she had to bear the loss of two of her boys, Thomas and Walter, who perished in the War. Thomas was her third son who in the early part of the century migrated to Canada with his wife Mary, whom he married in 1900. The couple settled in Midland, Ontario, with their two children and Thomas worked as a chauffeur. When the call to arms came he joined the 20th Btn Canadian Infantry and was attached to the machine gun section. It was while the Canadians were fighting to the southeast of Ypres that he was wounded and evacuated to a base hospital at Boulogne, where he died on 15 April 1916. He is buried in Boulogne Eastern Cemetery.

Walter, the sixth son, was a telegraph messenger with the Post Office before the War and also a Territorial soldier. He joined the 1/4th Dorsets in 1914 and went with them to Mesopotamia. He was one of the casualties of the attack on Ramadi Ridge on 28 September 1917 [1] and his body was interred in Baghdad (North Gate) Cemetery. A year after Walter's death his mother placed an item in the *Chronicle*'s 'In Memoriam' column which included this short verse, which might have given her some comfort knowing that it was very unlikely that she would visit her sons' graves.

> *A soldier's grave, a touching thing,*
> *Where loving hands no flowers may bring.*
> *But God in his great loving care,*
> *Will find our dear one lying there.*

[1] For details of the attack see Samuel Dimond.

Cpl Reginald John Vallard – aged 25
2nd Btn Dorsetshire Rgt – 15371

L/Cpl William Charles – aged 40
SS Cairnstrath, RMLI – PO/7577

Both are commemorated on the Cenotaph [1]

Reginald Vallard. (Source: S. Vallard.)

William Charles and Reginald Vallard were step-brothers. William was born in Fordington on 19 February 1877 to Louisa Charles and the following year she married William Theophilus Vallard from Yetminster, and the couple set up home in Cuckhold's Row.

Their fourth child Reginald was born in 1891 and on the outbreak of war he went to Mesopotamia to fight against the Turks. It is possible that, given the date of his death, 22 April 1916, Reginald was one of the majority of the 2nd Btn Dorsets who were besieged in Kut but more likely he formed part of a composite unit known as the Norsets, which consisted of drafts from the 2nd Norfolks and men of the 2nd Dorsets who had been absent from Kut for one reason or another when it fell to the Turks.

A failed attack on the Turkish positions at Sanniyat on 8/9 April 1916, in which Lt John Johnson [2] was killed, was not the last attempt to break the line there in an effort to relieve the besieged men at Kut. On 21 April orders for another assault arrived but, in hindsight, the prospects for success were not good. Many of the troops of the Meerut Division, of which the Norsets were part, were inexperienced and the British units which had been thrown together lacked cohesion. Added to these factors was the debilitation of the men, brought about by the flooding of the River Tigris, which led to trenches being flooded to a degree that some soldiers had to flee for their lives from the torrents.

The Norsets started their attack on the 22nd without the benefit of a heavy barrage, which allowed the Turkish troops to fire unmolested on the advancing battalion. Before clearing their own lines the men had to traverse three trenches full of water and then progress into no man's land, which was 400 yd wide and 1 ft deep in water. The fire they faced was heavy, as were the casualties they sustained, some of which seem to have been inflicted by their own machine guns trying to enfilade the Turkish lines. Another effect of the terrible conditions became evident when those men who got near to the enemy trenches found that their rifles were clogged with mud. With so many useless rifles the attack was going nowhere and eventually the troops had to retire. Of the 44 men of the Norsets that were killed, the Dorsets contributed 18, one of whom was Reginald. He is commemorated on the Basra Memorial and Portland (Dorset) War Memorial.

At the age of 17 William Charles joined the RMLI and served for 23 years on 11 different ships, principally cruisers, both at home and in the Far East. He was on *HMS Duke of Edinburgh* when she was involved in picking up survivors off the P&O ship *Dehli* which ran aground off the Moroccan coast in December 1911. On 31 January 1917 William was retired from the Marines but wasted no time in getting back to sea by enrolling in the Royal Fleet Reserve the very next day.

Sailors have many superstitions, one of which is that it is unlucky to change the name of a ship. This was certainly true of the 2,128-ton cargo ship *Felbridge*, which was renamed *Cairnstrath* when it was sold in 1901. Lurking beneath the waves in the early hours of 4 August 1917, 6 miles SSW of the Isle de Pilier in the Bay of Biscay, Oberleutnant Renhold Saltswedel waited in the submarine *UC.71* for his next victim to come into torpedo range. His chosen target was the *Cairnstrath* which, with William on board, was in transit from Bilbao to the Tyne, carrying a cargo of iron ore. When the torpedo that was unleashed from *UC.71* hit the ship it sank almost immediately and 22 of the 23 crew perished, including William. The German U-boat commander went on to sink a total of 111 merchant vessels before being killed by a mine in December 1917. William's body was not recovered and he is commemorated on the Portsmouth Naval War Memorial.

[1] William appears on the Cenotaph twice, as W. Vallard (mistakenly) and as W.C. Charles.
[2] See John Johnson.

Cpl William George White – aged 33
2nd Btn Dorsetshire Rgt – (3)8069
Cenotaph and St George's

Climbing up Fordington Hill from King's Road one could easily miss the gap in the houses which is Hillside Terrace. It consists of just ten properties, the end one of which was occupied by Richard and Louisa White. Richard worked as a brewer's labourer. All four brothers of the household served in the Army during the War but William, the second eldest, was both soldier and sailor. Before joining the Dorsets in August 1914 he had already served 9 years in the Navy.

The young blacksmith's mate signed up for 12 years at the age of 19 and it has to be said that in regard to his relationship with the Senior Service he may have been on the same ship as his officers but was not always sailing in the same direction. He spent much of his early service in Australia and it was there that he first got into trouble, deserting for 4 days from *HMS Mildura* in Melbourne. Neither did William like his next ship, *HMS Ringarooma*, from which he again went on the run. For these offences he was sentenced to 90 days' hard labour. William's record did not improve and there are further instances of him being confined to the cells. However, despite his misdoings his service record does state that his conduct was generally considered to be good or very good. Finally, having served 9 out of his 12 years William parted from the Navy in 1908, when he left *HMS Hampshire* and eventually found his way back to Dorchester, where he settled, gaining employment with Eddison and Matteo's Steam Roller Works.

Despite William's previous poor relationship with authority he joined the Dorset National Reserve and then enlisted in the Dorsets at the beginning of the War, fighting in France until he was wounded. On recovery he was sent to the 2nd Btn in Mesopotamia where, like Reginald Vallard, he was a casualty of the attack on Sanniyat on 22 April 1916. After the battle had stalled the Turks raised the Red Crescent, indicating that they were sending out stretcher-bearers to collect their wounded. The British did the same but the Turks did not allow them to collect those wounded that lay in or behind their lines. In the

Chronicle of 1 June among the long list of missing was Cpl William White, suggesting that he may well have been one of those men the stretcher-bearers could not reach. Eventually, the authorities determined that he died of his wounds on the 24th. His name appears on the Basra Memorial.

Pte Walter Edward Early – aged 21
2nd Btn Australian Infantry – 582
Cenotaph

Victoria Buildings consists of a small terrace of cottages which, externally, have hardly changed since they were built. They are not easy to locate; if you want to visit them you will have to leave your car in Salisbury Street and walk around the corner into Salisbury Fields where they mark the northern limit of this peaceful urban space, which still feels like a compromise between a village green and a park. Walter Early was brought up at No.7 by his parents Walter, a coach builder's labourer, and Francis. Doubtless Walter played at being a soldier many times with his friends on the grass outside his house, not knowing that some day he would be fighting for his life in a very different environment.

Sometime during the first decade of the 20th century Walter decided to migrate to Australia where he settled in New South Wales and found employment as a builder's labourer. He decided to fight for his home country on 17 August 1914 by enlisting in the 2nd Btn of the 1st Infantry Brigade of the Australian Army.

The name Anzac Cove has a very special meaning for Australians. Not only was it the first occasion that they went into battle as a single nation [1] but also it was the place where so many of their soldiers were slaughtered in the debacle of the Gallipoli campaign. Walter's part in that campaign began on 18 October 1915 when he embarked from Sydney Harbour onto the troopship *Suffolk*. The jetty was full of onlookers and relatives and the troops had some difficulty in marching to the ship, the CO remarking in his diary that, 'the police were quite unable to keep the crowd clear of the approach to the jetty'. [2] The *Suffolk* left Sydney in heavy rain and with an angry sea, and several men were seasick, but after practising boat stations, they settled down to contemplate an uncertain future.

The 2nd Btn disembarked in Egypt on 8 December with orders to go to Cairo to prepare for the campaign. The following April, after intense training, the Australian forces were ready to go into battle and on the 5th Walter boarded the *SS Durfflinger*, a captured German merchant ship, and set sail for the Gallipoli peninsula. Just before 6 am Walter climbed down from the ship into a small boat that was to land him on the enemy's shore. He may or may not have felt reassured by the colonel's parting message: 'You are soon to go into action. Your training has made you fit for it, and I have the greatest confidence in your courage and resolution. Just one word – keep a cool head, and listen to the fire orders of your officers. When you shoot, let every bullet find its mark; when you bayonet, see that you stick it in'. [3] Forty five minutes later the Australian troops landed on the beach and started to establish a bridgehead. It was not long before the 2nd Btn were receiving requests from all quarters to reinforce those already engaged in the fighting and sustaining heavy casualties. Losses within the 2nd Btn began to rise quickly and by the end of April 34 of their men had been killed, 251 wounded and 155 missing.

On 2 May Walter was in the trenches when the order came to prepare for an attack on the Turkish positions. The assault was a failure, during which Walter went missing, and after a court of enquiry it was established that he was killed in action. The news of his death and his belongings, which included a birthday book, two hairbrushes and a gospel, were delivered to his parents who had moved from Victoria Buildings to 4 Harvey's Terr. His body was never recovered and he is commemorated on the Lone Pine Memorial, Gallipoli.

---

[1] Prior to 1901 Australia consisted of a number of independent states.

[2] War diary of the 1st Australian Infantry Bgde, written by Col H.N. MacLaurin.

[3] Ibid.

Pte John Frederick Sargent – aged 19
1st Btn Dorsetshire Rgt – (3)7037
Cenotaph and Holy Trinity

(Source: Mr A. McIntyre.)

When John Sargent was born on 9 August 1896 his father was already 70 years of age and he was to know his son for just 4 years before he died, leaving his wife Mary, who was 30 years his junior, to look after their only son and two daughters. The family originally lived at 27 Glyde Path Rd but after her husband's death Mary moved just round the corner to 35 Colliton St, also the location of Dorchester Boy's School, which doubtless John attended. After leaving that school he did not get what one might call a regular job but instead spent his time up at Came Down Golf Club caddying for two brothers, Ernest and Reginald Whitcombe. The Whitcombes were a remarkable golfing family. Came Down appointed Ernest to be the club Professional and later his mother Bessie was appointed stewardess to the club and brought her other two sons, Charles and Reg, to live on the premises. The family stayed there for 17 years and Charles Whitcombe and his two brothers represented Great Britain in the Ryder Cup in 1935. Reg won the British Open, whilst brother Charles led the championship on numerous occasions but never won the claret cup.

John did not wait to be called up for the War but enlisted when he was 18 and went to join the 1st Btn Dorsets at Ypres in April 1915. In that year the battalion fought the Battles of Gravenstafel Ridge, St Julian and Bellewaerde Ridge, before making the journey south, by train to the Somme area, at the end of July. After a year of trench warfare the men were settling into the routine of 7 days in the front line, alternating with periods in the rear for rest and training. John was a keen letter writer and some of the correspondence between him and his mother and his sister Winnie survives. Their contents illustrate how letters provided the soldier with not only news from home but also a constant reminder of what they were fighting for, and when expected correspondence did not arrive great anxiety was expressed. Then, of course, there was the all-important parcel, a very tangible connection with the family. John, like many men, constantly enquires as to when the next one will be arriving. He writes very little about the battlefront, except to comment on the weather and his minor ailments, and his writing has a cheerful and optimistic tone.

On 23 April 1916, after a month out of the line, the battalion was moved to the Thiepval sector and on the night of 7/8 May there was an intense bombardment on the British trenches during which John was killed. Two weeks after his death his platoon commander sat down and penned the following letter to his mother: 'Dear Mrs Sargent, I am sorry not to have been able to write to you before but we have only just got out of trenches. May I offer you my sincerest sympathy for your great loss. I saw your son and his companions soon after the unfortunate occurrence. A shell had burst near the dugout. They were in there in peace. I don't think they suffered any pain. As his platoon leader I am deeply sorry to lose such a good fellow.' John is buried in Athuile Military Cemetery, Somme.

Stoker 1st Class Walter John Smith – aged 25
HMS Queen Mary, RN – K/6811
Cenotaph and St Peter's

Leading Stoker Frederick Wills – aged 26
HMS Queen Mary, RN – S/113649
Cenotaph

In the early dawn of 31 May 1916 two stokers were working very hard in the bowels of *HMS Queen Mary* as the battle cruiser headed towards the Skagerak, off the coast of Denmark. Walter Smith and Frederick Wills were about to take part in the Great War's one and only major sea conflict, the Battle of Jutland, and the 150 ships of the British Grand Fleet were about to engage the 99 ships of the German High Seas Fleet.

Admiral Scheer [1], leader of the High Seas Fleet, realised that he could not take on the British force in a standing battle because of its superior size but, instead, sought to even up the numbers by luring some of the British battle cruisers out of Rosyth, by sending a decoy fleet, led by Admiral Hipper [2], into the North Sea. Once the British ships arrived they would find the main part of the German navy waiting for them. Fortunately for the Royal Navy, they were able to decode the German wireless messages and as a consequence, by midnight on 30 May, Admirals Jellicoe [3] and Beatty [4] were at sea 5 hours before the Germans left the port at Wilhelmshaven. Parts of the respective fleets met off the northeast coast of Denmark, the main bodies of ships remaining out of sight.

On the afternoon of 31 May Beatty's and Hipper's ships fought a running battle in which the *Queen Mary* took part but Walter and Frederick would have known little of the battle that was going on above their heads. The *Queen Mary* was directing her fire on the battle cruiser *Seyditz* and scored two hits before the *Derfflinger* started firing at the British ship and it soon started to take effect. By 4.20 pm the *Queen Mary* had been struck twice, the first shot igniting one or both of the forward magazines which broke the ship in two. The second shell struck a gun turret and was followed by an explosion. The aft portion of the ship shook, rolled over and sank. Walter and Frederick were among the 6,097 British sailors killed on that day, 1,124 of whom were on the *Queen Mary*.

Walter, who was born on 15 July 1891, was the son of Henry and Rose Smith who in 1901 were living at 12 Railway Terr, just a few doors away from the Benjafields. [5] Later they moved to 22 Friary Lane. Walter joined the Navy 2 months before his 19th birthday, leaving his job working at Reduit, the house in Culliford Road owned by Dorchester solicitor Henry Huxtable, where he worked with his father as a gardener. According to the *Chronicle* he was a well-known boy around Dorchester and liked. [6] Walter joined the *Queen Mary* on 4 September 1913 and, except for a short period in 1914 when he worked on the repair ship *Cyclops*, stayed with her until she was destroyed.

Frederick was nearly 2 years older than Walter and enlisted the day before his 24th birthday. Before joining a ship he did his training at *Victory II*, the Royal Navy's training depot in South London, and it is quite possible that the two boys met there between February and September 1913. Frederick was the son of Mr and Mrs Charles Wills of 6 Durngate St and worked as a farm labourer in his pre-navy days. An entry in his service record suggests that he may have had a girlfriend or fiancée back home, as it states that he sported a tattoo on his forearm consisting of two hearts and the word 'MIZPAH'. [7] Walter and Frederick are both commemorated on the Portsmouth Naval Memorial.

[1] Admiral Reinhard Scheer.
[2] Admiral Franz von Hipper
[3] Admiral John Jellicoe
[4] Admiral Sir David Beatty
[5] See William Benjafield.
[6] *Chronicle* 6/7/1916.
[7] The word, taken from the book of Genesis, symbolises an emotional bond between two persons.

Ordinary Signalman Leonard Stephen Thompson – aged 18
HMS Southampton, RN – J/29255

L/Cpl Walter John Thompson – aged 26
1st Btn Dorsetshire Rgt – 16077

Both are commemorated on the Cenotaph and St George's

As the new decade opened in 1910, Sarah Ann Thompson was unaware that by its closing she would have lost her husband and two of her sons. Sarah married John Thompson in 1888 and their first child Walter came along a year later. At that time the family was living at Brick-Kiln Common, Broadmayne, where John worked as a carter on a farm. Then, sometime in the '90s, the family came to Dorchester and moved into 13 High St, Fordington, next to a coffee house run by the Bartlets. Tragedy first struck the family in 1912 when John died; then, when the War arrived, Ann was faced with the prospect of four of her sons going off to fight, perhaps never to return.

As a boy Sarah's fourth son Leonard regularly attended St George's Church Sunday School and was a member of the Church Lads' Brigade and the Band of Hope. He entered the Navy at the age of 17 and after training at *HMS Ganges* and *Victory I* joined *HMS Southampton* as a signaller. At the Battle of Jutland, the background of which is described in the stories of Walter Smith and Frederick Wills, [1] the *Southampton* was flagship of the 2nd Light Cruiser Squadron. At 10.25 pm on 31 May 1916 five ships were seen sailing on a parallel course to the squadron, each trying to identify the other without giving away which side they were on. The row of ships turned out to be German and the leading four opened fire on the *Southampton*. What happened next was described in a letter from Lt A.N. Peters to Leonard's mother: 'During most of the day we had been under fire, and he and all of them had worked splendidly. Then, at night we once more came into action with a superior force at almost point blank range, and in a few minutes he and the others were no more. They were all buried at sea … I, as his signals officer am deeply grieved at losing him myself; he was always so willing and hard working.' [2] Leonard was one of 35 killed and 41 wounded in the action and is commemorated on the Portsmouth Naval Memorial.

Four weeks after Leonard had perished the telegram boy once again visited the Thompson household, this time with news that Walter Thompson, Sarah's eldest boy, had died. However, the recipient on this occasion was not his mother but his wife Bessie, whom he had married barely a year before. Walter died of wounds on 2 July while fighting with the 1st Dorsets on the Somme. He is buried in Warloy-Baillon Communal Cemetery Extension, Somme.

---

[1] See above.
[2] *Chronicle* 15/6/1916.

L/Cpl Herbert Stewart Angell – aged 27
42nd Btn CEF – 418747
Cenotaph, St Peter's, Holy Trinity and Thomas Hardye School Roll of Honour

The 1901 census shows Arthur and Sarah Angell living at 8 High East St with their three children. They ran a boot-making business, their daughter Sarah was employed by the County Council as a pupil teacher and Arthur, the eldest son, was a plumber. Their youngest child, Herbert, aged 11, was attending the Grammar School, for which he had gained a scholarship the previous year. He regularly went to Sunday school at Holy Trinity and was a member of the choir. Like his older brother, Herbert also became a plumber and moved to Bristol to work for Collin and Son, Sanitary Engineers. Then in 1910 he made the decision to seek his fortune in another part of the British Empire and on 12 May boarded the steamship *Royal Edward* bound for the port of Quebec in Canada. From there he travelled on to Montreal, where he settled and became a mining engineer.

Herbert answered the call of his mother country by enlisting in the 42nd Btn Royal Highlanders of Canada on the 29 April 1915. The battalion sailed for England on the *SS Hesperian* in June and commenced a period of training and assimilation into the 7th Canadian Infantry Brigade, at St Martin's Plain Camp, Folkestone, until September, when the Highlanders headed for France. Herbert was killed in his first major action, the battle for Mount Sorrel. On 2 June 1916, the day of his death, the 42nd, together with the Princess Patricia's Canadian Light Infantry, were desperately defending the line fronting Hooge and

Sanctuary Wood near Ypres. The area offered an excellent observation point over the Ypres Salient and the Germans were determined to capture it. The day opened with a devastating artillery fire which destroyed many of the Canadian trenches. The 42nd were in reserve but were called up to join a force that would counterattack the enemy, but the operation was aborted and instead they were told to hold the line. The Canadian attack eventually took place at 7.10 am the next day but failed with heavy losses. Capt. Chaplain Walker wrote a letter to Herbert's mother in which he said, 'No historian can ever fully relate the glorious deeds of our men on that occasion. I passed through the thickest of it with them, and am a witness to their super-human valour.' [1] Herbert is commemorated on the Menin Gate Memorial.

[1] *Chronicle* 15/2/1917.

L/Sgt William Arthur Geard – aged 35
1st Btn Dorsetshire Rgt – 5356
Cenotaph

From a British perspective, if there is one day during the 4 years of the Great War that symbolises the destruction and carnage of that conflict it has to be 1 July 1916, when 57,470 British troops became casualties, of which 19,240 [1] were killed or died of their wounds. The Pals battalions, like those from Accrington, Grimsby, Leeds and Sheffield, suffered terribly, and although by no means on the same scale, Dorchester too made its contribution to the figures. Three of the men who appear on the town's memorials were killed on this date, two from the 1st Dorsets and one from the Somerset Light Infantry. In addition, Walter Thompson of the 1st Dorsets died of wounds. [2]

William Geard was born in Twerton near Bath in Somerset, the son of Amos, a market gardener, and Jane. His connection with Dorchester came when he married Annie Hustings in the local Registrar's office on 25 August 1914. At the time, William was encamped in the Barracks and Annie was living at 11 Dagmar Terr. A baby was born a few months later which would grow up not knowing its father.

Following William's wedding he was sent to France, where he joined the 1st Dorsets and fought with them for almost 2 years. Now, it was 1 am on 1 July 1916 and L/Sgt Geard and his men were marching into dugouts at Blackhorse Ridge, situated behind the British lines, to the southwest of Thiepval. Each was carrying emergency rations, two bombs, two extra bandoliers of ammunition and two sandbags. Before the impending battle, the CO addressed the troops, asking them particularly to avenge the deaths of two officers whom he believed had been murdered by the Hun. [3] It appears that the men were in good spirits, a Lt Douie suggesting that, 'The proceedings were marked by no high seriousness, and occasionally degenerated into hilarity …'. [4] After all, British guns had fired 1,500,000 shells onto the enemy's trenches and barbed wire, so surely there could be little resistance.

Before the Dorsets could commence their assault they had to get to the British front line by passing through Authuille Wood and then along Dumbarton Track. The Dorsets were not in the first wave of attack and Sgt Geard and his men proceeded into the wood where they were to await orders to advance. Another sergeant who was there on that day was Ernest Shepherd, who recorded what happened next: 'We had a terrible dose of machine gun fire sweeping us through the wood, could not understand why. If front and second lines had been carried, enemy machine guns would be out of action. We found the reason quick enough.' [5] The reason was simple. The distance from the edge of the wood to the British line was only about 100 yd but the exit track was targeted by German machine guns. There was no alternative way forward than to make a dash for it. The first sections made their move and were scythed down, followed by other groups of men who did little better. Over half of the 1st Btn's casualties for the day occurred crossing this short stretch of open country. Of those who got to the British front line, six officers and about 60 men ventured out into no man's land, where all the officers were hit and only about 25 men reached the objective. The remainder of the Dorsets were still in their own trench, which now was full of dead and wounded. Later that night they were joined by the remainder of the small party that had made the attack. Counted among the dead on that day was William, whose body was recovered and buried in Blighty Valley Cemetery, Somme.

[1] Figures taken from *The Somme*, Peter Hart (W & N Military, 2005).
[2] See Walter Thompson.
[3] Capt. Algeo and Lt Mansel-Pleydell went into no man's land of their own volition to locate some machine guns; neither returned.
[4] Regimental history.
[5] Rossor, 1987.

Pte William Percy Membury – aged 32
1st Btn Dorsetshire Rgt – 3/7501
Cenotaph, Holy Trinity and St George's

The Membury family was well known in Dorchester and had a long association with the Army. Robert Membury, with his wife Lilian and their two sons Reginald and William, lived at 43 Colliton St, where he ran the Model Brass Foundry which cast the bronze plaques that are on the Cenotaph. Robert and his two sons were keen Volunteers and Territorials with the Dorsets. William, the eldest son, served for 17 years, while his father received the long service medal, and they both became prominent musicians in the Volunteer Band. In the community, father and son were both members of the Dorchester Fire Brigade. When William left school he was apprenticed as a decorator to Mr G. Barber and after serving his 5 years went to work for William Stovey, house decorators in Durngate Street. When he was 21 William married Lilian Wilson in Holy Trinity Church and the couple first went to live at 18 Victoria Buildings, where their two girls were born, and then moved to 23 Duke's Ave.

Given their interest in the military it was no surprise that William and Reg made a beeline for the Depot Barracks on 21 August 1914 to enlist in the Dorsets. After the initial questions to determine their qualifications for enlistment it was time for the medical. William passed with flying colours but Reg was found to have a heart murmur and was turned down. So, it was Reg who the next day waved his brother off as he departed for the training camp at Wyke Regis before leaving for France. William joined the 1st Btn

William (front left) with brother Reginald (front right) and other Dorset Territorials.
(Source: Mr G. Membury.)

at Ypres in February 1915. He fought with them without serious incident, except for a spell out of the line due to rheumatism, until 1 July 1916 when he was killed in the same action as William Geard. The details of his death were given in a letter from a Sgt Maj. Miller to his parents: 'We are all exceedingly sorry at the death of your son, who was killed in the advance by a bullet from the enemy. He had previously been selected to accompany an officer who, with the assistance of a few men, including your son, had to ensure that communication was maintained with the troops on our flanks, so you will realise that he had to be exposed to the enemy while we were advancing. Although your son had a dangerous task to perform he never for a moment shirked from his duty, and carried on with his orders until he had the misfortune to be shot.' [1] William was interred in Lonsdale Cemetery, Somme. William and Reg were obviously very close, which is indicated by an embroidered postcard William sent his brother in 1915, with the words, 'From a loving brother Will – to a loving brother', and as if to echo the feelings Reg had a black-edged memorial card printed with similar sentiments.

[1] *Chronicle* 24/8/1916.

In Loving Memory

OF

WILLIAM PERCIVAL MEMBURY,

The beloved Brother of

REGINALD CHARLES MEMBURY,

Who died for King and Country

July 1, 1916, Aged 32.

IN THE BATTLE OF SOMME.

Card printed for William's memorial service.
(Source: Mr G. Membury.)

Pte Reginald Luke Prince DCM – aged 29
1st Btn Somerset Light Infantry – 128564
Cenotaph

The letter that Mary Prince received from the King did not contain the usual words of condolence but congratulated her on having six sons serving in the Army. Mixed with her pride at receiving the letter must have been some regret that her husband, who had died in 1897, was not alive to share it. By the close of the War she may have even envied her husband, who did not live to know that three of his sons died in battle and two were discharged from the Army as unfit for duty. Only one son appears on a Dorchester memorial, although all of them were born in the town. In 1891 the family, headed by their father Arthur, a carpenter, were living at 3 Maie Terr.

The son who is commemorated on the Cenotaph is Reginald, who served with distinction in the 1st Btn Somerset Light Infantry until he was killed in action on 1 July 1916. He was a regular soldier who sailed to France with his battalion on 22 August 1914. On 8 March 1915 he was in an advanced trench, opposite Ploegsteert Wood, operating a telephone, when he was severely wounded in the mouth by a piece of shrapnel. Despite this, he continued to maintain communications and for this act of gallantry he was awarded the DCM. In addition, a month later, news came through that he was to receive the Russian gallantry award of the St George Medal (3rd Class). This silver medal was a degree of the Order of St George awarded by the Tsar to allied servicemen for acts of merit.

On 1 July 1916 the 1st Somersets suffered a very similar plight to that of the 1st Dorsets. Their objective was to capture the line around the Quadrilateral Redoubt which consisted of an old system of trenches. Their fate was witnessed by Sgt A.H. Cook, who was among the first to go over the top. He described how all at once the machine guns opened up with a murderous fire, men falling like nine pins, and when the few men who survived reached the enemy trench they found that, although it had been badly damaged by the artillery, the German troops had been safe in their dugouts. 'Jerry was popping up all over the place, behind and on our flanks and throwing grenades at us from all angles … dead and dying were lying everywhere ….' [1] It is not known whether Pte Prince reached the German line but he did perish in the attack and became one of the 1st Btn's 463 casualties for that day. He is buried in Serre Road Cemetery No.2, Somme.

The other sons of Mrs Prince who gave their lives were Bertie and Joseph. Sgt Bertie Prince had been with the Colours for 13 years and was serving with the Royal Munster Fusiliers when he was killed on 20 November 1917, aged 27. His brother Joseph was 39 when he died on 30 September 1918 fighting with the 1st Btn Dorsets during the Battle of the St Quentin Canal. One cannot begin to imagine what effect the loss of three sons had on Mary Prince. After the War she moved to Weymouth to be near what was left of her family.

---

[1] Great War Forum: http://1914-1918.invisionzone.com/forums/index.
php?showtopic=56080.

Pte Humphrey Bull – aged 51
Depot, Dorsetshire Rgt –11663
Cenotaph and St George's

Humphrey Bull and his brother George worked for the local council and were often seen around the town. Having retired from the Army George worked as a labourer on the roads, but like William Bussell and James Bishop he was keen to help the war effort, despite his advanced years. Consequently, he rejoined the Dorsets and was employed as an orderly under Sgt Winzar in the recruiting office at the Depot.

Humphrey was married to Elizabeth Moors and the childless couple lived at 6 Mill St. He died on 4 July 1916 and is buried in Fordington Cemetery. His was another impressive military funeral in the town, the wheeled bier passing through the streets of Fordington proceeded by a firing party of the Gloucestershire Rgt, with arms reversed and a military band playing the 'Dead March'. At the front of the procession was Mr Evan Dobell, the undertaker, followed by the mourners on foot. At the graveside the firing party did their duty and then fixed bayonets and presented arms whilst the Last Post was played. Following the service the military contingent marched briskly away from the solemn scene, the band playing a stirring tune.

Maj. Denzil Hughes-Onslow – aged 53
6th Btn Dorsetshire Rgt
Cenotaph and Holy Trinity

Colliton Park is now the home of Dorset County Council but previously it formed the garden and grounds of Colliton House, a fine building of the 16th century. Living there in 1911 were Denzil Hughes-Onslow, his wife Marion, their son Nigel and eight servants. The Hughes-Onslows originated from Scotland and since their arrival in Dorchester in the 1880s had stamped their mark on the town. The *Chronicle* informed its readers that, 'they were deservedly popular in society circles and among all classes of society, and their generosity and charity won them grateful esteem'. [1] Denzil was the proverbial all-round sportsman. A good horseman, he frequently rode to hounds and he and his wife were for many years associated with the County Council

(Source: www.ww1photos.com.)

Hunt Ball. Locally, he was a keen supporter of Dorchester's cricket, football and athletic clubs, especially the Dorchester Cricket Club, of which he was the captain and mainstay, not just with the bat but also with his purse. Therefore, it was no surprise to the people of the town that when War was declared he moved his family out of their home and handed it over to the Red Cross to use as a hospital.

Denzil was born in Balkissock, Ayr, on 20 December 1862 and between the ages of 15 and 18 went to Charterhouse School, where the boy gave no indication of the man to come. He was an average pupil, did not excel in games, nor was he a leading member of any school society. On leaving Charterhouse he entered Sandhurst Military Academy and was commissioned into the Cheshire Regt in August 1884. He then transferred to the Dorsets in 1887 and in the following year married Marion Oliver from Laggan, Ayrshire. Doubtless it was his duties with the Dorsets that brought them to live in Dorchester. On 6 April 1892 Denzil's allotted time in the Army was up and he took his pension, but far from retiring he again joined the regiment on the same day and remained with it until finally parting in 1904, as a major.

A close friend wrote, 'When war broke out Maj. Hughes-Onslow was offered the command of the Prison Guard [2] in the town. This post would have enabled him to continue to live in ease and comfort in his own home. But he refused to accept it, telling me more than once that it was not the best he could do.' [3] Instead, Denzil joined the 6th Btn Dorsets, one of the service battalions, and spent a year at Wareham Camp. It was whilst he was there that he read in the *Chronicle* that a German prisoner who was suffering from spotted fever, a very contagious disease, was being lodged at the Masonic Hall in Prince's Street. This incensed him so much that he wrote an emphatic letter on the matter to the town council, saying that he had an interest in the case because his house had been lent for use as a hospital on the same terms as the Masonic Hall and he was surprised that the prisoner had been brought there, rendering it useless for the treatment of allied soldiers who were sick and wounded. Indeed, he considered it a gross breach of faith and felt that he was reflecting the concerns of the people of Dorchester. Mr C.A. Smith, who was present at the meeting at which the letter was read out, said that the officer was only expressing what they all felt. Alderman Fudge then stood up and commented that the Masonic Hall was never intended for German prisoners, no matter what the disease, and pointed out that nobody in the town had done more for the sick and wounded than Hughes-Onslow. This, indeed, appears to have been the case. A friend of his, writing to the *Chronicle* after his death, pointed out that Denzil had defrayed many of the running costs incurred at the Colliton House hospital from his own money: 'It was enough to mention a deserving case of sickness. It was always, "We will defray the cost".' [4]

Denzil had more immediate matters on his mind when he went to France with the 6th Btn commanding C Coy in July 1915. However, it was not long before he felt it necessary to make his feelings known once again. The battalion was at the Ypres Salient and after several days of heavy rain found themselves having to sleep in a well-manured field, without tents. The next morning, in reply to Denzil's question about why his men had to endure such terrible conditions, the Brigadier pleaded that, 'They [the powers that be] thought we should prefer it'. Denzil's sardonic reply of, 'Oh, did you, perhaps you'll join us next time' settled the matter and a few tents were produced. [5]

During his service in France Denzil was wounded several times. On 16 June 1916 he received a shrapnel wound to his face, was sent home and offered 6 months' leave, which he refused and resumed his duties as soon as he was able. For his part during the action in which he was wounded he was mentioned in Despatches. He was again wounded slightly on 7 July and again on the 10th, the day that he was killed. Lt-Col Rowley, the battalion commander, described his second in command's death in a letter to his wife, Mrs Rowley: 'Onslow was killed yesterday morning. He was writing a Despatch to me (which he never finished), and was shot dead by a stray bullet through the back of the head. He slept in the same place the day before and it seemed quite safe. Earlier in the day he had been wounded in the hand; but only a scratch. He died a soldier's death and without pain or knowledge of how he was killed. He was so universally liked throughout the regiment, so honest and true, and I have indeed lost a real friend, and his death has cast a gloom over the whole battalion.' [6]

Further down the chain of command there was further praise for their CO. An RQMS gave his own views of Denzil in a letter to his father: 'We lost a dear old Major – Major Hughes-Onslow – one of the old stock and brave as a lion. After our bombing officer was killed, he took command of the bombers in a splendid bit of work until he himself was hit. [7] He had no cause to do it, except it was the British in him that made him do it. We brought his body down and gave him the last rites of a brave officer. The whole regiment turned out to pay their last tribute to one of England's bravest.' [8] Signalling Sgt John Rogers, in a letter to his aunt living at 32 Trinity St, wrote, 'Poor Major Hughes-Onslow was a hero. A braver man has not fought in France, and he was loved by all the regiment. He was a father to the men, always visiting them in the trenches, no matter what the conditions were.' [9] Denzil was buried in Meaulte Military Cemetery, south of Albert in France, and is commemorated on the Ballantrae Memorial, with those of the Laggan Estate and Barr parish church, Ayrshire.

[1] *Chronicle* 27/7/1916.
[2] This refers to the guard at the German POW camp.
[3] *Chronicle* 20/7/1916.
[4] Ibid.
[5] Regimental history.
[6] *Chronicle* 20/7/1916.
[7] Presumably this refers to an occasion previous to the day Denzil was killed.
[8] *Chronicle* 27/7/1916.
[9] *Chronicle* 20/7/1916.

Pte Reginald Sturmey Chilcott – aged 20
1/4th Btn Dorsetshire Rgt – 3442
Thomas Hardye School Roll of Honour

The Chilcott family farmed at West Knighton and Little Mayne Farms, just outside Dorchester, and like many successful farmers Walter Chilcott sent his son Reginald to the local grammar school for his education. Reginald was born in 1896 and when the time came to go to War enlisted in his county regiment at the Depot Barracks. He was put into the 1/4th Btn and was serving with them in Mesopotamia when he died, on 13 July, of either one of the many diseases prevalent in that theatre of war or of an accident. He is buried at the Basra War Cemetery and commemorated on the memorial inside St Peter's Church, West Knighton.

2 Lt Claude O'Connell McSwiny – aged 19
9th Btn Shropshire Light Infantry
Thomas Hardye School Roll of Honour

Claude McSwiny came from an eminent military family. His father Myles served as a Fleet Surgeon [1] in the Royal Navy and his grandfather on his mother's side was Lt-Gen. Sir William Bellairs C.B., KCMG, who saw active service in the Crimea, the Zulu Campaigns and South Africa. His great Grandfather Lt-Gen. William Bellairs fought with the 15th Regiment of Hussars at the Battle of Waterloo and then went on to become one of Queen Victoria's bodyguards. Claude was born in Malta in February 1897 and after his father's retirement he and his family went to live at 103 Dorchester Rd, Melcombe Regis. Given his military background it was natural that when it

(Source: www.ww1photos.com.)

came to schooling his parents should choose to send their son to Dorchester Grammar School, which was well known for its active Officer Training Corps. As well as joining the Corps Claude was in the school choir alongside two other lads who died in the War, Charles Budden and Alfred Meadway, [2] and was captain of the school football team.

Claude obtained a commission with the 9th Btn Shropshire Light Infantry and at the age of 19 was leading men, some of whom were probably twice his age. He went to France in May 1915, where he was attached to the 7th Btn, fighting at St Eloi and in the Ypres Salient. He was killed on the first day of the Battle of Bazentin Ridge at the Somme on 14 July 1916. It had been decided that the attack on the Ridge should take place at dawn, so throughout the night the young lieutenant and his men had been patiently waiting in no man's land for the off. At 3.30 am the men rushed forward expecting to find the German wire cut by the earlier artillery bombardment, but when the first wave arrived at the wire it was intact and not one soldier could get through. By now the Germans were aware of the attack and, with successive lines of British soldiers arriving at the uncut wire causing congestion, found an easy target. The remaining Shropshires withdrew to their own trenches, regrouped and then made a fresh attack which was more successful. This time the men managed to cut the wire, then entered and held the German line against five counterattacks until they were relieved. At the inevitable body count it was found that out of the 614 of the battalion that started the attack 473 were reported dead, wounded or missing.

Claude's mother received a telegram to say that her son was one of the missing, closely followed by another confirming his death. According to one source his body was buried where it fell, on the ridge above Caterpillar Valley. [3] He is also commemorated on the Thiepval Memorial. After Claude's death his mother also received two letters from people who knew her son. The first was from the Adjutant of the 3rd Btn who said, 'we who knew his true value here, as we all did, can truly sympathise with you in your loss', and a brother officer wrote, 'What a man he was, and only nineteen; he was always the same cheerful boy, whether in the trenches or out. He was a comfort to his men under shell fire; he was always steady and kept his nerve when all were falling round him. He was a man, yet only a boy in years.' [4]

[1] Rank equivalent to a Naval Commander.
[2] See Charles Budden and Alfred Meadway.
[3] De Ruvigny, 1922.
[4] Ibid.

Pte Frederick Ernest Read – aged 31
1/4th Btn Dorsetshire Rgt – 2623
Cenotaph and St George's

Frederick was the youngest son of Elizabeth and George Read of Belle Vue Terrace, Maumbury Way. George was employed as a gardener in the Borough Gardens whilst his two sons set up an enterprise selling oil, wood and confectionery from their home. The *Chronicle* [1] told its readers that Frederick volunteered for service in the early years of the War and after training in England joined the 1/4th Btn Dorsets in Mesopotamia in June 1916. Little remains of Frederick's service record apart from the few badly burnt pages that tell how he died. He was admitted to No.33 General Hospital at Makina Masus, where he died on 14 July 1916 from the effects of heat. He was buried in Basra War Cemetery. The high temperatures in this theatre of war were a real problem for the British army. For instance, the regimental history records that out of a draft of 60 sent up the river in June 1916, of which Frederick may have been one, only 11 reached the Btn, the remainder having to be admitted to hospital with the effects of the sun. In daytime shade temperatures of 49 degrees it was impossible to work and at night it was impossible to sleep before midnight. Sleeping outside one's tent had its own dangers, as Reginald Dabinett found out. [2]

[1] *Chronicle* 3/8/1916.
[2] See Reginald Dabinett.

Pte William Alfred Gill – aged 22
2nd Btn Royal Munster Fusiliers – 3/5839
Cenotaph

Recruitment officers like Sgt Winzar were already familiar faces on the streets of Dorchester before War began and, when the posters went up in 1914 to say that the country was looking for patriotic men, lots of local lads went to hear them speak at the Corn Exchange. Among the audience at one of the meetings was a young shop assistant named William Gill, who went on to enlist in the 5th Btn Royal Irish Lancers. He did not remain with them but was later attached to the Royal Munster Fusiliers, and went as one of the reinforcements to the1st Btn in Gallipoli in May 1915. Whilst there he received several wounds and was sent home to recuperate, and after recovering was then sent to France where he joined the 2nd Btn.

In July 1916 the 2nd Btn moved from the Loos area to the Somme for the great offensive. The Munsters did not take part in the debacle of the first day but reached Albert on the 10th and then took up positions at Contalmaison, 4 km northeast of Albert. They attacked on the night of the 16th and took the first and second line of German trenches, then rapidly moved on to the third. It had been fighting of the hardest hand-to-hand kind, the battalion history recording that, '… the bayonet on this occasion, playing a more important part than the bullet'. [1] Two days later, on the 18th, the Germans launched a counterattack which was beaten off but not without casualties. It was during this fighting that William was killed. He is buried in Gordon Dump Cemetery, Ovillers-Boiselle, Somme.

Three days before William's death a postcard from him, addressed to his parents Alfred and Mary, fell through their letterbox at 1 Maude Rd. In it, their son recounted an incident that had recently happened to him. With three other comrades and an officer, he was sent off to cut some wire entanglements and his comrades were quickly shot. The officer after fell wounded and William went to him and conveyed him to a place of safety. Perhaps his gallant action was of some solace to his parents in their grief.

---

[1] Westlake, 1994.

Pte Ernest James Standfield – aged 21
2nd Btn Dorsetshire Rgt – 16310
Cenotaph and St Peter's

Ernest was the eldest son of James and Emily Standfield who lived at 10 Durngate St. When he left school he joined his father working as an upholsterer's porter before enlisting in the 2nd Btn Dorsets. He died on 16 July 1916 in one of the military hospitals in Amara, Mesopotamia, from illness or an accident and was buried in Amara War Cemetery. Nearly 2 years later, Ernest's parents received news that must have filled them with dread – their other son Joseph had been wounded in the shoulder, but fortunately it was not fatal and he survived the War.

In 1933 it was found that salts in the soil in Amara Cemetery were eroding Ernest's gravestone, so his was one of over 4,000 that were dug up and replaced with a screen wall which has his name inscribed upon it.

Sapper Charles William Jeffery – aged 21
25th Air Line Section, Army Signal Corps – 77109
Thomas Hardye School Roll of Honour

Charles was the only son of William and Emma Jeffery of Weymouth. His father was a printer, who may have been associated with Jeffery Bros, printers at 4 St Mary St. In addition, he was sub-postmaster at Chapelhay Post Office, although, presumably because printing was a full-time job for him his wife Emma appears to have looked after the post office side of things, and when William died in 1923 she took over the role of sub-postmistress.

There were fine schools in Weymouth but such was the reputation of Dorchester Grammar School that William and Emma decided that their son should go there instead. During the War Charles served as a Sapper with the Army Signal Corps in Mesopotamia, where his job with the 25th Air Line Section was to erect and maintain overhead communication lines. He died of accident or illness on 18 July and is buried in Basra War Cemetery. Although Charles is not listed on the Thomas Hardye School Roll of Honour he should be. On speech day in July 1917 the headmaster included his name in the list he read out of old boys who comprised the roll. [1]

---

[1] Chronicle 2/8/1917.

Pte Frederick Tibbs – aged 42
Royal Defence Corps – 24587
Fordington Cemetery

Frederick Tibbs was a family man from Napton, near Rugby in Warwickshire, where he was employed at the local cement works. On 9 September he went to the recruiting office to enlist, where he was medically examined and found to be physically fit to serve, despite being laid up for 15 weeks the previous winter. He became a driver in the ASC but it was not long before his poor health put him into hospital, where he was diagnosed with nephritis and rheumatism. An Army Medical Board at Aldershot was told that Frederick suffered from continual pain in his back and legs and that his heart was dilated and enlarged. As a consequence he was discharged.

Having been invalided out of the Army Frederick joined the Royal Defence Corps and was posted to Dorchester. The Corps, which was made up of men who for one reason or another were not able to fight, had the job of protecting vulnerable places such as ports, water towers and gas works, and in Dorchester they also provided guards for the German POW camp. On Friday 21 July 1916, at Poundbury Camp, Frederick complained of feeling ill and appeared to be in great pain. He was seen by the MO at the military hospital in the Depot Barracks and died. The police were called as a matter of course and PC Payne, after

A military funeral in Dorchester, turning from Cornwall Road into Great Western Road. (Source: The Keep Military Museum.)

gathering all the facts, laid them before the Coroner who ordered a post-mortem, which found that he had died of disease of the heart and other organs.

During the course of the War Dorchester saw many impressive military funerals, including Frederick's. As well as the usual firing party, military band, funeral bier and carriages of mourners the procession was followed by 80 soldiers of his company. The whole procession moved slowly and solemnly down the High Street to the tune of the Dead March, on its way to Fordington Cemetery where he was buried.

Pte Horace Edward Young – aged 29
11th Btn Royal Fusiliers – G/17382
Fordington Cemetery

Horace Young was brought to Dorchester for treatment after being seriously wounded while serving in France, and it was necessary to amputate his leg. The *Chronicle* assured its readers that 'Everything that was possible in the way of skilled attention and careful nursing was done for him, but this proved unavailing'. [1] Horace died in the County Hospital on 22 August and was buried in Fordington Cemetery. He was a native of Paddington in London and left behind a wife Annie and a child to mourn his loss. Annie was present at the funeral, her wreath consisting of a harp with a broken string.

[1] *Chronicle* 32/8/1916.

L/Cpl Harry Stallard – aged 34
1/4th Btn Royal Berkshire Rgt
Cenotaph

Harry Stallard was born in Coleshill, Berkshire, and in 1903 he married Elizabeth Sarah Puzey. He was serving with the 1/4th Btn Berkshires on the Somme when he died of wounds on 25 August 1916. He is buried in Etaples Military Cemetery, Pas-de-Calais. It has not been possible to establish why he appears on the Dorchester Cenotaph, neither the 1911 census nor the 1918 register of electors showing anyone having an obvious connection with him living in the town. Neither was there anyone representing him at the opening ceremony of the memorial. The CWGC shows that his wife was living in Birmingham after his death.

Pte Percy Haskett Easley – aged 24
6th Btn Dorsetshire Rgt – 10142
Cenotaph and Holy Trinity

In an age where the predominant form of transport was still the horse the occupation of groom was still popular with young men, who if they were successful might go on to become coachmen. Percy Easley and his two brothers were all grooms, two working in a livery stable and one with a private family. In 1911 the boys were living with their father William, a house painter, and their two sisters but they were only five of the nine children born to their mother Elizabeth who had died in 1908, the others having grown up and probably left home.

Percy enlisted in the 5th Dorsets on 27 August 1914, aged 21 years, stating that he had spent a short time in the Household Cavalry. Initially, he must have impressed his seniors because by November he had been promoted to the rank of corporal, when the newly formed battalion was training at Grantham, Lincolnshire. The stripes remained on his arm for just 6 months when, in April 1915, he was court marshalled for 'Conduct to the prejudice of good order and military discipline'. [1] The deed that brought the charge was a fight with a private and the punishment was reduction to the ranks. Two months later he was in trouble again when he was absent at reveille on 13 June and did not reappear until the next day. For this he was given 10 days' Field Punishment No. 2, which was unusual given that he was still in England. [2]

In July Percy had something else to concentrate his mind, when he went off to fight in the ill-fated Gallipoli campaign, where he was shot in the ear and had to be evacuated to hospital at Mudros for 2 months. After returning to duty it was not long before he was back in hospital, in November 1915, this time with a bout of dysentery. In January 1916 the battalion moved to Egypt, but instead of going with them Percy returned home and went into a VAD hospital in Rugby, where the MO diagnosed that he was suffering from diabetes and that he was not well enough to undertake even light duties. But, the Army was hungry for men and eventually Percy was considered fit enough to return to the Front where, after being posted to the 6th Btn Dorsets, he was attached to the 9th Btn Devonshire Rgt.

The 9th Devons had been involved in the great struggle on the Somme since the beginning and sustained nearly 500 casualties in the first 3 days of battle. On 3 September 1916 they were at Mametz and the following day unexpectedly ordered to Montauban, Somme, then forward into the line from where they were to attack the village of Ginchy. This they did but had to retire after German counterattacks. During the fighting Percy went missing and was eventually listed among those who died on 4 September, although his body was never found. He is commemorated on the Thiepval Memorial. Percy's personal effects, which consisted of some letters and photographs, were returned to his father at 12 West Walks.

[1] Army form B.121, SR.

[2] Field Punishments were normally awarded when the men were in the field of battle and there was no time to hold a court marshall. For an explanation of Field Punishments see Douglas Crooke.

Sgt Reginald Scriven – aged 30
1/4th Btn Dorsetshire Rgt – 358
Cenotaph and Holy Trinity

Reginald Scriven was a well-known face around Dorchester, especially with the congregation of Holy Trinity Church, where, as a boy, he was a member of the choir and, on the death of his grandfather, succeeded him as verger. He was also secretary of the Holy Trinity branch of the Church of England Missionary Society and when he went to war he became secretary of a similar branch formed within the Dorset and Wiltshire Regiments abroad.

In civil life Reginald worked as a clerk with Henry Duke and Son, auctioneers and land agents, who then had their premises at 40 South St. In military life he was a long-term member of the Dorset Territorials and proceeded with them to India in October 1914, where it was understood that they would complete their training as a garrison force before being sent to France. As often happened in the Army expectations were turned on their head when the men of the 1/4th were sent not to France but to Mesopotamia, to protect British oil interests.

When Reginald's mother Eliza opened an envelope from the Army she would have been quite justified in asking, Why me? Within the previous 12 months her husband Walter and one of her daughters had died and now she had news that Reginald was lying dangerously ill in a hospital bed.. Subsequent letters from him to friends and relatives were reassuring, '... full of cheer, and contained the hope that he would soon be on duty again'. [1] Alas, it was not to be; he succumbed to his illness on 7 September and was buried in Basra War Cemetery.

[1] *Chronicle* 21/9/1916.

L/Cpl Wilfred Albert Bascombe – aged 19
5th Btn Dorsetshire Rgt – 17542
Cenotaph

Wilfred, who was known by his second name Albert, was born in Poole in 1897, the second eldest son of Edwin, a journeyman carpenter, and Bessie. During the War he served with the 5th Btn Dorsets and his name appeared among the list of casualties published by the *Chronicle* on 5 October 1916.

Following the horrors endured in Gallipoli the men of the 5th Btn joined the Western Front in July 1916, coincidentally making the trip from Egypt in the troopship *Transylvania*, upon which Charles Pope was later to drown. [1] On 16 September 1916 the Dorsets, together with the Lancashire Fusiliers, took over the line around Mouquet Farm (called Mucky Farm by the British and Moo Cow Farm by the Australians) near the village of Pozières, Somme, which consisted of three sets of ruins and at the time the Canadians reported that it had been captured. It turned out that the portion behind the German line was still definitely in enemy hands and the troops there were making it very hot for the Dorsets who were sheltering in very shallow trenches. There ensued a bombing battle which the 5th Btn eventually won but not before sustaining casualties. Their 3 days in the front line cost them 13 killed and missing, and four officers and 37 OR wounded. Among the dead was Albert who died on the 18th. He is commemorated on the Thiepval Memorial.

[1] See Charles Pope.

Pte David Payne – aged 29
2nd Btn Dorsetshire Rgt – 8363
Cenotaph

29 April 1916 was one of the most humiliating days in the history of the Dorset Regiment and the British Army. On that day Sir Charles Townsend surrendered to the Turkish forces at Kut-al-Amara after the town had been besieged for 5 months. Inside Kut was what was left of the 6th Poona Division, which included the 2nd Dorset Btn. When the troops found themselves surrounded there was no undue alarm because they felt that it was just a matter of time before they would be relieved, but despite several attempts to chase off the Turks, each one failed. Meanwhile conditions inside Kut were becoming desperate. For the first month of the siege the Turks attempted to storm the British defences but after being repulsed decided to use a new weapon – starvation. The battalion history describes what it was like inside the defences: 'Thus from the beginning of 1916 onwards the story of the 2nd Dorsets in Kut was one of gradual starvation … many men when laden with rifle and equipment could barely move from the reserve trenches to the front line.' As the siege lengthened rations were reduced, the men were eventually compelled to eating weeds and grass, and medical supplies were inadequate to treat those who were poisoned and those suffering from disease and illness. On the day of surrender the casualty roll for the 2nd Dorsets was 35 men killed and 47 died of disease, leaving approximately 400 prisoners of the Turks.

When the widow Edith Payne received news at her home at 21 Friary Lane in August 1916 that her son David was among the men taken prisoner at Kut she may have felt some sense of relief that he was at least alive and being looked after, albeit by the enemy. But what she did not know was that he was among 11,800 soldiers who had left Kut-al-Amara with their captors on 6 May on a terrible march of over 700 miles to Anatolia, during which they were ill-treated and abused, resulting in 1,000 of them dying on the journey. A Lt Harvey painted a graphic picture in his diary of the conditions the men had to endure: '6 May – Before we had been very long on the march we found our loads of kit and food a great burden, many men fell out through fatigue and were beaten along by the escort. Mahomed Russi rode up and down the column slashing with his whip at men every few yards … 7 May – Rations were issued in the evening, when we received four of the usual black biscuits per man. By this time we had found that the best way to eat them was to pound them as small as possible with the heel of the boot, soak them for a couple of hours, and then boil for a time … 11 May – This was a very hot and tiring march and numerous cases of flogging occurred through men being exhausted and falling out; no effort was made to provide any conveyance for those who were sick, several of whom fell out and were never seen again.' [1] Of the 350 [2] Dorsets that left Kut, David Payne was one of only 140 who answered at the roll call at Bagtsche Station before he was taken to the POW camp at Kasamuni. Already weakened by sand-fly fever, jaundice and malaria David died on 20 September 1916. The vast majority of men taken at Kut perished long before the Armistice and only 70 of the Dorsets survived to be repatriated. David is commemorated on the Basra Memorial.

---

[1] Diary of Lt-QM F.A. Harvey, 2nd Btn Dorsetshire Rgt.
[2] Four hundred men actually survived the siege but some were exchanged for Turkish prisoners and did not undertake the march.

L/Sgt George Thomas Ford – aged 24
5th Btn Dorsetshire Rgt – 8777
St George's

Following the fighting at Mouquet Farm, in which Wilfred Bascombe was killed, the 5th Dorsets were taken out of the line from 19–26th September to rest, first at Albert and then at Englebelmer, before preparing for the next attack. This was planned to take place on 26 September, when a major assault was to be made to push the Germans off the high ground of Thiepval Ridge, a formidable task which by the end of the day would produce another three names for Dorchester's memorials.

George Ford was living in East Ham with his parents and eight siblings when he decided to give up his job as a pawn broker's clerk and join the Army. He enlisted in the Dorsets in December 1909, aged 17, and was posted to the 1st Btn where he spent his time on home service before the War, including a spell in Belfast. It was while he was at Farnham in Hampshire that he was confined to camp for smoking on a march. When the battalion returned to Dorchester he was admitted to the military hospital in March 1913 with a serious rupture to his thigh sustained in a football match, which for a while threatened his military career. It may have been then that he met Kathleen White from Mill Street, resulting in their marriage on 3 April 1914. Five months later he went off to France and on 27 January 1915 their daughter Kathleen was born. It is not clear whether he saw his child but he may have done so when he was sent back to England in March 1915, after being shot in the right leg. It was 8 months before he was posted abroad again, this time as one of the re-enforcements to the 5th Btn in the Dardanelles, when the worst of the fighting for the Dorsets was over.

Now, on 26 September 1916, the newly promoted L/Sgt Ford was waiting in a trench for the order to take his men into the attack. If things went well they would force the Germans off Thiepval Ridge and then go on to capture the Zollern and Stuff Redoubts. At 12.35 pm the whistles blew and the men advanced through the German artillery barrage without many casualties. The men were about half way across no man's land when they were caught by a second barrage which had a disastrous effect. All four company commanders were hit, dozens of men went down and the scene was one of utter confusion. Even so, the remainder continued towards their targets, eventually reaching the Zollern Redoubt, where they dug in the next day. The 5th had suffered heavily in the battle; of roughly 600 in action nearly two-thirds were casualties, including 122 men killed or missing. Among the missing was George.

Kathleen did not get official notice that her husband had been killed in action until January 1918. Two years after that she was informed that George's body had been exhumed from the battlefield and was to be buried at Regina Trench Cemetery, Courcelette, Somme, and she wrote to the Army requesting a photo of his grave, a service that the YMCA were providing at a cost of 7s 6d for three copies. There the matter may have ended, except for a letter from the Infantry Record Office, dated 2 October 1923, informing Kathleen that a wallet and some remnants of correspondences had been found on George's body when it was dug up. The letters she wrote in reply make interesting reading; not only do they show how desperate she was to have things belonging to her husband returned, but also they reflect in their language the attitude that 'ordinary folk' had to authority: 'In reply to your most kind letter, I shall be very thankful to have any things that have been found belonging to my husband no matter how dirty it is, if you will be so kind to send it to me …' and 'Many thanks on your kindness for sending me my husband's wallet and correspondence as I was very thankful for it, but I would like to know if you can tell me how did anyone find the wallet … I hope it will not be giving too much trouble to find out how they got the wallet for me. I thank you so much dear Sir if you could let me know …'. [1] Unfortunately, any reply she received no longer exists.

---

[1] Letter dated 7/10/1916, SR.

Pte Herbert Hiscock – aged 20
5th Btn Dorsetshire Rgt – 3/7086
Cenotaph and St George's

Standing at 5 ft 1½ in tall and weighing just 7 st 10 lb, with a sallow complexion, Herbert Hiscock did not present a picture of someone who would prove to be a thorn in the side of the British Army. He was born in 1896, the only son of Samuel, a basket maker, and his wife Selina, and the family lived at 41 Colliton St. After Herbert left school at 14 he soon got into trouble and ended up in Bugley Reform School in Wiltshire. When he joined the Dorsets in January 1914, giving his occupation as hawker and admitting that he had served time for poaching, his parents surely hoped that the ways of the military would sort him out, but Herbert had other ideas. If there was one prominent feature of Herbert's first year of service with the 3rd Btn at Upton Camp it was his absence. During that period he was absent without permission on no less than seven occasions, the periods of absconding ranging from a few hours to 11 days. On one occasion he and another soldier, named William West, were apprehended by PC Montague in Dorchester and kept in the cells until a military escort arrived the next morning. After August 1915 he seemed to settle down to army life for a while, that is until July 1916 when he was charged with 'falling out without permission'. [1]

In September 1916 Herbert was sent to fight in Gallipoli with the 5th Btn and having survived that he then went with them to France, where he was killed in action in the attack on Thiepval Ridge on 26 September. [2] In April 1918, Selina was sent her son's personal effects, which consisted of some letters and photographs, and when she acknowledged them she added a heart-rending note: 'I received the letters and photos safe, which belong to my dear son. I thank you for sending on. I shall keep for his sake, sorry to lose him, the only one to look after his mother, which he promised to do for his father's sake.' [3] Herbert's father had died in 1912 and his two sisters had left Dorchester, leaving him as the only provider to his mother. Selina, perhaps affected by the tragedies in her life, did not outlive her son for long. She died on 16 October 1919 and with her went the family's ties with Dorchester. Herbert is remembered on the Thiepval Memorial.

---

[1] SR.
[2] See George Ford for details.
[3] SR.

Sgt Arthur Beaumont Taylor – aged 31
5th Btn Dorsetshire Rgt – 14835
Cenotaph

Henry Screen, a carriage builder living at 24 Fordington High St, and his family had more reasons than most to celebrate on Christmas Day 1913. It was the day his second eldest daughter Edith was to marry Arthur Taylor, a 23-year-old clerk from Leamington Spa. The couple were duly married but like so many at the time the opportunity to set up home was curtailed by the needs of their country.

When the call came Arthur kissed his wife goodbye and doubtless told her not to worry. The people of Dorchester, in general, first became aware of his death through the births, marriages and deaths column of the *Chronicle* on 10 May 1917, which included the following item: 'Previously reported missing, now reported killed in action on 26 September 1916, Sgt A. Beaumont Taylor, husband of Edith Taylor of Dorchester, eldest son of Mr and Mrs Taylor of Stockport.' Arthur died in the attack on Thiepval Ridge, together with three other Dorchester men of the 5th Btn Dorsets. [1] His name is listed among the thousands of others on the Thiepval Memorial.

---

[1] See George Ford for details of the fighting at Thiepval Ridge.

Pte James George Samways – aged 22
5th Btn Dorsetshire Rgt – 14468
Cenotaph and Post Office Memorial

James Samways was born in Fordington on 19 November 1894, when his parents Jane and James were living in Mill Street. Later they moved back to Piddlehinton, his mother's place of birth. When James Junior joined the Army he was working for the post office. He was wounded whilst serving with the 5th Btn Dorsets and died on 26 September. He is buried in Abbeville Communal Cemetery, Somme, suggesting that he may have been taken to one of the hospitals in Abbeville before he passed away.

Rifleman William Peckham – aged 30
17th Btn London Rgt – 573065
Cenotaph and St George's

The Peckhams were not a long-established Dorchester family but moved to the town in the 1890s. Henry Peckham worked on the railway as a locomotive driver and he, his wife Susan and their children lived at 1 York Terr. Their son William joined the Dorsets and was later transferred to the 17th Btn London Rgt, more commonly known as the Poplar and Stepney Rifles. Initially recruited from men who lived in the East End of London it was part of the 47th London Division.

1 October was the date upon which William was about to enter into what would turn out to be the last major British offensive during the first Battle of the Somme. The village of Eaucourt-L'Abbaye had seen heavy fighting in 1916 and now it was the turn of the 47th London Division to attempt to capture it. With the 19th and 20th Btns of the 47th on their right the Stepneys set off into no man's land at 3.15 in the afternoon but only got as far as the German wire, which had not been cut by the artillery barrage. Unable to take their objective and harassed by German bombers, they had to withdraw. William was killed in the attack and after his body was recovered from the battlefield it was buried in Warlencourt British Cemetery, Pas-de-Calais.

Rifleman Frederick Pidden – aged 30
2nd Btn [1] Royal Irish Rifles – 5113
Cenotaph

(Courtesy of Swindon Collection, Swindon Library.)

When the Military Service Act of 1916 introduced conscription it also set up local tribunals to hear appeals from individuals seeking exemption from service. Two tribunals met regularly, one covering Dorchester and the other the surrounding rural area.

Jane Pidden attended the Dorchester tribunal in June 1916 and told them that her husband had died in 1914 and that she had also lost a son, Frank, in 1910. Moreover, she also pointed out that although she had another six sons, five of them were already serving, leaving the 22-year-old Thomas at home. The clerk to the tribunal said that Col F.G. Wheatley, the military representative, advised that the tribunal should give the case every consideration owing to the particular hardship to her. Mr Merrick, the tribunal member said, 'you have done very well for the Army,' to which she replied, 'Yes, sir, I have done my little bit', which brought forth cries of, 'Hear, hear'. Questioned as to her means Jane replied that she only got 10s 2d a week from the Government and of that she had to pay rent of 7s 6d. Accordingly, her son was granted exemption from serving on the grounds of domestic hardship. [2]

With five sons serving in the Army the chances of Jane losing at least one of them were high. Frederick was the second eldest of the brothers and lived with his mother at 8 Alexandra Rd which was just over the tracks from the GWR station, where he worked in the Traffic Department as a carman, delivering parcels. Frederick died of his wounds on 2 October whilst fighting with the 2nd Btn Royal Irish Rifles during the Battle of the Somme and was interred in Bailleul Communal Cemetery.

[1] CWGC shows 8th Btn.
[2] *Chronicle* 15/6/1916.

Acting CSM Sidney James Milledge – aged 36
26th Btn Royal Fusiliers – 19561
Thomas Hardye School Roll of Honour

Sometime between 1879 and 1881 Zillwood and Clara Milledge returned to Weymouth, the town of their birth, after living in London. As well as their three children, they took with them their cook and housemaid, and moved into Lennox Street. Zillwood was a land surveyor and they sent their son Sidney to Dorchester Grammar School. On leaving school Sidney found employment as a bank clerk with the Wilts and Dorset Bank and in 1903 married Elizabeth Simmons from Devon. The couple settled in Bournemouth, presumably because of Sidney's work.

When deciding which regiment he wanted to join Sidney naturally decided on the 26th Btn of the Royal Fusiliers. Known as the Banker's Battalion it was raised by the Mayor and City of London in July 1915 and was composed mainly of bank clerks and accountants. On 31 August 1916 the Fusiliers arrived on the Somme and was involved in some of the heavy fighting, particularly on 15 September when it lost 244 men attacking Flers Trench. At the beginning of October Sidney was back in camp with his men helping to prepare them for a further attack in the same area and on 3 October the Bankers took up positions in Flers Trench, relieving the 3rd Btn New Zealand Infantry Bde. The war diary for the period in which Sidney was killed records, 'The Btn remained here during the 4th & 5th – during this time it was subject to fairly heavy shelling' [1] and it was probably during this bombardment that he died. His body is one of 3,580 men buried in the Australian Imperial Force Burial Ground, Flers, Somme.

[1] War diary.

2 Lt Wilfred Harold Vine MC – aged 29
2nd Btn York and Lancaster Rgt
Cenotaph and Thomas Hardye School Roll of Honour

Among the usual war news and casualty lists the following headline appeared in the *Chronicle* on 2 November 1916: 'Lieutenant Wilfred Vine Killed in Action – One of the Bravest'. The article then went on to exclaim that, 'The friends – and how many there are – of the widely-known young Durnovarian Lt Wilfred Vine, have been deeply moved by the news that he has fallen on the field of honour.'

Wilfred was the son of Richard Vine who had been in business as a corn merchant in Dorchester since about 1887, with premises at 8 High East St. Richard also lived on the premises, with his wife Fanny, daughter Nellie, who was born in California, and son Wilfred. The business prospered to the extent that they could afford to buy 'Brightside', 20 Cornwall Rd, one of the newly built villas overlooking the Borough Gardens. When it was time to consider Wilfred's education it was decided to send him to the Grammar School and after completing his education he qualified as an accountant, joining the family firm. By 1911 he was managing the company. Wilfred married Vivienne Mullins from Liverpool and by then the couple were living at 16 Alexandra Rd, a 2-minute walk from his parents' house. It would appear that Wilfred was quite a character, the *Chronicle* declaring that, 'By his never-failing bonhomie, Wilfred Vine was a "hail fellow well met". [1] A member of the Dorchester Dramatic Society, with which he appeared in many Hardy plays, he was also a very good comedian, often in demand to perform on stage and at social gatherings. His talents were not confined to the stage; he was also a keen sportsman, achieving considerable success on the cycle track.

Wilfred enlisted in the Royal Engineers as a Sapper on 10 August 1914 and rapidly gained his sergeant's stripes, before catching someone's eye as officer material. Consequently, on 7 November 1915 he was transferred to the York and Lancaster Rgt with a commission as 2 Lt. After his death, Wilfred's Captain, in a letter to his wife, felt compelled to mention that, 'Your husband was famous throughout the battalion for his great cheerfulness and good humour under all circumstances; and as for his courage I might add that he was one of the bravest men who ever walked'.

Wilfred's bravery was recognised when he was awarded, belatedly, the Military Cross in November 1916 for his part in the Battle of Morval on the Somme on 25 September 1916. The citation reads: 'For conspicuous gallantry in action. He led his platoon with great courage and determination, assisting to capture two machine guns and 150 prisoners. He has previously done fine work.'[2] The fine work referred to included being wounded on two occasions. Wilfred was killed in action while leading his men in an attack on 12 October during the Battle of Ancre. He is commemorated on the Thiepval Memorial.

---

[1] *Chronicle* 2/11/1916.
[2] *London Gazette* 14/11/1916

Capt. Douglas Heron Marrable – aged 57
Assistant Instructor in musketry

Lt Edmund Douglas Marrable – aged 25
105th Bty, RFA

Both are commemorated on the Cenotaph

Dorchester became the county town of Dorset for a number of reasons, not least because it was there that the county assizes were held and it was the home of the county jail, which, in turn, led to the development of other administrative and legal services being established, including the High Court and County Court. These courts were administered through the combined post of Registrar and High Bailiff of the County Court and the District Registrar of the High Court and in 1899 the position became vacant. It was filled by Douglas Marrable, a solicitor from London, who brought his family to the town and moved into The Corner House, 41 High West St. Douglas was the son of a mining engineer and his mother Madeline was a talented artist, whose works are collectable today. [1] His wife was Laura and they had one son and three daughters.

It was not long before Douglas was making an imprint on the lives of the people of Dorchester. His two loves were sailing and shooting and he was instrumental, along with Col Tweedie, [2] in founding the Dorchester and District Rifle Club, which continues today as the Dorchester and District Rifle and Pistol Shooting Club. He became its honorary secretary and also took time in supervising the local scout troop on the range. He was also a prominent freemason and became Worshipful Master of his Lodge. [3] Douglas became involved in local politics and served on the town council for 3 years and was vice-chairman of the Dorchester and Fordington Conservative Club.

Military matters had interested Douglas from an early age. As a young man he had been a member of the Royal Naval Reserve and when War was declared he immediately offered his experience and skills in musketry to the authorities, at the age of 56. His offer was accepted and in the winter of 1914/15 he could be found at Wool in the Purbecks, training men of the Northumberland Fusiliers. So good was his tuition that his battalion went on to win the brigade prize for shooting. The Army realised what an asset they had in Douglas and asked him to go to Winchester with a commission of lieutenant to train other troops. This he did and then went on to North Yorkshire, where he put men of the Border Rgt through their paces.

Before the War Douglas had contracted a chest complaint that sent him to Madeira to recuperate and when he next went to Salisbury Plain, promoted to captain, he found that the open windy rifle range was no place for a man with a weak chest. His condition reoccurred and got progressively worse, and as a consequence he asked to be transferred to the Reserve so that he could recover at home. This was duly granted and he returned to Dorchester. Such was his character that before he had recovered fully he found a new job, this time as secretary to the county military tribunal, dealing with appeals for military exemption. This work was very demanding and entailed extensive travel around the county and it was on a visit to Bridport that he caught a chill from which he never recovered. He resigned his post and died shortly after, on 12 October 1916. He was buried in Dorchester with military honours. As well as appearing on the Dorchester Cenotaph Douglas's name appears on the Freemason's Roll of Honour.

Edmund, the only son of Douglas and Laura, served with the 105th Bty, RFA as a lieutenant. As the War progressed and air to land communications improved, aircraft were being used increasingly to help artillery batteries register their guns on enemy targets. That may have been why Edmund was seconded to an RAF training unit in Kent. Wye Aerodrome no longer exists but in 1916 the former farmland became the home of No. 20 Reserve Squadron RFC and in May 1917 home to 42nd Training Squadron. On 25 April 1918 Edmund was a passenger in an Avro Trainer flown by Lt Cyril Whelan when it collided with a Sopwith Pup, flown by 2 Lt Alwyne Levy. Both machines fell to earth, crashing near the Golden Bull public house in Kennington near Ashford, and all three of the officers were killed. Edmund has a war grave in Kennington Cemetery. His widowed mother received the news of her son's death at her home in Belgrave Square, London.

[1] Madeline Frances Marrable (1833–1916).
[2] See Arthur Caruthers-Little.
[3] Douglas was elected as a freemason in London on 11 September 1889, at the same meeting that Dr Thomas Barnardo was elected.

Rifleman Robert Laird – aged 34
17th Btn King's Royal Rifle Corps – A/200040
Cenotaph [1] and Thomas Hardye School Roll of Honour

On 21 November 1880 the Depot Barracks in Dorchester had an addition to its personnel by the name of Robert Laird, tenth child of the family of Quartermaster Sgt John Laird of the Dorsetshire Rgt. John and his family were living in family quarters, which were situated in a block immediately behind and running parallel to the Little Keep.

John Laird had brought his new bride Agnes to England from Ireland in 1858 and a year later enlisted at Liverpool in the 75th Rgt of Foot. Fortunately, Agnes, was not destined to be one of those army wives who were forever following their husbands around the world or having to spend years at home waiting for them to return. Of John's 38 years with the Colours he only served abroad on one occasion, for a period of 2 years in the East Indies. In 1881 he transferred to the 39th Rgt of Foot which, in the same year, was amalgamated into the Dorsetshire Rgt, and thus John found himself in Dorchester as QMS at the Depot. Its reputation for having an active and successful Officer Cadet Corps may have been the reason why John sent Robert to the local grammar school, although the boy still had to meet the requirements of the entrance examination.

By 1901 Agnes had died and Robert had left home, living and working in Bridport as an articled clerk with the firm of Austen Wretham, and he was still with them when he enlisted in the 5th Btn London Rifle Brigade on 1 December 1915. At some time he transferred to the 17th Btn KRRC and was killed on 15 October 1916. The day before his death orders had been received to send two companies of his Btn forward to support the Black Watch, who were clearing enemy trenches at the Schwaben Redoubt, north of Thiepval. At 5 pm the next morning the Germans launched two counterattacks and whilst they were repulsed, three of the Rifle Corps men were killed and 25 wounded. It is likely that one of those killed was Robert, who was buried in Tincourt New British Cemetery, Somme. It was perhaps fortunate that neither of Robert's parents had to endure the grief brought about by his death, his father having died in 1910. Instead it was his sister Elizabeth who received the sad news in Dorchester at 18 Bridport Rd.

---

[1] The Cenotaph incorrectly shows K.E.A. Laird.

Cpl William James Downton – aged 25
10th Btn Durham Light Infantry
Cenotaph and St George's

William was the second eldest son of John Downton, a bootmaker, and his wife Elizabeth. The family were long-time residents of Fordington Hill, living at No. 7. When William left school he served his apprenticeship with the grocer Richard Boon, owner of Boon's Stores at 11 Cornhill. He also sang in the St George's Church choir for many years. Later, James left Dorchester and moved to Ringwood in Hampshire and when the call to serve came he joined the Hussars, later transferring to the DLI. William was with D Coy, 10th

Btn fighting at Le Souich and Brevillers in the Battle of Arras when he died of wounds on 16 October and was buried in Etaples Military Cemetery. His elder brother Charles served with distinction in the Dorsets and received the Meritorious Service Medal for conspicuous bravery in the field.

Pte William Charles Mayo Dean – aged 30
Royal Flying Corps – 2245
Cenotaph and St George's

From the day of his birth William Dean was surrounded by the sounds of the military. His father Charles was a well-known recruiting sergeant at the Depot Barracks and William lived with his parents and two brothers in staff quarters. By 1914 Charles had been long retired, the family had moved out of the Barracks to 15 Harvey's Buildings in Holloway Road and the boys were all working. William was employed as a fitter with Messrs Thurman and Co., Ironmongers, who then had their premises at 17 South St. [1] He joined the firm as an apprentice and had a reputation as a practical joker. One person who was subjected to his pranks was a blacksmith by the name of Young, a surly fellow and unpopular with the rest of the staff. On one occasion William told Young that he was required in the office and when he left the forge put down the metal bar he was about to start work on. In his absence the young apprentice heated the bar to blue heat and placed it back on the bench. Returning from his fool's errand Young got quite a shock when he picked up the hot piece of metal. William did not wait to be accused of committing the crime and fled into Colliton Street.

Employees of Thurman's. William Dean is far right standing next to Young, the blacksmith. (Source: Mrs E. Rowbotham.)

It was not surprising that when War arrived all three of Charles' sons joined the Army and he must have been very proud when they all decided to enlist in the Dorsets. William went into the 1/4th Dorsets and sailed with them to India before going on to Mesopotamia. Then, in August 1915 someone noticed that he had some special skills to offer and he was selected for service as a mechanic with the RFC. For William, it was a fateful move because he was attached to Gen. Townsend's ill-fated force and became a prisoner of the Turks at the surrender of Kut-al-Amara on 29 April 1916. William endured the terrible conditions of captivity until 22 November, the day he died. [2] His body lies in Baghdad (North Gate) War Cemetery.

For William's mother Sarah it was the second family death in under a year. Her brother Harry, who was a private at the Depot, died in July 1915. [3] But that was not the end of her grief, for she was hit by a trilogy of tragedy when Charles died 5 months after his son, the *Chronicle* describing him as 'A well-remembered soldier and father of soldiers – a familiar figure in the streets of Dorchester, with his recruiting ribbons. A professional soldier of the old school. Served 21 years in the Dorsets.' [4]

[1] In 1921 Thurman's moved to 64 High West St next to the County Museum, where it remained until closure in 1979.
[2] Reports on the terrible conditions endured by the Turkish prisoners were widely reported in the international press and questions were asked in the House of Commons. The stories included those of physical abuse, lack of medical care and starvation. See William Mahar.
[3] See Harry Mayo.
[4] *Chronicle* 26/4/1917.

Pte William George Mahar – aged 27
2nd Btn Dorsetshire Rgt
Cenotaph

The Mahar and Shorto families were not only neighbours but also linked by marriage and tragedy. Within the two families an uncle and two cousins were to perish during the Great War. [1] Living at No. 3 Miller's Close in 1901 was William Mahar, his wife Charlotte and their two children Emma and William, and next door at No. 4 lived Charlotte's brother George Shorto and his family who were also destined to lose a son. Death was further associated with No. 3 when William and Charlotte moved out, to be replaced by the Fickus family who lost father and son.

William and Charlotte's son William did not appear at Miller's Close in the 1911 census; instead he was listed among the soldiers of the 2nd Btn Dorsets serving in Poona, India. Four years after that he was on another less desirable roll call, that of the men of the battalion who were besieged in the town of Kut in Mesopotamia. William survived the siege and set off on the long trek to Turkey with fellow Durnovarian David Payne. [2] After the 700-mile journey he was sent to Afyonkarahisar in central Turkey, where prisoners from the Gallipoli campaign were being held. By mid-1916 most of the OR Kut prisoners had been sent to work on the railroad in the Toros mountains, but a few remained, those who acted as batmen for the officers and those who were too ill to travel, and it was likely that William was one of the latter.

Another soldier, John Still, was a prisoner at Afyonkarahisar and wrote about the terrible conditions incurred by the men: 'Afyon is vividly remembered by the prisoners who were already there. Some of them naked, many half out of their minds with exhaustion, most of them rotten with dysentery, this band of survivors was received with deep sympathy by the rest, who did all they might to restore them, small as their own resources were. In very many cases it was too late. The sick men were placed in the camp hospital; but this was a hospital in not much more than the name, for though there was a Turkish doctor in attendance with some rough Turkish orderlies, medicines were non-existent, and a man too ill to look after himself had a very poor chance. Deaths were frequent; the dead were buried by their comrades in the Christian cemetery of the town.' [3]

In the archives of the Dorset Rgt there is a file of 'unofficial death reports' which contains a sheet stating that a death certificate for Pte W. Mahar had been received from the Red Crescent [4] indicating that he had died on 25 October 1916. He was buried in the local cemetery and later his body, along with other Allied dead, was transferred to Baghdad (North Gate) Cemetery.

---

[1] See Harold and Bertram Shorto.
[2] See David Payne for a description of the march.
[3] Still, 1920.
[4] The Turkish equivalent of the Red Cross.

Gnr Arthur Henry Cecil Smith – aged 17
106th Siege Bty, RGA – 121987
St George's

There is no obvious evidence as to the identity of the person who appears as A.H. Smith in the official records but a clue lies in the births, marriages and deaths column of the *Chronicle* on 30 October 1919, which reads, 'In ever loving memory of our dear son, Gunner A.H.C. Smith, who died of wounds October 25, 1916'. Records show that the person referred to was Arthur Smith, the son of Herbert, a stone mason, and Rose who lived at Harman's Cross near Swanage. Arthur is buried in Puchevillers British Cemetery, Somme, and also appears on the Swanage War Memorial.

Pte Arthur Edwin Hurst – aged 29
1/4th Btn Dorsetshire Rgt
Cenotaph, Holy Trinity and St Peter's

The 1891 census shows the 2-year-old Arthur Hurst living in Pease Lane (now known as Colliton Street). Arthur was one of 11 children born to Mary and her husband William who was employed in the town as a joiner and cabinet-maker. According to the *Chronicle* Arthur was a very popular boy in the town who had a wide circle of friends, particularly in the sporting arena, where he excelled in football and was a keen gymnast. He was employed by W.J. Durden, plumbers and decorators, and attended Holy Trinity Church. There he was not only a member of the bible class but also took on the irksome chore of pumping the bellows for the church organ.

Arthur was also a member of the Dorset Territorials before the War and continued with them when the 1/4th Btn was created. He went with them to India in October 1914 and thence to Mesopotamia. There he was attached to a machine gun section and in an engagement with the Turks was wounded in the arm and the thigh and had to be taken to the base hospital. He was able to write a letter to his parents telling them that he was making a good recovery but this was overtaken in transit by the official notice that he had died on 26 October 1916. He is buried in Basra War Cemetery.

Pte William Symes – aged 36
1st Btn Dorsetshire Rgt – 6270
Cenotaph and St George's

The person listed on the above memorials as W. Symes of the Dorsets is probably William Symes who was wounded and died in King George's Hospital, Lambeth, London, on 31 October 1916. His death certificate gives his address as the Depot Barracks, Dorchester, and his regiment as the 1st Btn Dorsets. [1] SDGW shows that he was born in Dorchester, which suggests that he was the William Symes who in 1911 was serving in the Navy, while his wife Emma was living in Devonport. He died from a gunshot wound to the stomach and intestinal obstruction, and was buried in Nunhead All Saints' Cemetery in South London.

---

[1] The CWGC shows him with the 5th Btn.

Bombardier Percival Vine MM and Bar – aged 28
1st Trench Mortar Bty, RGA – 24502
Cenotaph and St Peter's

No. 16 Salisbury St, sitting next to what was the Baptist Church Hall, [1] has, like many houses, a name plaque but this one is a little different, suggesting that there is more to the name than just the owner's wish to personalise their property. 'The Old House At Home' relates to the fact that the building had a long history as a hostelry, reputedly going back to the 18th century. [2] Thomas Vine, who managed to combine the jobs of carpenter and publican, and his wife Annie were running the pub in 1891 and it remained with the same family until the 1930s. Thomas and Annie had three soldier sons, Horace, Edgar and Percy, the former two serving in the Army Ordnance Corps and the RAMC, whilst Percy, the eldest, went into the RGA.

As a lad Percy Vine was employed at the Post Office as a telegraph messenger and then became a clerk at Mr C.H. Smith's County Stores, opposite the Corn Exchange in High East Street. [3] The *Chronicle* described Percy as 'A young fellow of splendid physique, he was a born footballer, and in his position at back he was a veritable tower of strength to any team, as may be gathered from the feet that he had been known to kick the ball from one goal to the other.' [4] At the age of 18 Percy joined the RGA and served with the 63rd Coy in Malta, before going to France in March 1915, where he was assigned to a TMB. Although Percy was one of Dorchester's most decorated servicemen he was not killed in battle but in the comparative safety of his billet. One of his officers wrote in a letter to his parents: 'I most deeply regret to inform you that your son was killed during a bombardment on the place in which we were billeted on the afternoon of 31 October. His death was absolutely instantaneous, and his loss is a very great blow to the battery. He was one of the bravest and coolest men I have ever met. He was buried in a small military cemetery here and a cross has been erected over his grave, which is always well looked after.' [5] In this case the officer's comments were fully justified and not just aimed at giving Thomas and Annie some comfort. Six months after their son's death they received, from the War Office, the MM with the addition of a bar for two acts of gallantry carried out by their son. He was awarded the medal initially, in September 1916, [6['for harassing the enemy with trench mortars for 12 days in a certain sector, whereby the enemy was forced to evacuate most of his positions.' [7] The second award occurred after his death. [8[Percy's body lies in the Albert Communal Cemetery, Somme.

The Vines' other sons got through the War but not without mishap. On 11 October 1917 an article appeared in the *Chronicle* stating that Edgar, of the RAMC, was lying dangerously wounded in a base hospital in France but fortunately he recovered. Another son, Horace, was not so lucky. He too was seriously wounded and had to have an arm amputated.

---

[1] The hall is currently being used as a museum.

[2] Strange, 1995.

[3] The property is currently a shop that sells beds, but the floor of its entrance gives away its former use, consisting of a mosaic with the words 'The Stores'.

[4] *Chronicle* 9/11/1916.

[5] *Chronicle* 7/12/1916.

[6[*London Gazette* 12/9/1916.

[7]] *Chronicle* 3/5/1917.

[8] *London Gazette* 8/12/1916.

2 Lt Bertram Temp Collier – aged 19
25th Btn Northumberland Fusiliers

2 Lt Ernest Stebbing Collier – aged 29
9th Bde, RGA

Both are commemorated on the Cenotaph and St Peter's

Thomas Collier was a civil servant which may explain why he spent over 25 years in South Africa, where he married and his four children were born. When he retired he returned to England and settled in Bournemouth, where he was living with his wife

Annie, their two daughters and youngest son Bertram in 1911. The eldest son Ernest remained in South Africa.

Bertram was born in 1897 in Cape Colony and was still a young lad when he left his homeland. After finishing school he went into one of the new professions that had emerged out of the beginning of the Edwardian period, that of motor engineer. On 30 September 1914 he swapped four wheels for two, when he enlisted in the 2/9th (Cyclist) Btn Hampshire Regiment, based in Chichester. However, he was not destined to pedal around the south coast for long. In April 1915 he was granted a commission as 2 Lt with the 16th Btn Northumberland Fusiliers, moving on to the 31st Btn before going to France where he again moved, this time to the 25th (2nd Tyneside Irish).

The 2nd Irish were one of four Irish Pals battalions raised in Newcastle-upon-Tyne and like so many of the Pals they were almost wiped out on the first day of the Somme, in their case before they even reached their own front line. In early November 1916 the 25th were in the area of Steenwerk, Nord, to the east of Armentières and on 17 November Bertram's father received a letter informing him that his son had 'died in 2nd Australian Casualty Clearing Station at 7.00 am this morning, 5/11/16 from gunshot wound penetrating abdomen'. [1] After Bertram was buried in Trois Arbres Cemetery, Steenwerk, the Army set to work clearing up his personal affairs. The young lieutenant had credit of £7 17s 6d on his mess account, which was paid into his estate, and his personal effects, which included his watch, nail clippers and silk handkerchief, as well as the usual letters and photographs, were returned to his parents at 13 Cornwall Rd.

Ernest Collier, back row left, with fellow students at St John's College, Johannesburg. (Source: St John's College, Johannesburg.)

Despite remaining in Africa Thomas and Annie's other son Ernest managed to find a way of supporting the cause. When hostilities commenced the South African authorities were only too aware of their border with German Southwest Africa, and when the British Government asked Prime Minister Louis Botha if he could raise a force to invade what is today's Namibia he said that he could. After quelling a revolt by Boers who were sympathetic to the Germans 67,000 South African troops invaded the province in March 1915, completing their task on 9 July, when a surrender was signed. Ernest played his part in the fighting by enlisting as a private in the South African Medical Corps at the beginning of the War and then going on to serve with them in Egypt and France for 13 months, before going to cadet school. He emerged as 2 Lt of the RGA. He returned to the Front in May 1916 and was serving with the 9th Bde as Signalling Officer when he was killed in action on 2 April 1918. His is the only Commonwealth War grave in Blerancourt Communal Cemetery, Aisne. Back home Ernest was mourned by his widow Bessie whom he had married in December 1916.

[1] SR.

Sgt Maj. Joseph Grosse – aged 57
Depot, Dorsetshire Rgt – 12207
St George's

On 9 November 1916 another impressive military funeral took place in the town. The *Chronicle* report tells us that it was 'The Last Post' [1] for a much-respected first-class warrant officer of the Dorsetshire Rgt. The coffin contained the body of Joseph Grosse and was carried from his house at 1 Maumbury Way to the waiting hearse by six CSMs of the Dorsetshire Rgt. The cortege included the band of the RDC, a firing party of the East Lancashire Rgt and a detachment of the Dorsets, under the command of a Lt Portman. Together with the family the procession set off on the short journey to Weymouth Avenue Cemetery, accompanied by the sound of Handel's Dead March from Saul and after the interment the regulation volley was fired over the grave followed by buglers playing the Last Post. The chief mourners around the grave were his wife and daughter. Both of his sons were serving in the War, one a prisoner in Germany. Joseph was a member of St Peter's Church congregation and the rector, the Rev Coote, gave a touching address bearing witness to the fine character and bearing of the deceased who had served his Heavenly King as well as his Earthly King.

Joseph Grosse was born in Winthorpe, Nottingham, and served with the Dorsets for 30 years before retiring with the rank of RSM. His wife was Clarissa Hawke, whom he married in 1875 in Plymouth. After his retirement Joseph got a job as a gardener but as a Reservist could not resist the call to duty. He may have felt somewhat insulted when he found that he had to re-enlist as a lowly private in September 1914, but he was immediately promoted to sergeant major and went to Bolton Park, Grantham, helping to train the regiment's first Service Btn. He then returned to Dorchester to work at the Depot until he was discharged through illness on 13 March. He died on 6 November.

[1] *Chronicle* 16/11/1916.

Pte Alfred Pearce – aged 32
10th Btn Royal Warwickshire Rgt – 2056
Cenotaph and St Peter's

Alfred Pearce was born at Wyke Regis in 1884, son of farm labourer Charles and his wife Mary. The family moved to Higher Burton, just outside Dorchester, in the 1890s where Alfred was employed as a carter on one of the local farms. In 1901 he married Dorchester girl Ada Pearce and in 1911 they resided at 12 Salisbury St, just a few doors away from the Old House at Home, where Percy Vine's family lived. [1] Alfred was then working as a brewer's labourer, probably at Eldridge Pope's brewery, and he and Ada had a 1-year-old daughter.

When it was time to go to War Alfred enlisted in the Warwickshire Rgt and served with them in France. On 8 November the 10th Btn moved into Stuff Trench to the northeast of Thiepval to relieve the 7th Btn South Lancashire Rgt. The trenches were in a very poor condition and Alfred and his fellow soldiers immediately set to work repairing them and improving the drainage. During the next two nights patrols were sent out into no man's land and a few casualties were incurred. On the 10th the war diary records that there was considerable enemy shelling in the evening and by the end of the day Alfred and another man, Ernest Yeomans, had been killed. Alfred's body lies in the Villers-Bretonneux Military Cemetery, Somme.

----

[1] See Percy Vine.

Pte Alma Victor Martin [1] – aged 29
7th Btn West Surrey Rgt – G/21773

Pte Albert Ernest Martin – aged 34
6th Btn Dorsetshire Rgt – 3/7431

Both are commemorated on the Cenotaph and St Peter's

The Society of Dorset Men in London's *Year Book* for 1917/18 contains the photographs of two brothers of one of their 'most enthusiastic members'. The man referred to was Arthur Martin who was a prominent member of the Society. He was the eldest of three brothers and had an illustrious career, firstly with Lord Northcote when he was Governor General of Australia and then with the American industrialist Daniel Reid, known as the 'Tinplate King'. Arthur was described in the *Year Book* as one of the most enthusiastic of the overseas Dorset Men who had canvassed his American friends to raise funds for the Creature Comforts Fund for Dorset Soldiers and Sailors. [2] Arthur and his brothers Victor and Albert were the sons of Charles and Sarah Martin who in 1901 were living at 18 Frome Terr, where they were neighbours of Ernest Clarke's family. [3]

Victor was the youngest of the sons and before joining up in June 1915 he worked as a postman in Weymouth and prior to that as an attendant at the county asylum. It was there that he met his future bride Edith, who was working there as a nurse. They married in 1914 and their son Gerald was born a few months before his father's death. Victor initially

enlisted in the Dorsets but was then transferred to the 7th Btn West Surrey Rgt. In November 1916 the West Surreys were seeing out the last few days of the Battle of the Somme and on the day Victor was killed, the 13th, they were marching to Albert in preparation for an attack on Desire Trench, near the village of Grandcourt. He is commemorated on the Thiepval Memorial.

In his youth Victor, in common with his brothers, had been a keen local footballer and his death occasioned the *Chronicle* to observe that, 'it is a melancholy fact that within the space of a few weeks three noted Dorchester footballers have died for King and Country – namely, Bombardier Percy Vine, Pte George Thomas and Pte Martin.' [4]

Albert, the second eldest son, was born in 1883 and after leaving school worked for several years as a porter at the Victoria Hotel, Weymouth. He married a Weymouth girl, Emily Legg, in 1909 and 2 years later they could be found living at 2 Standfast Rd with their two children. Albert joined the Dorsets early in the War and fought with the 6th Btn in France.

At the beginning of May 1917 the battalion moved into the Arras area and on the 12th supported an attack on Cupid Trench, which although successful left the Dorsets in what the regimental history describes as 'a hot corner'. The position was held until the 15th when it was decided to withdraw because of alarms of a big counterattack. This came as the

Dorsets were withdrawing and the platoon commander, 2 Lt Goodson, described in a letter to Albert's mother that, 'your son was killed in action on the night of the 15th, while gallantly withstanding the onset of large masses of Germans', adding 'I always found him a willing and capable soldier'. [5] Albert is buried in Brown's Copse Cemetery, Roeux, Pas-de-Calais.

[1] The memorials show V.A. Martin. The Cenotaph wrongly lists him under the Dorset Regiment.

[2] At the cessation of the War the fund had a surplus, some of which was donated to the County Hospital, where a plaque commemorating the donation can still be seen.

[3] See Ernest Clarke.

[4] *Chronicle* 12/12/16.

[5] *Chronicle* 7/6/1917.

Pte William Henry Dunford – aged 37
1st Btn Dorsetshire Rgt – 17080
Cenotaph

Before leaving Dorchester to go off and fight in the War William Dunford handed his watch to his brother Jack, telling him that he might as well have it as he would not be coming back.[1] What caused such certainty in William's mind is unknown but it proved to be true. William was born in King Street, Fordington, in 1879, the son of Thomas, a maltster, and his wife Emily. They later moved to Victoria Buildings, Fordington Hill, where they lived next door to Walter Early's family before settling at 2 Alington Terr. [2] By 1901 William had left the family home and moved to Fisherton Anger where he worked as a labourer.

William was with the 1st Btn Dorsets at the beginning of the winter of 1916/17. The weather was wet and the first frosts when they thawed turned the ground into a quagmire. The Battle of Ancre commenced on 13 November and on the 16th part of the 1st Btn was occupying some captured German trenches near Mailly-Maillet, Somme. The following day, when William was killed, working parties were sent out to dig trenches and they were subjected to heavy shelling and he was probably killed in the bombardment. He is commemorated on the Thiepval Memorial.

[1] This fact was told to me by a relative.
[2] See Walter Early.

Pte Leonard Ralph Archer – aged 18
2nd Btn Hampshire Rgt – 29498
Cenotaph and St Peter's Church

Ralph Archer, as he was known, was the son of John and Alice. The family lived at 9 The Grove and John was employed by a local family as a coachman. Tragically, Ralph's mother died when he was just 2 years old and after her death his father moved the family to 15 Mountain Ash Rd.

Ralph could not have been with the 2nd Hampshires very long when he was killed. During November the battalion were working 3 days in the line, 3 days in support and 3 days in reserve. On the 21st it was Ralph and his colleagues' turn to go into the trenches at Les Boeufs on the Somme and relieve the Newfoundland Rgt. Nothing spectacular happened the next day, except that one soldier is recorded as killed in action, namely Leonard Archer, who is commemorated on the Thiepval Memorial.

Pte George William Thomas – aged 31
1st Btn Dorsetshire Rgt – 16822
Cenotaph and St Peter's

First-hand testimony on the fate of a soldier is sometimes provided by his CO but in the case of George Thomas the information came from one of his friends with whom he was serving in France. Mr A.R. Churchill recorded some of his recollections of the War in the *Dorset Year Book*. Among them was the following: 'During the few days I was at Rouen, I met a fellow townsman, George Thomas, who, in peacetime, ran a one-man hairdressing saloon at the bottom end of Durngate Street, near the Crown Inn. He was a useful footballer, and played for Dorchester Thursdays, and although much older than I was, we were close friends, having something in common; our trade. George was serving with the 1st Btn, then holding the line at La Bass, [1] where they had been transferred after suffering heavy casualties in attacking the Thiepval bastion on 1 July, the opening day of the Somme. He was never robust, and now, having just been discharged from hospital, he looked very pale and drawn. We had a chat about our home town and also about the conditions up at the Front. He had obviously been through a terrific ordeal and was not too confident of his eventual survival. His gloomy forebodings were unhappily fulfilled; he died of wounds received at the Battle of Ancre in November and was buried at Warlincourt Halte British Cemetery, Pas-de-Calais.' [2] George died on 22 November and his parents, George and Mary, received the news of their only son's death at their home at 1 Alington Terr, from where George ran his hairdressers.

---

[1] The writer meant La Basée.
[2] *Dorset Year Book* 1960/61, published by the Society of Dorset Men in London.

Pte Benjamin Daniel Steirn – aged 41
1st Btn Dorsetshire Rgt – 3/7421
Cenotaph and St George's

It could be said that the military was central to Benjamin Steirn's life. He was eldest son of a farrier in the RHA and spent a large part of his early years living in Woolwich, the home of the Royal Artillery. When he had to make a decision on his own future he might have followed to his father's branch of the services like his brother Frank but instead he joined the Royal Navy, where he served for 7 years before being transferred to the National Reserve. In 1898 Benjamin married Mary, a girl from Woolwich, and by 1911 they had moved to Dorchester, where they were living with their children and Mary's mother at 23 Alington Rd. Benjamin was now working as a house painter whilst Mary and her mother took in laundry.

When War came Benjamin was unable to go back into the Navy so instead volunteered for the Dorsets, wasting no time by enrolling 2 weeks after the declaration of hostilities. He served with the 1st Btn until 16 June 1915, when he was discharged as being no longer physically fit for war service. Returning to Dorchester, Benjamin did not work again, except for a short period with the Whitehead Torpedo Works at Portland Harbour. A few days before his death he was admitted into the County Hospital for an operation but his body was too weak to stand the shock and he died on 23 November. His wife and five children attended the military funeral which was held at Fordington Cemetery, where he rests.

Pte William George Squibb – aged 28
2nd Btn Hampshire Rgt – 29724
Cenotaph

William was born in 1888, the son of George and Eliza Squibb who lived in a cottage at Middle Farm, Dorchester, where his father was employed as a groom. When William was eight his mother died, possibly when giving birth to his brother Charles, who was born in the same year. After his wife's death George moved to Winterborne Steepleton, where he lived with his son who worked as a farm labourer. In the early summer of 1916 William married his cousin Elizabeth Squibb but the marriage would prove to be a short one. On 25 November of the same year William died of wounds while fighting with the 2nd Hampshires on the Somme. He is buried at Grove Town Cemetery, Meaulte, Somme.

Pte Charles James Benger – aged 26
2nd Btn Royal Fusiliers – G/4027
Cenotaph and St Peter's

In an age of patriotism and Empire the Great War provided the perfect opportunity for newspaper writers to display their prose with flourish, whilst at the same time encouraging men to join the brave lads fighting at the Front. The style of writing used then, which even in today's world of the tabloid press seems overdramatic, was ably demonstrated in the *Chronicle*'s report on the death of Charles Benger: 'Everybody who knew that fine manly soldier, Pte Charles Benger, of the Royal Fusiliers, will hear with deep regret that he was killed in service on December 4th, and will feel much sympathy with his parents, Mr and Mrs Charles Benger, of 3, Maie Terr. The sad news, which came to hand so shortly before Christmas, makes a grievous break in the family chain of the four stalwart sons and five daughters of whom their parents are so justly proud. Mr and Mrs Benger's eldest son Mr John Benger, so well known and much respected as hallkeeper of the Dorchester Municipal Buildings, Sergeant-at-Mace to the Mayor and Corporation [1] of Dorchester and a valued member of the Fire Brigade, is "doing his bit" by way of military service in the Dorchester Coy, Dorset Volunteer Regiment; and his two other sons, Henry and Ernest, are both in the Army and serving in France. Pte Charles Benger, whose death we have to deplore, was the third son. He served his apprenticeship as a hairdresser and barber with Mr H.W. Perham, and while in Dorchester, before he went to a situation in London, his tall athletic form – he stood six feet two in his socks – was well known on the football field. Charles Benger was not the lad to wait either for compulsion, or even for Lord Derby's attestation scheme. [2] The first week in September 1914, when the war was yet green he joined Kitchener's Army, and during his 27 months of soldiering on active service had quite exceptional experience. He first fought on the Western Front, whence he was invalided with frostbite, in that first terrible winter of 1915, when our army leaders had much to learn in the way of trench construction and sanitation and equipment for preserving the health of our men against that formidable foe, "General Winter". On recovering he went to Gallipoli, then to Egypt, and finally to another front – to receive his mortal stroke.' [3]

Dramatic as it may seem this obituary is by no means untypical and despite what may appear to be the free use of hyperbole the esteem in which Charles was held was certainly endorsed by his platoon officer, when he wrote in a letter to his mother, 'The qualities that Pte Benger possessed as a soldier were everything to be desired, and in everything to be admired. He was always most devoted to his duty, and ever willing to perform his share of the work – and that to the full. During his service he endeared himself to his comrades one and all; a true, noble son, who made the supreme sacrifice gallantly. His body lies in a grave which we have carefully registered on the map.' [4] The 2nd Btn war diary entry for 5 December 1916 is short and to the point. It reads, 'Briqueterie Camp – Trenches drying up slightly. Casualties. Other Ranks – 1 killed, 1 wounded.' The anonymous OR killed was Charles. The final comment in the officer's letter suggests that his body was given a temporary grave from which it would later be transferred to a cemetery. However, despite the assurances given, it seems that his body was not recovered and instead his name appears on the Thiepval Memorial.

[1] The Corporation or Town Council.
[2] Following the initial rush to join up numbers were dwindling by the spring of 1915. The 'Derby Scheme' was introduced and allowed men to sign up and then return to their homes until they were needed. One of the attractions of the scheme was that they wore a grey armband with a red crown, thus avoiding being accused of shirking.
[3] *Chronicle* 28/12/1916.
[4] Ibid.

Pte Charles Henry Sawyer – aged 31
1st Btn Border Rgt – 22795
Cenotaph and St George's

After Charles Sawyer married Alice Woodsford at Dorchester Registry Office in April 1905 the young couple decided to turn their backs on their rural upbringing and head for London. Charles was one of six sons of John and Ruth Sawyer, a family of agricultural labourers who had followed the available work around the county, living in Littlebredy, Netherbury and Puddletown. Alice was the daughter of Sarah and Joseph, a shepherd from Up Sydling. With their son Arthur, Charles and Alice settled in Wandsworth where Charles worked as a carman, delivering goods around the capital.

On 12 May 1915 Charles arrived at the recruiting office at Kingston-upon-Thames thinking that his work with horses would make him an ideal candidate as a driver and when asked if he was prepared to be recruited into the East Surrey Regiment replied, 'Yes, for transfer to ASC'. With the logic peculiar to the Army he was transferred to the Border Regiment and fought with the 1st Btn at Gallipoli and in France.

WWI provided an ideal environment for the spread of diphtheria, a highly contagious disease that thrives among people in overcrowded and insanitary conditions. On 24 October 1916 Charles was admitted to hospital with the condition and died on the 27th. He was buried in Heilly Station Cemetery, Méricourt-l'Abbé, Somme. After her husband's death Alice returned to her home county, settling in Dorchester. His personal effects, which included two pipes, a toothbrush and two religious medallions, were sent to her home at 28 Miller's Close.

1917
The Battle Front

France and Belgium

The Arras Offensive, 9 April–16 June

In the spring of 1917 the French proposed an offensive at Arras while the British were to provide diversionary attacks in the same area. The British attacks began on 9 April and comprised the following engagements:

First Battle of the Scarpe, 9–14 Apr; Vimy Ridge, 9–12 Apr; First Battle of Bullecourt, 10–11 Apr; Second Battle of the Scarpe, 23–24 Apr; Battle of Arleux, 28–29 Apr; Third Battle of the Scarpe, 3–4 May; Second Battle of Bullecourt, 3–17 May.

The British operations led to some success but the French offensive was a failure.

Battle of Messines, 7–14 June

Famous for the explosion of 19 mines under the German lines. The subsequent infantry attacks succeeded in pushing the Germans off the Messines Ridge.

Third Battle of Ypres, 31 July–6 November

Commonly called Passchendaele, the Third Ypres was the battle that was fought in the mud. After the start, the rain came down and it did not stop for weeks. No less than 4.25 million shells were fired in the preliminary bombardment but the mud made it very difficult for the British infantry, who were successfully repelled by the Germans in most places. The battle trudged on until 10 November, with the British capturing Passchendaele Ridge. The principal phases of the operation were:

Battle of Pilckem Ridge, 31 Jul–2 Aug; Battle of Langemarck, 16–18 Aug; Battle of Menin Road, 20–25 Sept; Battle of Polygon Wood, 26 Sept–3 Oct; Battle of Broodseinde, 4 Oct; Battle of Poelcapelle, 9 Oct; First Battle of Passchendaele, 12 Oct; Second Battle of Passchendaele, 26 Oct–10 Nov.

Battle of Cambrai, 20 November–7 December

A large-scale attack was launched by the British at Cambrai against the Hindenburg Line. The infantry were supported by 450 tanks and the assault came as a complete surprise to the Germans. After gains on the first day the fighting continued and on 30 November the Germans counterattacked with 20 divisions pushing the British back, almost to their starting point.

Mesopotamia

Having captured the town of Kut, Gen. Maude went on to take Baghdad on 17 March. Although recognising the need to consolidate his position, he decided instead to attack and in mid-March launched the Samarrah offensive. The offensive, during which the British seized the Samarrah railway and the town of Falluja, was completed successfully but at the great cost of 18,000 casualties. Operations in Mesopotamia then wound down for the summer, although an unsuccessful attempt to capture the garrison at Ramadi did take place in July. In late September Maude decided to have another crack at the town and on 29 September the garrison surrendered. He then went on to take Tikrit on 6 November.

Palestine

Having pushed the Turks from the Sinai peninsula, Sir Archibald Murray set his sight on Gaza, in Palestine. His two attempts to clear the Turks from the area around Gaza in the spring were disastrous and led to him being recalled to London and replaced by Sir Edmund Allenby. In November Allenby captured Gaza and set out to achieve his remit from the British Government to proceed to Jerusalem and secure it by Christmas. En-route the British fought an action at El Mughar Ridge on 13 November and then went on to occupy Jerusalem on 11 December.

Salonika

In May the British gained a considerable amount of ground and repulsed strong counterattacks by the Bulgarians. [1]

---

[1] See Thomas Winwood.

1917
Roll of Honour

Pte Alfred Charles Seal – aged 19
9th Btn Devonshire Rgt – 22611
Cenotaph

The Cenotaph shows an A.L. Seal who was serving with the Dorsets when he died but the available evidence suggests that his name was put there in error, or he served with that regiment before transferring to the Devons. There is no A.C. Seal listed in the Dorset Rgt's Roll of Honour but SDGW does show him with the Devons, even though they complicate matters by misspelling his name as Leal. The matter is clarified by CWGC which shows him as A.C. Seal, son of Charles and Emily Seal of 19 The Grove. In 1911 we do, indeed, find Alfred living with his parents at this address, plus his two sisters and a couple of boarders. His father was employed as a carman with Dorchester Corporation.

One can understand why so many soldiers in war are fatalistic about their chances of survival. The often-heard comment of 'Well, if it has your name on it ...' sums up the attitude well. Alfred's fate was determined by the fact that out of the 1,100 men of the 9th Devons who were to retire to billets at Bertrancourt, Somme, on 5 January 1917, he was one of 50 who were detailed to remain in trenches. The reason for this was that it had been decided that an attempt should be made to recapture a position known as Hope Post from the Germans. By 6.20 pm the Devons had done their job but at a cost. Out of 16 casualties Alfred was one of three men recorded in the war diary as 'missing, believed killed'. He is commemorated at Serre Road Cemetery, Somme.

2 Lt Reginald Brook Holding Webb – aged 21
Indian Army Officer Reserve
Cenotaph, Holy Trinity and Thomas Hardye School Roll of Honour

Reginald Webb was born in Beverley, Yorkshire. His father was serving as a lieutenant in the East Yorkshire Rgt, which meant that the family lived in various places in England and abroad, including India. There is no evidence that they ever lived in Dorset but when it came to Reginald's education he was sent to Dorchester Grammar School.

The Indian Army Officer Reserve (IAOR), which in 1914 consisted of a very small number of retired officers, became a holding unit for newly commissioned men of the Indian Army before they were sent to a regular regiment. Reginald was commissioned into the IAOR on 9 July 1915 and then posted to the 53rd Sikh, Frontier Force, fighting in Mesopotamia as part of Gen. Maude's revitalised army. At the beginning of December 1916 Maude was confronted by two systems of Turkish defences to the north of Kut which had to be captured. The Allied troops dug their own positions over the next few weeks and came within 300 yd of the enemy's line. Then, on the night of 8/9 January 1917, in an attempt to occupy parts of the Turks' trenches, four separate raiding parties were organised, including one of the 53rd Sikhs. In what has been described as 'a singularly bloody and desperate affair', [1] all of the officers on the raids went missing and most of the rank and file. Reginald had been given the temporary rank of captain for this assault and was last seen leading his men into the night. He is commemorated on the Basra Memorial.

There remains the question of why Reginald's name should appear on the Dorchester Cenotaph and Holy Trinity Church Memorial. The answer may lie in the fact that his brother Bertie Webb may have been the person of that name who is shown on the 1918 Register of Electors living at 3 Cornwall Rd.

---

[1] Chandler, 1919.

Cpl Alfred John Valler – aged 20
5th Btn Dorsetshire Rgt – 12722
Cenotaph

When young Alfred Valler joined the Dorsets on New Year's Day 1915 he had a big reputation to live up to. That reputation belonged to his father, RSM Alfred Valler, a veteran of the regiment who came out of retirement to fight in the War. He was a well-known resident of Dorchester, living at 35 Glyde Path Rd and then at 15 Duke's Ave with his wife Alice and their family, and as an experienced NCO he was welcomed with open arms by the 5th Btn. The official history of the Dorsets comments, 'In securing RSM Valler's services the 5th were fortunate. He was to prove one of the Battalion's mainstay; an ideal man for the post.' [1] Alfred showed his mettle in Gallipoli during the attack on Turkish trenches between Hetman Chair and Susak Kuya in August 1915. Having lost most of his men he was ordered to withdraw from an impossible position but being the man he was he had other ideas. '... the RSM was contemplating going back into it with such men as he had got to make a finish of it, as all the rest of the Battalion had gone.' [2] He did not go in again and lived to see the end of the War. Alas, the same could not be said for his son.

Like his father, young Alfred also fought with the 5th Btn in Gallipoli and then went with them to France in July 1916, taking part in the September attack on the Zollern Redoubt. [3] Later, on 10 January 1917, he, with the remainder of his company, moved into the British front line near Beaucourt for an attack the next day. The prospects were not good; very little was known of the German positions, the ground was so muddy that the troops could only move slowly and the nature of the land made concealment impossible. Zero hour came at 6 am and two companies advanced into the darkness accompanied by an artillery barrage. Their objectives were successfully accomplished but, unluckily, when daylight came it was with freezing fog and a blinding snow-storm. The Germans then made a sudden counterattack, which drove the Dorsets from the trenches, several being cut off while retiring. By the end of the day 26 of the battalion had been killed, 92 were missing and 52 wounded. Alfred was among the severely wounded and died 3 days later. He was buried at Varennes Military Cemetery, Somme.

[1] Regimental history.
[2] Ibid.
[3] See George Ford.

Pte Kenneth MacDonald – aged 26
4th Australian Trench Mortar Bty
Fordington Cemetery

The *Chronicle* of 15 February 1917 reported that 'Kenneth MacDonald, one of the gallant Anzacs whose deeds of heroism in the Operations in the Gallipoli Peninsula will be immortalised, passed away on Wednesday.' The son of Hector MacDonald of Glasgow, Kenneth was in Australia when war broke out, and formed part of one of the first contingents that left the Antipodes to fight for the motherland. He took part in the fierce fighting at the Suvla Bay landing and was later invalided to England with an attack of enteric fever.

Presumably at some time during his sick leave Kenneth found himself in Dorchester, for it was there that he married Hilda Gill of 1 Maud Rd in the last quarter of 1916 and a daughter Ivy was born of the union the following summer. Unfortunately, the infant would never know her father, as he died whilst his wife was pregnant. When Kenneth was well he returned to the fighting but was wounded at Gueudecourt on the Somme in January 1917. He was sent home to the Royal Victoria Hospital, Southampton, [1] and it was there that he died on 7 February. His body was returned to Dorchester on 8 February and rested in St Mary's Church until his burial the next day in Fordington Cemetery.

[1] The Royal Victoria Military Hospital was built after the Crimean War to train army nurses and doctors and to treat patients and ensure their swift return to duty. Southampton was chosen as its location so that patients could be taken there straight off the ships in the docks.

Pte Alfred Henry Stainer – aged 30
5th Btn Dorsetshire Rgt – 18172
Cenotaph

Alfred was the eldest son of mason's labourer John Stainer and his wife Mary Jane and when he was 21 he married his older cousin Charlotte. Alfred was one of those unfortunate soldiers whose death was caused by the unsanitary conditions of war when, whilst serving with the 5th Btn Dorsets on the Western Front, he was taken ill with dysentery, from which he died on 11 February. His body was interred in Etaples Military Cemetery. At the time of his death his widowed mother was living at 20 The Grove.

Pte Henry Elliot – aged 47
Royal Defence Corps – 12706
Fordington Cemetery

The elevated site used for the German prison camp in Dorchester is a pastoral delight in summer but in the winter it can be cold, wet and windy. To protect the prisoners from the elements wooden huts were built, similar to those shown on the proverbial POW films. When it came to guarding the prisoners the job was initially given to soldiers of regular regiments but in 1917 the Royal Defence Corps was established and they took on the role. However, unlike the Home Guard of WWII they were not just recruited locally but came from far and wide and whilst the enemy captives were ensconced in their heated huts their guards were sleeping in bell tents.

January 1917 was particularly wet, the *London Times* reporting that thousands of acres were under water across the land. [1] Living in tents in such weather was hardly conducive to healthy living and so it was no surprise when one of the prison guards, Henry Elliot, was admitted to the County Hospital with bronchitis. He did not recover from his illness and passed away on 14 February. He was buried in Fordington Cemetery with full military honours.

[1] *London Times* 1/1/1917.

Pte William Ernest Gosling – aged 34
1/4th Btn Royal Hampshire Rgt – 204114
Cenotaph

Frederick Gosling had reached the rank of colour sergeant and on retirement settled in Dorchester with his family at 19 Maie Terr. His second son William joined the regiment in 1899 and served with the Colours for 8 years, six of which were spent in India. When the 1st Btn arrived home in Gosport in 1907, he got a job in Southampton docks with the LSWR, but 'the soldiering instinct took control of him on the outbreak of war, and shortly afterwards he joined another regiment'. [1] He chose the Hampshires and it was not long before he was back in India with the 1/4th Btn. After what the Chronicle described as a considerable time of inactivity he volunteered to join the fighting in Mesopotamia and sailed from Bombay on 28 December 1916.

After an unsuccessful attack on the Turkish forces at Sannaiyat on 17 February 1917 Lt-Gen. Maude decided to attempt a crossing of the River Tigris, whilst, at the same time, launching another attack on Sannaiyat. William was one of those who had to cross the river just before light on the 23rd and everything went well until the first craft was about two-thirds across. Then, the Turks opened up with shell and rifle fire. Lt R.B. Stokes, a Sapper present at the time, commented, 'Hell of a morning, bullets flying free all the time and we were shelled continuously'.[2] By the end of the day the Hampshires had incurred 100 casualties and the Turks had withdrawn from their position. William was among the casualties, killed in action. He is commemorated on the Basra Memorial.

[1] *Chronicle* 22/3/1917.
[2] Carver, 2003.

Able Seaman Harry Shirley – aged 20
HMS Paragon, RN – J/25493
Cenotaph

On the night of 17 March 1917 the destroyer *HMS Paragon* was patrolling in the Dover Straits. As part of the Dover Patrol she was checking the submarine barrage that had been laid down to prevent German submarines from entering into the Straits which was not only busy with merchant shipping but also carried the armada of craft taking men and supplies to the War in Europe. At about 10.50 pm a German destroyer flotilla sailed into the area with the object of breaking the barrage and encountered the *Paragon*, which immediately began to flash a challenge. The response was swift and decisive; a single torpedo accompanied by gunfire hit the *Paragon* which broke in half and she sank within 8 minutes. Unfortunately, some of the ship's own depth charges exploded killing some of the survivors. Of the crew of 77 only two survived.

Among the bodies that were not recovered was that of Harry Shirley, whose parents lived at 25 Alexandra Rd. Harry was born in January 1897 in Bagshot, Surrey, where his family settled after his father's premature retirement from the Army after being wounded. At the age of 16 young Harry left his job as a gardener and joined the Navy as a boy sailor and, after training at *HMS Impregnable* in Devonport, served on a number of capital ships, including the cruiser *Endymion* and the battleship *Agincourt*. He joined the *Paragon* on 14 June 1916, which up to the point of her sinking had had an uneventful career. Harry is commemorated on the Portsmouth Naval Memorial and his name appears in the Dover Straits Memorial Book, which is kept in Dover Town Hall.

5th Engineer Officer John William Pitfield – aged 25
HMHS Asturias, Mercantile Marine
Cenotaph and St George's

The one thing that connected all the places where William Pitfield lived during his working life was the London to Weymouth railway line. He was born in Dorchester and as a young man went to work as a ticket inspector with the LSWR in London. It was there that he met Annie Adams whom he married and took to Weymouth where they had their only son John, in January 1892. William was now an engine driver and the job meant another change of house, this time to Bournemouth, where their daughter Edith came into the world. The family finally settled in Dorchester where they resided at 'Chapel Lawn', 114 Maumbury Way.

At 19 John Pitfield, like his father, was employed on the railway but then decided on a career change and joined the merchant navy as an engineer. At just after midnight on the morning of 21 March 1917 the villagers of Salcombe in Devon were woken by the sound of motorboats moving into the estuary and they were asked to bring blankets and clothing to the survivors of a ship that had been torpedoed off the coast. The vessel concerned was the hospital ship *Asturias* which was on passage to its home port of Southampton after discharging about 900 wounded at Avonmouth. The single

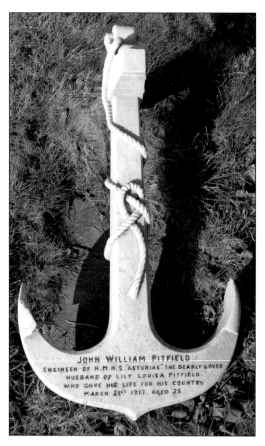

John Pitfield's grave in Weymouth Avenue Cemetery.

torpedo, which came from the German submarine *UC 66*, damaged the rudder and entered the engine room where John would normally have been working. The Captain grounded the ship in Starehole Bay, whilst those on board climbed into the boats, but John was not among the survivors. He was one of the 42 crew members who were either killed outright or died of their wounds after being brought ashore. His body was returned to Dorchester and buried in Weymouth Avenue Cemetery.

As one can imagine the attack on the hospital ship caused considerable outrage and was widely reported in the British and American press. According to a member of the RAMC on board, the ship was sailing with full navigation lights and the large red crosses on the sides of the vessel were clearly visible. A statement of apology was issued by the German Ambassador, who claimed that the ship was mistaken as a troop transporter, as she carried the normal navigation lights of a steamer and the crosses on her sides were not illuminated.

Pte Ernest Henry Mills – aged 23
2nd Btn Dorsetshire Rgt – 16412
Cenotaph and Holy Trinity

The 2nd Dorsets had been involved in the hardest of the fighting to reach Baghdad in Mesopotamia and on 17 March 1917 the city was taken without a fight. The next task of the Anglo-Indian force was to encircle the defeated Turkish troops before they could rendezvous with the main force. The British Gen. Keary intended to squeeze the retiring Turks between his own army and that of the retreating Russians; however, unbeknown to him the revolution in Russia had gained hold and the Russians had ceased operations in Persia, leaving him to pursue the Turks alone. Meanwhile, 4,500 Turkish troops had dug in on high ground at the foot of the Jebel Hamlin Mountains, behind two canals. Keary decided to begin an attack on them on 25 March, after bridging the canals. At 9.30 pm on 24 March the Dorsets were among the soldiers who filed across the second canal to prepare for the assault next morning, an attack that would result in the death of three Dorchester men.

The Dorsets advanced with their brigade at first light and soon realised that they not only were opposing a very well prepared force, but also had to negotiate a very confusing landscape, consisting of a labyrinth of mounds and gullies. Some progress was made but by 7 am the enemy fire was so great that the men could progress no further. At 8 am a strong counterattack developed and the 2nd Btn made a stand, selling their lives dearly. By the early afternoon Gen. Keary came to the conclusion that nothing more could be done and ordered the Dorsets to withdraw. The 2nd Btn incurred 200 casualties and included in the 100 or so that went missing was Ernest Mills of Dorchester.

In September 1917 Ernest's sister received a letter at her home in Maie Terrace from a soldier telling her that her brother had been killed, but it was not until March 1919 that she received official notification. Ernest, a railway porter, was the youngest son of William and Emily Mills, both of whom had died before the War. He is commemorated on the Basra Memorial.

L/Cpl Malcolm Mitchell Loveless – aged 23
2nd Btn Dorsetshire Rgt – 16364
Cenotaph

On 12 April 1917 the *Chronicle* published a letter from Mr Smith of the Dorset County Stores, High East Street, which read: 'I regret to inform you that one of my most trusted young men, Malcolm Loveless has been killed in action. Personally, I thought a great deal of him. He was a cheerful, sunny soul, whom everyone liked, and now he has given his life for his country I feel bound to give him this public testimony of my greatest respect. His name must now be added to the Dorset Roll of Honour.' [1] Malcolm worked at the County Stores for 17 years and lived with his aunt, Mrs Moore of 8 Durngate St. He was not a native of Dorchester but was born in Athelhampton, a hamlet to the east of Dorchester, and was brought up in various parts of the county due to his father's occupation. In 1901 the family was living at Cranborne Manor, home of the Marquess of Salisbury, where his father Fred was a caretaker gardener.

Malcolm was another young soldier who was killed in action at Jebel Hamlin on 25 March. [2] His name joined those of Ernest Mills and Thomas Adams on the Basra Memorial.

[1] *Chronicle* 12/4/1917.
[2] See Ernest Mills.

Pte Thomas Adams – aged 33
2nd Btn Dorsetshire Rgt – 16409
Cenotaph and St Peter's

Thomas Adams was the last of the trio of Durnovarians to die at Jebel Hamlin on 25 March but unfortunately it is not clear who he was. A clue to where he was living is in the fact that he is mentioned on the memorial plaque inside St Peter's which commemorates 'members of the parish who gave their lives'. However, the waters are somewhat muddied by the fact that the Rev Filleul [1] reported in the All Saints' church magazine of September 1917 that, 'Thomas Adams, reported missing on 25 March must, I fear be also amongst the lost', suggesting some connection with that church. The most likely candidate is the Thomas Adams who lived at Alington Terrace in Durngate Street, as the others all came from Fordington. His father was Robert Adams a fish dealer and his mother was Elizabeth. In any event, Thomas is remembered on the Basra Memorial.

---

[1] Rev Samuel Filleul

Pte Bertie Silas Dyer – aged 28
2nd Coy, RAMC – 66138
Cenotaph

Blink and you will miss the entrance to Agra Place in Dorchester. One feature of the town is the number of terraces that are tucked away from the hurly-burly of normal street life and Agra Place is one of them, situated at the end of South Street, on the eastern side. Living at No. 1 in 1891 were Frederick and Mary Jane Dyer with their four sons, including 4-year-old Bertie. As well as being employed as a gardener Frederick was an ardent member of the Salvation Army, of which he was treasurer of the local Corps, which then had its headquarters in North Square. His son Bertie attended Sunday school in his boyhood and became an equally committed Salvationist as his father. With a particular gift for music he was a member of the Salvation Army band and also the Corp's secretary.

By 1901 the circumstances of the Dyer family had changed somewhat. Mary Jane had become a widow and was now living at 14 Prospect Terr, and two daughters had been added to the family between censuses. Bertie had entered into the world of new technology when he started a bicycle repair business in Greyhound Yard at the other end of South Street. In March 1914 he married Mary Ingram and the couple set up home at 14 Dagmar Terr, on the newly developing Victoria Park Estate.

When Salvationist Bandmaster Barnes was called up for military service a popular choice of deputy was made in bandsman Dyer, who held the post for the short period before his own enlistment in the Army on 6 August 1916. Bertie joined the RAMC and was posted to the 2nd Coy and then joined the largest of the hospital ships, *HMHS Aquitania*. This luxurious Cunard liner, which had previously seen service as an armed merchant cruiser and troopship, now carried 4,182 beds and Bertie transferred to it on 6 September 1916, not realising that he was far from fit. He had been suffering from nephritis for over a year and his symptoms got worse, necessitating his removal to Connaught Hospital at Aldershot. Unfortunately, little could be done for him and he died on 27 March 1917.

Bertie was brought back to Dorchester and given a Salvation Army funeral. The service was held outside his home, where two of his favourite hymns were sung before the cortege left in procession for Fordington Cemetery, the band he loved so much leading the way.

Pte Hedley Beck – aged 28
2nd Btn Wiltshire Rgt – 26734
Cenotaph

Three years before the outbreak of war the widow Elizabeth Howe was running a bakers and confectioners at 17 Cornhill, with the assistance of two of her children, Sidney and 24-year-old Beatrice. Meanwhile, in Tiverton, Devon, Reginald Beck operated an ironmonger's business with the help of his 20-year-old brother Hedley. We do not know when or how the two families first met but in 1915 Beatrice and Hedley married in Dorchester and it appears that they then lived in the town. On 21 March 1918 the following article appeared in the *Chronicle*: 'MRS BECK'S BEREAVEMENT – Mrs Hedley Beck of 17 Cornhill has received official announcement that her husband, on active service, who has been missing since 9 April last, was killed in action on that date. Warm sympathy will be felt for Mrs Beck, whom within a short time has been bereaved by mother, brother and husband.'

In the early minutes of 9 April 1917 the men of the 2nd Btn Wiltshire Rgt were waiting to go over the top, as part of a major offensive on the German Hindenburg Line. At 1.30 am a party went forward to attack a target known as The Mill, southeast of Arras, but met with considerable resistance and had to retire with heavy casualties. At 5.30 am the main attack commenced. The distance between the assembly positions and the target was about 2,000 yd and when the battalion moved off it was not long before they encountered considerable hostile shelling, which persisted throughout the attack. To reach their objective the troops had to cross two sunken roads and it was between these that they were met by withering machine gun fire. Despite this, the remaining troops pushed forwards to the German barbed wire, only to find that although it had been damaged it still provided an impassable barrier. By this time the Wiltshires had been considerably depleted and those who were left retired to one of the sunken roads they had just crossed. They managed to consolidate their position and held out until the evening despite heavy shelling of the road and retired after being relieved by the 16th Manchesters. It had been a black day for the 2nd Btn and when the roll call was made it was discovered that casualties sustained during two attacks amounted to 16 officers and 365 OR. Hedley was among the casualties but his body was not found. He is commemorated on the Arras Memorial.

Gnr Arthur Edward Williams – age unknown
9th Btn King's Royal Rifle Corps – A/1760
Cenotaph

The Cenotaph shows the name A.E. Williams as serving with the Rifle Brigade. The most likely candidate is an Arthur Edward Williams of the 9th Btn Rifle Bde, born in Fordington, living in Wells, Somerset, and enlisted in Taunton. He died of wounds on 14 April 1917 [1] and was buried in Duisans British Cemetery, Etrun, Pas-de-Calais. Although he was born in the town, I have been unable to trace his family with certainty, although the 1901 census does show an Arthur E. Williams, born 1880, living at 3 Albert Rd.

---

[1] SDGW shows the 14th but the CWGC gives the 12th.

Gnr Arthur Edwin Prowse – aged 28
11th Bty, 165th Bde, RFA
Cenotaph and St George's

(Source: Mr R. Prowse.)

Life must have been difficult for Robert and Caroline Prowse in the 1890s, trying to bring up their eight children in the overcrowded and unhealthy environment of Mill Street. Robert worked at Eldridge Pope's brewery for over 30 years and it was with the help of his employer that he was able to improve his family's circumstances by moving them to 1 St George's Rd, on the edge of town. By the 1911 census we find that Caroline had produced 13 children, 11 of whom survived, and that the family was now residing at 18 Alington Rd.

Arthur was the fourth eldest son and like his father worked for the brewery. In February 1916 he joined the Army and proceeded to France in September. He was serving with the 165th Bde RFA when he was killed on 15 April 1917, during the Arras offensive. He was buried in Roclincourt Valley Cemetery, Pas-de-Calais. In a letter to the bereaved parents the officer in charge of his battery wrote,
'Your son was a very gallant and a very good soldier. He was in my section and one of the best men I had. I could always trust him to do anything and he always did his best.' [1] The Chaplain of the unit wrote a very touching letter to Arthur's brother, in which he said, 'In a little grave near the gun which he served I laid to rest your brother with three of his comrades, all of whom were respected and loved by their officers and fellow men. The life and sacrifice of your brother will help us to love the things for which he died, and to hate with an ever-increasing hatred the things which caused his death.' [2] In remembrance of their son Robert and Caroline placed a notice in the *Chronicle* on the anniversary of his death, containing the following verse:

> *He nobly answered duties' call,*
> *His life he gave for one and all.*
> *A loving son, a brother kind,*
> *A beautiful memory left behind.*

[1] *Chronicle* 3/5/1917.
[2] Ibid.

L/Cpl Frederick William Goldring – aged 36
6th Btn Dorsetshire Rgt – 17421
Cenotaph

The name Pease Lane has long disappeared from the maps of Dorchester. Now it is named Colliton Street; a quiet, narrow thoroughfare running behind High West Street, it was once a busy little community with a public house, a shop, blacksmith's and the Dorchester Boy's School. In 1881 the population of the lane increased by one, when Annie Goldring gave birth to a baby son which she and her husband William named Frederick. Annie already had one son, Walter, and would go on to produce six more children, of whom only two would outlive her. By 1891 the family had moved house to Great Western Terrace off Maumbury Way, and the 1901 census shows them residing at 5 Victoria Rd. Frederick was then 19 years of age and it must have been of some pride to his parents that he was working as a clerk in a chartered accountants office, something that in those days would have been seen as a step up from his father's job as a porter in a wine merchants. By 1911 Annie and William had moved to 9 Alexandra Rd.

When war came Frederick went to the recruiting office in Dorchester and joined the Dorsets, being posted to the 6th Btn. In April 1917 the 6th Dorsets were in the Arras region preparing to take part in an offensive on the German Hindenburg Line. After an unsuccessful attack on 12 April, which the regimental history described as 'a melancholy waste', the Dorsets retired to Arras Caves. The possible circumstances surrounding Frederick's death on the 22nd are recorded in the battalion war diary: 'Whilst Btn was filing out of Caves, a shell fell just at the head of the exit killing 6 and wounding 6 ….' Alternatively, a notice inserted in the *Chronicle* by his parents suggests that he went missing before he was declared killed in action, intimating that Frederick died in battle. [1] Whatever his fate, he is commemorated on the Arras Memorial.

---

[1] *Chronicle* 26/7/1917.

Pte Albert Charlie Etheridge – aged 20
1st Btn Duke of Cornwall's Light Infantry – 31696
Cenotaph

The sign hanging at the entrance of Antelope Walk, Cornhill, gives some indication of its former use. The Antelope Hotel was one of Dorchester's coaching inns and among the staff working there just before the War was Albert Etheridge. He lived with his parents Alexander and Emily at 4 Burleston Terr, Maumbury Way, [1] and it may well have been the case that his father also worked at the Antelope as an ostler. Albert enlisted in the Dorsets and was at some time transferred to the 1st Btn DCLI, serving with them in France.

On 19 April 1917 the Cornwalls were holding part of the Front running from the Arras–Lens road to the Souchez river, which was being subjected to heavy shelling, sniper and machine gun fire. The 23rd was the date chosen for a second attempt to penetrate the German line in what would become known as the Second Battle of the Scarpe. Facing Albert and his comrades were very strong German defences, protected by three extensive fields of barbed wire. Zero hour for the assault was set at 4.30 am and the Cornwalls moved up to the assembly line the evening before. Then came the sleepless night, waiting for the order to advance into no man's land. At 4.45 am the men were on the move, accompanied by an artillery barrage. They eventually reached the German wire to find that the British guns had not done their job and it was still largely intact. Under fire, they had to seek refuge in shell holes. There next developed a fierce bombing battle with the Germans in their trenches but no further headway could be made and the remaining men retired and established a line a little further back. By this time casualties were severe but the Cornwalls held their position until 9 pm, when they were relieved by the 14th Royal Warwicks. Albert was among those killed in action on that day and is commemorated on the Arras Memorial.

[1] Now 41 Monmouth Rd.

Pte Arthur John Rendell – aged 27
12th Btn Hampshire Rgt – 31974
Cenotaph

The Green [1] and Hansford families had at least two things in common. Firstly, at different times they both lived at 69 Holloway Rd and, secondly, they both had reasons to grieve because of the War, the Greens losing two sons and the Hansfords a son-in-law. Florence Hansford was the daughter of Henry who worked as a labourer with the town council, and it may well have been through him that she met her future husband Arthur who was similarly employed. Arthur was the son of John and Caroline Rendell and although born in Dorchester he spent most of his childhood in other parts of the county, as his father followed the demands for his work as an agricultural labourer. Florence and Arthur married in the Dorchester Registrar's Office on 11 May 1913 but the marriage was fated to be a short one. Arthur joined the Dorsets but then found himself in Greece fighting against the Bulgarians with the 12th Btn Hampshires.

Had Arthur been able to read C.T. Atkinson's regimental history of the Hampshire Rgt, published after the War, he might have been forgiven for reporting sick on 23 April 1917. The next day his battalion was about to launch an attack and sitting in his trench he would have read the following: 'Nobody who had faced the Petit Couronné and the neighbouring defences for several months could have had any illusions about the desperate character of the venture. Our bombardment had done little damage to the Bulgarian defences, their trenches having largely been blasted from the solid rock, the wire had not been very effectively cut and our guns had quite failed to master those of the enemy, who had every advantage in observation and knew the ranges to a nicety.' [2] But, of course, Arthur and his fellow soldiers of the 12th Btn did not know the situation; they did not know that the wire was still largely intact or that the enemy's guns were waiting for some sign of movement upon which they could let fly their barrage of death.

The 12th Btn began its advance at 9.45 pm up a narrow gully and as it did so the shells began to fall among the men. The steep sides of the gully made matters worse and it soon turned into an inferno, the Hampshires' way blocked by the dead and wounded of the Devons ahead of them. Despite this some of the Hampshires did manage to get through the wire and gained a foothold on their objective, only to invite further shelling and enfilading fire from their right. Then, the counterattacks began, making the whole position untenable and a withdrawal was ordered.

The attack had been a disastrous failure and inevitably casualties were high. The Hampshires lost15 officers and 249 OR were casualties. The Devons incurred over 400 casualties. Arthur was killed and is remembered on the Doiran Memorial, northern Greece.

---

[1] See Thomas Green.
[2] Atkinson, 1952.

Capt. Thomas Ralph Okeden Winwood MC – aged 31
B Bty, 99 Bde, RFA
Cenotaph and St Peter's

Among the families listed in the 1919 edition of *The County Families of the United Kingdom* [1] is that of Thomas Henry Rickets Winwood. In 1885 this retired army officer and Justice of the Peace was living in the Manor House at Wellisford, near Wellington in Somerset, and in that same year his wife Mabel gave birth to their first son, Thomas. By the time he was six the family had headed south to the coast and moved into 17 Brunswick Terr, one of an imposing row of houses in Weymouth. As befitting his place in society, when it was time for young Thomas to go to school he boarded at Clifton College, Bristol, and then Winchester College, but on completing his schooling he did not attempt to enter the usual doors to employment offered by such an education but decided to seek his fortune abroad. He headed for Argentina and then, around 1908, moved to Canada where he worked as a rancher for a couple of years, after which he had earned enough to buy his own ranch in Millarville, Alberta. Thomas obviously kept contact with his homeland because, in 1911, he visited and married Mabel Katherine Middleton of Bradford House, Bradford Peverell, a village to the west of Dorchester. Thomas then returned to Canada and continued ranching until misfortune struck; when he found that he could not pay his creditors and after being served with a summons for bankruptcy, he lost his ranch. He continued to work in Canada for a while, returning to England to answer the writ.

Despite his financial problems, or perhaps because of them, Thomas entered the War by applying for a temporary commission, declaring his experience with horses and giving the address of his next of kin as Rothesay House, Dorchester, where his parents were living. [2] His commission was granted and 9 months later he disembarked to France with the 99th Brigade, RFA but was not destined to stay there for long. Thomas was on his way to one of the lesser known areas of conflict, the Front in Greece.

With its strategic position and well-known animosity towards the Turks, Greece was wooed by the British and the French to join them in the War. However, the Greeks were unwilling to commit to the Allies, probably largely due to the Pro-German sympathies of their king who had married the Kaiser's daughter. However, they did allow British and French forces to disembark at Salonika, en route to help Serbia, but by the time the Allied forces were ready Serbia had fallen and the Austrians and Bulgarians were poised on the Greek border. The Allies turned Salonika into a huge fortified camp and during 1916 they made steady advances towards the enemy. An attempt to break the Bulgarian defences began on 22 April 1917 and became known as the Battle of Doiran. Thomas took part in the initial assault, which consisted of bombarding the Bulgarian lines with 100,000 shells, followed up by infantry attacks on 24th and 25th but, after much bloody fighting, the British troops were repulsed. Throughout the battle a fierce artillery duel took place and William, who had been promoted to temporary captain on 28 October 1916, became one of the 12,000 British casualties. S. Sayers describes Thomas's death in his biography of 'Ned' Herring, [3] 'Herring served as an Artillery Observer, directing fire in support of the 22nd Division's attack from a point on Pip Ridge. There was a furious artillery duel. 20 minutes after Capt. Thomas Winwood took Herring's place as forward observer the observation post took a direct hit from an enemy shell killing Winwood.' [4] Shortly before his death Thomas performed an act of gallantry for which he was awarded the Military Cross. His body was interred at Karasouli Military Cemetery, Greece.

The telegram telling Mabel of her husband's death was sent to her at Bradford Peverell on 5 May and his belongings were eventually returned after she had gone through what must have been a distressing time trying to get them from Canada where they had been inadvertently sent. Thomas's parents heard the news at Syward Lodge, Dorchester, where they had recently moved. The Winwoods had become a well-known family in the town; Thomas Senior was a prominent member of Fordington Church and he and his wife let the children of the Mill Street Mission use their garden for picnics.

There is a sad postscript to the story of Thomas Winwood. His service record contains a letter sent from a Nan Berry to his CO, explaining that she had written to Thomas in reply to a letter from him informing her of a dear friend's death, but her letter had been returned unopened. The officer had then to inform her that since her friend's death Thomas had also been killed.

[1] Walford, Edward (1919) *The County Families of the United Kingdom*. Vol. 59.
[2] Rothesay House was once the home of Llewelyn Powys, the writer, and during WWII it was used as a hostel for Land Army girls.
[3] Lt-Gen. the Hon. Sir Edmund Francis Herring, KCMG, KBE DSO, MC, ED, QC (1892–1982).
[4] S. Sayers, 1980.

Pte George Young – aged 25
1st Btn Dorsetshire Rgt – 9759
Cenotaph and St Peter's

George Young was a regular soldier from Lymington, who joined the Dorsets in May 1914. He did his training with the 3rd Btn before being posted to Belfast and it has to be said that his first few months were not without incident. George seemed to have a problem with NCOs. In August, for instance, he was punished for hesitating to comply with an order, then in October he was found guilty of threatening a lance corporal, and finally, in December, he received 14 days' detention for swearing at one.

This incongruity with his immediate superiors did not prevent him being posted to the

1st Btn in France where things only got worse for him. In March 1915 George was admitted into hospital with frostbite and he was returned to the UK for 5 months, after which he was sent back to the Front on entrenching duties. His return to the 1st Btn occurred on 16 January 1916 but it was not long before he was absent again, this time through an infection of the middle ear. After a spell in a rest camp it was back to the battalion, just in time for the Battle of the Somme, where he was severely wounded in the arm on 2 July, resulting in another return to Blighty for treatment and recovery. After discharge from hospital George arrived in Dorchester where a young girl was waiting for him. Lily Cheeseman was a Dorchester lass who lived at 14 Friary Lane with her parents, and on 19 October the couple were married at St Peter's Church. Lily had 2 months with her new husband before she had to wave goodbye to him, not knowing that it would be the last time they would embrace.

George rejoined the 1st Btn resting at Berteaucourt, Somme, just before Christmas. January 1917 brought with it the Battle of Ancre, fought in a winter described in the regimental history as 'the worst experienced during the War'. April came accompanied by snow and one day George left his machine gun section to join the queue of men reporting to the MO. He was referred to 36th Casualty Clearing Station, Heilly, before being admitted to hospital, where he died from pneumonia on 27 April. His body lies in Cayeux Military Cemetery, Somme.

Four months after George's death his new bride received the few effects of his that would add to her memories of him. They consisted of letters, photographs, razors, two religious books, a ring, belt, dice and pocket book.

Sgt George James Knight – aged 24
1st Btn Somerset Light Infantry – 9777
Cenotaph and St Peter's

By 1917 the people of Dorchester knew that if they turned to page four of the *Chronicle* they were likely to see yet another list of casualties or, worse, details of a relative, friend or acquaintance who would not be returning home. On 31 May the newspaper reported that 'Another well-known Durnovarian has made the supreme sacrifice'. The Durnovarian in question was George Knight, who was born in Dorchester, the eldest son of George and Elizabeth Knight, and as a child he lived in Glyde Path Road, where he doubtless played with his neighbour Alfred Valler, another victim of the War. [1]

George Junior worked as a butcher's assistant, prior to enlisting with some of his friends just before war was declared. He proceeded to the Front in May 1915 and was wounded in the July. He did not return to the firing line until September 1916, just in time to take part in the1st Btn's fighting in the mud around the Ypres Salient. In the spring of 1917 George, who had now gained three sergeant's stripes, was training in preparation for the Arras campaign, which began on 9 April. The 1st Somersets took part in three major attacks in the period up to 13 May and incurred nearly 450 casualties. George was killed in action on 9 May and is commemorated on the Arras Memorial.

---

[1] See Alfred Valler.

Pte Percy Frederick Blandamer – aged 18
6th Btn Dorsetshire Rgt – 16260
Cenotaph

As the 19th century turned into the 20th railway labourer Philip Blandamer and his family were living at Sandford, near Wareham, but he had connections with Dorchester where he was born and where he had cousins living. Philip married Elizabeth Clothier from Bath in 1886 and 10 years later she gave birth to their youngest son Percy, who after leaving school found a job as a garden boy.

Percy entered the War when he enlisted in the Dorsetshire Rgt and served with one of the battalions that were stationed in the Far East, from whence he was invalided home. After 2 months' convalescence he was transferred to the 6th Btn, which had been fighting in France since July 1915. In early May 1917 the 6th were preparing for a big offensive around 'The Scarpe' near Arras. This started on the evening of the 12th and continued until the 15th and in the bitter fighting that took place both Percy and Albert Martin [1] were killed. Percy died on 14 May and is commemorated on the Arras Memorial. His mother, a widow since 1910, was living at 18 Dagmar Rd.

[1] See Albert Martin.

Pte William Richard Newberry – aged 27
Machine Gun Corps – 42756
Cenotaph

There is some confusion with this person because his name is misspelt as Newbury on the Cenotaph, although he does appear correctly as Newberry in an addition of the St George's Church magazine and the death of a W.R. Newberry appeared in the 'Deaths' section of the *Chronicle* on 14 June 1917. William Newberry was born in Miller's Close and lived next door to Bertram Shorto, who was also a victim of the War.[1] His parents were Richard, a porter in a wine store, and Annie. In 1911 William married Martha Swyer and lived in Weymouth where he worked on the railway.

When war came William joined the Dorsets and at some time transferred to the MGC. Unfortunately, the unit he served with is not recorded so it is not possible to be precise about where he was killed in action. However, we do know that he died on 16 May and is remembered on the Arras Memorial.

[1] See Bertram Shorto.

Sgt William James West – aged 26
53rd Bty, 2nd Bde, RFA – 57633

Pte Cecil Ernest West – aged 19
2nd Btn Worcestershire Rgt – 207407

Both are remembered on the Cenotaph

Dorchester was not slow in taking on the new modes of transport that were developing at the turn of the century. Alfred Tilley was selling bicycles at the bottom of South Street, Edward Channon was making motor cars in High East Street and people like Arthur Caruthers-Little [1] could be seen riding about the town on their splendid motorcycles. But, contemporary photographs show that despite these new inventions it was the horse that still provided the predominant means of transport. Shop keepers had their own carts and horse-drawn vans, carriers came in from the villages on Wednesdays and Saturdays loaded with goods, and the big houses in the town, like South Court and Wollaston House, had their stables, which provided employment for men like James West who worked in Dorchester as a groom.

In 1886 James married Sarah Trevett and they went on to have seven children but tragically only two lived beyond 1918. Three of them died of natural causes, whilst two of the boys, William and Cecil, perished in the War. William was born in 1891 when his parents were living in Icen Road [2] and when he left school he obtained employment with the *Chronicle*. He answered his country's call at the beginning of the War, disembarking for France on 11 September 1914. He was killed at Mazingarbe near Fromelles on 18 May 1917, while serving with the 53rd Bty of the RFA. William was buried in Philosophe British Cemetery, Pas-de-Calais.

The widow Sarah, who had lost her husband in 1908, received the news of her son's death at her home at 7 Victoria Bldgs, Fordington Hill, and mixed with her feelings of grief must have been those of anxiety for her son Cecil who had just reached the age of eligibility for the Army. Cecil worked as an assistant for Joseph Hodder, the butcher, at 14 High East St and originally signed up with the Dorsets before being transferred to the 2nd Worcesters. He had only been at the Front for about 3 weeks before he was wounded on 6 June 1918 and died on the same day in a hospital near Esquelbecq in Nord. His headstone stands in Esquelbecq Military Cemetery. A report on Cecil's death appeared in the St George's Church magazine, accompanied by the following verse:

> *West went to fight for what we cherish best,*
> *And, facing death, home to his God went West.*

---

[1] See Arthur Caruthers-Little, who owned a motorbike and sidecar.
[2] Now part of Icen Way.

Pte Charles Henry Pope – aged 25
5th Btn Dorsetshire Rgt – 18045
Cenotaph, St Peter's and St George's

On the platform of Dorchester South railway station a young soldier said goodbye to his wife and little boy. . Stepping onto the train heading for Southampton, he did not know that he would never see them again. [1] Charles was attached to a Lewis Gun Crew as part of the 5th Btn Dorsets and had barely 12 months' service under his belt when he was fatally wounded. He died on 23 May in a military hospital at Boulogne and was buried in Boulogne Eastern Cemetery.

Charles was born in Dorchester, the son of Alfred and Annie Pope of Harvey's Buildings, Fordington Hill, and as a boy he attended All Saints' Church, where he was a chorister and had the unenviable task of working the bellows on the organ. When he left school Charles got a job as an upholsterer with the firm of Hannah and Holland, [2] where he worked for 11 years before joining up. In 1914 he married Susan Mowlam and little William arrived a year later. The couple lived at 8 Fordington Hill, and it was there that Susan received a letter from a 2 Lt L. Pool, who wrote, 'As Lewis gun officer to the battalion I hasten to offer you my sincerest sympathy. My work brought me into contact a lot with your husband, and I had formed a high opinion of his work. He was at the time acting as my storeman, and I had put him on that job as I knew that I could rely on him to carry out the necessary work in a thorough way.' [3]

[1] Churchill, A.B. (1960) Where are the Bhoys of the village?. *Dorset Year Book 1960/61.*
[2] Hannah and Holland, with premises at 8 South St, provided all sort of services, including upholstery, cabinet-making, undertaking and insurance.
[3] *Chronicle* 3/5/1917 and 14/6/1917.

Pte William Bussell – aged 64
Depot, Dorsetshire Rgt – 11673
Cenotaph

William Bussell could often be heard in the streets of Dorchester before he was seen. Military bands were a familiar sight in the town and William was the bass drummer of the 'Old Volunteers' and is one of the oldest men to appear on Dorchester's Great War memorials. Born in 1853 he lived with his parents, Charles, a coal carrier, and Sarah, in Miller's Close at the bottom of The Grove. When he left school he went to work at the Eldridge Pope brewery as a labourer and in 1876 married Francesca Lane, the daughter of another coal carrier. At some time William became a regular soldier for a while

Commemorative scroll presented with the memorial plaque to William's next-of-kin. (Source: Mr D. Bussell.)

with the Cheshire Rgt and on return to civilian life went back to labouring.

The family lived at 29 Colliton St, where Francesca died in 1900. When the War came along William was determined to do his bit but was too old to go to the Front. Instead, he was duly enlisted in the Dorsets and found a job in the Sergeant's Mess, where he worked with James Bishop [1] until he died of natural causes in the military hospital on 30 May 1917. William was buried with full military honours in Fordington Cemetery but his son Herbert, the only living child of seven born to him and Francesca, could not be there to see his father interred as he was serving abroad.

[1] See James Bishop

Gnr Arthur Edward Ashton – aged 34
57th Trench Mortar Bty – 202595
Cenotaph and St Peter's

Kate Petts' father was a railway engine driver, which possibly explains why she lived at 2 Railway Cottages, Prince of Wales Road. In 1906 her father died, which probably meant that she and her mother had to leave their cottage and in 1911 they were residing at 21 Monmouth Rd. Also living there at that date as a boarder was Arthur Ashton, who was employed by the County Council as an assistant schoolmaster. Kate worked as a shop assistant in a drapers shop. Whether Arthur, who hailed from Bristol, knew Kate before he came to Dorchester, or whether love blossomed between the couple after he moved in we do not know. In any event, the couple married in 1911.

Arthur was fighting with the 57th Trench Mortar Bty in the Messines area near Ypres in June 1917. On 2 June he was killed in action, 5 days before the huge explosion of mines under the German lines that announced the beginning of the Battle of Messines. He is commemorated on the Ploegsteert Memorial.

Gnr Charles Benjamin Trevett [1] – aged 37
110th Wessex Heavy Bty, RGA – 315472
Cenotaph, St Peter's and Post Office

Charles Trevett was born in 1881 in Upwey, between Dorchester and Weymouth, where his father was the local postman, and when the time came for him to find a job he too joined the Post Office and became a rural postman at Maiden Newton, northwest of Dorchester. In 1908 Charles married Ethel Male, a school mistress from Radipole, the parish adjacent to Charles' birthplace. By 1911 he was delivering mail in Dorchester where the couple lived at 3 Damers Villas, Damer's Rd.

Charles went to war in 1916 with the Wessex (Hampshire) Heavy Bty of the RGA and died of pneumonia on 2 June 1917, in a hospital near the town of Peronne, France. His body was interred in La Chapelette British and Indian Cemetery, Somme. After the War, Ethel migrated to Canada.

[1] There is some confusion over the name. The Cenotaph and St Peter's have Trevitt, the Post Office memorial has Trevett. The census returns indicate that the latter is correct.

L/Cpl John James Riglar [1] – aged 29
9th Btn Royal Dublin Fusiliers – 12725
Cenotaph

The River Frome, which caresses the northern perimeter of Dorchester, has a distinct kink in it just before it opens up in front of Frome Terrace. The reason for this is that it was once diverted to drive the machinery of Friary Mills which stood on that spot. Next to the mill was a row of cottages known as Clifton Terrace and it was at No. 2 that 2-year-old John Riglar resided in 1891 with his parents, John, a bootmaker, and Susan. Ten years later the family was living on the other side of town at 4 Dagmar Rd and John Junior was working as an errand boy with a local grocers. Tragedy first struck the family when Susan died at 46 and the father was left to raise nine children on his own. The young John left home before 1911 to live in Southampton, where he worked as a railway porter.

In August 1915, John went off to join the Gallipoli campaign and having survived that then went to France and fought with the 9th Btn RDF. It is unlikely that he got much sleep the evening of 6 June 1917; British guns were pounding the German lines and the predominant thought in his mind was that he was about to go into battle. Then, at 3.10 am, the ground shook under his feet when 19 huge mines exploded under the German line, killing approximately 10,000 of the enemy and destroying most of the defences on Messines Ridge. It was now time for the 9th Dubliners to advance and, after capturing the village of Wytschaete near Ypres, they went on to secure their objectives. John was killed in action on the following day, the 8th, and is commemorated on the Menin Gate Memorial.

---

[1] Cousin of Richard Riglar.

Capt. William John Whale – aged 39
163rd Siege Bty, RGA
Cenotaph and St Peter's

Florence Turner was the daughter of a Dorchester postman and lived her early years in Trinity Street. Unfortunately, she did not grow up knowing her father as he died when she was three. Florence lived with her mother and on leaving school became a dressmaker's apprentice before specialising in millinery. It is quite likely that she met her future husband William when a detachment of artillerymen came to the barracks.

William Whale was born into the artillery, the son of John, a gunner master sergeant, and his wife Margaret. John retired from the Army and the family lived in Woolwich, near the home of the Royal Artillery, where he worked as a clerk. Having been immersed in military life it was probably of no surprise to the family when their son William, at the age of 21, gave up his job as a clerk and joined the gunners. He signed on for 7 years and either extended his service or returned to civilian life and went into the National Reserve. Certainly, in 1911 he was still a soldier with the rank of sergeant. William would not be the only soldier to come to Dorchester and end up marrying a local girl, as other stories in this book show. Florence and William married in Dorchester in 1904 and at the time of his death the family home was at 'Greystone', 7 Maumbury Rd.

There is some uncertainty about where William fought during the War. His Medal Roll Card states that his first steps on foreign soil were trod in France, with the 163rd Siege Bty, on 27 September 1916. However, it appears that he had been fighting before that. Among the papers that make up William's service record is a letter from Florence to the Foreign Office, asking them to contact the American Embassy in Istanbul to establish whether her husband had been taken prisoner or wounded.[1] The reply was that nothing was known of his fate. We do not know the reason for William's apparent disappearance but Florence must have been greatly relieved when she eventually heard that he was safe. William had received a commission as 2 Lt in March 1915 and was promoted to the rank of temporary captain in France.

Siege batteries consisted mainly of heavy howitzers which, unlike other lighter artillery, were static, which meant that if located by the enemy they were particularly vulnerable. On 14 June 1917, at 3 pm, William's battery saw an SOS flare in the sky, indicating that someone needed artillery support and each gun responded by firing six rounds. At the same time, the Germans had an observation balloon up and must have pinpointed where the guns were located. At 5.55 pm shells began to fall around William at the rate of ten a minute and when they stopped at 6.20 William lay mortally wounded, together with two other officers and three men who had to be taken to hospital with shell shock.

Capt. Whale died in the 74th Field Ambulance Station on the same day as he was wounded and was buried in Dickebusch New Military Cemetery near Ypres, alongside eight other soldiers of the RGA. In addition to receiving her dead husband's belongings, which included his watch, watch case and tobacco pouch, Florence was sent a bill for £8 7s 6d, which represented outstanding monies he owed the officers' mess and outstanding wages to his servant.

---

[1] Letter dated 6/3/1915, SR.

Nurse Constance Mary Hodges – aged 41
Cenotaph

Constance Hodges is the only woman to appear on any of the WWI Dorchester memorials. The Hodges' presence in Dorchester dated back to the time her grandfather John established a firm of wine importers and merchants in High East Street and became Mayor of the town in 1860. His eldest son John continued the family business, married Sara Rankin and had 11 children. The boys took up diverse occupations, one becoming an electrical engineer, another Naval Attaché to the British Embassy in London and another Assistant Secretary to the Governor of Nigeria.

Of the girls in the family, Anna, who was called Constance, was educated at Romanoff School for Girls in Surbiton, Surrey, as were her younger sisters Elinor and Margaret. She then decided to go into nursing and in 1911 was working as a Sister in a private nursing home. When war came she volunteered her services to the military. She unfortunately died from blood poisoning at the Urmston VAD Hospital at Eastbourne, Sussex, on 22 June.

Henry Sprake – aged 38
6th Btn Dorsetshire Rgt
Cenotaph

Henry Sprake was born at Quarlestone Farm, Winterborne Stickland, near Blandford, where his father William was a successful farmer of 300 acres, employing nine men and three boys on the land and three servants in the house. After William died in 1910 Henry moved to 9 Marian Terrace, Dorchester, where he lived with his mother Sarah. The only clue we have as to Henry's military career is contained in a letter that was sent to the Town Clerk saying that he had been a member of the 6th Dorsets and had died of pneumonia at his home on 25 June.

Ordinary Signaller Walter Reginald Paull
– aged 18
HM Trawler Charles Astie, RN – Z/1859
Thomas Hardye School Roll of Honour

Great War memorials take many forms, from the plain to the statuesque. Some schools and churches have Rolls of Honour instead, whilst others have Remembrance Books. Lloyd's Bank published a Memorial Album, which consists of photographs of its staff who died, with a note of where they worked. One of the photographs in the album is that of Walter Paull.

Walter was the eldest son of Laura and William Paull of Puddletown, where William was the local postmaster. Walter was sent to Dorchester Grammar School and after he left joined Lloyd's Bank as a clerk in their Bridport branch. On 27 September 1916 he enlisted in the Royal Navy and trained as a signalman. Before he could join a ship he had to be able to send and receive semaphore at eight words per minute, read Morse flags and use an Aldis lamp, as well as have a working knowledge of naval flags and pennants. After reaching the required standards Walter was posted to *HM Trawler Charles Astie* which had been requisitioned for military duties. On 26 June 1917 the trawler was escorting the steamer *Hartland* from Tory Island, off the northwest coast of Ireland, to Inishowen on the mainland, when it collided with a mine which had been laid off Fanad Point by the German submarine *U-79*. All 17 members of the crew perished and Walter is commemorated on the Plymouth War Memorial.

Pte Joseph Hubert Lock – aged 37
2nd Btn Dorsetshire Rgt – 25695
Cenotaph and St Peter's

A 1610 map of Dorchester has the area we know today as North Square marked as 'The Shambles'. This was the market area of the town, more specifically where the butchers had their shops. Three hundred years later there were still a number of butchers in the Square and a market, with a slaughter house just round the corner in Colliton Street. 1 North Square was the home and premises of J. Marvin Lock, the third generation of his family to be butchers in the town. Joseph also had a shop at 28 South St but his business interests were not just confined to selling meat. He had coal depots at Dorchester's two railway stations, delivering house, steam and gas coal, and coke to customers in the town and surrounding rural areas. He also offered 'Hauling of every description, undertaken by compound road locomotives' [1] and farmed 270 acres in Fordington. To keep his enterprises going Joseph employed a number of Dorchester lads and his sons were also in the business.

For local employers one of the obvious problems brought on by the War was that their workforce was constantly being depleted by the needs of the military and for Joseph, whose businesses relied almost entirely on a male workforce, the impact was potentially ruinous. When conscription was introduced in 1916 his problems were exacerbated and in June of that year he appeared before the Dorchester Town Military Appeals Tribunal seeking conditional exemption for three of his employees. He justified his need by stating that one employee hauled coal, mainly to army camps, whilst another only had one eye. The third was his youngest son Joseph. All three of the cases were adjourned pending medical reports. [2]

The outcome of the appeal board in respect of the first two men is unknown but Joseph was found fit and enlisted in the 2nd Dorsets, joining them in Mesopotamia. The official report on his death states '19 July 1917 – died in the 21st British Stationary Hospital, Baghdad from the effects of heat due to exposure whilst on military duties'. [3] A report on his death was published in the *Chronicle* on 2 August in which sympathies were extended to Annie, his wife of 6 years, and his parents. Joseph was buried in Baghdad (North Gate) War Cemetery.

---

[1] Taken from an advertisement appearing in *Kelly's Directory 1915*.
[2] *Chronicle* 15/6/1916.
[3] Army form 2090a, The Keep Military Museum.

Air Mechanic 1st Class Harold Frank Moore – aged 19
RNAS – J/28710
Cenotaph, Holy Trinity, St Peter's and Thomas Hardye School Roll of Honour

On Saturday 28 July 1917, the 9.31 evening train arrived at the GWR Station in Dorchester. There was nothing extraordinary in that, but what was special on this occasion was that it carried a coffin draped in the Union Jack. The body within was that of Harold Moore, a young Durnovarian who was making his last journey home. Harold's body had travelled

Harold Moore's grave in Weymouth Avenue Cemetery.

from Howden in Yorkshire where he had been serving as an Air Mechanic with the RNAS.

Harold, born 26 November 1897, was the son of William, a sergeant in the Dorset Rgt, and Annie. He was educated at the Grammar School and attended Holy Trinity Church, where he was one of the leading choir boys under the Rev H. Bowden-Smith. The family lived at 15 High East St. On the 18th anniversary of his birth and standing just 5 ft 4 in tall Harold joined the Navy as a Boy Sailor and commenced training on *HMS Impregnable*, a 121-gun former first-rate ship of the line. After serving on the armed cruiser *HMS Endymion* he transferred to the newly formed RNAS. With the rank of Air Mechanic 1st Class Harold was sent to RNAS Howden, which had been established to counter German submarine attacks on British shipping on the northeast coast.

Those who knew the *Airship C/11A* might have considered that it had a jinx on it. Built at Kingsnorth on the Isle of Grain in Kent it had previously lost a propeller on landing and then been wrecked and rebuilt. On 21 July 1917 *C/11A*, under the command of Temporary Lt William Hervey, took off from Howden with its crew, consisting of Harold, who with another man was acting as Coxswain, and a Telegraph Operator named Harry Ward. Somewhere over the River Humber the airship burst into flames and plummeted into the water, killing all on board.

Harold's body was recovered and returned to Dorchester and as a mark of respect the officers and men of Howden provided the headstone to his grave, a splendid cross mounted on three plinths. The centre of the cross bears a ship's wheel and the letters RNAS. His funeral took place in Weymouth Avenue Cemetery on the day following his arrival in the town, the *Chronicle* reporting that 'the remains of the young patriot were interred in their last resting place in the cemetery in the presence of many spectators'. [1]

As is often the case with death during war, irony played a part. Harold was due to come home on leave on the previous Saturday but put it off to coincide with his father's leave from the Army. He did indeed arrive on the same day as his father but not to exchange war stories.

[1] *Chronicle* 2/8/1917.

Pte Horace Edwin Hanham – aged 23
2nd Btn Dorsetshire Rgt – 17658
Cenotaph and St George's

Sgt Douglas Bailey Hanham – aged 29
4th Btn East Surrey Rgt – 36965
St George's

Horace Hanham was the second Dorchester soldier to die of heat stroke in Mesopotamia within a week. The regimental history of the 2nd Btn makes several mentions of the hostile conditions the men had to work in and the high rates of sickness, pointing out, for instance, that in the month of Joseph Lock's and Horace's death, operations at Ramadi had to be cancelled because of the extreme temperature and that 'The battalion was lucky to escape having to march in such dreadful heat'. [1]

Horace was the son of Thomas, a sergeant of the Dragoon Guards, and Mary who lived at 2 Alington Rd. A one-time member of All Saint's Church choir, Horace worked as a grocer's assistant and a year before his death married Mary Jane Wilkins from Broadway, Weymouth. He died at No. 16 Casualty Clearing Station in Baghdad on 22 July and was buried in Baghdad (North Gate) Cemetery. His name also appears on the memorial of St Nicholas' Church in Broadwey.

The East Surrey Rgt lost over 6,000 men in the War and Horace's older brother Douglas must have thanked his lucky stars on Armistice Day that he was not among them. However, like Edward Pope he was one of those on whom the conflict had left a legacy. On 8 May 1921 he died from tuberculosis at his parents' home, his family at his bedside. His grave can be found in Fordington Cemetery.

---

[1] Regimental history.

Pte Bertie Andrew Frampton – aged 22
2nd Btn Dorsetshire Rgt – 16313
Cenotaph and St Peter's

Bertie Frampton was the son of Henry, a dustman, and Emma, who gave birth to 12 children, nine of whom were still alive in 1911. The family was living at 15 Icen Way then and their 15-year-old son, Bertie, was working in the town as a newspaper boy.

There is some confusion about the cause of Bertie's death. The *Chronicle* and All Saint's Church parish magazine both reported that he went missing on 25 July1917 in Mesopotamia, whereas the official history of the Dorsets and his Medal Roll Card both say that he 'died' on the same date, suggesting his death was caused by illness or injury. The 2nd Btn were not engaged in any fighting around the time of his demise but were encamped at Kadhimain, Bagdhad, so there is no obvious reason why he would have gone missing. Alternatively, he may have died whilst a prisoner of the Turks after the fall of Kut. The fact that he has no known grave and is remembered on the Basra Memorial suggests that there was no body to bury in a military cemetery, although a soldier was often buried where he fell. Whatever the circumstances, the grief felt by his mother was just as intense, especially as she was already mourning the loss of her husband, who had died the previous year.

Lt-Col John Brough CMG, MVO – aged 43
General Staff, 61st Division
Cenotaph and Thomas Hardye School Roll of Honour

John Brough and his younger brother Alan were both pupils at Dorchester Grammar School who went on to achieve senior rank in the Army. Their father William was a colonel in the RHA and in 1901 was living at Vicarage Farm House, Pound Lane, Fordington, with his daughter Elizabeth, his wife Annie having died. In 1911 the 69-year-old retired army officer was living at 56 High West St with two servants.

John was born in Punjab and had a diverse military career. He trained at the Royal Military Academies of Greenwich and Sandhurst and before the War served with the Royal Navy and was part of the West African Frontier Force which was set up to garrison British colonies in that area. He also served as a Royal Marines gunnery officer on several ships. In 1914 John was promoted from major to lieutenant colonel and took part in the West African Campaign, which was conducted in order to capture the German colonies of Togoland and Kamerun. [1] At the end of the campaign, in 1916, he returned to the UK and was employed on special duty with the Heavy Section Machine Gun Corps, a secret section of the Royal Artillery. The HSMGC was developing Britain's new weapon, the tank, and John has been credited as the man who prepared the first force of them for action. As well as helping in the training and strategy of using this new mechanised assault unit he spent much of his time demonstrating the armoured vehicles to military leaders and dignitaries, including King George V.

In 1916 the question arose as to whether the limited number of tanks produced so far should be used in the Somme offensive, or whether they should wait for more to be built. Haig decided to use what they had and John prepared to get the crews ready. However, for some unknown reason he was, in effect, sacked on the eve of their deployment and ended up with a desk job in London. Later, on 25 July 1917 John went with the 61st Division (2nd South Midlands) and joined the Fifth Army in Flanders as a staff officer. He helped with preparations for the Third Battle of Ypres and 2 days later presented a draft training schedule for the attack to his senior officers.

On 30 July a L/Sgt Gibbs was searching the French countryside for a missing British officer who had disappeared without reason, when he came across a body in a hedgerow. It was that of John Brough, who was holding his service revolver in his hand and had a gunshot wound in his temple. On 31 July a court of enquiry commenced where the MO, Capt. Scanlon, reported that two bullets had been found, indicating that John had twice pulled the trigger. The reason for his action was not known. There was no suicide note, though some witnesses close to him testified that he had become worried about his work and appeared morose and dejected. From the Army point of view, soldiers only committed suicide if they were mad or cowards and John had proved to be no coward, having been mentioned three times in Despatches while serving in Africa. The court of enquiry chose the other option and concluded that he had shot himself whilst temporarily insane, caused by worry. The date of his death was recorded as 29 July and he was buried in Longuenesse (St Omer) Souvenir Cemetery, Pas-de-Calais. His medals were sent to his sister Elizabeth.

John's father received the usual telegram from the War Office at the Junction Hotel in Dorchester and this was shortly followed by a letter stating that his son had died of self-inflicted wounds. The implications were unthinkable. John would not be listed among the fallen because he had died a dishonourable death. His father immediately wrote to the War Office asking them to state in the public record that he had died of wounds, but his pleadings were rejected, a pencil note being scribbled on the letter that if he wanted that then he would have to publish his own notices in the newspapers. Locally, William was treated more kindly, the *Chronicle* reporting, simply, that his son had died of wounds. This was echoed in the obituary that appeared in the 1917/18 *Dorset Year Book*.

[1] Now Togo and Cameroon.

Pte Reginald William Scott – aged 20
8th Btn Seaforth Highlanders – S/5500
Cenotaph

Located at the bottom of Mill Street and facing the former mill, the Swan Inn was a popular pub, especially with the local gypsies. The hostelry closed in the 1980s but retains the sign of its former use. Licensees of the pub for over 20 years were George Scott and his wife Harriet. Originally, George was listed as the licensee but it looks as if he changed his employment to that of butcher because in the 1911 census Harriet is listed as the licence holder. George's brother Arthur had a fishmongers at 18 South St.

Reginald was George and Harriet's third son who worked for Boon's Stores at 11 Cornhill, before joining the Army at the age of 18. He fought with the 8th Btn Seaforth Highlanders and was killed in action on 31 July at Passchendaele. He was buried at White House Cemetery, northeast of Ypres.

CSM Herbert Moody – aged 27
8th Btn Somerset Light Infantry – 27850
Cenotaph

Herbert Moody was another out-of-town man who married a Dorchester girl. He was born in Sherfield-on-Loddon, Hampshire, the eldest son of Walter, a groom and gardener, and Annie. Herbert worked as a market gardener and enlisted in the Wiltshire Rgt in Salisbury, later transferring to the 8th Btn SLI. In the latter part of 1916 he married Ethel Perkins in Dorchester and they set up home at 16 Alexandra Rd. As was so often the case with wartime marriages it was destined to be very short.

On 30 July 1917, between 10 and 11 pm, three companies of the 8th Btn moved up to Shell Hole Line, Westhoek, and two others occupied shell holes in the vicinity. They were preparing for a major offensive by about 100,000 men, on the 31st, in what would be recorded by history as the Battle of Passchendaele. The Somersets, who were not involved in the first stage of the battle, entered the conflict at 7.50 am and it was not long before the first reports on progress were arriving, by runner and pigeon, at HQ. The Btn captured several enemy positions and consolidated them, but during the fighting Herbert went missing. He is commemorated on the Menin Gate Memorial.

Pte Ernest William Webber – aged 33
2/4th Btn Dorsetshire Rgt – 202019
St Peter's

The son of a farm labourer, Ernest Webber was born in the village of Bloxworth, 14 miles to the east of Dorchester, on 4 December 1883. Emily Brushett was the daughter of William, a Dorchester shoemaker, and lived at 46 Icen Way. On New Year's Day 1909 the couple were wed in the town and then went to live in Warmwell, where Ernest was employed as a gardener. The following year they had a child named William.

The 2/4th Btn Dorsets had spent the first 2½ years of the War in India when, in the middle of March 1917, they received orders to move to Bombay to embark for active service overseas. Then, when they got to Poona they were told that their overseas holiday had been cancelled and instead they would form a garrison in Bombay. Some of the battalion remained at Poona to look after the arsenal at Kirkee and Ernest may have been among them. According to official records he died on 1 August, presumably from either illness or accident, but curiously there is no mention of him being buried. Instead his name appears on the Kirkee Memorial, Poona.

Pte John Reginald Hare – aged 21
2nd Btn Inniskilling Fusiliers – 43877

Cpl Edmund Lamb MM – aged 35
2nd Btn Leinster Rgt

Both are remembered on Holy Trinity

On Thursday 14 February 1919 an 'Interesting and picturesque ceremony' [1] took place in Dorchester. The town was basking in sunshine when, shortly before 11 am, a large detachment of soldiers, comprising the Depot Coy, companies from the Agricultural Corps and some soldiers who had been repatriated from Germany and Turkey, marched to a designated site and formed three sides of a square. Next, a group of civic dignitaries arrived in procession, preceded by the mace bearers and brought up in the rear by Mr Payne, the Town Beadle. [2] The dignitaries included the Mayor, Councillor G.J. Dennis, the Deputy Mayor, several aldermen and councillors, and officers of the council. They were all present to witness the presentation of two military medals.

At 11 o'clock, a Gen. Jackson, who was accompanied by his brigadier, presented the first medal to Driver Bartlett of Littlebredy, who had put an enemy gun out of action under heavy fire. After the name of the recipient of the second medal was read out a mother stepped forward to collect it, receiving 'a sympathetic reception' [3] as the medal and ribbon were handed to her. The General expressed the hope that all would try to follow the example of self-sacrifice and devotion to duty that the recipients had displayed, setting aside selfishness and working for the whole community.

The mother collecting her son's medal was Lavinia Hare, someone upon whom death was to visit again and again. She was born Lavinia Lee and married Edmund Lamb in Weymouth in 1881, and the following year gave birth to a son, also named Edmund. In 1888 her husband died and Lavinia was left with three young children to bring up. She married Metropolitan policeman Walter Hare and went to live with him in Sloane Square, London, where they had a child, John Reginald. The family returned to Dorchester sometime after 1911, where the couple ran the Old Ship Inn in High West Street for 2 years. Having been an ex-policeman made Walter an ideal candidate as landlord of the inn, which was a favourite watering hole for troops at the barracks and witnessed more than the occasional fracas. Walter suddenly died in 1919, making Lavinia a widow once again. But, her husbands' deaths were not the only reasons for Lavinia to grieve; she also lost John and Edmund.

John, who like his father was a police constable in London, was called up for military service on 12 January 1917. Initially he was put into the London Rgt but soon after arriving in France was transferred to the 2nd Btn Inniskilling Fusiliers, part of the 96th Bde. He was fighting with them for less than 2 months when he was gassed on 25 July and sent to be treated at the 54th General Hospital in Boulogne. He was dangerously ill and died on 1 August from the poisoning. Lavinia was informed of her son's death and was sent his belongings, which included his Ingersoll watch, two packets of spearmint and a card of buttons. He was buried in Wimereux Communal Cemetery, 3 miles north of Boulogne.

While his mother began her grieving John's half-brother Edmund was fighting with the 2nd Btn Leinster Rgt in France, but within 5 weeks he too was gone, killed in action on 7 September at Passchendaele. On 28 September his name was listed in the *London Gazette* among others who had been awarded the MM for gallantry. Edmund is commemorated on the Tyne Cot Memorial, Zonnebeke, Belgium. Two years after his death Lavinia sent the following touching epitaph to her two boys to the *Chronicle*: [4]

> *Could their mother have clasped their hands,*
> *The sons she knew so well.*
> *Or kissed their brow when death was near,*
> *And whispered 'my sons farewell'.*
> *I seem to see their dear sweet faces,*
> *Through a mist of anxious tears.*
> *But a mother's part is a broken heart,*
> *And a burden of lonely tears.*
> *We miss you, for we loved you,*
> *As memories we recall.*
> *The parting with our dear ones,*
> *Was the saddest day of all.*

[1] *Chronicle* 20/2/1919.
[2] The Beadle was an officer responsible for maintaining order.
[3] *Chronicle* 20/2/1919.
[4] *Chronicle* 11/9/1919.

Gnr Archibald Colin Bell – aged 33
160th Siege Bty, RGA – 87710
Post Office Memorial

Archibald Bell was a Hampshire lad who was born in Southsea in 1884, the son of Francis, a builder's assistant, and Catherine. Leaving Hampshire, he came to Dorset, got a job as a postman and in 1911 was lodging with shepherd Tom Foot and his family at Grimstone. Just up the road from Grimstone, in the village of Sydling St Nicholas, lived Caroline Gifford and she and Archibald were married on 6 April 1915. Eight months after his marriage Archibald enlisted in the Army Reserve at Cerne Abbas and was mobilised in May 1916. He became a gunner with the RGA and was sent to France in September 1916, serving with the 160th Siege Bty.

On 1 August 1917 Archibald's battery was positioned at La Chapelle Farm near Ypres, where they were engaged in a tit-for-tat artillery battle with the Germans. There were few days that were casualty free and on 10 August Archibald's name was added to the list of those killed, along with nine other men of the 160th. He is buried in Klein-Vierstraat British Cemetery, West-Vlaanderen. It was 5 months later that Caroline received her husband's personal effects, which included two of his pipes with tobacco pouch, some photographs and a broken mirror.

Pte Reginald Bertie Dabinett – aged 31
2nd Btn Dorsetshire Rgt – 201820
Cenotaph

The two men posing before the photographer wore British Army tropical uniform comprising tunic, shorts and topi helmet. Behind them was an appropriate backdrop painted with a palm and to one side was a table covered in a leopard skin. Thousands of soldiers had similar photographs taken, the backdrop varying according to the theatre of war. The two men in this particular piece of artwork were brothers Bertie and Reginald Dabinett, both of whom served in India with the 1/4th Dorsets and who were two of the eight sons of George Dabinett, a house painter, and his wife Louisa. The family were well known in the town, especially Reg who, as the *Chronicle* pointed out, was 'in the front rank of local footballers and popularly known as "Little Titch", he was one of the most skilful components

Reginald (left) with his brother Bertie (right). (Source: Mrs J. Caddy.)

of the winter game in the district, and had been selected to play for the county'. [1], [2] Before joining up Bertie worked for some time at Holy Trinity Church Rectory and Reg was a carriage painter at Channon's, coach builders. Reg's occupation was of some use to him in India. In a letter, he told his brother Arthur that he had been excused duty for 2 weeks whilst he painted the Captain's gig. Reg definitely had an eye for the main

Part of a letter from Reginald to his sister, dated 15 September 1916, with references at the top to a popular song and to the 'wicked war'. (Source: Mr A. Wilson.)

chance. When he enlisted he gave his religion as C of E, and consequently had to parade in the Indian heat with other soldiers of his denomination and march 2 miles to the local church, carrying his rifle and 20 rounds of ammunition. He then decided to change his religion to that of Chapel, not because of some spiritual revelation but simply because the local chapel was only 100 yd from the barracks. As he pointed out in his letters, 'you have to be artful in the army'. [3]

Reg and Bertie were both regular letter writers while in India and their missives make interesting reading. Bertie's letters mainly concern themselves with life back home, the Dorchester boys he came across in the course of his duty and the telegraphy course he was sent on. Reg's indicate his interest in the local life, like the 'curious habit' of the Sikhs who took off their shoes before entering a house, or the women who went out of their way to avoid contact; the myriad of insects waiting to strike a man down and the plethora of half-wild dogs. One thing that they both complained about, incessantly, was the terrible heat. Bertie, somewhat graphically, wrote, 'You will not see any of the fellows very fat out here, as you sweat the fatness out of you, you are sweating more or less from the time you get up in the morning until last thing at night.' [4] Reg explained that sometimes the heat was so bad at night he had to take his bed outside to sleep.

The brothers were stationed together in Jullundur, until Reg was drafted to Mesopotamia in the autumn of 1916, where he was attached to the 2nd Btn. Inevitably, because the battalion was frequently on the move, his letter writing decreased but he continued to write postcards to Bertie who passed on the news of his brother to their parents. The reason for Reg returning to India is not clear. He may have been one of the regular group soldiers returning from Mesopotamia to rest or possibly the cause was more serious. On 31 July 1917 he wrote a letter to his parents from the military hospital in Poona. As well as admitting patients with the usual illnesses and injuries the Kirkee hospital was the only one in the area that dealt with cases of men who had been bitten by animals. Reg had been bitten on the face one night by a prowling jackal but his letter indicated that there was little reason for his parents to be anxious because he was on the mend and was looking forward to an extended period of leave in Bangalore, where the weather was much cooler. He also said that he would have liked to have sent home to his sister Cissie one of the beautiful, large butterflies prevalent around the hospital. A month later his parents received the news that their son had died of rabies on 22 August. He was buried in Bangalore (Hosur) Cemetery. Bertie returned to Dorchester after the War, married and worked in the town as a painter and decorator.

[1] *Chronicle* 20/9/1917.
[2] See photo on page 14.
[3] Letter 22/6/1916.
[4] Letter 28/7/1916.

Pte William Hellier – aged 32
2nd Btn Dorsetshire Rgt – 17837
Cenotaph

William was the eldest of three soldier sons of Henry and Mary of 33 Fordington Hill. Prior to joining the Dorsets he worked for J. Marvin Lock [1] and before that as a dairy hand for Mr Child's dairy at West Stafford. William was serving in Mesopotamia when he died of enteritis, in No. 3 General Hospital, Basra, on 26 August 1917. He was buried in Basra War Cemetery and after his death his parents placed the following verse in the *Chronicle*:

> *Sleep on dear one, in a far off land,*
> *In a grave we may never see.*
> *But as long as life and memory last,*
> *We will always think of thee.*

[1] See Joseph Lock.

Pte Montague Harold Sargent – aged 19
5th Btn Dorsetshire Rgt – 17623
Cenotaph and St George's

The memorials correctly show M.H.S. Sargent, although Montague was known by and served as Harold. He lived at 12 Harvey's Buildings and was the eldest son of George, who described himself as a journeyman baker, and Rose. Harold was wounded with the 5th Btn Dorsets and died in one of the base hospitals at Boulogne on 6 September 1917. He was buried in Boulogne Eastern Cemetery. A year after his son's death George received a second blow when Rose died.

Flt Sub-Lt Noel Stafford Wright – aged 18
Royal Naval Air Service
Thomas Hardye School Roll of Honour

(Source: www.ww1photos.com.)

Dr Walter Wright practiced as a GP in the town of Wool and then got the important public post of physician, surgeon, MO and public vaccinator for the Winfrith district of the Wareham Poor Law Union, which also included the job of Admiralty surgeon. He and his wife Caroline had three sons; the second named Noel was sent to the Dorchester Grammar School to be educated.

In those early days of flight and with the surname of Wright doubtless Noel often had his leg pulled after he joined the RNAS as a pilot. He flew with the 1st Squadron, attached to the Hawke Btn of the Royal Naval Division, and was killed in France. On 18 September Noel was flying with Capt. J Manley RFC over the British side of the lines near Neuve Église, Belgium, when their Sopwith Triplane Scout collided with a Spad VII biplane. Noel and Capt. Manley were killed and were buried in Bailleul Community Cemetery.

Pte Jessie Walter Harmer – aged 35
6th Btn Oxfordshire and Buckinghamshire Light Infantry
Cenotaph

It has not been possible to find a connection with this man and the town of Dorchester. He is the only J.W. Harmer who died serving in the Ox and Bucks LI but there is no evidence that he or his relatives lived or were born in the town. Neither was he represented by anyone at the unveiling ceremony of the Cenotaph.

Jessie was born in Ewelme, Oxfordshire, the son of William and Mary, and the 1911 census shows him still living there working as a gardener. In 1914 he married Elizabeth Winterborne. Jessie died of wounds on 20 September 1917 and is buried in Cement House Cemetery near Ypres.

Gnr Frederick Groves – aged 31
278th Siege Bty, RGA
Cenotaph and St George's

Doubtless Annie Groves extended her sympathies to her neighbours in Hillside Terrace in the spring of 1916 when they were informed that their son William White [1] had died of wounds in Mesopotamia. Almost a year later she too would answer the knock on her door that would change her life forever.

Frederick Groves was born at Godmanstone just outside Dorchester and moved to the town with his parents, William and Lucy. He spent 4½ years in the county police force before going to work for J. Marvin Lock, butcher and coal merchant. [2] In 1911 he married Annie Day of Beaminster and the following year their daughter Freda was born. Frederick was a gunner on one of the four 6-inch howitzers belonging to the 278th Siege Bty and went with them to France on 18 March, just 6 months before he was killed in action, on 25 September. His body was interred in the Menin Road South Military Cemetery, 2 miles east of Ypres.

[1] See William White.
[2] See Joseph Lock.

L/Cpl Samuel Bertie Dimond – aged 27
1/4th Btn Dorsetshire Rgt
Cenotaph

In the Mesopotamian campaign Gen. Maude chose the month of September 1917 to deliver a knockout blow to the Turks at Ramadi. A previous attempt in August, in temperatures of over 122 degrees in the shade, had failed. The Turks had established a garrison at Remadi comprising 100 cavalry, 100 artillery and 3,000 infantry troops and were well dug in. The landscape was featureless, except for a few ridges that hardly earned the name. The 1/5th and 2/5th Gurkhas supported by Dorsets were given the job of capturing Ramadi Ridge which was just 17 ft high and the approach to it offered no cover. The attack was made on 28 September and the Gurkhas had no difficulty seizing it, but on nearing the crest they came under heavy fire and were reinforced by some of the Dorsets. The men were very exposed to the Turkish troops just 1,000 yd away and had to endure artillery, rifle and machine-gun fire but after more of the Dorsets were committed to the fierce fighting the position was eventually secured. However, so exposed and precarious was the position that it was decided to withdraw under cover of darkness. The next day the attack was renewed and the Turks surrendered, leaving the town of Ramadi in Allied hands.

Samuel was one of three soldiers who appear on Dorchester's memorials who were killed in the fighting on the 28th, the others being Harry Eady and Harry Sturmey. According to SDGW, Samuel lived in Dorchester, although there is no other evidence of him doing so. He was one of 15 children born to Elizabeth and Henry Dimond and he spent some of his childhood in Compton Valence, a village to the west of Dorchester. Samuel is buried in Baghdad (North Gate) Cemetery.

Sgt Harry Cecil Eady – aged 27
1/4th Btn Dorsetshire Rgt – 200635
Cenotaph [1]

In 1911 the tiny village of Tincleton, which lies 5½ miles east of Dorchester, consisted of about 40 families and boasted a post office and school. Sarah Eady was the school headmistress, living at the schoolhouse with husband Henry, a commercial clerk, and their four children, George, Mabel, Harry and Daisy. When it was time for Harry to earn a living he followed not his father's but his mother's profession by becoming an assistant schoolmaster. It appears that he taught in one of the schools in Dorchester because in the 1911 census he is shown boarding at 9 Bridport Terr with the family of Douglas Crooke, who also gave his life for his country. [2]

Harry was a Territorial before the War and a good shot. There is a photograph of him, dated 1912, among a group of soldiers who made up Sgt Scott's winning shooting team. In the photo Sgt Scott wears his Volunteer Long Service medal, which was awarded to him in 1909. A fishmonger by trade, he enlisted in 1896. Harry remained with the Territorials on the outbreak of hostilities, serving with the 1/4th Btn in Mesopotamia. He was killed in action during the attack on Ramadi Ridge [3] on 28 September and was buried in Baghdad (North Gate) Cemetery.

[1] Harry Eady is wrongly listed on the Cenotaph as W. Eady.
[2] See Douglas Crooke.
[3] See Samuel Dimond for details of the engagement.

Sgt Scott's shooting team. Harry Eady is third from left, back row. Left to right, standing: Pte R. Foster, Pte Hurst, Pte C. Eady, Pte J. Joy, Pte T. Dowd, Pte S. Howe, Pte H. Barnes, Pte E. Wilson. Sitting: Pte B. Norris, Sgt C. Old, Sgt A. Scott, Cpl H. Moore, Pte M. Gilday. (Source: Mr C. Eady.)

2 Lt Leonard Baker Spicer – aged 23
9th Btn King's Own Yorkshire Light Infantry
Cenotaph and St George's

By 1915 James and Mary Spicer had been running the little grocers and post office on the corner of Fordington Green and Duke's Avenue for at least 10 years. Today, the post office has closed but the grocers is still there, as is the attached residence of Bedloe House where they lived. When their son Leonard left school he joined the family business but when the War came he joined the migration of young men leaving the town for the Front. Leonard enlisted as a private in the King's Own Scottish Borderers and fought with them in Gallipoli before being transferred to the KOYLI. He must have been a good soldier because on 24 April he was commissioned as 2 Lt.

At the beginning September 1917 the 9th Btn were in bivouacs on a railway cutting south of Zillebeke, southeast of Ypres, and Leonard had spent the previous month helping to prepare his men for an attack on German lines, which was to take place on the morning of 4 October. On the night of the 3rd/4th the troops moved up to the assembly trenches near Polygon Wood and by 5 am they were ready. At 6 am the British barrage opened up as the Yorkshires made their way into no man's land and into the darkness. The German guns returned fire but Leonard and his comrades managed to get away before the worst of it fell onto the line. Fighting his way through mud up to his knees in the 'The Swamp', as the men nicknamed it, it became a veritable killing ground, and when the advancing troops were subjected to a withering machine-gun fire, bodies of his comrades began falling around Leonard.

The battalion went on to confront the strongly held position of Juniper Trench but instead of defending it the Germans attempted to withdraw. However, Leonard saw what was happening and the battalion's war diary recorded the result: '2 Lt Spicer by a quick manoeuvre cut off the majority of these who gave themselves up'. [1] At about noon, enemy troops were seen advancing out of the village of Gheluvelt and in response to this a party of men, under Leonard, were sent out with two Lewis guns and a Vickers to flank the advancing men and bring enfilading fire to bear down upon them. Later in the day communication with Leonard and his party ceased. Initially it was believed they had been cut off and made prisoner, but they were never seen again. He is commemorated on the Tyne Cot Memorial.

Pte Joseph Diskett Moggeridge – aged 22
1/6th Btn Gloucestershire Rgt
Cenotaph

When Jane Moggeridge completed her census form in 1911 she was unable to record her husband because he was not present, not an unusual situation for her and her children because Henry Moggeridge was a merchant seaman and often away from home. On such occasions her eldest son Joseph was the man of the house. When it was time for Joseph to set up his own home he tied the matrimonial knot with Florence Andrews in the summer of 1916. Florence, who lived at 20 Dagmar Rd, was the daughter of Edward who worked as a platelayer with the LSWR.

Joseph served with the 1/6th Btn Gloucesters and was killed on 9 October 1917 during the Battle of Poelcapelle, part of the Passchendaele offensive. He is commemorated on the Tyne Cot Memorial. After Joseph's death his wife placed an item in the 'In Memorium' section of the *Chronicle* on 10 January 1918 with a short verse that summed up the frustration of those who were unable to say goodbye to their loved ones at their time of death:

> *If I could have raised his dying head*
> *Or heard his last farewell,*
> *The blow would not have been so hard*
> *To the one I loved so well.*

Pte Herbert Nelson Frampton – aged 20
1st Btn West Kent Rgt – 205334
Cenotaph

Charles and Helen Frampton had five children, all of them boys, and they lived at 29 Great Western Rd. Charles worked as a platelayer with the GWR and Helen was employed as a dressmaker. Their fourth eldest son was baptised Herbert and given the second name of Nelson, probably after the great British hero, something that was not an uncommon thing to do at that time. He grew up among his family and friends as Nelson and it was with that name that he joined the Dorset Yeomanry and later transferred to the West Kent Rgt.

On 24 October 1917 the West Kents returned to the front line after resting at Ridge Camp near Ypres, with orders to attack German positions northwest of Gheluvelt, near the Menin Road. Zero hour came at 5.40 am and the attackers advanced in a quagmire, which was to determine the success of the assault. The mud impeded the attacking troops, almost prevented communications, and choked the rifles and Lewis guns. The result was the worst day in the 1st Btn's experiences of the War. Practically no men of two companies returned and many of the wounded could not extricate themselves from the mud, suffering a slow and painful death. Twelve out of 16 officers became casualties, as did 348 of 581 OR, of which 225 were killed or missing. Nelson was one of the latter and is commemorated on the Tyne Cot Memorial.

Pte John Rhodes – aged 31
254th Coy, Royal Defence Corps
Fordington Cemetery

John Rhodes, who was employed in Dorchester as a driver with the RDC, was taken ill and admitted to the County Hospital. After 2 or 3 months' treatment he died on 26 October. He was a native of Fulham and originally enlisted in the 12th Btn London Rgt. John was given a full military funeral and buried in Fordington Cemetery.

Pte Harry Legg – aged 19
Middlesex Yeomanry – 230822
Cenotaph

Walter Legg was born in Dorchester but moved to the USA, where he and his wife Agnes started a family. On repatriating, the family first settled in Wakefield, Yorkshire, where Walter worked as a steel temperer. By 1911 they had returned to Dorchester and were living at 22 Olga Rd, with Walter working as an insurance agent. Henry, the youngest of the Legg family, was born in Wakefield but grew up in Dorchester. During the War he served with the Middlesex Yeomanry in Egypt.

In October 1917 the Yeomanry were holding two strong points on the El Buggar Bir Girheir line, prior to an assault on the city of Beersheba on the 30th. On the morning of the 27th Maj. Lafone, the CO, received orders to hold on to one of the positions at all costs against a superior Turkish force. The attack lasted for several hours and was supported by intense shelling and machine-gun fire. Most of the small force had been either killed or wounded when Lafone ordered the remainder to withdraw, personally covering their retreat. The position was eventually overrun and Maj. Lafone was awarded the VC for his bravery. Harry was among those killed and was buried in Beersheba War Cemetery.

Pte Douglas Harold Crooke – aged 21
2/23rd Btn London Rgt
Cenotaph

In 1911 the Crooke family, who came from Birmingham, were living at 9 Bridport Terr. Douglas was at school, his father was working as a furniture salesman and the family had three lodgers. By 1914, when Douglas enlisted in the Army at 17, he was living in Battersea in London and joined the newly formed 2/23rd Btn London Rgt at Clapham Junction.

The first year of his army career was spent at home and it was not long before he got into trouble. On 15 May 1916 he committed the sin of being insubordinate on parade and was given 14 days' detention, followed a month later by an admonishment for being absent on parade a few days before he was due to leave for France. The regiment remained in France until November when they shipped to Salonika, where they stayed until June 1917.

Douglas's next move was to Egypt and within a week he was punished again, this time for insolence to an NCO. The punishment he received was a standard one for soldiers while fighting in the field of battle. Field Punishment No. 1 replaced flogging in the British Army in 1881 and consisted of the convicted man being shackled in irons and secured to a fixed object, like a stake or a gun wheel, for up to 2 hours in 24 for a maximum of 21 days. As the main object of the punishment was to humiliate and to set an example the man was placed in the open and there were even stories of victims being 'crucified' within the range of enemy guns. Field Punishment No. 2 was the same as No. 1 but the prisoner was not tethered to a fixed object. Douglas received the maximum sentence of 21 days and with it the reputation as a troublemaker. His next dose of FP1, this time for 14 days, came on 12 November 1917 for the trivial offence of losing a biscuit from his iron rations 'due to neglect'. [1] Clearly he was not very happy about this because 3 days later he was given another 16 days for insolence. Whether Douglas learnt his lesson or not we will never know because he died of wounds on 9 November, possibly as a result of fighting in the battle for Beersheba. He was buried in Beersheba War Cemetery.

[1] SR.

Pte Harold Manfield – aged 24
6th Btn Royal Irish Rgt – 11209
Cenotaph and St George's

The first news that Bessie Manfield had of her son Harold's death was in a letter from the military chaplain who buried him, telling her where the body was at rest and that he had placed a wooden cross over the grave. Then came a letter stating that he was wounded and in hospital, which brought confusion in her mind and a little hope. Perhaps the chaplain had been mistaken in some way and her son was alive. But no, the official announcement, dated 5 December 1916, arrived soon after to say that Harold had been killed. According to official sources he died in battle with the 6th Btn on 20 November and was buried in Croisilles Railway Cemetery, Pas-de-Calais.

As if these circumstances were not devastating enough, this tragedy came on top of another recent bereavement. The previous May, Bessie's husband Oliver, who worked as a wheelwright, was crushed to death by a cart. The couple had moved to Dorchester from Crewkerne sometime in the first decade of the 20th century and in 1911 they were living at 16 Mill St but then moved to 10 York Terr, next door to Walter and Louisa Hardy [1] who also lost a son in the War. A year after Harold's death Bessie placed a notice in the 'In Memoriam' column of the *Chronicle* which included the following:

Could I have been there in the hour of death,
To catch the last sigh of his parting breath,
His last feint whisper I might have heard,
And breathed in his ear just one parting word.
In the bloom of his life death claimed him,
In the pride of his manhood days.

---

[1] See Frederick Hardy.

Pte Frederick Walter Edwin Dawe – aged 20
1/1st Queen's Own Dorset Yeomanry – 230860
Cenotaph

Frederick was born in Dorchester, the son of Edwin, an upholsterer, and Mable, and although the family moved away he appears on the Cenotaph because his uncle George lived in the town. During the War Frederick served the Dorset Yeomanry, fighting the Turks in Egypt.

In 1917 the forces of the British Empire took their operations in Egypt into Ottoman Palestine where they fought two unsuccessful battles at Gaza in March and April. At the end of October, after 6 months of preparations, Beersheba was captured and a week later the whole of the Gaza to Beersheba line. On 19 November the Yeomanry Division pushed on into the hills and the following day units encountered strong resistance at Beitunia. Early on the 21st the Turks delivered a counterattack, engaging the Dorsets. The war diary records, 'Turks advanced strongly on right flank about 1500 hrs and regiment was ordered to retire about 1600 hrs. Retired under heavy fire and sustained heavy casualties'. Frederick disappeared in the fighting and was never seen again. He is commemorated on the Jerusalem Memorial.

Drummer Harold Willoughby Shorto – 21
2/4th Btn Dorsetshire Rgt – 200435

Pte Bertram Shorto – aged 37
1st Btn Dorsetshire Rgt – 5821

Both are commemorated on the Cenotaph

In Edwardian Dorchester it was not uncommon to find branches of the same family living close to one other. David and Emma Shorto lived at No. 14 Miller's Close for over 30 years and brought up their family there. When their son George married he and his wife Jane moved in next door, while daughter Charlotte married William Mahar and settled at No. 3.

George and Jane had a family of their own and their second eldest son Harold worked as an errand boy to an oil merchants when he left school, and when it was time to do his duty he served with the 2/4th Dorsets in Egypt. In November 1917 Harold was literally on the road to Jerusalem and on the 21st reached the village of Biddu. It was soon cleared of the enemy and the Dorsets continued towards their objective of Bire. It was not long before they came under heavy fire from a ridge and it was probably then that Harold was killed. He is buried in the Jerusalem War Cemetery.

One of Harold's uncles was his father's brother Bertram, who when his father died moved with his mother into No. 6 Miller's Close. Bertram worked as a bricklayer and went off to war in August 1914 with the 1st Btn Dorset Rgt. His Medal Roll Card indicates that he was a prisoner of war, which accounts for why he was buried in Berlin South Western Cemetery. The official records indicate that he died on 9 December 1918.

If one wanted to see how local communities within Dorchester were affected by the War Miller's Close provides an example. It consisted of about 30 houses situated at the bottom of The Grove, its entrance signposted by the Compasses public house, and during the War the telegram boy would visit the Close on six occasions to deliver the news of a death. At No. 1 was John Holland, the father of Arthur who was killed in 1915; at No. 23 lived Jane Davis who was widowed in 1918; and at No. 19 was the Fickus family who lost a father and a son. The Shorto family living in Miller's Close, as stated above, lost two family members. [1]

---

[1] See William Mahar, Arthur Holland, Reginald Davis and Frederick Fickus.

Pte Herbert Thomas Peasley – aged 38
2nd Btn Wiltshire Rgt [1]
Cenotaph

Herbert Peasley and Edith Richardson were both natives of Bath and married in 1908. As a young man Herbert followed his father into the drapery trade and it may have been this profession that brought the young couple to Dorchester, where Herbert found work in the town as a draper's assistant. The couple lived at 7 Ashley Rd.

In response to the declaration of War Herbert initially joined the Dorsets but later transferred to the 2nd Btn Wiltshire Rgt, serving with them on the Western Front. The 2nd Btn's war diary records that their artillery bombarded Ghulevelt Polderhoek near Ypres on the morning of 28 November 1917. Later in the day the enemy retaliated, causing three casualties, one of whom was probably Herbert. He was buried in Hooge Crater Cemetery near Ypres.

---

[1] On the Cenotaph he is listed under the Dorsetshire Rgt.

Pte Ernest James – aged 22
7th Btn Somerset Light Infantry – 265685
Cenotaph and St George's

To the south of Dorchester, hidden from the nearby heavy traffic of the Weymouth to Dorchester road, is the small parish of Winterborne Herringston. In 1881 Thomas James was working at Herringston Farm as a labourer/domestic servant and living in the dairy house with John Shepherd and his family. In a cottage on the estate there was also living the Amey family, which included daughter Emily. Thomas and Emily courted, were married in 1884 and went on to have 13 children. The 1911 census shows that ten of the children were still living at home, sharing five rooms which included the kitchen. The family remained at the farm, probably up to the time of Thomas's death in 1913, when Emily lost the home that went with her husband's job and moved to 7 Brownden Terrace, Cromwell Rd, Dorchester.

Ernest, their second youngest son, enlisted in the Dorsets and was then transferred to the SLI. In November 1917 the SLI was part of the 20th (Light) Division who were about to take part in the Battle of Cambrai, which commenced on 20 November and included the use of 400 tanks. After hard fighting the 20th Division advanced as far as the village of Masnières in Nord, and elsewhere many other areas were taken from the Germans. In Britain, the success of the British Army was treated as a great victory and church bells rang out for the first time since 1914. However, the Germans were preparing for a counterattack, which they launched on 30 November, the day that Ernest was killed in action. Most of the British gains were wiped out and on 4 December Haig ordered a withdrawal. The casualties during the battle had been high, over 40,000 on each side, one of which was Ernest. He is commemorated on the Cambrai Memorial, Louverval, Nord, France.

Pte Albert Vincent Keats – aged 27
2/6th Btn Gloucestershire Rgt – 37326
Cenotaph and St George's [1]

When Albert Keats was born in 1890 his parents William and Elizabeth were living at Hope Quay, Weymouth, with William's parents. Interestingly, it may well have been the case that the family knew that of Ernest James who was killed just 2 days before Albert. Albert's grandfather William, a sailor, was born at Winterborne Herringston when the James family were there. When Albert left school he took up his father's profession of cabinet-maker and moved out of the family home to work in Parkstone, Poole, and on 17 April 1911 he married Emily Hobbs, the daughter of a carter, in her local church of St George's, Langton Matravers, near Swanage. The couple settled in Dorchester, living at 24 Duke's Ave a few doors away from William and Hersella Loveless.

Like Ernest James, Albert fought at the Battle of Cambrai, but with the Gloucesters. As part of the 61st (South Midland) Division the 2/6th Btn was not involved in the initial attack but held back in reserve and when the Germans made their counterattack it was ordered up to reinforce units in the area under attack near La Vacquerle. Albert was killed in action on 2 December and is buried in Cagnicourt British Cemetery, Pas-de-Calais.

---

[1] St George's wrongly shows A.D. Keats.

View from the tower of St George's, Fordington, looking west. Duke's Avenue can be clearly seen. This short road illustrates the effect of the War on small communities. No less than nine families living there had connections with someone who had died in the War. (Source: From the private collection of Mr S. Poulter.)

Pte Oscar Gerald Payne – aged 27
4th Btn Royal Fusiliers – 59495
Cenotaph and St George's

Oscar Payne was born in Piddletrenthide, one of the villages that takes its name from the chalk stream that runs through the Piddle valley. The family lived at Middle Tything and his father worked as a newsagent. In 1911 we find that Oscar had left the rural life and was living in the small town of Tenbury in Worcestershire, working as a grocer's assistant but he came back to Dorset to marry Matilda Thomas, a Dorchester lass, in 1913. Matilda was the daughter of Henry and Flora and lived at 14 Culliford Rd. Oscar's first entry into the Army was with the Dorset Yeomanry but at some time he was posted to the 4th Btn Royal Fusiliers, also known as the City of London Rgt.

On 9 December 1917, after a week in the trenches opposite the French village of Pronville, the Fusiliers moved into a camp behind the British line near Mory, between Arras and Bapaume. The weather was described in the battalion war diary as cold and wet but at least Oscar was able to take a hot bath. Three days later he was back in the trenches which were subject to constant shelling and local attacks by the enemy. Added to this the Fusiliers had to cope with their own artillery firing short into the area they occupied. On the 14th the battalion was relieved by the 8th East Yorkshire Rgt and the Fusiliers counted the cost of holding this part of the line for the short period. It amounted to three OR killed, one died of wounds and three wounded. Oscar was among those killed. He died on 14 December and is buried in Mory Abbey Cemetery, Pas-de-Calais.

Sgt Thomas Wilfred Dowden – aged 26
1st Btn Royal Fusiliers – 229277
Cenotaph and St Peter's

Living two doors from each other in Icen Way, Thomas Dowden and William Vincent [1] may well have been playmates when they were children. Three years older than William, who lived at No. 44, Thomas and his parents lived at No. 46. Both were to die in the War. Thomas moved to London before 1911 and worked as a railway porter, boarding in Wandsworth with the brother of Percy Easley, another Dorchester casualty. [2] At the time of their son's death Thomas's parents were living at 18 Frome Terr, two doors away from the Clarke family who also lost a son. [3]

In September 1918 the parishioners of All Saints' Church read the following entry in the parish magazine: 'I fear that there can be little hope that Sgt T. Dowden can still be alive. He was announced as missing after the Cambrai fight some months ago, and his name has not appeared amongst lists of prisoners. He used to sing in our choir as a boy, and was a constant attendant at the Bible Class at the Rectory. His death is a sad blow to his invalid mother.' [4] Hope for Thomas's friends and relatives had been kept alive by an article in the *Chronicle* the previous July, reporting that 'Anxiety is felt as to the fate of Sgt T. Dowden, Royal Fusiliers, of Dorchester who was reported missing on December 30th. Two privates of his company are prisoners of war in Germany.' [5] All hope disappeared when his mother received official confirmation that her son had indeed been killed in action on 30 December 1917. Unfortunately, the battalion war diary gives no indication of how Thomas died. He is commemorated on the Thiepval Memorial.

[1] See William Vincent.
[2] See Percy Easley.
[3] See Ernest Clarke.
[4] *Dorchester All Saints' Monthly Magazine.* Dorset History Centre (PE/DO(AS)/MG 1).
[5] *Chronicle* 28/2/1918.

1918
The Battle Front

France and Belgium

In the spring of 1918 the Germans launched a series of large operations (known as the Spring Offensive) that were designed to break conclusively the allied line in several places and win the War before the American forces became effective.

Operation Michael, 21 March–5 April

The first offensive, codenamed 'Operation Michael' and known as the Kaiserschlacht (Kaiser's Battle), was launched on 21 March and aimed at the British on the Somme. After an intense barrage the infantry attack came as a complete surprise to the British and the contents of many battalion diaries written at the time show the utter confusion and desperation as the British retreated, outnumbered three to one. Despite the gain of territory the Germans ran out of steam, because of overextended supply lines and exhausted men. Subsequent engagements in defence of the British line included the following:

> Battle of St Quentin, 21–23 Mar; First Battle of Bapaume, 24–25 Mar; First Battle of Noyon, 25 Mar; Battle of Rosières, 26–27 Mar; First Battle of Arras, 28 Mar; Battle of Avre, 4 Apr; Battle of Ancre, 5 Apr.

Operation Georgette, 9–29 April

'Operation Georgette' was aimed at the Allied line around the River Lys in Flanders and on the first day the Germans captured 4 miles of ground behind Portuguese-held trenches, followed the next day by an attack on the British Second Army. Once again the British troops had to retreat under the weight of the oncoming forces, to such a degree that they lost many of the places, like Messines and Passchendaele, that they had given so many lives for previously. The engagements fought during the Lys offensive were:

> Battle of Èstaires, 9–11 Apr; Battle of Messines, 10–11 Apr; Battle of Hazebrouk, 12–15 Apr; First Battle of Kemmel Ridge, 17–19 Apr; Battle of Bethune, 18 Apr; Second Battle of Kemmel Ridge, 25–26 Apr; Battle of Scherpenberg, 29 Apr.

Third Battle of the Aisne, 27 May–6 June

On the morning of 27 May over 4,000 German guns opened up on the Allied line on the Chemin Des Dames Ridge, and the British, packed into the trenches in their sector, suffered heavy casualties from the accurate shelling, before the infantry attack came. Once again taking the Allies by surprise, the Germans smashed through parts of the line and advanced through a 40-km gap in the defences. By 6 June they had advanced to within 60 km of Paris but had to make a halt on the River Marne. The reasons for this were, again, a lack of supplies and reserves of troops, plus the fact that the Allies, which now included the newly arrived Americans, were mounting counterattacks.

Second Battle of the Marne, 15 July–5 August

This was the last German large-scale offensive and was a diversionary tactic to disguise a major attack in Flanders, against the BEF. Despite gaining some ground the Germans failed to make a breakthrough and on 18 July the French launched a counterattack, aided by British, American and Italian troops. By 20 July the Germans had withdrawn to the positions they had occupied at the beginning of their Spring Offensive.

Allied advance to victory

In July the Allies began a series of attacks on the German line. The principal operations involving British troops on the road to victory were as follows:

> Battle of Amiens, 8–11 Aug; Outtersteene Ridge, 18 Aug; Battle of Albert, 21–23 Aug; Battle of the Scarpe, 26–30 Aug; Battle of Bapaume, 31 August–3 Sept; Battle of Drocourt-Queant, 2–3 Sept; Battle of Havrincourt, 12 Sept; Battle of Epehy, 18 Sept; Fifth Battle of Ypres, 28 Sept–2 Oct; Battle of St Quentin Canal, 29 Sept–2 Oct; Battle of the Canal du Nord, 1 Oct; ; Advance in Artois, 2 Oct–11 Nov; Battle of Beaurevior, 3–5 Oct; Battle of Cambrai, 8–9 Oct; Battle of Coutrai, 14–19 Oct; Battle of the Selle, 17–25 Oct; Battle of Valenciennes, 1–2 Nov; Battle of the Sambre, 4 Nov.

Mesopotamia

After the capture of Ramadi the next target for the British was Khan Baghdadi, which was taken on 27 March with the aid of 400 Ford lorries. The final battle of the Mesopotamian campaign occurred on 29 October when Sir William Marshall's forces secured the Mosul oilfields.

Salonika

At the beginning of the year the Allies were ready to make a major attack in an effort to end the fighting. The British did not get involved in the operation until 15 September, when with Greek troops they made an attack in the Lake Dorian area, with disastrous results. British and Greek losses totalled 7,103 and the Bulgarians withdrew from their positions.

1918
Roll of Honour

Boy Mechanic William Ernest Parsons – aged 17
Royal Flying Corps – 156739
Cenotaph and St Peter's

Sapper Arthur William Parsons – aged 39
9th Canadian Railway Troops
Cenotaph

The name of Parsons adorned the front of a grocery shop at 31 High East St for a hundred years and many a Durnovarian through the generations has enjoyed the aroma of freshly ground coffee wafting through the open door as they passed. Charles Parsons purchased the shop in 1871 from Mr Potter, his employer. A prominent citizen, Charles was a leading light in the establishment of the Plymouth Brethren in the town, reportedly holding services in his store in Durngate Street before a church in Acland Road was built. When Charles retired the business passed to his son Ernest.

Parsons' shop in High East Street.

Ernest was married to Emma and in 1901 their first son Willie was born. Willie attended Dorchester Commercial School which, as well as providing the basic curriculum, taught those skills required for office work and business. His school report for 1909 shows that he was particularly strong in English and his conduct was excellent, and the *Chronicle* described him as 'One of the brightest and most promising scholars that Mr Victor Dodderidge ever had'. [1] Despite receiving an education geared for commerce Willie's real interests and talent lay in mechanical science and he became quite an expert at operating the school's telegraph system. The school had its own scout troop, of which Willie was a member, and he went on to receive the coveted award of King's Scout.

In 1914 Willie was not old enough to go to war so instead drove his father's motor car, petrol restrictions permitting, collecting and delivering grocery orders. Keen to help his country, as a scout he did his bit on the home front, be it at some cost to his education. His father received a letter in September 1914 from the Commandant of the Dorset National Reserve, pointing out that the scouts were due back at school after carrying out duties for the military since the beginning of the War, and that Mr Dodderidge, the headmaster, had decided to leave it to each parent to decide whether their son should continue their studies or continue 'to help the officers who are working almost night and day at their military duties', also adding, 'Therefore I write to beg you on patriotic grounds to allow your son to go on as he is doing. He is giving valuable help to the Country in this tremendous crisis in her history by doing work which would otherwise have to be performed by a young soldier, to the detriment of his military training'. [2]

(Source: Mr K. Parsons.)

When Willie was old enough he informed his parents that he wished to join the RFC as a mechanic. Ernest applied on his behalf on 3 November 1917 and was informed that Willie just fell into the qualifying age bracket, which was 15–17½. [3] Having satisfied the educational requirements and given satisfactory references, one of which was provided by Mr Jackman of the YMCA, [4] Willie was accepted into the RFC as a boy mechanic and started at the School for Technical Training at Haldon Camp, Tring, in Hertfordshire.

According to the Adjutant at Haldon Camp the first indication that all was not well with Willie was when he reported sick on 10 January 1918 with a cold and then on the 18th with what was diagnosed as impetigo. He again paraded before the MO on the 23rd with a swollen face and showing signs of albumin in his urine. It was only then that it was recognised that there might be something seriously wrong with the young recruit and he was admitted to the Isolation Hospital the next day. In a letter to his parents from hospital Willie was quite matter of fact about his illness and there appeared to be little reason for Ernest and Emma to be unduly anxious [5] Then, on the 26th they received a telegram informing them that Willie was dangerously ill.

Ernest immediately left for Tring, where he arrived the following day, in time to be with his son during the last hours of his young life. He died the same day of scarlet fever.

Back in Dorchester, his funeral service on 7 February was conducted by a missionary of the Plymouth Brethren to Central Africa and attended by a large number of townspeople. The days that followed brought many letters of sympathy, including one from Willie's CO saying, 'It has been a great blow to the section, for he was universally liked – and the whole flight have expressed their desire to be present at the funeral'. [6]

Among the letters of condolence one stood out. It came from a colleague of Willie's, L/Cpl Dunkerley, who slept in the same hut. He told how his friend had reported sick every morning for 8 days before being admitted to hospital and that, 'The Medical Officer ought to have known his case was serious before all that time passed. They don't seem to care much'. [7] By writing such a letter Dunkerley had committed what in the eyes of the authorities was an offence and he asked not to be mentioned in any subsequent complaint. We do not know how far it went but it appears that Ernest made some representations, the evidence for which is contained in two letters. The first was from the Adjutant at Haldon who stated that an investigation had taken place but gave no indication of any conclusion arrived at. The second letter was from Willie's schoolmaster and scoutmaster, Mr Medway, in which he wrote, 'I am very sorry to think that his bright career has been cut off by the carelessness of those whose duty it was to have given him every attention' [8]. Willie's sad story ends there. His family remained in Dorchester, a Jack Parsons becoming mayor. Parsons' shop finally closed in the 1980s, after moving into Cornhill, and with it went part of Dorchester's history.

Arthur, the younger brother of Ernest, was born in June 1879 at 31 High East St. He attended Dorchester Grammar School, where he took a prominent part in athletics and on completing his studies became an assistant at Bascombes, the drapers. He then went to live in Cardiff for a while before making the decision to join his sister Louisa and her husband Ernest in their migration to Canada. Arthur arrived in Montreal on the SS *Kensington* on 20 May 1906 and found work as a salesman. At his Attestation into the 9th Canadian Railway Troops in January 1916 he stated that he had already served with the 16th Field Ambulance for 2½ years, suggesting that he was a Territorial before the War. The Canadian Railway Troops were part of the Canadian Pioneers and had the job of maintaining the allied railway network.

In October 1918 his unit was working in the Vimy Ridge area, Pas-de-Calais, when Arthur was taken ill with severe pneumonia, from which he died on 13 October. He was buried in Beaulencourt British Cemetery. For Louisa, Arthur's

(Source: Mr A. Parsons.)

sister, as for so many Canadians, the name Vimy Ridge represents both grief and pride. [9] As well as losing Arthur, her son Charlie was killed there.

[1] *Chronicle* 7/2/1918.
[2] Letter dated 12/9/1914.
[3] Letter dated 6/11/1917.
[4] Letter dated 7/11/1917.
[5] Undated letter.
[6] Letter dated 28/1/18.
[7] Letter dated February 1918.
[8] Letter dated 14/2/1918
[9] The Canadians captured Vimy Ridge from the Germans in April 1917, incurring 10,602 casualties, comprising 3,598 killed and 7,004 wounded.

L/Cpl Stanley George Lee – aged 30
1/4th Btn Dorsetshire Rgt – 201126
Cenotaph, St Peter's and Post Office

Stanley is one of the 11 postal staff of the district who gave their lives in the War. He was born at Winterborne Herringston, the son of George and Fannie. Soon after his birth, the family moved to 13 Friary Lane, Dorchester, where George worked as a coachman. When George died, Stanley had to leave school prematurely to help support the family. At 13 he was working as a telegram boy with the post office and later gained promotion to postman. In 1912 he married Emma Symonds of Wincanton. Stanley joined the Dorsets in Dorchester and served with the 1/4th Btn in Mesopotamia, where he died of accident or illness on 15 February. He was buried in Amara War Cemetery.

L/Cpl Herbert John Atherton – aged 25
9th Lancers and 8th Squadron Machine Gun
Corps – 519879
Cenotaph

In 1911 Florence Atkins lived with her parents, Benjamin, a coal porter, and Mary, at 1 Maud Rd. Also residing there was a boarder, John Mallory, who worked as a labourer with the GWR and it was probably through him that she met her future husband. Herbert Atherton, a Welshman from Cardiff, worked in the traffic department of the GWR as a porter. (One of his work colleagues was Frederick Pidden, who died in October 1916. [1]) Herbert and Florence married in 1915 and their daughter Marie was born soon after.

(Courtesy of Swindon Collection, Swindon Library.)

Herbert enlisted in the 9th Lancers and was later

transferred to the 8th Squadron MGC. Unfortunately, the war diary for this unit is not available after February 1918 so we do not know what fighting he was involved in just prior to his death. He died of wounds on the 11 March and was buried in Tincourt New British Cemetery, Somme. He is also remembered on the GWR Memorial located in the ticket office at Chester railway station. After her husband's death Florence placed a notice in the *Chronicle* which included the following verse:

> *We cannot know what pain he bore,*
> *When with that blow he fell.*
> *God called him to a perfect peace,*
> *From those who loved him well.*

---

[1] See Frederick Pidden.

Pte Reginald Joseph Lucas – aged 28
20th Btn Durham Light Infantry – 54237
Cenotaph and St Peter's

On 2 May 1918 the *Chronicle* reported 'Another home in Orchard Street on which bereavement has fallen is that of 29'. Living at that address was Ada Lucas and hers was the fourth house in the street to receive the dreaded telegram during the course of the War. Others were the Colliers at No. 24, the Martins at No. 7 and the Painters at No. 30. [1] In fact, Reginald Lucas's death brought sadness to more than one house in Orchard St; his parents lived at No. 18 and an uncle at No. 5.

When Reginald was born his parents were living in Mill Street and moved to 7 Frome Terr in the 1890s. At 21 he was working as a porter for Henry Ling, the printer, at 23 High West St. He was also an agent for the sale of the *Chronicle* and in his spare time was a member of St Peter's gymnastic club. His marriage to Ada Cornick took place in St Peter's Church on 5

(Source: Mrs J. Mercer.)

August 1912 and they chose to live near their relatives in Orchard St, where their three children were born.

Reginald was called up and attested at No. 3 RFA Depot Hilsea in Hampshire on 13 November 1916, and was then sent for training to Rugeley Camp on Cannock Chase. However, his association with the gunners lasted less than 2 months, as he was transferred to an infantry battalion, the 13th DLI, joining them in France on 12 February 1917. Between 20 and 25 September Reginald took part in the Battle of Menin Road Ridge. His battalion was part of a force tasked with securing the hotly disputed 'Tower Hamlets Spur' and took part in the second phase of the attack on 'Green Line', astride the Menin Road. Their first objective was to capture the 'Blue Line', which they did and were consolidating the position when the Germans massed for a counterattack, causing the DLI to send up an SOS flare.

In response the British artillery opened up in support and the Germans were broken up. The next day the guns were required to help the 13th once again when, during a German attack, things became so desperate that even the battalion's headquarters personnel had to take up arms. The fighting had been costly for the Durhams, with 48 men killed, 181 wounded and 16 men missing.

On the third day of the battle Reginald was taken by the 6th Australian Field Ambulance to a Casualty Clearing Station with a wound. His service record indicates a shrapnel wound to his hand but the later hospital diagnosis was that he had been shot in the arm just below his left shoulder. The confusion is compounded by a photograph of him with his right arm in a sling but this may have been an inaccuracy when the photograph was produced. In any event, Reginald's wound was severe enough for him to be sent home where he was treated at Wharncliffe Military Hospital, Sheffield.

Reginald spent 4½ months in England, during which he was able to spend some time with his family and friends. It was then time for him to rejoin his unit. Had Reginald been posted back to the 13th Btn his life might have been spared but while he was in England they had been taken from the battlefields of France and sent to fight in Italy. So, instead was sent to join the 20th Btn at Etaples on 17 March 1918. In less than a week he was dead.

On 22 March the men were improving trenches after an advance towards Vaulx-Vraucourt, about 5 miles from Bapaume. That night they had to retire behind the line and the battalion diary recorded 'the rest of the night passed off uneventfully'. [2] However, in war, words like 'uneventfully' take on a new meaning and do not exclude men from being killed. At the end of the day the 20th added another three men to its roll of honour.

After a month of not hearing from her husband Ada was alarmed and wrote to the Army saying she was anxious as he always wrote to her regularly. In reply, she received two letters from the Infantry Record Office, both dated 23 April and signed by different people. One said that as far as they were aware he was fit and well, the other proffered the news that he had been killed in action on 28 March. The usual machinery then went into action, to settle any outstanding monies owed, returning personal possessions and eventually dispatching Reginald's medals and commemorative plaque, but that was not quite the end of the story.

Ada was desperate to know where her loved one's body was located. Six years after his death, some identity discs were sent to her with his name on. Reginald had previously told her that he had marked his discs so that if they were ever returned she would know they were definitely his. She was not convinced and wrote to the authorities saying that now surely they must know where his body was. Unfortunately, their reply does not exist, but we do know that Ada died without knowing if her husband's body was ever found. [3] Reginald's name was added to the Arras Memorial. His daughter Winifred Lucas, who was born on 18 February 1917, did not grow up to know her father but had one token of his love – a postcard sent by Reginald from the Front with the words 'To my darling Babe with her loving dad's love and kisses'.

---

[1] See Horace Collier, Victor Martin and William Painter.

[2] WD.

[3] Information supplied by a relative.

Pte John Mayo Biggs – aged 40
23rd Btn Royal Fusiliers – 48639
Cenotaph and Holy Trinity

In 1881 Thomas Biggs, a wine importer, and his wife Annie were living at 3 High West St and 2 years before that, on 22 November 1879, they celebrated the christening of their only son John Mayo at St Peter's Church. By 1901 they had moved into 4 Cornwall Road, one of the smart villas overlooking the Borough Gardens, where John doubtless spent many hours of his childhood playing. When John grew up he qualified as a brewer, but not content with staying in Dorchester he moved to Hemel Hempstead, where he became the owner of the Star Brewery, and like so many Dorset ex-patriots joined the Society of Dorset Men in London. Back in Dorchester his mother was widowed in 1911.

For his part in the War John joined the Royal Fusiliers and at the time of his death was serving with the 23rd Btn. The 23rd, which had been formed in the Cecil Hotel in The Strand, was known as the First Sportsmen's [1] Btn and had been fighting in France since June 1915. When the great German offensive started in March 1918 the men were resting at Equancourt, Somme. They had no inclination of the rout that was about to take place. The first sign of a breakthrough came when shells started landing in their camp and during the days that followed John and his comrades had their hands full trying to repel German attacks, at the same time endeavouring to make a tactical withdrawal. From 12 March to the end of the month the battalion was severely ravaged, with over 550 casualties, and such was the degree to which the fusiliers were overwhelmed that over 200 of the casualties, of which John was one, were reported as missing. The official date of his death was given as 25 March.

It was over a year before Annie Biggs was notified officially that it must be assumed her son had been killed. John is commemorated on the Arras War Memorial and appears on the war memorial in Hemel Hempstead.

---

[1] The 23rd Btn Royal Fusiliers was one of two Sportsmen's battalions. They were largely made up of men who had made a name for themselves in sports such as golf, football, cricket and boxing and had been given dispensation to recruit men up to the age of 45.

Lt-Col Alan Roderick Haig-Brown, DSO – aged 40
23rd Btn Middlesex Rgt
Holy Trinity

Alan Haig-Brown's connection with Dorchester came through the family of Alfred Pope, the brewer. Alan's father was the Rev William Haig-Brown, headmaster of Charterhouse School, which was attended by several of the Popes' sons. The connection was strengthened further when Alan married Violet, the second of Alfred's four daughters, in 1907.

Educated at his father's school and at Pembroke College, Cambridge, Alan left university with a classics degree and went to Lancing College to work as a master. The pay of a schoolmaster was somewhat meagre so he supplemented his earnings by writing freelance for the newspapers, mainly on the subjects of sport and nature. In sport his forte was football and not just writing about it. He got his Blue at Cambridge on the football field and later played as an amateur for the professional teams of Tottenham Hotspurs and Brighton and Hove Albion. He combined his love of nature, field sports and fishing with his writing skills and had several books published, including *Sporting Sonnets* and *My Game Book*.

Alan's first interest in the military emerged at Lancing College, when he was appointed Lieutenant of the Cadet Corps, and when it changed to an Officer Training Corps he took command, until December 1915, when he was appointed second in command of a service battalion of the Middlesex Rgt. He went with them to France and when their CO Lt-Col Ash was killed at the Somme in September 1915 Alan was promoted to lieutenant colonel and took over the battalion. After taking part in the Battle of the Somme in 1916 the 23rd Btn moved to the Ypres area and it was there that he was mentioned in Despatches in April 1917. In June he was slightly wounded and awarded, in the same month, the DSO. Later in the summer the strain of continuous fighting around Messines and Wystchaete had its effect on him and he returned to England for rest in a hospital.

On returning to duty in October Alan learned that the 23rd were off to the Italian Front to help stem the thrust of the German/Austrian armies but then plans were changed. When the Russians left the War, following their revolution, it meant that thousands of German troops could now be moved to fight on the Western Front and because of this Alan's battalion was moved back to France.

When the Germans launched their vast offensive on 21 March 1918 the battalion were in billets, but 4 days later they were fighting a desperate rear-guard action in a field near Achiet-le-Grand, Pas-de-Calais. Withdrawal was left until the enemy almost enclosed them and Alan was directing the retirement of his men when he was killed instantaneously by a machine gun at close range. He was buried in Achiet-le-Grand Memorial Cemetery and his name also appears on the Shoreham-by-Sea Memorial and Lancing College Roll of Honour.

Pte Reginald Charles Bright – aged 24
1st Btn Worcestershire Rgt
Cenotaph

There is no documentary evidence to prove that Reginald lived in Dorchester, except for the entry in SDGW which states 'Living in Dorchester'. The connection with the town comes through his sister Violet who married a Paul Morton in Dorchester in 1915. In support of this the 1918 register of electors shows Albert John Bright, Reginald's brother, living with the Mortons at 9 St Martin's Rd.

Reginald was born in Lymington, Hampshire, where, in 1911, he was living with his mother and sister Violet and was employed as a shop assistant in a boot retailers. On 23 March 1918 his battalion, the 1st Btn Worcesters, were holding a much extended river line at Pargny on the Somme against German advances. Reginald died of wounds on 28 March and was buried at Assevilliers New British Cemetery, Somme.

Pte Francis George Pearce – aged 36
23rd Btn London Rgt – 718069
St Peter's

Francis Pearce (known by his second name George) lived with his parents Mary and Charles, an agricultural labourer, in Buckland Ripers, a village near Weymouth. George later went to live in Dorchester where he worked as a carman and his home address was 18 Charles St.

In December 1915 George enlisted and was put in the National Reserve with the 3rd Dorsets to await mobilisation, which for him came on 21 March 1916. He did his training at Wyke Regis and was then transferred to the London Rgt, going to France on 28 June. He fought with the 12th Btn without any mishap, except for a couple of spells in hospital with diarrhoea and fever, and in January 1918 was posted to the 23rd Btn. On 5 April he was helping to fight off a German offensive near the village of Bazentin-le-Petit, 6 miles northeast of Albert, when he was hit by a shell fragment which fractured his right thigh. Unable to get back to his unit he was taken prisoner and died of his wounds on the 8th. It is unclear whether his body was returned for burial or whether he was buried by the Germans in a temporary grave. In either case, he was later transferred to Delville Wood Cemetery, Somme.

Pte Walter John Kingman – aged 25
2/4th Btn Dorsetshire Rgt – 200755
Thomas Hardye School Roll of Honour

Walter Kingman's father, also Walter, was the tenant of Duddle Dairy farm at Bockhampton, 3 miles to the east of Dorchester, where he lived with his wife Martha and their five children. Walter Junior, the eldest son, was sent to Dorchester Grammar School for his education and then worked on the family farm. He enlisted in the 2/4th Dorset Rgt and served in Egypt.

The object of British operations in Palestine in April 1918 was to break the Turkish line in the neighbourhood of Berukin near Jaffa and push the Turks towards the sea. The first step was to capture and occupy a line between Berukin and Rafat and the 2/4th Dorsets' part of the assault was to capture and hold a high hog's back called Three Bushes Hill. Accordingly, early on 9 April Walter joined the advance towards the hill and after a short fight it was secured. At 7.45 am the Turks made a determined counterattack on the Dorset's left flank, occupied by B Coy. It was repulsed, but heavy shelling meant that the men had to withdraw to the hindmost edge of the hill, with the Turks taking up a line on the leading edge. Now the opposing troops were facing each other only 50–100 yd apart. Then, D Coy, on the right flank, reported their position as serious and all HQ staff were called upon to join the fight. In addition to the Turkish infantry assault the Dorsets were encountering heavy artillery fire, during which one man had an extraordinary escape from death. A shell landed by Sgt Collis and blew off both his arms and a leg, which in normal circumstances would have meant certain death, but he was standing by the first-aid post at the time and the MO immediately applied tourniquets and he lived to tell the tale.

Reinforced by two companies of Indian infantry the Dorsets hung on to their position for the rest of the day, repulsing a series of attacks, until things quietened down in the late afternoon. Then, with the advent of night the enemy came again, the two sides firing at each other at point-blank range. The regimental history describes the position the next morning as 'not a very comfortable one'. Tenaciously the 2/4th and the Indians clung on to their position until they were relieved on the night of the 10th/11th by an Indian regiment. The 2 days' fighting had been costly for the Dorsets, with around 90 men killed or wounded. Among those killed on the 9th was Walter. His body lies in Ramleh War Cemetery, which contains 3,300 Commonwealth graves from WWI.

Pte Henry Cook – aged 19
2nd Btn Hampshire Rgt – 78198
Cenotaph and Holy Trinity

Henry was born in 1898, the son of Alice Cook. He lived at 37 High West St, where his grandfather ran a cabinet-making business, and he attended the Grammar School. He was killed while serving with the 2nd Hampshires in France.

After holding Spree Farm near Ypres against German assaults, the 2nd Hampshires were at Haslar Camp on 9 April 1918 when news of a new attack came. Arriving at Watou, 12 miles east of Ypres, Henry and comrades climbed onto a bus bound for Bailleul and continued along the Armentières road before coming to a sudden halt at 4 pm. The battalion was told that it had to deploy immediately as the Germans had taken Steenwerck and were advancing. Patrols were sent out and the forward companies got as far as Steenwerck railway station and dug in. The next morning further patrols were sent forward to see what the situation in Steenwerck was like and found it heavily defended, with the Germans sending their own patrols up the railway line to gather intelligence on the strength of the British. At 6 pm shells started to fall among the Hampshires, followed by an attack by German infantry. This attempt was promptly and successfully checked, but the day's casualties came to 40 killed and missing and 52 wounded. Henry was among the dead and his name appears on the Ploegsteert Memorial.

Cpl Arthur Farnham – aged 31
38th Bde, RFA – 102258
Cenotaph and St Peter's

The early months of 1918 were an anxious time for Eliza Farnham, whose son Arthur had been wounded in France. But now was a time to be joyful. He was on his way home from the hospital where he had been treated and would soon be arriving on the train. Doubtless she went to the station to meet him, but he did not arrive.

Arthur worked for Lord Digby's hunting stables at Minterne House, 10 miles north of Dorchester, which may have influenced his decision to join the RFA, where horses were an integral part of a fighting team. He had been serving with the 24th Bty of the 38th Bde RFA for over 2 years when he was wounded and sent home on Christmas Eve 1917 to be treated at Novar Red Cross Hospital in Aberdeen. Having recovered from his wounds he boarded a train, to spend 10 days leave with his mother. Tragically, instead of stepping off the train his dead body was found on the morning of 11 April 1918 alongside the track just outside Lancaster. At the coroner's inquest the jury returned a verdict of 'Found dead on the line', there being no evidence of how he died. Arthur did eventually return home to be buried in Dorchester Cemetery.

Lt-Col Thomas William Bullock – aged 43
1st Btn Dorsetshire Rgt
Cenotaph

In any walk of life there are those who sit back and do only what is required, and those who, with enthusiasm and commitment, try to improve things. Thomas Bullock came under the latter category. Born in London, the son of Fanny and Samuel, a Superintendent of Wrecks with the Board of Trade, Thomas received his education at Wilson's Grammar School in Camberwell and at King's College, afterwards deciding on a career in the Army. He was commissioned as 2 Lt in October 1900 with the 1st West India Rgt, which was part of the Regular Army that spent most of its time in the British colonies of the Caribbean. Before going off to exotic climes, he spent some time at the Hythe School of Musketry on the edge of Romney Marsh. Then it was off to Barbados to join the regiment, where his organising skills were soon recognised and he was made adjutant in 1904, at the age of 30. It was in Barbados that he met and married Constance Wade, the daughter of a doctor. Following periods in Bermuda and Jamaica, the West India Rgt received orders to move to West Africa, and it was Thomas's job to superintend the transfer. Ever conscious of the plight of his men, while serving in Africa he did useful work trying to alleviate the effects of malaria among the men.

In 1908 his career took another path when he moved to the 23rd Btn London Rgt where after 2 years he was promoted to captain and transferred to the Dorsets, there being appointed Recruiting Officer for the county and Adjutant of the Special Reserve. In 1914 his wife sadly died, leaving him with two motherless sons..

That same year, when the order for mobilisation arrived in Dorchester the immediate need was for someone with the ability to turn the first rush of civilians into soldiers, for which Thomas was well suited. Accordingly, he was made adjutant and attached to the 3rd Btn and after 4 days of feverish activity, staff working under flares at night, the first batch of new recruits marched out of the Depot Barracks heading for training camps at Wyke Regis, Weymouth and Upton, Ringstead. In December 1915 Thomas was promoted to major, after which he went to France and was attached to the General Staff, but the following June he was invalided home and it was probably then that he married his second wife, Milicent White.

Many songs emerged from the Great War, some of which took a swipe at senior officers. One contains the lines 'Forward Joe Soap's Army marching without fear, with our brave commanders safely in the rear'. It is true that sometimes HQ officers like Thomas were well behind the lines, but sometimes they were not, and in any case they were not immune to enemy artillery fire. On 12 April 1918 [1] Thomas, now a lieutenant colonel, was at the 1st Btn HQ at Douchy, between Arras and Albert, when an enemy shell fell, killing him. He was buried in Bienvillers Cemetery, Pas-de-Calais.

In a letter, Thomas's successor adjutant wrote, 'The men are all very cut up about the loss of the Colonel. Their letters are full of it, and in several cases I have read, "He was the best Commanding Officer we ever had. He was always so considerate and looked after the welfare of the men"', [2] and the unit's MO wrote, 'He is the finest Colonel I have ever had without a doubt, and always his first care was for his officers and his men, and he used to be most careful to see that they were as comfortable as possible, and was continually asking men whether anything could be done for their comfort and health'. [3] Thomas's reputation was not his only legacy. Whilst at Wyke Camp he published a pamphlet with another officer entitled 'An Aid to Instructors', which went to eight editions and was used extensively by the Army.

[1] The regimental history gives the 12th, although the Roll of Honour, the CWGC and SDGW give the 11th.
[2] Du Ruvigny, 1922.
[3] Ibid.

Pte Tom Martin – aged 24
2/4th Btn Dorsetshire Rgt – 200876
Cenotaph

The 1901 and the 1911 censuses for The Grove, Dorchester, both show Tom Martin living with his mother Harriet with, in both occasions, his father absent, although Harriet states that she is married. A reason for this is hinted at in the birthplace of Tom's brother, which is shown as Cairo, suggesting that the father may well have been a soldier serving abroad. Tom too was kitted out in khaki uniform suited to the North African climate when he enlisted in the 2/4th Dorsets and went to serve with them in Egypt.

On the night of 10/11 April 1918 the Dorsets were relieved of their position on Three Bushes Hill [1] after practically 96 hours of continuous fighting and marching, and in the casualty clearing station medical staff were busy tending the wounded and dead. Tom probably died of wounds there on 12 April. He has no known grave and is commemorated on the Jerusalem Memorial.

[1] See Walter Kingman.

Pte Frank Wheatcroft – aged 28
1st Btn Dorsetshire Rgt – 9037
Cenotaph

One day in 1976 a house in Weymouth was being cleared, following death of the occupant. An observant relative who was helping noticed something in the builder's skip that looked interesting and on further investigation took from it some medals, a 'Dead Man's Penny' [1] and some letters and photographs. Having retrieved the artefacts he saw that they

Frank Wheatcroft. (Source: Mr M. Goddard.)

related to a Frank Wheatcroft, a name that was not familiar to him, so he took them home and started to trace the person to whom they belonged. Nineteen years later he was able to pass them on to their rightful owner, Frank Wheatcroft's great nephew Mervyn.

More than 100 years before the above event Louisa Palmer married a solder, Frederick Wheatcroft of the 2nd Dorsets, in 1889 and their first child Frank appeared soon after. The three lived at 10 Grove Buildings from where the parade ground bugle at the Depot Barracks could be heard. It appears that the family then moved to Openshaw, Manchester, the husband's home town, where their second child was born. Unfortunately, Frederick started to show signs of mental illness, which affected his army career and resulted in the couple parting, Fred remaining in the North and Louisa returning to live in Dorchester with her two children. To make ends meet she worked as a charlady and when her son Frank got a job with the *Chronicle* he was able to add to the family's income.

Frank became a Territorial with the Dorsets and doubtless knew other local part-time soldiers like the Membury brothers. [2] Then, just before his 21st birthday, he decided to become a full-time soldier with the same regiment and after enlistment was posted to the 1st Btn, serving in Belfast. Frank was a sober man but a few misdemeanours are recorded on his conduct sheet, including breaking out of barracks in civilian clothes without a pass and neglect of duty.

On mobilisation the 1st Dorsets went to France and Frank fought with them through the early battles of Mons, the Marne, La Bassée and Armentières, and was in the Ypres sector in January 1915 when he was mentioned in Despatches for gallant conduct. He remained with the 1st Btn through 1916 and then in June 1917 he was given some well-deserved home leave, during which he married Evelyn Osmond of Cerne Abbas.

By 1918 Frank was a very valuable commodity; he was an experienced soldier who had been tested on the battlefield and could pass on that experience to fresh recruits from home. However, any amount of experience could not account for the German shell that had a soldier's name on it. One day in April, Frank was standing outside a shelter in the line near Ayette, Pas-de-Calais, when a shell exploded nearby, fatally wounding him. He died on 13 April and is buried in Bac du Sud Military Cemetery, Bailleuval. Evelyn remarried in 1925 and her treasured mementos were passed on through her second family.

---

[1] The commemorative plaque sent to next of kin was also known as the Dead Man's Penny or the Widow's Penny. See photo on page 236.
[2] See William Membury.

Driver Wilfred Arthur George Bowring – aged 18
73rd Bty, RFA – 24024
Cenotaph and St George's

Wilfred Bowring was born in Fordington in 1900, the eldest son of John, a bricklayer's labourer, and Flora. The family of seven children lived at 20 Short's Lane, off Mill Street. Wilfred worked for Marvin Lock who ran several businesses in the town, as well as being a farmer. [1] In his spare time Wilfred was a member of the Boys' Life Brigade, which was attached to the Mill Street Mission, and after his death one of the officers of his company referred to 'his manly straightforward character'. [2]

Obviously eager to join the War Wilfred signed up voluntarily in August 1917, a fortnight before his 18th birthday, and became a driver with the 73rd Bty, RFA. He died on 16 April 1918 at a base hospital near Boulogne, from the effects of being gassed, and is buried at Wimereux Communal Cemetery, Pas-de-Calais.

[1] See Joseph Lock.
[2] *Chronicle* 2/5/1918.

Pte Reginald Walter Davis – aged 23
1st Btn Royal Warwickshire Rgt – 27754
Cenotaph and St Peter's

In 1911 Sarah Davis was widowed at the age of 31, leaving seven children without a father. The family was living in Burton Bradstock in West Dorset, where her husband Charles had worked as a mill hand. Reginald, their third eldest son, worked in the local dairy and moved into Dorchester when he married Elizabeth Climo and settled at 23 Miller's Close. Reginald joined the Army but died of his wounds on 19 April, perhaps sustained the previous day when the his regiment, the 1st Warwickshires, took part in the Battle of Bethune. He was buried in Lapugnoy Military Cemetery, Pas-de-Calais.

Pte Thomas Voss – aged 40
6th Btn Dorsetshire Rgt – 18116
Cenotaph

Tom Voss was a native of Dorchester, the son of William and Sarah, and had previously been granted a certificate of exemption for war service, doubtless because he worked as a striker and furnace man for the Lott and Warne foundry, which was doing war work. He was employed by them for over 20 years when, about 15 months prior to his death, he left their employ, said goodbye to his wife Mary and his children at their home at 43 Monmouth Rd, and went off to France to fight and die for his country.

In March 1918 Tom and the remainder of the 6th Dorsets were in the front line north of Havrincourt, Pas-de-Calais, digging, laying barbed wire and patrolling, but most of all they were waiting; waiting for the tremendous German attack that was anticipated any day. It began at 4.45 am on the 21st with a bombardment of high explosive and phosgene gas shells and at 8 am the first infantry attacks arrived, which continued into the next day, the enemy using the terrible Flammenwerfer (flamethrower) weapon. On the 23rd the battalion held its own for most of the day but withdrawal was inevitable and the Dorsets retired, fighting a rear-guard action. During the fighting on that day Tom was severely wounded in the back and taken to a casualty clearing station, where it was decided that he required hospital treatment. He was sent to East Leeds Military Hospital but succumbed to his injuries on 22 April. Tom's body was returned to Dorchester where he was accorded a full military funeral before being buried in Fordington Cemetery.

L/Cpl William Alfred Painter – aged 28
3rd Btn Dorsetshire Rgt – 27120
Cenotaph and St Peter's

The sound of bells ringing from the tower of St Peter's Church was nothing new to the folk of Dorchester but on Sunday 29 May 1918 they had a mournful tone. The bell ringers had muffled the clappers and were playing a Grandshire Triple in commemoration of one of their own. William Painter had been not only a former ringer at St Peter's but also a regular member of the choir. The *Chronicle* informs us that he was 'a well-known and esteemed young Durnovarian' [1] who regularly attended the YMCA and took a great interest in the 'Harriers Club', which was associated with Pope's brewery.

William's parents were Henry, a labourer, and Mary Ann who were living at 5 Frome Terr when he was born in 1890 and after completing his education he gained employment with Longman's of 4 Cornhill, printers and booksellers, where he worked in the binding department. After a while William decided on a change of occupation and joined the county constabulary, working as a PC in Wareham, and when War broke out he became 'one of the stalwart lads who discarded the blue for the khaki, and in due course proceeded to the Front'. [2] He was both wounded in the arm and suffering from pneumonia when he was sent back to England, where he spent several weeks recovering. After visiting his parents he returned to his regiment on 21 March 1918 but within a month he lay dead in a British base hospital after a recurrence of his illness.

William died on 21 April and was buried in Etaples Military Cemetery. Back in Dorchester his name was inscribed on a memorial to those members of the Salisbury Diocesan of Bell Ringers which was placed within St Peter's Church. His name was also listed on the County Constabulary Memorial, outside police HQ in Dorchester. [3]

[1] *Chronicle* 2/5/1918.
[2] Ibid.
[3] This memorial has since been moved to the police HQ at Winfrith.

Cpl Edgar Henry Hunt – aged 27
7th Btn Queen's Own West Kent Rgt – 205329
Cenotaph, St Peter's and St George's

Edgar Hunt, the son of Harry, a domestic coachman, and Mary, was born in the village of Thornford, 4 miles southwest of Sherborne. In the 1890s the family moved to Broadmayne near Dorchester and then into the county town itself. The 1911 census shows Edgar working as a groom in Harrow, Middlesex, and in 1915 he married Gertrude Gladwell in Stow, Suffolk.

On the day of Edgar's death, 26 April 1918, the 7th West Kents were being relieved from the front line after being almost wiped out defending their area of the Somme battlefield against the German's Spring Offensive. Over a period of 3 weeks, during March and April, they had lost 40 officers and over 1,000 men. On the 24 April the decimated battalion again went into action to try to regain some of the losses but had to retire. German snipers and machine-gunners then crept forward to harass the British troops and Edgar may have been killed by one of these.

For his mother, who received the news of her son's death at 1 Duke's Ave, Edgar's loss was the second of two recent deaths, her husband having passed away the previous year. Edgar's name was added to the Pozieres Memorial, Somme.

Pte Edwin Reginald Voss – aged 23
137th Coy, Machine Gun Corps (Infantry) – 61239
Holy Trinity

Louis Voss ran his cabinet-making business from his home at14 Prince's St, aided by his youngest son Edwin. Edwin was described by the *Chronicle* as 'very popular in the town', [1] who, in his spare time, was a Territorial with the Dorsets. Therefore, it was no surprise that he joined the county regiment at the beginning of the War. On the day he was killed in action, 27 April, he was attached to the 137th MGC, fighting in Egypt. He is buried in Ramleh War Cemetery, Israel. His brother Louis, who was working for the Government, was on a brief visit to his parents when the news of Edwin's death arrived.

---

[1] *Chronicle* 16/5/18.

Pte George Ernest Pitman – aged 22
2/14th Btn London Rgt [1] – 512382
Cenotaph

Only one George Pitman, who served with the London Rgt, is recorded as having been killed in the Great War. SDGW shows him as George Ernest, born at Wyke Regis and living in Weymouth. He was the youngest son of Henry and Eliza and the family was living at 4 Chickerell Rd, Weymouth, in 1911, but it has not been possible to establish his connection with Dorchester.

George was killed in action on 1 May, when the 2/14th London Rgt was engaged in bitter fighting with the Turks east of the River Jordan in Egypt. On the same day another soldier of his battalion, Richard Cruikshank, won the VC. Despite being wounded several times, he tried consistently to deliver a message from company HQ to his platoon, which was sheltering in a wadi. George is buried in the Jerusalem War Cemetery.

---

[1] Listed under 'Rifle Rgt' on the Cenotaph.

Pte George Gibbs – aged 24
1/4th Btn Dorsetshire Rgt –
201742
Cenotaph and Holy Trinity

A young soldier stands perfectly
still in front of the camera, in
the shop of Mela Ram and Sons,
photographers in Peshawar,
India. He was Pte George Gibbs
and the photograph was to be
a New Year gift to his mother
Fanny back home in Dorchester.

Fanny was born in Buckland
Newton, a village northeast of
Dorchester, and she married
Frederick Gibbs who lived in the
nearby village of Piddletrenthide.

(Source: Mr M. Gibbs.)

In 1879 she gave birth to the first of 11 children, 9 of whom lived to adulthood, and in the
second half of the 1890s she and her family moved to Dorchester, possibly victims of the
agricultural depression. Once in the town, Frederick found work as a bricklayer's labourer
and they lived at 55 Icen Way.

George and William were the last two children born to the family and with 2 years
between them the boys were close. Both had an interest in keep fit and both joined
the Territorials. They worked as errand boys, George for Mr J.T. Godwin, the china
merchant on the corner of High West Street and Trinity Street, [1] and William for a
grocers shop, and would have been well known around the town. Like the Membury
brothers, [2] they went together to the Depot Barracks to join the Dorsets, in their case
receiving consecutive service numbers. They were both posted to the 1/4th Btn and
probably made the same journey to India, not knowing what lay ahead of them. As was
the case of the Dabinett brothers, [3] the two were destined to be parted when they
got there, when William was sent to Mesopotamia as a Despatch rider, attached to an
armoured motorised battery.

At first William delivered his messages on his horse named Blossom but as the War
caught up with new technology he swapped Blossom for a motorcycle. One day William
turned up on his bike at the base in Peshawar where George was posted and the two were
given an hour to chat before William had to return to his unit with his Despatches. This
parting was to stay forever in William's memory as the last time he saw his brother. George
died from pneumonia at a station hospital on 23 May and his name is recorded on the
Delhi Memorial (India Gate). Oddly, it is unclear whether his parents received his medals,
as his name was deleted from the Medal Roll for some reason.

[1] The site is now occupied by The Horse with the Red Umbrella tearooms.
[2] See William Membury.
[3] See Reginald Dabinett.

Driver Wavil Francis Ford – aged 26
'A' Signal Depot, Royal Engineers – 19930
Cenotaph

It was the lot of every mother with sons to fear that one day they might be called away to war. For Eliza Ford, with seven sons, that thought must have been in her mind increasingly as the talk of war turned from conjecture to certainty. Her fears were compounded by the fact that there was a considerable lobby in the country for introducing conscription, headed in Parliament by Winston Churchill.

At the turn of the century Eliza was living at 7 Duke's Ave with her husband Frederick, seven sons and one daughter. Frederick worked as a foreman joiner with the firm of Charles Slade in Acland Road and when their second eldest son Wavil left school in 1902 he went to serve an apprenticeship as a carpenter under his father. That completed, he then decided to join the Royal Engineers at age 18 and in April 1911 he could be found with the 56th Coy RE, at Bulford Camp on Salisbury Plain.

Wavil went to fight in France in August 1914 but was gassed at Ypres the following spring, which necessitated his return to the UK, where he was treated and sent back to the Front. However, Wavil was far from well, his nervous system had been badly damaged by the gas and he developed neuritis. Once again, he was sent back to the UK but despite months of treatment at Lord Derby's Hospital near Warrington he died on 24 May 1918.

Frederick and Eliza arranged for Wavil's body to be returned to Dorchester for burial. The funeral cortege left their home, now at 2 Icen Way, on 28 May and made its way silently, for they had declined the offer of a band, to Weymouth Avenue Cemetery, where the burial took place with full military honours. Any fears that Eliza had about her sons were justified. In addition to losing Wavil, two of her other sons were injured by the War. Fred, a gunner in the RFA, was in the County Hospital fighting malaria and Charles was discharged from the Dorsets owing to injuries.

Lt-Cmdr Paul Thomond Methuen – aged 31
Royal Navy
Cenotaph and Holy Trinity

Standing just inside the western boundary of Roman Dorchester, the magnificent frontage of West Walks House, with its Etruscan pillars and balcony, looks out across the Borough Gardens to the villas in Cornwall Road. Residing there in 1915 was the Rev Paul O'Bryen Methuen, his wife and their daughters. Paul, the Methuen's only son, had entered the Royal Naval College, Dartmouth, in May 1901 and was made Cadet Captain, passing out third highest among his fellow cadets as a midshipman in August 1902. In November of that year he joined the Drake class cruiser *HMS Good Hope*, flagship to the admiral, and after gaining further qualifications was promoted to lieutenant and transferred to *HMS Exeter*, serving in the Mediterranean and Atlantic. In December 1908 the ship gave assistance to victims of the Messina earthquake of 1908/9 [1] and, in thanks, he and his fellow officers were awarded the Messina Medal from the King of Italy.

Paul now started to specialise in gunnery and after undertaking a training course, where he received the highest qualifications possible, he worked on the staff of the school before being posted as Gunnery Lieutenant to the battleship and gunnery training ship *HMS Queen*. Before the War the ship had been stationed at Portland; then in 1914 she went off with the newly promoted Lt-Cmdr Methuen to join the Dover Fleet, patrolling the Channel and supporting troops fighting in Belgium by bombarding the coast. In March 1915 the *Queen* took part in the ill-fated Dardanelles Expedition where Paul did good work, his CO describing him as 'a very able and efficient executive and gunnery officer, of whom I have the highest opinion. He rendered valuable service throughout the Dardanelles operations'. [2]

Paul was serving with the Grand Fleet on *HMS Hercules* when he came home on leave in the spring of 1918. Apart from a case of appendicitis in October 1916, he seems to have had good health during his naval career, but while at home on this occasion he complained of feeling ill and was diagnosed with typhoid fever, from which he died on 26 May. Three days later his funeral service took place at Holy Trinity Church, followed by burial in Weymouth Avenue Cemetery. The usual gun carriage used for military funerals was not available so the coffin was carried through the streets on a wheeled bier followed by two bluejackets [3] and three carriages of mourners. Among those standing at the graveside when three volleys were fired were several officers from the Depot Barracks and Poundbury Camp. For an objective view of Paul's contribution to the Navy and his character we have only to look at the short comments that were written on his service record by his COs wherever he served. Words like 'zealous', 'hard working' and 'highest opinion' predominate.

---

[1] The earthquake took place on 28 December 1908, killing between 100,000 and 200,000 people.
[2] *Times* obituary 6/6/1918.
[3] This seems to have been a popular term at the time for policemen in uniform.

Pte Kenneth Frederick Hyde – aged 19
2nd Btn Royal Berkshire Rgt – 44850
Cenotaph and St Peter's

The nature of South Street changed considerably in the 19th century, from a mixed commercial and residential thoroughfare to one consisting mainly of shops. William Hyde ran his watch-making and jewellery business at 1 Napier Terr, at the bottom of South Street, a couple of doors up from the Railway Tavern. Living above the shop with him, in 1914, were his second wife Alice, his youngest son Kenneth and daughter Lucy from his previous marriage.

Initially, Kenneth enlisted in the Hampshire Rgt but was then posted to the 2nd Berkshires. He died of wounds on either 27 May or 11 June [1] and is commemorated on the Soissons Memorial, Aisne, France.

---

[1] The CWGC gives 27/5/1918 and SDGW 11/6/1918.

Pte Frederick Samuel Hardy – aged 19
2nd Btn Devonshire Rgt
Cenotaph and St George's

(Source: Mr R. Hardy.)

On 20 May 1918 Frederick Hardy wrote a letter to his brother William, informing him that he had been in France for 2 months, just in time to celebrate his 19th birthday. The tone of the letter suggests that the writer was cheerful and relaxed, as he had every right to be, as his unit, the 2nd Devons, had recently taken over some French trenches at a spot in the Aylette Valley that had been barely touched by the War. He was surrounded by verdant pasture and trees, where the local villagers worked in the fields almost up to the front line and where the War must have seemed a long way away. However, things were about to change. Reports and rumours that a major German attack was imminent were confirmed by two enemy prisoners who were captured. The Devons did not have to wait long, the attack came the next day.

The Germans opened the Battle of the Aisne at 1 am on 27 May with a ferocious barrage of 4,000 guns and mortars along a 30-km front. The Devons were in Reserve and Frederick and his colleagues in 'A' Coy were able to shelter in some tunnelled quarries at the Bois de Buttes, near where they were waiting. At 4 am, with all communications cut and the tunnels untenable, the CO ordered the men to their fighting positions on the edge of the Bois de Buttes, not knowing that the enemy had already infiltrated their flanks. By 5 am regiments in the front line were beginning to fall back, whilst the Devons were being machine gunned by enemy aircraft. Within an hour they were isolated from the rest of the Division, their foremost three companies ripped apart. In desperation a Lt Tindall of 'C' Coy ordered his men to fix bayonets and rushed into the incoming Germans. He and almost all of his men perished. At 9.30 am all that remained of the 2nd Devons was a small group of men surrounding their CO at HQ. Out of ammunition, they crawled out of their shelters and took what was left from their dead comrades, but resistance was futile.

In Bois de Buttes there is a memorial commemorating the 23 officers and 528 men of the 2nd Btn who were killed, wounded or went missing. Frederick was not killed in action until the 31st and may have been among the 40 or so soldiers who managed to evade the Germans by swimming across the River Aisne in an attempt to return to British lines. He is commemorated on the Soissons Memorial. At the time of Frederick's death his mother Amelia was living at 11 York Terr on Fordington Hill, having been widowed. She could not accept the fact of her son's death and always left a light on in the house at night to welcome him home. Both of Frederick's brothers had an eventful war. Walter was invalided out of the Army in 1917, whilst George, who went all through the War with the 6th Btn Dorsets, spent time with Dunster Force, [1] and then in 1919 joined 238th Special Brigade, a force that went to Russia to fight against the Bolsheviks. He was discharged in November 1919 after receiving a gunshot wound to his right knee.

[1] Dunster Force, named after its creator Maj. Gen. L.C. Dunsterville, was created in 1917 from select troops form the Commonwealth armies. Its purpose was to help set up and train local forces that would hopefully prevent the invasion of British India via Persia.

Rifleman Seaward James Cook – aged 23
1/8th (City of London) Btn (Post Office Rifles) – 372323
Post Office Memorial

Seaward was born in Rusper, Sussex, the son of Walter and Alice. In 1900 his father died and it appears that he went to live with his grandparents who lived at Kingston near Corfe Castle. At the time of the 1911 census Seaward was at 10 Monmouth Rd, Dorchester, the house of his uncle John Clewes, and was working as a post office messenger. The fact that he appears on the Post Office Memorial for Dorset suggests that perhaps he was boarding with them at the time. In 1916 he married Clara Brain from Westbury-on-Severn, Gloucestershire, and they went to live in South London. Seaward was wounded and probably died in one of the three casualty clearing stations that had been set up in the village of Ligny-St Flochel, Pas-de-Calais. He died on 16 June 1918 and was buried in the cemetery that bears the village's name.

2 Lt Gerald Arthur Hawkes – aged 25
521st Siege Bty, RGA
Cenotaph and Thomas Hardye School Roll of Honour

Annie Hawkes gave birth to a boy in 1894 but she would not know her son as she died in childbirth or very soon after. His father Thomas eventually remarried to Emily Humphrey and the family lived in Weymouth, where he had his cabinet-making business. Thomas obviously had an eye for an opportunity and saw that a mass-market for ready-made household furniture was developing. Accordingly, he became a director in the company of Hawkes, Freeman Ltd, 'general house furnishers, ironmongers, undertakers, house agents, furniture removers and funeral furnishers', [1] with premises at 40/41 St Thomas' St.

Business obviously flourished for Thomas and he was able to send Gerald to the Grammar School in Dorchester, where, after finishing his studies, he successfully completed an entrance examination for the Civil Service. It is quite possible that he was working in London as a civil servant when he joined the Queen's Westminster Rifles and disembarked to France on 4 December 1915. On 8 April 1917 he was commissioned as 2 Lt and attached to the 521st Siege Bty, RGA. On 3 July 1918 he died of wounds and is buried in Aire

Communal Cemetery near St Omer, Pas-de-Calais. Gerald had married and at the time of his death his wife Frances was living at 12 Cornwall Rd.

[1] *Kelly's Directory 1915.*

Sapper Cecil Frederick Chappell – aged 20
HQ Signals Coy, Royal Engineers
Post Office Memorial

On the 25 July 1918 the *Chronicle* carried an article reporting that the body of Cecil Chappell had been buried in Weymouth Avenue Cemetery. Present at the funeral were representatives of the local postal service, including Walter Drew, the District Postmaster, for whom Cecil worked before the War. Cecil Chappell was not a Dorset man but born in Guernsey, the son of Alexander, a house painter, and Ada. Cecil was serving with the Royal Engineers when he was admitted to Netley Hospital suffering from 'throat trouble'. [1] He died on 19 July.

[1] *Chronicle 27/7/1918.*

Boy 1st Class, Edward Curtis – aged 17
HMS Arlanza, RN – J62963
Cenotaph

At age 17, Edward Curtis is one of the youngest of the names appearing on Dorchester's Great War memorials. His father Alfred had been a colour sergeant in the Army and when he retired ran a coffee tavern at 17 The Grove with his wife Louisa. She gave birth to 11 children, the youngest when she was 44 years of age. Their son Edward was born on 6 April 1901 and when he was 15 he joined the Navy as a Boy 2nd Class on *HMS Impregnable*, Plymouth. After training he was promoted to Boy First Class and joined his first ship the *HMS Arlanza*.

The *Arlanza*, a liner of the Royal Mail Steam Packet Company on the UK to River Plate service, was requisitioned by the Navy in 1915, fitted with some guns and became an armed merchant cruiser, joining the 10th Cruiser Squadron blockading German merchant ships. On 23 July 1918 an accident took place on the ship, when a shell exploded prematurely, killing Edward and two of his shipmates, Able Seaman John Gregory and Trimmer Archibald McLachlan. Edward's body was buried at sea which left Louisa, like thousands of other mothers, with no grave to visit. So, when her husband died the following year she added Edward's name to his headstone in Weymouth Avenue Cemetery, joining father and son in death. Edward is also remembered on the Plymouth Naval Memorial and the Training Ship Mercury Roll of Honour.

Pte Henry William Wood – aged 38
1st Btn East Kent Rgt – G/14135
Cenotaph and St Peter's

On 3 April 1917 a wedding took place in Holy Trinity Church. Both the bride and groom were marrying somewhat late in their lives, both aged 37, but with a war on who knew when the next opportunity would come along. Alice was a schoolteacher, the daughter of James Pitfield, a Dorchester cabinet-maker, and at the time of her marriage she was living in All Saint's parish. The groom William Wood was a Devonian and was doubtless wearing his uniform of the Middlesex Rgt on his wedding day. On that joyous occasion neither knew that in little more than a year Alice would be a widow.

After the wedding William went off to war and on some date must have been transferred to the 1st Btn East Kents, the Buffs, as he was with them during the advance of the 6th Division in Flanders. He was killed in action on 2 August. Alice received the news of her husband's death at 37 Glyde Path Rd, where she was living. William is commemorated on the Tyne Cot Memorial.

Rifleman Reginald Berry King – aged 18
1/17th Btn London Rgt – 38762
Cenotaph and St Peter's

Charles King came to Dorchester from Taunton in the second half of the 1880s with his wife Florence and daughter Mabel. They moved into 45 Standfast Rd in Fordington and Charles worked in the town as a baker. It was not long before the family began to grow and by the time the new century came along Florence was pregnant with their eighth child, Reginald. When the boy had completed his education he found a job with the china and glass merchant R.B. Whittingham at 7 High East St, where he worked until he was called away to war in September 1917.

At the beginning of August 1918 Reginald was at the Front with the 1/17th Btn London Rgt, near Warloy in Picardy, where the men were occupying Lavieville Trench. Generally, things were pretty quiet with only the odd casualty, but on the 9th three deaths were recorded, [1] one of whom was Reginald. His body was interred in Warloy-Baillon Communal Cemetery.

Back in Dorchester, on the day following Reginald's death, an eerie coincidence occurred in the King household, now living at 2 Icen Way, when the parents found his pet canary dead at the bottom of its cage.

[1] WD.

Pte Albert [1] Victor Tizard – aged 31
1/7th Btn Royal Warwickshire Rgt
Cenotaph

Anyone walking through the Borough Gardens in the early 1900s might well have received a 'marning zur' greeting from Walter Tizard who had worked there for many years as a gardener for the town council. Walter lived a stone's throw away from the gardens at 21 Victoria Rd with his wife Harriet and their children. Their eldest child was Albert, who in 1908 went to work for Lings, booksellers, stationers and printers, as a machinist in their print shop at 23 High East St. In 1910 he married Alice Attawool from Portland and settled in Dorchester at 8 Dagmar Rd, and their first child Alfred was born the following year. By December 1915 Albert had enlisted in the Army, the number of his children had risen to five, and the family had moved to 33 Fordington Hill.

Albert enlisted in the Reserve and mobilised into the 1/7th Btn Warwickshire Rgt on 2 May 1916, disembarking in France on 17 September. The following May he was admitted to a military hospital in Rouen with some problem relating to his thumb. Whatever it was, it was serious enough to get him invalided home where he was able to spend time with his family, including new daughter Grace. Albert's sick leave lasted 6 months and then it was time for him to return to France, but not for long. Two days after his return to the battalion they were shipped off to fight on the Italian Front.

On 16 August 1918 Albert was acting as stretcher bearer during fighting in the area of Asagio in northeast Italy when he was killed instantaneously by an enemy shell. The major of his battalion said of him, in a letter to Alice, 'He was an extremely good stretcher bearer, one of the type one hates to lose and finds very hard to replace. He was not one of those who slacked his duty', and then added, 'The memory of a good man who has died is better than the presence of a coward who has stayed at home and shirked'. [2] One wonders if the widow with six children all less than 9 years of age, agreed. She did at least receive some tangible help from the government, when in 1919 she was granted a pension of 42s 2d per week. Albert was buried in Barenthal Military Cemetery, Vicenza.

[1] In the *Chronicle* and in the 1901 census Albert is called Alfred, suggesting that he used both names. All his military records refer to him as Albert, as does the 1911 census.
[2] *Chronicle* 5/9/1918.

Pte Elwood William Falls – aged 23
4th Canadian Mounted Rifles, 2nd Central Ontario Rgt
Fordington Cemetery

Elwood was one of the soldiers who came to Dorchester to be treated at one of the military hospitals. He was a student, the son of William and Catherine Falls of Meaford, Ontario, and enlisted in the Canadian Army on 23 April 1917. He died on 25 September 1918 and was buried in Fordington Cemetery.

(Source: Veterans Affairs Canada.)

2 Lt Harold Amey – aged 25
7th Btn Shropshire Light Infantry
Cenotaph and St Peter's

On the afternoon of Friday 7 September 1917, a wedding took place at All Saints' Church in High West Street. The bride, Annie Coombe, a local schoolteacher, wore a cream coat-frock trimmed with ivory satin and carried a bouquet of pink carnations and lilies. She was the daughter of Francis Coombe, the licensee of the Crown Inn, Salisbury Street. The groom was on leave from his regiment in France and was dressed in the smart uniform of a sergeant of the Dragoon Guards. For Annie it must have been a day of mixed feelings. On the one hand there was the joy of her marriage and seeing her beloved, but on the other was the knowledge that, after their short honeymoon in Bournemouth, he would be returning to the Front, where he had already been severely wounded in the hand.

Harold Sansom Amey was the son of Frederick Amey, a grocer's assistant, and Annie, who at the time of his birth were living at 1 Salisbury Terr with their nine children. After leaving school Harold worked as a printer with the *Chronicle* and was also a Territorial soldier with the 4th Dorsets. At the age of 19 he decided on a change of employment and 'took the King's shilling' [1] on 11 March 1911, signing up with the 2nd Dragoon Guards, otherwise known as the Queen's Bays, for 7 years with the Colours and 5 years in Reserve. The Queen's Bays, as part of the 1st Cavalry Brigade, was one of the first regiments to go abroad with the BEF and Harold disembarked in France on the 15 August 1914, just in time to take part in the Battle of Mons and the subsequent retreat. He was soon promoted to the rank of corporal and by September 1916 was wearing the stripes of sergeant. He remained in France for the duration of the War, fighting in many of the major battles, but not with the same regiment. Following a training course, he was granted a commission of 2 Lt and transferred to the 7th Btn Shropshire Light Infantry. Like the Queen's Bays, the 7th served in France for the entire war and suffered more casualties than any other battalion in the Shropshires.

On 27 September 1918 Harold was preparing his men to go into battle. The objective was to aid in the capture of the village of Flesquieres, southwest of Cambrai. Flanked by the Royal Scots Rgt on one side and the Royal Scots Fusiliers on the other the 7th Btn attacked the German lines at 5.20 in the morning with, what the war diary described as, 'a magnificent dash'. Despite severe opposition, Harold's battalion captured 350 German prisoners, but not without loss themselves. He was among the 38 men killed from his battalion. Some of the officers who saw Harold fall wrote to Annie bearing tribute to her husband's popularity in the regiment and to his great gallantry, which contributed in no small degree to the capture of a strong enemy position. The *Chronicle*, on the 24 October, informed the people of Dorchester of a letter Annie had received from the Keeper of the Privy Purse, which read, 'The King and Queen deeply regret the loss you and the army have sustained by the death of 2 Lt H. Amey in the services of his country. Their Majesties truly sympathise with your sorrow'. Harold is buried in Morchies Australian Cemetery, Pas-de-Calais.

---

[1] For many years a soldier's pay was one shilling per day. By 'taking the King's shilling' a recruit was accepting entry into the Army.

Pte Reginald John Mills – aged 24
5th Btn Dorsetshire Rgt – 22414
Cenotaph

By September 1918 reports were coming in daily to the headquarters of the 5th Dorsets of the great advances being made by the Allied armies. On 28 September the battalion made its way forward to the Front to relieve the Northumberland Fusiliers and the next day sent out patrols along the Sensée Canal, as a preliminary to an attack later in the day. They began the assault but then received a message that it had been postponed, only to be told less than an hour later that the postponement was cancelled. They advanced once again but were unable to get very far and were driven back. On 1 October the battalion resumed their attack, the objective being the well-defended Aubencheul-Abancourt railway. The 5th were generally making good progress but on their right the men of A Coy began to fall from machine-gun fire. The Germans' stubborn resistance was more than the Dorsets could deal with and it was not until they were reinforced by Northumberland Fusiliers that they were able to take the railway. Notwithstanding the success, casualties had been high: 51 men killed or missing and 212 wounded.

One of those killed on 1 October was Reginald Mills, a well-known Dorchester lad who had been at the Front since August 1914. He was the eldest son of John Mills, saddle and harness maker, who had his shop at 14 High West St, and Louisa, and the family lived at 11 Victoria Rd. When John left school he worked for two of the town's popular grocers, Fare's Stores at 19 High West St and Wright and Son at 19 High East St, and he regularly attended the Congregational Church, where at a memorial service tributes were paid to him, one being that 'No guile was found in him'. [1] One cannot imagine how his mother felt at the time, having lost a son, brother and nephew within a week. Reginald is buried in Sucrerie Cemetery, Pas-de-Calais.

[1] *Chronicle* 14/11/1918.

Pte Frederick Herbert Smith – aged 31
5th Btn Dorsetshire Rgt – 10151

Pte Alfred Thomas Smith MM – aged 34
89th Field Ambulance, RAMC – M2/132294

Both are commemorated on the Cenotaph

The Smith brothers Frederick and Alfred died less than a fortnight apart, in October 1918. Frederick entered the War at its inception, joining the Dorset Rgt on 26 August 1914, and was involved in some of the worst fighting, including the Gallipoli campaign, where he was wounded in the foot, the Somme and the 3rd Battle of Ypres.

As the War was coming to a close the 5th Dorsets were stoutly hanging on to their precarious position at the Aubencheul-Abancourt railway near Cambrai. The regimental history records that, despite the German shelling, 2 October was a quiet day with few casualties, but the same could not be said of the following one. The 3 October brought continued shelling without a continuance of the battalion's good fortune. The lieutenant colonel was badly wounded, and the chaplain and a doctor were killed, as were four stretcher bearers. Counted among those killed was Frederick and as no other casualties were recorded he was presumably one of the stretcher bearers. Frederick's remains were recovered with those of five other men but unfortunately they were not recognisable and only

Frederick Smith, standing back left. (Source: Mrs G. Broughton.)

one identity disc was found, that belonging to Frederick, which was not attached to any of the bodies. Because of this Frederick does not have an individual grave but is remembered on a special memorial in Sucrerie Cemetery.

While Frederick was in action with the Dorsets near Cambrai his brother Alfred was fighting a different battle near Neuve Eglise, the battle to get wounded men to a place of safety, which often had to be done in circumstances of great danger. During a battle the artillery of both sides would aim their shells at the roads behind the opposition's front line, to hinder reinforcements and ammunition being brought up. These same roads were used by the ambulance drivers.

On 5 September 1918 the 89th Field Ambulance was preparing to receive casualties from an impending attack, their job made more difficult by hostile artillery fire. Alfred's work at this time earned him the MM. [1] The citation reads as follows: 'During the operations of 4th and 5th September this man showed the greatest gallantry and bravery whilst engaged in the evacuation of wounded from the regimental aid post in front of English Farm to a car loading post on the Neuve Eglise road. Immediately after "Zero" he brought the Ford ambulance car straight to the regimental aid post whilst the road was being heavily shelled and he continued to evacuate the stretcher cases from the regimental aid post for 36 hours, notwithstanding heavy shelling of the road at short intervals. By his coolness, daring and endurance he was mainly responsible for keeping the regimental aid post clear, and the

Alfred Smith (left) with his ambulance. (Source: Mrs G. Broughton.)

speedy evacuation thus obtained was undoubtedly instrumental in saving many lives. His work throughout was beyond praise.' [2] Whether Alfred was wounded on that day or later on is unknown, but in any event he died of wounds on 14 October and was buried in Ypres Reservoir Cemetery.

Frederick and Alfred were two of the nine children of Fred and Caroline and spent their early childhood in King Street, moving to 18 Fordington Hill in the 1890s and later settling at 1 Standfast Rd. Before the War, Frederick worked as a cowman and Alfred as a groom. Their father Frederick had already lost his wife in 1913 and in exchange for his sons' lives he received their medals, including Alfred's MM, memorial scroll and death plaque. The chances of him seeing his boys' graves were summed up in a verse he inserted in the 'In Memoriam' column of the *Chronicle*: [3]

> *We do not know what pain they had,*
> *And did not see them die.*
> *We only know they nobly fell,*
> *And could not say goodbye.*
> *Buried in a foreign land,*
> *Their grave we will never see.*
> *But deep within our hearts,*
> *We'll keep their memory.*

[1] *London Gazette* 11/2/1919
[2] WD
[3] *Chronicle* 14/11/1918.

Pte Harry James Tompkins – aged 22
2nd Btn Dorsetshire Rgt – 9841
Cenotaph and Holy Trinity

Five days after Britain declared war on Germany Harry Tompkins stood before the attesting officer at the Depot Barracks, for the second time, trying to join the War. On the first occasion it was his teeth that let him down. He hardly presented the figure of a tough fighting man, standing at 5 ft 3 in and weighing under 8 st. But the British Army had a reputation of making men out of boys and Harry would go on to have a very eventful time, almost making it through to the Armistice. He was the younger of two soldier sons of Henry, a bricklayer, and his wife Alice. He lived at 7 Colliton St and despite his size was probably very fit because of his work as a golf caddy. Doubtless he knew John Sargent, a fellow caddy who also lived in Colliton Street. [1]

After a year serving at home with the 3rd Dorsets, Harry was posted to the 5th Btn and fought in Gallipoli. There he was wounded in the foot on 13 August 1915 and sent home for treatment on the hospital ship *Franconia*. His destination was the 2nd Southern General Hospital in Bristol, where he spent 8 days before being released to recuperate. On 10 December he embarked on *RMS Kinfauns Castle* bound for Mesopotamia. Harry landed in lower Mesopotamia on 7 January 1916, where he fought with the 2nd Dorsets, surviving the Kut siege. The following June, thanks to an attack of colitis, he was on the hospital ship *Sicilia* bound for Bombay. One of the advantages for men serving on the Western Front over those serving in Mesopotamia was that if they were sick or injured they were sent back home with the possibility of seeing their loved ones, whereas for those in Mesopotamia it was a trip to the British base hospital in India.

It was not until October that he rejoined his unit but it was not long before another attack of colitis sent him back to India. Such was the seriousness of Harry's illness on this occasion that a medical board deemed him unfit for fighting service and he was sent home to England, where he was taken off the strength of the battalion. One would have supposed that he might then have been either invalided out of the Army or put on home duties but this was not the case. Instead Harry joined a course on how to use a Lewis gun, which he passed with flying colours. It was almost a year before he returned to the 2nd Dorsets, just in time for their move from Mesopotamia to Palestine, which took place in April 1918.

The Dorsets had been moved to Palestine to reinforce the advance of Gen. Allenby's army which was pushing the Turks northward on the coastal plain. During the first 5 months there they had not done much fighting but were about to go into action as part of a plan to attack the enemy's defences, on 19 September. The Dorsets' first objective was to capture well-fortified trenches at Brown Hill, situated about 3 miles northwest of Jaffa, which once taken would enable them to go on to take a second line.

With the 4th Wiltshires on their left and the 105th Mahrattas on their right the battalion advanced, accompanied by artillery barrage which cut the Turkish wire. The men poured into the enemy trenches, dealing easily with those defenders who did not surrender or run off. They then pushed on to their second objective which they took with little resistance. The 2nd Btn's casualties had been relatively light; about 50 men had been hit, one of whom was Harry. He was shot in the left buttock and taken to the 36th Casualty Clearing Station and thence to a hospital in Gaza where he died on 5 October. His headstone stands in Gaza War Cemetery.

[1] See John Sargent.

Pte John Thomas Jolliffe – aged 20
5th Btn Dorsetshire Rgt – 203175
Cenotaph and St George's

Tucked away behind Monmouth Road, South Western Cottages is a small terrace of homes that look out over the London to Weymouth railway line. On the other side of the line there is a similar group of cottages which once had exactly the same name but have now been amalgamated into Prince of Wales Road. As the name suggests they were once owned by the LSWR and were used to accommodate staff. Living at No. 22 in 1911 was John Jolliffe, a railway guard, his wife Mary and their six children.

The Jolliffe's second eldest son was named John and like his father he also worked for the LSWR. As a young lad John was a bugler in the Boys' Brigade and 'a lad of bright attainments and a general favourite of those with whom he came into contact'.[1] He answered the call of his country in late 1916 or early 1917 and joined the 5th Dorsets. On 9 September 1917 he was wounded and gassed and died on 5 Oct 1918. [2] His body lies in Duisans British Cemetery, Pas-de-Calais.

[1] *Chronicle* 17/10/1918.
[2] See Reginald Mills and Frederick Smith.

Pte Charles Robert Winzar – aged 25
5th Canadian Railway Troops – 404242
Cenotaph and St George's

Charles Winzar was born in Dorchester on 1 July 1893, the only son of Robert and Martha. The family lived at 40 Trinity St, from where his father ran his decorating business. At the age of 19 Charles decided to seek his fortune in Canada and migrated to Toronto, where he found employment as a waiter with the recently opened Bowles Restaurant. Later, he joined the Canadian Army, in April 1915, serving with the 5th Canadian Railway Troops. He died in a military hospital of dysentery on 9 October and his headstone can be found in Aire Communal Cemetery.

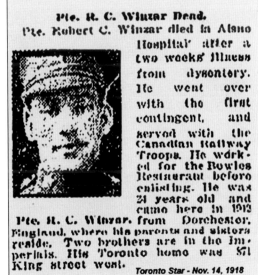

Pte. R. C. Winzar Dead.
Pte. Robert C. Winzar died in Alano Hospital after a two weeks' illness from dysentery. He went over with the first contingent, and served with the Canadian Railway Troops. He worked for the Bowles Restaurant before enlisting. He was 24 years old and came here in 1913. Pte. R. C. Winzar. from Dorchester, England, where his parents and sisters reside. Two brothers are in the Imperials. His Toronto home was 571 King street west.
Toronto Star - Nov. 14, 1918

(Source: Veterans Affairs Canada.)

Pte Reginald James Bascombe – aged 19
15th (County of London) Btn Civil Service Rifles – 535078
Thomas Hardye School Roll of Honour

In February 1916 the *Chronicle* carried a notice that a Dorchester Grammar School boy, Reginald Bascombe, had successfully passed the Civil Service entrance exam for established clerks. Born in August 1898, Reginald came from Tyneham, in Purbeck, where his parents James and Bessie farmed at Battington Farm. After his exam success Reginald entered into the Civil Service by obtaining the post of clerk in London, where he lived in Brixton, very close to his uncle Fred.

Reginald enlisted on 4 August 1916, one month before his 18th birthday, and not surprisingly signed up with the 15th (County of London) Btn Civil Service Rifles. Like the Post Office Rifles and the Inns of Court Rgt the Civil Service Rifles was largely recruited from employees within that profession. After 6 months in the Reserve Reginald was sent to France to help make up the numbers of the battalion, which had been severely depleted by the battles of the Somme and Butte de Warlencourt. He survived the fighting at Ypres and Bourlon Wood in 1917 and the German Spring Offensive of 1918, when the Rifles were reduced at one stage to just a handful of men. On 4 October 1918 he was granted 2 weeks' leave in the UK and doubtless was looking forward to seeing his family. When he landed at Southampton an aunt and uncle, who happened to live there, met him and it was while he was staying with them that he was taken ill and died of pneumonia on 20 October. His grave can be found in Southampton (Hollybrook) Cemetery.

Pte William Francis Moull – aged 26
11th Btn Royal Sussex Rgt – 2/11844
Cenotaph

On 7 October 1917 a wedding was conducted by the Rev Bartelot at St George's Church, Fordington. The groom was a young lance corporal [1] of the East Surrey Rgt named William Moull, who hailed from London. Standing next to him at the altar was Alice James, the daughter of Vandelow and Matilda of 16 Short's Lane, off Mill Street. Sadly, this would prove to be another marriage that would not have a chance to blossom, thanks to the War.

William set foot in France on 19 January 1915 with the East Surreys and at some stage transferred to the 11th Btn Sussex Rgt, with which he fought on the Western Front until just before the end of the War. In July 1918 his battalion was absorbed into the West Kents as part of the 75th Bde, which was renamed the 236th Brigade and sent to fight in North Russia on 17 October 1918.

The seizure of power by the Bolsheviks in Russia brought with it some serious concerns for the Allies, including the fear that a stockpile of war materials and equipment at the port of Archangel might get into the hands of the Germans. It was also hoped that helping the White Army to defeat the Bolsheviks might lead to the re-establishment of an Eastern Front. Accordingly, the 236th Bde embarked at Dundee to join an international fighting force. William was killed in action on 21 October, not long after he landed, and is commemorated on a memorial in the Murmansk New British Cemetery.

[1] The marriage certificate shows him as a lance corporal but in all other sources he is referred to as a private.

Pte Cyril Arthur Legg – aged 18
1st Btn Hampshire Rgt – 29117
Cenotaph

At a time when the average size of a family was much larger than today overcrowding in Dorchester was not uncommon. Such was the case of Arthur Legg's family, which lived at 5 Hillside Terr, off Fordington Hill. The cottage had three bedrooms, which in 1911 were being shared by Arthur, his wife Fanny, their five daughters and three sons, include three children under five.

The nature of the warfare in which their eldest son Cyril was involved, in October 1918, was very different to the previous years of attrition in the trenches. The 1st Hampshires were now fighting a more open form of battle where the more rapid advances that were being made left no time for trench digging. On 20 October the battalion went into action, marking the second stage of fighting along the River Selle, Picardie, behind which the Germans were trying to make a stand. There were no complicated trench systems to be captured and no swathes of barbed wire to be cut, and the local villages were intact instead of consisting of smoking piles of rubble. Cyril and his comrades spent two nasty days on 20/21 October dug in east of the village of Haspres, in heavy rain and under constant shelling by the enemy, which consisted largely of gas shells. Cyril was killed in action on the 21st and was buried in St Vaast Communal Cemetery, Nord. He is also commemorated on the war memorial of St Nicholas' Church, Broadway.

Bombardier John Aiken – aged 25
Dorsetshire Bty, RFA and RHA – 12650, 860368
Cenotaph

When Elizabeth Ellen Woods married John Aiken in 1885 she entered into the nomadic life of an army wife. Her husband John was an Irishman, an infantry sergeant and 15 years her senior. They were married in Elizabeth's home village of Alverstoke in Hampshire but it was not long before the couple were on the move. Their eldest child Clara was born in Pembroke a year after their marriage, followed by Ada in 1888. It was sometime between Ada's birth and 1893, the date that their eldest son John was born, that the family moved to Dorchester, after spending a period at the army barracks in Burnley. By 1901 John Senior had retired from the Army and was working as a labourer at the Barracks in Dorchester, where the family lived. John died in 1913 and left his wife with seven children to bring up. [1]

John Junior was employed as an engine cleaner in 1911 but, given the environment in which he grew up, it was no wonder that he was also a part-time Territorial soldier like so many Dorchester boys. When War was declared he was quick to join up and enrolled in the Dorset Bty, RFA, sailing off to India and serving at several stations in the North-West provinces of that continent. John had been absent from home for a long time and Elizabeth must have been eagerly awaiting his return. Alas, it was not to be. Instead, a cablegram was sent to her home, now at 22 Prospect Terr, from the War Office, informing her that John was dangerously ill. This was followed a few days later by another saying that he had succumbed to his illness, in Lahore, on the 21st October. He is among more than 1,800 British soldiers commemorated on the Kirkee War Memorial, situated within the Kirkee War Cemetery. The fact that John's body was not buried in Kirkee Cemetery suggests that he was interred elsewhere; in a grave that it was considered would be difficult to maintain.

Elizabeth placed the following touching verse in the 'In Memoriam' column of the *Chronicle*, which appeared on 31 October 1918:

No mother's care did him attend,
Nor o'er him did a father bend.
No sister there to shed a tear,
No brother by, his words to hear;
Sick, dying in a foreign land
No father by to take his hand.
No mother near to close his eyes,
Far from his native land he lies.
The kill was short, the shock severe,
Our hope in heaven that we may meet
And then our joy will be complete.

---

[1] John's younger brother Joseph was killed in WWII.

Pte William Thomas Manels – aged 18
3/4th Reserve Btn Dorsetshire Rgt – 4346
Cenotaph

The 4th Reserve Btn Dorsets spent the whole of the War at home, training officers and men before they were posted to overseas units. It had various homes, including Bournemouth, Salisbury Plain and Cheddar, and in the spring of 1918 orders came for it to move further afield, namely to Northern Ireland. With the unrest in Ireland this new posting was certainly livelier than Salisbury Plain and was more akin to those who were serving on the Indian Frontier.

In the summer of 1918 the 4th Dorsets received a new recruit into its ranks in the form of William Manels, an 18-year-old lad from Dorchester. He was the youngest of the three children of John and Frances who, before moving to the county town, ran a bakery in Broadmayne, a village 4 miles to the southeast of Dorchester. At some point they decided to quit Broadmayne and moved to Dorchester and at the turn of the century were living in Loud's Mill Cottage, St George's Road, where John worked as a miller at the adjacent mill.

William (far right) with his parents and brothers Arthur and Reginald. (Source: Mr B. Manels.)

[1]
The history of the 4th Btn Dorsets records that during the winter of 1918 it had suffered badly from the ravages of the septic pneumonia epidemic caused by the influenza pandemic which spread across the world and caused more casualties than the Great War. Officially the influenza pandemic did not cause fatalities in the British Army until the summer of 1918. Previous deaths of pneumonia were mostly attributable to the terrible wet and cold conditions endured by the men or to post-wound infections, particularly gas, which affected the lungs. In the cold, raw climate of Londonderry the soldiers started to go down with the disease 'and not a few succumbed'. [2] Among those who yielded to it was William, who died on 25 October. His body was returned to Dorchester and he was buried in Weymouth Avenue Cemetery, his parents attending from their then address at 7 Greening's Court, High East Street. At the graveside the Last Post was played by a bugler of 2nd Coy, Dorchester Boys' Brigade, of which William had been a member.

[1] Loud's Mill has been converted into a residential property.
[2] Regimental history.

Boy 2nd Class John Cyril Lake – aged 15
HMS Impregnable, RN – J92386
Weymouth Avenue Cemetery

At 15 John Lake was the youngest Dorchester casualty of the Great War. His parents were Herbert, a maltster's labourer, and Elizabeth, and the family lived at 8 Icen Way. On 10 September 1918 John joined *HMS Impregnable*, the Royal Navy's training establishment at Devonport. His navy career had hardly started when he died of bronchopneumonia on 29 October, another victim of the flu pandemic. His father's misery caused by his young son's death was compounded by the death of his wife in the same year.

Pte Elisha John Owers – aged 20
1st Btn Somerset Light Infantry – 31231
Cenotaph

Elisha Owers was born in Dorchester, the son of John, a farm labourer, and Bessie, and the family lived at 3 Gregory's Buildings in Mill Street. Elisha died in one of the military hospitals at Le Treport near Dieppe, of illness or accident, on 1 November and is buried in Mont Huon Military Cemetery, Le Treport.

Pte Thomas James Mowlem [1] – aged 31
6th Btn Wiltshire Rgt – 26671
Cenotaph and Holy Trinity

Thomas Mowlem was born in the village of Plush in the Piddle Valley, 10 miles to the north of Dorchester, and like most of the boys in an area dominated by agriculture he worked on the land. In 1916 he married 23-year-old Gertrude King, who had worked as a parlour maid for the author Thomas Hardy at Max Gate. The couple were married in Dorchester and chose to live at 39 Prince's St. Thomas was serving with the 6th Btn Wiltshire Regt when he died of disease or injury on 2 November. He is buried in Terlincthun British Cemetery, Boulogne.

[1] Thomas's surname is mistakenly recorded as Mowlen by the CWGC.

Pte Lionel Robert James – aged 19
443rd Agricultural Coy, Labour Corps – 555872
Cenotaph and St Peter's

On 2 November a soldier of the Agricultural Labour Corps, based in Dorchester, died in one of the town's military hospitals. The man was Lionel James, son of Alfred and Sarah James, of 3 Agra Place, South Street. Their son Lionel was working as a gardener when he joined the Dorsets on 11 October 1915 and went off to train at Wyke Regis with the 3rd Btn. He was there for 8 months, during which time, apart from a few minor misdemeanours, he managed to stay out of trouble and left with a report indicating that he was average at drill and musketry but it was considered that he lacked self-confidence.

Lionel was posted to the 1st Btn Dorsets and joined them on 2 July 1917, just in time for the German attack on the British positions at Nieuport, Belgium, on the 10th. A few days after the action, he was taken to a field ambulance station suffering from the effects of gas but was discharged to duty after 3 days. However, all was clearly not right with him. In the months that followed he required further treatment from the effects of the gas and also for trench feet, and in December it was decided that he was no longer fit enough to fight.

In cases where men were deemed unfit for battle but not bad enough to be invalided out of the Army it was normal to transfer them to non-combat units such as the Labour Corps, and so it was that Lionel found himself back in Dorchester with the 443rd Agricultural Coy. Doubtless his parents were delighted that their son was not only now in a safe environment but also in his home town. However, while Lionel was safe from Germans he became victim to a much more powerful enemy, the influenza epidemic of 1918. He succumbed to it on 2 November and was buried with full military honours in Weymouth Avenue Cemetery. Those present at the funeral included his comrades from the Labour Corps, RAMC staff and a VAD nurse from the hospital.

L/Cpl Edward John Blackburn – aged 30
13th Btn Devonshire Rgt
Cenotaph

Like the use of gas in the War, sniping was initially regarded as a dirty way of fighting. But, as its use by both sides escalated, it became acceptable and in December 1915 the British Army set up a school for snipers near Ypres. A sniper was required to be not just an excellent shot with a rifle but also a patient observer, sometimes watching the comings and goings of the enemy over a long period of time. He also had to feel confident about moving out of the line into no man's land without being detected.

Edward Blackburn was already a scout with the 13th Btn Devonshire Rgt when he took on the dangerous job of sniper. Having to remain in the same 'nest' for long periods meant that once he had made his first kill the opposition were determined to find his location and eliminate him and, if spotted, the artillery would be directed to send a shell over to his position. Sometimes, however, the situation was different and two snipers faced each other, the first with the opportunity of making the shot being the survivor. Such was probably the situation Edward found himself in at Festubert on 10 January 1916, when he was shot in the head by an enemy bullet. Fortunately, although he was unconscious for 16 hours, the wound was not fatal, but he was sent home and treated at University College Hospital, London.

It was deemed that Edward was not fit enough go back to the Front and instead he was retained at home on light duties. A later medical board determined that his ability to work had been decreased by 50% due to his very delicate health caused by 'stress of active service'. [1] His heart was found to be enlarged, with an excessive pulse rate and it had a murmur. Accordingly, Edward was invalided out of the Army on 30 May 1917 with a pension of 13s 9d per week, plus 2s 6d for his children.

Edward returned to Dorchester, where he lived with his wife Bridget at 9 North Square and found employment as a clerk in the local recruiting office of the National Service Department. He remained working there until he caught influenza which developed into pneumonia and died at home on 3 November. He was buried at Weymouth Avenue Cemetery.

---

[1] Medical report dated 9/5/1917 – SR.

Gnr William Ernest Barnard – aged 28
609th Coy, Labour Corps – 6088
Fordington Cemetery

William Barnard was from the East End of London and found himself in Dorset when he was transferred from the 6th Reserve Brigade, RFA, where he was a driver, to the 609th Coy, Labour Corps. The 609th, which had its headquarters in Dorchester, supplied labour for local farms. Born in 1890 William had been living with his parents, Walter and Ellen, at Manor Park, London, where he worked for the *Daily Telegraph* as a messenger, before he joined the RFA and went to France in September 1915. He died of pneumonia on 3 November in Dorchester 1918.

Cpl William Percival Trew MM – aged 32
2nd Btn Royal Munster Fusiliers – 20460
Cenotaph and Holy Trinity

Mr Edward Trew, who lived in Athelstan Road and was head of the *Chronicle*'s publishing department, received a letter from the sister-in-charge of a general hospital in Rouen stating that his son 'Billy' was dangerously ill with pneumonia. This was shortly followed by notification that he had passed away on 4 November. For Edward, this was his second loss in 5 years, his wife having died previously.

It might be said that William Trew was a soldier who 'got about a bit', having served in the Balkans, Egypt and France. At the beginning of the War he joined the Hussars, before being selected for the Royal Dragoon Guards, with which he trained at Newport, Monmouthshire, Tidworth and Salisbury Plain. After training William was attached to the Dorsets and served abroad with them, before finally joining the Royal Munster Fusiliers. He fought with the Munsters in Salonika and Egypt, as part of the 10th (Irish) Division, and in France with the 150th (York and Durham) Brigade. He is buried in St Sever Cemetery Extension, Rouen.

During the July prior to his death William had been home on leave and doubtless spent some time with his fiancée, Miss Sambrook, discussing the arrangements for their wedding which was to take place on his next leave which, alas, never happened. On 6 February 1919 the *Chronicle* proudly told its readers that Cpl Trew had not only been awarded the MM [1] for gallantry but also signed papers for a commission just before he died.

---

[1] *London Gazette* 14/5/1919.

Sgt Wilfred Frederick Cottell – aged 30
1st Btn Dorsetshire Rgt – 7962
St George's

There was little about the man who stood before the Attestation Officer at Winchester on 20 June 1906 to suggest that he would become a top drill instructor. Wilfred Cottell stood just 5 ft 2¼ in tall and weighed less than 8 st. He was born in Newport on the Isle of Wight, the son of George and Dorcas, and as a teenager was a Territorial with the Hampshires, but when he decided to enlist in the regular Army for 9 years he chose the Dorsets. Duly enlisted into the 3rd Btn the Army set about making a man out of him and after 6 months' training and a gym course the 18-year-old former painter had put on half a stone and grown an inch taller.

During his pre-war army career Wilfred spent some time with the regiment in Gosport and then with the 1st Btn in Belfast, where he was stationed on the outbreak of hostilities. But, instead of going with them to France it was decided that he should return to the UK as a drill instructor and, accordingly, he was despatched to the 3rd Btn in Dorchester with the new rank of sergeant, to put new recruits through their paces. Much of his time was spent at the training camp at Wyke Regis but he also worked in Dorchester, where presumably he met Gladys Shave, perhaps on a day he had an occasion to visit the pharmacist where she worked. The couple were married on 1 October

(Source: Mr J. Cottell.)

1916 and lived with her widowed mother at 11 Fordington Green. Soon after, however, the couple were parted when Wilfred was sent to work at an officer cadet school in Bath.

The reason for Wilfred joining the 1st Btn in France was colourfully described by the *Chronicle* on 21 November 1918: 'When the great German offensive of last spring was threatening and every available man had to be sent abroad to stem the torrent of barbarism, Sgt Cottell proceeded to the Front.' He joined his unit on 18 April and fought with them during the subsequent advance.

Two days before the Armistice Gladys received a letter from her husband saying that all was well but doubtless he was anxious for the War to end so that he could get home and see his 16-month-old son. It was not to be. Four days after the official cessation of fighting, while the rest of the country was celebrating, Gladys was informed that her husband was dead. Among the numerous letters of condolence sent to her was one from Wilfred's CO, Capt. William Lipscombe, describing how he met his end: 'I greatly regret to have to inform you of your husband's death in action on Nov 4th, on the occasion of crossing the Canal. [1] He was killed by a shell which landed quite close to him, and since there was no wound in him it is certain he died from the shock and felt no pain. His loss is deeply regretted by all who knew him as he was a very fine soldier and will be greatly missed by the battalion.' [2]

Another letter, this time from the Bishop of Salisbury, which one supposes was meant to offer her some comfort, read: 'God has thought fit to allow you to be afflicted in the War and He has taken away for a time one very dear to you. I write as your bishop to assure you of my deep sympathy and prayers for you that you may trust God through it all and bow to His will. You have much to comfort you that your dear one died for others, and still more that he will be lovingly and mercifully dealt with by One who died for him. Remember the nearer you keep to your Saviour, the nearer you will be to your dear one. May god bless you.' [3]

Wilfred's personal belongings, which included a religious book and a gold ring, were returned in April 1919. Gladys duly acknowledged their receipt, pointing out that the ring was of particular value to her but that a watch that had been returned was not her husband's and would they please look out for his and send it on. In the same letter she made a plea for the balance of monies due to her husband to be sent as soon as possible, as her baby was delicate and she needed the money to help pay her way. She eventually received the sum of £8 10s 8d. Wilfred was buried in St Souplet British Cemetery, Nord.

[1] This was the advance over the Sambre Canal.
[2] Letter dated 8/11/1918.
[3] Undated letter signed F.B. Sarum (Fisher Bishop of Sarum).

Commemorative plaque or 'Widow's Penny', sent to Wilfred's wife Gladys, and letter from Buckingham Palace. (Source: Mr J. Cottell.)

Pte Herbert Dart – aged 22
6th Btn Dorsetshire Rgt – 15888
Cenotaph and St George's

When Thomas Dart died in 1910 his wife Eliza still had all of her six children living at her home in Frampton, 6 miles northwest of Dorchester. Fortunately, three of the six were of working age and able to support their mother. Florence, the eldest daughter, was employed as a parlour maid, Margaret was a dressmaker, and two of the boys, Ernest and Herbert, both worked as under-gamekeepers on a local estate. Herbert died of wounds on 5 November 1918 whilst serving with the 6th Dorsets. He is buried in Caudry British Cemetery. He is also remembered on the memorial at St Mary's Church, Frampton.

There is an interesting and fortunate tale to relate about Herbert's sister Margaret, who early in 1915 was in Switzerland. Deciding it was high time to return home she made her way to a French port but because of delays for one reason or another arrived to find that her ship had sailed. She travelled on a later crossing and found, when she got home, that the craft she was intended to sail on had been sunk in the English Channel. [1]

[1] Story told to me by a relative.

Pte Thomas Meagher [1] – aged 41
Royal Defence Corps – 75522
Fordington Cemetery

Thomas hailed from Shadwell in London and served with the Royal Fusiliers before joining the Royal Defence Corps, presumably because he became unfit for active service. He might have been allocated work nearer to his home but instead was sent to Dorchester to guard German prisoners, not the most comfortable of occupations. Poundbury Camp was on an elevated site, exposed to wind and rain, and whilst the prisoners were accommodated in newly erected wooden huts with electricity and stoves, the guards had to put up with living in tents. The crowded conditions provided an excellent environment for the influenza epidemic to spread, and in October 1918 several Germans became victims. In November Thomas was taken ill and died in the County Hospital on the 10th.

[1] Thomas served in the Army under the name of Mears.

This photograph shows clearly the heated wooden huts used by German prisoners, and tents which housed the prison guards. (Source: The Keep Military Museum.)

Drawings made by German prisoners. Top: 'Under the chestnut tree' by Erich Streuber. Middle left: 'Office of camp 2' by Kurt Polent. Middle right: 'Dreaming' by K. Bartolmay. Bottom: Camp theatre (left) and recreation room (note the YMCA emblem) by H. Delfs. (Source: The Keep Military Museum.)

Post-War Roll of Honour

Sgt Richard Hodder Foster – aged 36
1st Btn Duke of Cornwall's Light Infantry
Weymouth Avenue Cemetery

Richard Foster was epileptic but it did not prevent him having a successful association with the military. A native of Dorchester, his parents were James, an ironmonger's labourer, and Louisa, and he grew up at 11 Prince's St. His first job was as a boy porter to two local doctors and he then became a chauffeur. In 1910 he married Margaret Shave, the daughter of a local retired farmer, and the couple settled at 25 Prince's St. When Richard was not working he spent some of his spare time with the local Territorials, so it was no surprise that he joined the Dorsets at the outbreak of War. He spent his time with the regiment on home service before being transferred to the Somerset Light Infantry and then to the DCLI.

On 4 October 1917 Richard's arm was badly crushed by a piece of shrapnel and after spending 6 months at a hospital in Manchester and another six in the VAD hospital at Colliton House in Dorchester he went to Perham Down Camp on Salisbury Plain, hoping to get a discharge. Before a decision was made, however, Richard had an epileptic seizure and died of heart failure on 12 November 1918.

Pte Stephen Male – aged 34
3rd Btn Dorsetshire Rgt – 17731
Cenotaph and St George's

Stephen Male served as a stoker at sea for many years before he and his wife Blanche settled down in Dorchester with their three children. The family lived at 10 Harvey's Buildings, Holloway Road, two doors away from Montague Sargent's family. [1] Stephen continued stoking, now at the town's gas works in Icen Way.

Although working as a stoker Stephen gave his trade as engine driver/fitter when he enlisted in the Army on 31 May 1917. He was posted to the 7th (Reserve) Btn Dorsets and trained with them for 5 months before joining the 3rd Btn with a view of a posting to India. However, when it came to the medical inspection doctors found that Stephen had a problem with his heart. The symptoms he displayed suggested that he had at some time suffered from syphilis but he assured them that he had not. Whatever the cause of his complaint, instead of going off to India Stephen was transferred to the Army Reserve (Class W) [2] in February 1917 and given the job of driving a road engine, on the understanding that he could be recalled to the Colours at any time.

The call back to arms came the following September, when Stephen was told to report for a medical before being mobilised once again. However, a medical board found him permanently unfit for military service due to valvular disease of the heart and he was officially discharged on 14 September 1917. Whilst the board did not consider that Stephen's condition was caused by his military service they did conclude that it aggravated it and accordingly he was awarded a pension. He lived for another year, then, after a short illness, died on 21 November 1918. His body was taken to Portland for burial.

[1] See Montague Sargent.
[2] Class W meant that it was considered that his services were more valuable in Civvy Street than they were to the military.

S/Sgt Frederick James Andrews – aged 41
Military Provost Staff Corps – W/1858
Cenotaph

Reporting on Frederick Andrew's retirement from the Army in December 1916, the *Chronicle* [1] made the following comment: 'A most interesting and meritorious military career, and one that it falls to the lot of but a few soldiers to lay claim to, has just been closed by the discharge of Staff Sergeant Frederick James Andrews after 22 years' service.'

Frederick was not a Dorchester man but was born in Wareham in 1877, the son of Frederick, a carter, and Emily. By 1891 the family had moved to Swanage, living at South Barn, and Frederick Junior was working as a labourer. Three years later he joined the Dorsetshire Rgt, which set him off on his varied military career. After a period in the Depot Barracks he went to Belfast and from there on foreign service to Gibraltar, Malta and India. It was while he was in the latter country that he transferred to the Indian Army and was posted to a field telegraph section, taking part in the Tirah Expedition, a campaign that took place in the mountainous region of the North-West Frontier. [2]

The Afridi tribe had for some 16 years been given a government subsidy to protect the Khyber Pass, but in August 1897 they suddenly arose and took over the strongholds held by their own tribesmen and attacked a number of other forts. The British replied by sending nearly 40,000 men with about 2,000 followers to put down the rebellion and whilst casualties were not high it was difficult fighting for the British. The terrain was ideal for the guerrilla warfare undertaken by the tribesmen and the extreme conditions, with snow, freezing rain and temperatures down to minus 27 degrees.

In contrast to the cold of the North-West Frontier Frederick's next posting was to South Africa to fight in the Boer War, but this was interrupted when he was sent to China as part of the force to put down the Boxer Rebellion. In June 1900 lightly armed followers of the Righteous Harmony Society Movement, or Boxers, besieged foreign embassies in Peking as part of a more general rebellion against imperial expansion, cosmopolitan influences and Christian evangelism. This action escalated when the Empress Dowager of China, acting on behalf of the Emperor, declared war on those foreign powers with embassies in the country and ordered all foreigners to be killed. As a consequence those who were vulnerable fled to the Legation Quarter of Peking where they held out for 55 days. Western powers sent a joint force of some 20,000 troops to rescue them, but several foreign ministers and their families were killed before its arrival. In August 1900 the international force took the city, subdued the rebellion and Frederick returned to South Africa.

By the time Frederick returned to Dorchester, in 1906, he had earned the India Medal, China War Medal and South Africa Medal. In addition, he had been awarded King Edward's Coronation Medal. While in Dorchester he met and married on 22 July 1906 Lucy Brushett, the fifth daughter of William Brushett, a boot-maker living at 46 Icen Way, and within the year they had their first child Eva. A study of the birthplaces of the children of service families can give some insight as to where the father was stationed, and the Andrews family are a case in point. Their first child was born in Dover, their second in Colchester and third in Devonport. In 1911 the family could be found living in Beachcroft Road Barracks, Colchester, where Frederick was a sergeant with the Prison Staff Corps.

At the outbreak of War Frederick was still in the Army and Lucy was living at 8 Shirley Terr, Dorchester, with her children.. Then, according to Frederick's Army service record, he was discharged on 22 November 1916 as being unfit for duty, although no details of the injury or illness are given. He then re-enlisted on 10 November 1917 and was immediately promoted to staff sergeant. But just over a year later, on 24 November, he died of pneumonia in Hereford General Hospital, another victim of the influenza epidemic. He is buried in Weymouth Avenue Cemetery.

---

[1] *Chronicle* 12/12/1916.

[2] A memorial to the men who fell in the Tirah Campaign can be seen in the Borough Gardens, in the northeast corner near the refreshment kiosk.

Gnr Stephen O'Brien – aged 45
1st Reserve Bde, RFA – 88804
Fordington Cemetery

Stephen O'Brien, an Irishman from Tipperary, spent most of his adult life in the Army and might have risen in the ranks had it not been for the demon drink. He commenced his military career in March 1889 when he joined the Royal Artillery at Preston in Lancashire, aged 18. Stephen was initially posted as a gunner to the 11th Bde; then, on the reorganisation of the RA on 1 July 1899, he joined 11th Bty RFA. His first 5½ years were spent at home, during which time he was granted Good Conduct Pay of 1¼d per week, which was taken away 2 years later and subsequently restored. In May 1893 he found himself standing before the local magistrate for some misdemeanour or other and was fined 25s 6d.

In 1895 Stephen's service with the Army was due to end but he applied for and was granted an extension for another 12 years and with it came a change of occupation to that of driver, and a move to one of the outposts of the Empire, India. There he was stationed on the North-West Frontier and took part in the Tirah Expedition. [1] Stephen's service in India ended in October 1899 because potentially he was now required in another part of the Empire where Britain was engaged in conflict, South Africa. The Irishman left India with three things to remind him of his service there: a bout of malaria, the India Campaign Medal and the Royal Humane Society's bronze medal for bravery. The citation that came with the latter award read as follows: 'On the 25th June 1899, Acting Bombardier A. Haynes was bathing in the Phalki nullah, Sialkot, India, when he was carried away by the rush of water, the nullah being swollen from heavy rain. O'Brien jumped in to his help, but owing to the strong current could not effect the rescue.'

Stephen duly arrived on the African continent on 4 November 1899 and took part in much of the fighting there.

After 5 years of serving abroad Stephen set foot on British soil once again, in November 1900, and was posted to a new unit. In his service record it is shown as A Battery but elsewhere it is referred to as 'Chestnut Troop', which was, and still is, the senior artillery battery in the Royal Artillery. Established in 1773 and equipped with only chestnut horses from the outset it got its name at the Battle of Waterloo, when the Duke of Wellington asked the whereabouts of 'the Chestnut Troop'. The name stuck and eventually became its official title.

In 1902 Stephen was once again due to leave the Army but instead signed on for a further 2 years. He did so when the Chestnut Troop was in Dorchester and it was there presumably that he met his wife-to-be, Louisa Drew, a girl from Cattistock. The couple married in 1903 and their son Stephen was born the following year. Now he was back home Stephen seems to have reverted to some of his former bad behaviour. Once again he forfeited his good conduct pay and, in addition, was reduced to 2nd Class pay and lost a good conduct badge. This may have been the straw that broke the camel's back for Stephen because after a short posting to Egypt he asked to be released from the Army. His last day of service was 25 March 1907 and the reference from his former employer was not going to help get him a job in civilian life. It read, 'Conduct bad, has been addicted to drink'. [2] Despite that, Stephen did find work, as an agricultural labourer and he and Louisa lived at Muckleford, 5 miles northwest of Dorchester.

Whatever Stephen's behaviour in the Army, and there are no specific details of his crimes, he undoubtedly was a fighting man and it was no surprise therefore that he re-enlisted in the Army a week after War was declared. The degree of his patriotism might be judged by the fact that he had a Union Jack tattooed onto his right forearm. He fought in France, where his old illness of malaria flared up again on two occasions, and in 1915 he went down with bronchitis. He recovered from these but the conditions of the Western Front were too severe for Stephen and after another bout of malaria, in November 1917, he was sent to a hospital in Newcastle and then discharged from the Army. He returned to Louisa and his four children at Muckleford and survived until 2 December 1918, when he died. After her husband's death Louisa moved into Dorchester and lived at 1 Hillside Cottages.

---

[1] See Frederick Andrews.
[2] SR.

Pte Leonard William Tattershall – aged 23
Motor Transport Detachment, ASC – DM2/170813
Weymouth Avenue Cemetery

Leonard Tattershall was an ex-patriot of Dorchester, who was born in the town in 1895, the son of Arthur, a builder's carpenter, and Alice, and in 1901 the family was living at 4 Prospect Terr. In the early 1900s they moved to Weston-super-Mare where they were living in 1911. All, that is, except for Leonard's elder sister Ethel, who either remained in Dorchester or returned to work there as an elementary school teacher, boarding with fellow teacher Mary Churchill at Rowan Villa, Prince of Wales Road.

Leonard was a private in the ASC and sometime during his time in the Army served in Salonika. He died on 3 December 1918 at the University War Hospital, Southampton, and his parents, who were then living in Birmingham, decided that his body should be returned for burial in the town of his birth.

Pte Frank Jones – aged 26
609th Coy, Labour Corps – 15363
Fordington Cemetery

Frank Jones was transferred to 609th Agricultural Coy, Labour Corps, from the 5th Reserve Rgt of Cavalry in August 1917. He was admitted into the hospital in the Depot Barracks suffering from influenza and was then transferred to the County Hospital, where he died of pneumonia and acute nephritis on 13 December 1918.

Pte Harold Roy Frost – aged 33
Machine Gun Corps (Infantry)
Cenotaph [1]

The Frost family's association with Dorchester came when Harold's grandfather came to the town to run the King's Arms Hotel in High East Street in the 1870s. When he retired his son Harry took over the business with his wife Elizabeth and it was there that their son Harold was born in 1885. The boy's early years were supervised by a live-in nurse and he was surrounded by the hotel's staff which as well as the usual chambermaids and bar staff included a 'billiard marker' and a 'boots'. By 1901 Harry had left the hotel trade and the family had moved to 16 Charles St. He became an agent for the railway and Harold, now 16, was serving an apprenticeship as a bicycle maker. Nine years later Harold married an Irish girl, Charlotte Telford, and the couple moved into a spacious eight-roomed house in South Walks.

Unfortunately, there is little evidence of Harold's war service so we have no indication of the circumstances that led to his tragic death. On 14 December 1918 his body was found at Rugeley Camp in Brereton, Staffordshire, hanging by the neck with a rope from a beam. An inquest was held on 17 December and a verdict of 'suicide whilst temporarily insane' was brought in. [2] His body was returned to Dorchester and buried in Weymouth Avenue Cemetery.

[1] Appears as R. Frost.
[2] Quoted from his death certificate.

Driver Frederick William Wallis – aged 24
D Bty, 310th Bde, RFA – 776496
Cenotaph

Frederick, who was born in West Knighton, a village 4 miles southwest of Dorchester, came to live in the county town when he married Rosie Kate Northover in 1914. The couple lived at 13 Dagmar Rd. He survived the War, serving with the RFA, and he and Rosie were doubtless looking forward to his demob. Unfortunately, it never came because he was taken ill in France and was admitted to No. 7 Stationary Hospital in Boulogne, where he died on 18 January 1919 following an attack of double pneumonia. Frederick is buried in Turlincthun British Cemetery.

Pte Arthur Leonard Payne – aged 39
8th Field Bakery, ASC – S/359744
Cenotaph

Arthur was born in Trowbridge, Wiltshire, the son of Samuel, a commercial traveller, and Caroline. Sometime in the 1880s the family moved to Dorchester and in 1901 was living at 5 Bridport Terr. In 1906 Arthur married Rosina Harding in Bristol and the family appear to have settled there, where he worked as a grocer. Arthur is buried in Janval Cemetery on the outskirts of Dieppe, which was the port where most of the Army's flour supplies were landed. Arthur may have been employed in that operation with the 8th Field Bakery when he died of accident or disease on 24 February 1919. At the time of his son's death Samuel was living at 31 Mountain Ash Rd, his wife having died in 1907.

L/Cpl Frederick Toogood – aged 39
5th Btn Wiltshire Rgt – 21130
Cenotaph and St George's

The mechanisation of agriculture had a profound effect on rural communities, as thousands of workers found that their services were no longer required on the land. But there were those who took advantage of the revolution and at the turn of the century it was still not uncommon to see two traction engines pulling a wagon and water cart along the roads of Dorset. These were the teams of men who worked the steam ploughs, offering their services to farmers who did not or could not invest in the necessary machinery themselves. These teams normally consisted of four men and a boy, and in April 1901 the local census enumerator for the Queen Camel area of Somerset caught up with one such group of men: George Eveleigh, the foreman, whose job included cycling ahead and finding work, Frederick Day, Arthur Squibb, the engine driver, Willie Stone, the cook, and Frederick Toogood, steersman, who presumably guided the plough as it made its journey across a field.

By 1911 Frederick ceased travelling and settled in Dorchester where he worked as a fruiterer's salesman and in 1914 he married Beatrice Whately in Yeovil, just before he went off to War with the Wiltshire Rgt. He embarked for the Balkans in September 1915 and sometime later was wounded. This necessitated his return to the UK, where he was treated at the military hospital in Blandford Camp, in his home county. It was there that he died on 25 January 1919.

Pte William Thomas Trevett – aged 34
2nd Btn Essex Rgt – 277609
Cenotaph

Monday 3 February 1919 was a day for Beatrice Trevett to put the flags out. After nearly 5 years away at war her husband William was finally returning home. At 2 years old his son Ronald would not know him but little Reggie, aged 6, had some knowledge of his dad, through the letters his mother received and the brief periods he was home on leave. For William's father Thomas, the feelings of joy at the prospect of seeing his son again were coloured by the fact that another of his sons, Albert, [1] had been killed in October 1917 while serving in France.

William had answered the call from King and Country on the outbreak of War and in 1914 went to India with the 2/4th Btn Dorsets, where he served for 2½ years. Then he went to Egypt, where, as the *Chronicle* proudly proclaimed, 'he was involved in all the activities in which our sons of Dorset have done such good work'. [2] At some stage during his time in Egypt he then transferred to the Essex Rgt.

After several days of happy reunion with his family William was suddenly taken ill and just 3 days later died of influenza and heart failure, on 11 February 1919. He died at the home of his aunt at 50 Icen Way and it was from there that his funeral took place 6 days later. William's Union Jack-draped oak coffin was carried to Weymouth Avenue Cemetery in a horse-drawn glass hearse and among the many floral tributes was one that had the following words attached: 'To my darling Daddy, from his own little boy Reggie.' [3]

[1] Albert does not appear on any Dorchester memorial.
[2] *Chronicle* 6/3/1919.
[3] Ibid.

Driver John George Adams – aged 33
337th Bde, RFA – 151163
Cenotaph

A person by the name of J.G. Adams appears on the Cenotaph and the most likely candidate is John George Adams. He was the only J.G. Adams recorded by the CWGC to have died while serving in the RFA and it does appear that he might have had some connection with Dorchester. According to the CWGC he was married to Alice Eliza Adams and the Absent Voters List for 1918 shows a John and Alice Adams registered in the town. If he is the correct person he was serving with the 337 Bde, RFA in Mesopotamia. On 9 May 1919, John was killed when a team of horses bolted and trampled him to death. He was buried in Baghdad (North Gate) Cemetery.

Pte Bertie Lawrence Burden – aged 25
2nd Garrison Btn Northumberland Fusiliers
Post Office Memorial [1]

Bertie Burden delivered post in the village of East Knighton where he lived with his parents, George, a farm labourer, and Mary, who took in washing. Bertie appears to have spent his time during the War in Mesopotamia and India, firstly with the Dorsets and then with the 2nd Garrison Btn Northumberland Fusiliers. He was serving with the latter at Poona when he died of sickness or accident on 8 July 1919. His name appears on the Kirkee War Memorial.

---

[1] The memorial shows 1/4th Dorsets.

Sgt Francis Edgar Dowd – aged 24
16th Btn Rifle Brigade – 6668
Cenotaph

Thomas Dowd had served as a soldier with the Dorsets but in 1901, at the age of 51, he was on pension, living just 2 minutes' walk away from the Depot Barracks. Living with him at 2 Maie Terr was his wife Elizabeth, 16 years his junior, and their six sons. Two years later Thomas died and Elizabeth was left to bring up the children whose ages ranged from 2 to 15. If we jump forward to 1911 we find all of the boys still at home and most of them now working, as was Elizabeth as a needle worker.

Francis Dowd was the second youngest son and when he left school joined the ranks of errand boys who pedalled their way around the town delivering goods to people's houses. He was part of the BEF and landed on foreign soil on 14 August 1914 with the ASC. Whilst serving with them he was promoted to sergeant and then in October 1917 transferred to the 16th Btn Rifle Brigade. Francis survived the War by just over a year but his health must have been affected for him to appear on the Cenotaph. He died on 9 December 1919 and his body lies in Weymouth Avenue Cemetery.

Pte Philip Bates – aged 20
5th Btn North Lancashire Rgt – 44868
Fordington Cemetery

Philip Bates was born in Burnley, Lancashire, the youngest of four sons born to John, a millwright in the cotton industry, and Hannah. Philip did not enter the War until 4 July 1918, and his poor health led to him being invalided out of the Army and then to his premature death from tuberculosis on 28 December 1919, aged 20. Although he is buried in Fordington Cemetery he did not die in Dorchester but in Southampton's Isolation Hospital. I have been unable to trace any connection between him and Dorchester or why he was buried in Fordington is a mystery.

L/Cpl Michael Tooley – aged 25
No. 2 Military Foot Police – P/14241
Cenotaph

When Michael Tooley died on 30 January 1920 this brought to an end the number of persons to be added to Dorchester's Great War memorials. Michael's father John was a gunner in the RHA and he and his wife Anna Marie were living at the barracks in Dorchester when Michael was born. Ten years later, the family were living at 34 The Grove and it seems that John had been put on light duties, working as a sweeper in the barrack's bakery.

When Michael left school he got a job with the *Chronicle* before following in his father's footsteps by joining the artillery. At 18 years of age he enlisted in the RGA at Weymouth, later serving with the 112th Heavy Bty in France, where he was gassed and received shrapnel wounds. Despite his wounds Michael survived the War and became part of the Army of Occupation on the Rhine, where, there being no immediate need for gunners, he became a military policeman. In January 1920 Michael was admitted to hospital, where he died on 30 January 1920. It was over a month before Michael and Anna heard about their son's illness, followed 2 days later by the official notification of his death. His body lies in Cologne Southern Cemetery.

The Unknown Warriors

It has not been possible to identify positively the following names (nor that of A.E. Williams and J.G. Adams, as already mentioned):

Cenotaph
> F.W. Cake (Dorsetshire Rgt)
> H. Drake (Devonshire Rgt)
> G.W. Herridge (Warwickshire Rgt)
> C. Lee (Labour Corps)
> J.H.D. Mills (RFA)
> W. Roberts (Staffordshire Rgt)

St George's
> J.H. Allen
> V. Charles
> C. Davis
> W.A. Hillier
> W.G. Legg
> R.T. Scott

Thomas Hardye School
> C.A. Johnson
> V. Powell

Remembering Today

Dorchester's strong connection with the military has long disappeared. Men in uniform are rarely seen in its streets, the infantry barracks has been partly demolished and what is left has been converted to other uses. The parade ground, upon which men were put through their paces by sergeant majors barking orders, is now occupied by offices and car parks. Now the only clue to the fact that the old buildings were occupied by the Dorsetshire Regiment lies in two words written above a doorway, 'Mons' and 'Shaiba', commemorating battles fought by the 1st and 2nd Btns, respectively. The artillery barracks has been replaced by an industrial estate and all evidence of its former use has disappeared, save for the riding school, the hospital and some buildings which are used by B Coy, 6th Btn, The Rifles, as a TA centre. The proud name of the Dorsetshire Regiment, too, has gone, but its history lives on through the excellent work of the regimental museum, which is housed in The Keep, the building through which thousands of men passed from civilian into military life.

It has been almost 100 years since the outbreak of that terrible conflict but it still catches the imagination. If anything, there has been resurgence in interest in the Great War, due partly to television and the fascination with genealogy. Such was the enormity

Dorsetshire Regiment memorial to the 4,060 Dorsets who lost their lives in all theatres of conflict during the Great War. Located on the start line of the first day of the Somme Battle (1 July 1916). (Courtesy of Capt. C.A. Parr MBE.)

Two photos of the artillery barracks' hospital, recognisable by the porch.
Above: A group of medical orderlies getting ready for Christmas 1914.
Below: The building today as part of the Grove Industrial Estate and in a semi-derelict state.

and complexity of the military, social and political aspects of the War that it continues to feed debate among academics, and each week, it seems, a new book on some aspect of it is published. The Western Front Association sets out to educate people about the War and the Dorset and South Wiltshire branch provides a source of information through its monthly talks and a forum for discussion. In addition, it has recently played a major role in commissioning a memorial to the Dorsetshire Regiment on the Western Front, thus perpetuating the memory of the regiment.

Locally, the people of Dorchester, like thousands of communities, continue to remember all those who have died as a result of war, by gathering around the cenotaph each November. The shop fronts surrounding the memorial have changed, as have the fashions of the day, but, other than these, a photograph taken at the eleventh hour in 2012 would not be dissimilar to one taken on 24 May 1921, when the cenotaph was unveiled. The civic and church dignitaries still turn out in their robes and youngsters from organisations such as the sea and air cadets line up in much the same place as did the boys of the Dorchester Grammar School Corps. Members of the British Legion have replaced those of the Old Comrades Association.

In one respect Dorchester differs from most British communities on Remembrance Sunday. Each year a wreath is laid at the foot of the German war memorial in Fordington Cemetery, commemorating those of the enemy who for a short period of time were residents of our town.

In June 2010 the footfall of marching soldiers was again heard in the High Street, when thousands turned out to welcome the 4 Btn, The Rifles, on their homecoming from Afghanistan. The Regiment was granted the Freedom of Dorchester in 2007. Each summer, Armed Forces Day, which is organised by the Royal Naval Association, affords another opportunity for townsfolk to pay tribute to all members of the armed forces. A march through the town is followed by events in the Borough Gardens, where Durnovarians of previous generations gathered to listen to military bands that were garrisoned in the town. The day starts with a parade of veterans, bands and dignitaries from North Square, through the town to the Gardens, where a number of events and a concert take place, the band assembled on the same bandstand as numerous previous ones did during the many decades of Dorchester's military occupation.

(Photo supplied courtesy of Leslie Phillips.)

Appendix A
Organisation of the British Army

For those readers unfamiliar with the British Army in the Great War, I have attempted below to give some idea of how it was organised, to help with reading the text.

- In the infantry a solder belonged to a battalion which was divided into a number of companies, which in turn are subdivided into platoons and sections. A battalion has about 1,000 men.
- Infantry battalions were organised into regiments, mostly based on geographical areas such as counties. Different battalions of a regiment did not normally fight side-by-side.
- Several battalions from the various regiments would be gathered to form a brigade. This consisted of about 5,000 men and was commanded by a division.
- Artillery units were also organised into brigades and were attached to infantry divisions. An artillery brigade was made up of several batteries of guns and an ammunition column. An artillery brigade, with a full complement of field guns, amounted to approximately 800 men. In addition to horse artillery and field artillery there were garrison artillery and howitzer brigades.
- A division was made up of several infantry and artillery brigades and was about 20,000 strong. As well as British there were Australian, Canadian, Indian and New Zealand divisions.
- Several divisions made up a corps and a number of corps formed an army. Five armies operated on the Western Front.
- Other army units like the Royal Engineers, the Royal Army Medical Corps and the Army Service Corps fitted in at various levels.

The Dorset Regiment

During the War infantry regiments like the Dorsets grew along with the need for additional troops. In August 1914 the Dorsets had two regular battalions: the 1st, which was serving in Northern Ireland, and the 2nd, which was halfway through serving a tour in India. These consisted almost entirely of regular soldiers, many of whom became casualties in the early months of the War and had to be replaced by raw recruits enlisted at the outbreak of war, known as 'Kitchener's Army'.

Born out of the Dorset Militia the 3rd Btn Dorsets was not to see active service abroad but spent the whole period of the War recruiting and training troops for the Front, taking in men from all corners of Britain. In early August three companies of the Btn went to billets at Wyke Regis [1] and one to Upton Camp. [2] The Btn was given the responsibilities of guarding railway tunnels and bridges, protecting the waterworks at Upwey and guarding the torpedo works at Smallmouth, [3] as well as the naval oil-tanks near Portland. It was also detailed to protect the coast around Upton Fort near Weymouth.

The 4th Btn, made up of part-time Territorial soldiers, was divided into three units. The 1/4th Btn fought in Mesopotamia and the 2/4th served in India and Egypt. The 3/4th did not see service abroad.

On the outbreak of War two new battalions came into being. The 5th Btn was created in August 1914 from the first flush of eager recruits and some of the old soldiers of the Reserve. It fought at Gallipoli and on the Western Front. The 6th was formed on 6 September 1914 and was originally intended as a pioneer battalion, but fate had it that it would fight in France for the whole of the War.

Four other battalions were created for the purposes of the War but none of them lasted the full term. They were the 7th (Reserve) Btn, the 1st (Home Service) Btn, the 2nd (Home Service) Garrison Btn and the 9th Btn (absorbed into the 6th Btn Wiltshire Rgt).

[1] Wyke Regis is part of Weymouth.
[2] Upton Camp was located at Ringstead in Dorset.
[3] The Whitehead Torpedo Works was set up in Wyle Regis in 1895. Ironically, it was an Austrian company.

Appendix B
Former Place Names in Dorchester

Aldhelm Villas, now 43–61 Damer's Rd.

Arnold Square was located off Mill Street.

Bell Street, now part of Icen Way.

Bridport Terrace, a terrace of houses in Bridport Road running west from Cornwall Road to the railway.

Brownden Terrace, now part of Cromwell Road.

Burleston Terrace, now part of Monmouth Road.

Chestnut Villas, now 12–26 South Walks Rd.

Cuckolds Row was part of what is now Holloway Road and in 1881, 48 families were living there. It included Pound House and Fordington Infant's School.

Dagmar Terrace, part of Dagmar Road.

East Parade, now 11–23 London Rd.

Gordon Terrace, now 33–47 South Walks Rd.

Gregory's Buildings was located off Mill Street.

Greyhound Yard, at the top of South Street, was replaced by the Tudor Arcade.

Grove Buildings was located at the lower end of The Grove.

Harvey's Buildings was located on Fordington Hill.

Hillside Cottages were a row of cottages on Fordington Hill.

Holloway Row, former name of Holloway Road.

Icen Road, now part of Icen Way.

King Street together with Tubb's Road and Standfast Road became King's Road.

Lester Square consisted of six properties off the lower end of Mill Street.

Loud's Road, named after Loud's Mill, was renamed St George's Road.

Maie Terrace was part of a development behind the Sydney Arms. When the development was completed it was named Tilley Town by the locals, after the name of the builder. Maie Terrace is now Prospect Road.

Marian Terrace was part of Culliford Road.

Maumbury Way in 1902 ran from Maumbury Rings to the Baker's Arms public house. The road from the Baker's Arms down to Barnes' Way was known as Monmouth Road. By 1911 a large number of houses had been built in the area and Maumbury Way was renamed Monmouth Road.

Mill Bank at Swan Bridge, where the old east gate of the town was situated; here a stream runs off the River Frome which once fed Fordington Mill. The raised south bank of the stream was known as Mill Bank.

Napier Terrace, a terrace of shops at the bottom end of South Street.

Pease Lane, now Colliton Street.

Prospect Terrace, part of Prospect Road.

St Martin's Road, now part of Bridport Road, it ran from the Top o' Town roundabout to the Waterworks.

Shamrock Terrace, part of Alfred Road.

Shirley Terrace formed part of Cambridge Road. It was replaced by a modern development.

Short's Lane ran off Mill Street.

South Terrace, a terrace of shops at the bottom of South Street.

South Walk's Terrace, now part of South Walks Road.

Standfast Road, now part of King's Road, it extended from Prince's Bridge to Fordington Cross.

Sydney Terrace, the terrace running west from the Sydney Arms on Bridport Road.

Tubbs Road ran from what we know today as the junction of London Road and King's Road down to Prince's Bridge.

Tubbs Row, the row of cottages adjoining the Swan Inn.

Nurses and patients celebrate Christmas in a hospital ward, probably at the County Hospital. (Source: Dorset County Museum.)

Sources

Most of the sources for this book have come from primary material. Much of the information on families has come from census returns, births, marriages and deaths records, and newspapers. Details of an individual's Army service have largely come from sources such as service personnel records, Medal Roll Cards and information collected by the Commonwealth War Graves Commission, and the Soldiers Died in the Great War database. Information on the operational side of individual military units was obtained from regimental histories and diaries completed by commanders in the field, on a day-to-day basis. The internet has some excellent sites on the history of the Great War but, as with all sources, their accuracy and validity have to be carefully considered.

Primary sources

Anonymous (1919) *Pope Book of Remembrance – Being a Short Summary of the Service and Sacrifice Rendered to the Empire in the Great War by One of the Many Patriotic Families of Wessex: The Popes of Wrackleford; with a Foreword by Thomas Hardy.* Privately printed, Chiswick Press.

Bishop, H.C.W. (1919) *A Kut Prisoner.* John Lane Co., New York.

Commonwealth War Graves Commission, Maidenhead, www.cwgc.org.

Dorchester All Saints' Church. Scrapbook containing extracts of monthly magazine, 1883–1932. DHC, Dorchester.

Dorset County Chronicle and Somersetshire Gazette. DHC, Dorchester.

Dorchester Town Council – papers relating to the erection of a war memorial in the town. DHC, Dorchester.

Dorset Year Books, 1914 –1921. Published by the Society of Dorset Men.

Dorset Yeomanry records. DHC, Dorchester.

Kelly's Directories of Dorsetshire, 1889, 1895, 1907 and 1915. DHC, Dorchester.

Library and Archives of Canada, http://www.collectionscanada.gc.ca/index-e.html: Service records of Canadian military personnel.

War diaries of Canadian forces.

National Archives of Australia, http://www.naa.gov.au/. Service records of the 1st Australian Imperial Force, 1914–1918.

National Archives, Kew, http://www.nationalarchives.gov.uk/:

Campaign Medal Rolls of British Soldiers, 1914–1918. Series WO 329.

Pension records of British Soldiers – NCOs and OR. Series WO364.

Royal Marines registers of service. Series ADM 159.

Royal Naval officers' service records. Series ADM 196.

Seamen's registers of services. Series ADM 138 and ADM 188.

Selected First World War and Army of Occupation War Diaries. Series WO 95.

Service records of Army officers of the Great War. Series WO339 and WO374.

Service records of British soldiers – NCOs and OR. Series WO363.

Nobbs, Gilbert (1917) *On the Right of the British Line*. C. Scribner's, New York.

Register of Electors for the Dorchester Borough and Absent Voters List, 1918. DHC, Dorchester.

Rossor, Bruce (1987) *A Sergeant-Major's War – Ernest Shepherd*. Crowood Press, Ramsbury.

Short Summary of the Attack by the 64th Brigade on the Morning of 8 October, 1917. Capts J.H. Frank and A. Day. War diaries of the King's Own Yorkshire Light Infantry. http://www.nationalarchives.gov.uk/.

Soldiers Died in the Great War database. Naval and Military Press CD.

Spackman, Tony (2008) *Captured at Kut, Prisoner of the Turks. The Great War Diaries of Col W.C. Spackman*. Pen and Sword Books, Barnsley.

Strange, Ivor (1995) *Time! Gentlemen Please! – Dorchester Pubs Remembered*. Self-published.

The London Gazette. http://www.london-gazette.co.uk/.

The London Times. http://www.thetimes.co.uk/tto/news/.

The Sufferings of the Kut Garrison During Their March into Turkey as Prisoners of War, 1916–1917. *Diary of Lt-QM F.A. Harvey, 2nd Battalion, The Dorsetshire Rgt*. The Keep Military Museum, Dorchester.

Secondary sources

Atkinson, C.T. (1924) *The Queen's Own West Kent Regiment, 1914–1918*. Simpkin, Marshall, Hamilton, Kent & Co., London.

Atkinson, C.T. (1952) *The Royal Hampshire Regiment, 1914–1918*. Robert Maclehose & Co., Glasgow.

Atkinson, C.T. (2001) *The Devonshire Regiment, 1914–1918*. Naval and Military Press, Uckfield.

Atkinson, C.T. (2003) *Queen's Own Royal West Kent Regiment, 1914–1918*. Naval and Military Press, Uckfield.

Banks, Arthur (1998) *A Military Atlas of the First World War*. Pen and Sword Books, Barnsley.

Campbell, Christy (2007) *Band of Brigands*. Harper Collins, London.

Carver, Field Marshal Lord (2003) *The National Army Museum Book of the Turkish Front, 1914–1918*. Pan Books, London.

Chandler, Edmund (1919) *The Long Road to Baghdad*. Cassell, London.

Cochrane, T.A. (1995) *A Phoenix Rising*. Percydale Press, www.percydale.com.

Colledge, J.J. (1969) *Ships of the Royal Navy*. Greenhill Books, Barnsley.

Cotton, Vera E. (1924) *Durnford Memorial Book of the Great War*. Medici Society, London.

Dane, Edmund (1917) *British Campaigns in the Nearer East*. Hodder and Stoughton, London.

Draper, Jo (2001) *Dorchester Past*. Phillimore, Andover.

Farndale, Gen. Sir Martin (2003) *History of the Royal Regiment of Artillery, Western Front, 1914–1918*. Naval and Military Press, Uckfield.

Grey, Maj. W.E. (1929) *2nd City of London Regiment (Royal Fusiliers) in the Great War*

(1914–1918). Regimental Headquarters, London.

Holmes, Richard (1999) *The Western Front*. BBC Worldwide, London.

Marquis De Ruvigny (1922) *De Ruvigny's Roll of Honour: A Biographical Record of His Majesty's Military and Aerial Forces Who Fell in the Great War 1914–1918 (Military Rolls)*. Naval and Military Press, Uckfield.

Nicholson, G.W.L. (1962) *Official History of the Canadian Army in the First World War: Canadian Expeditionary Force 1914–1919*. Queens Printer and Controller of Stationery, Ottawa.

Penberthy, Maj. E. (1920) *An Account of the Training and Organisation of Snipers in the British Armies in France*. English Review, London.

Sayers, S. (1980) *'Ned' Herring – A Life of Lieutenant-General the Honourable Sir Edmund Herring*. Hyland House, Melbourne.

Steel, Nigel and Hart, Peter (1994) *Defeat at Gallipoli*. Macmillan, London.

Still, John (1920) *A Prisoner in Turkey*. John Lane, New York.

Terraine, John (2002) *The Western Front*. Pen and Sword Books, Barnsley.

Various authors (2002) *History of the Dorsetshire Regiment, 1914–1919*. Three volumes. Naval and Military Press, Uckfield.

Ward, S.G.P. (2005) *'Faithful': The Story of the DLI*. Naval and Military Press, Uckfield.

Westlake, Ray (1994) *British Battalions on the Somme*. Leo Cooper, Barnsley.

Wood, Maj. W. de B. (1925) *The History of the King's Shropshire Light Infantry 1914–1918*. Naval and Military Press, Uckfield.

Wylly, Col H.C. (1924) *The Border Regiment in the Great War*. Naval and Military Press, Uckfield.

Wyrall, Everard (2002) *History of the Somerset Light Infantry (Prince Albert's), 1914–1918*. Naval and Military Press, Uckfield.

Wyrall, E. (2003) *Gloucestershire Regiment in the War, 1914–1918*. Naval and Military Press, Uckfield.

Wyrall, Everard (2004) *History of the Duke of Cornwall's Light Infantry*. Naval and Military Press, Uckfield.

Websites

Ancestry – www.ancestry.co.uk
Battle-of-Jutland – www.battle-of-jutland.com
Canadian Great War Project – www.canadiangreatwarproject.com
Findmypast – www.findmypast.co.uk
First World War – www.firstworldwar.com
Hellfire Corner – www.hellfirecorner.co.uk
Historical Directories – www.historicaldirectories.org
Naval-History – www.Naval-History.net
The Long, Long Trail – www.1914-1918.net
The Wardrobe – www.thewardrobe.org.uk
U-Boat Net – www.uboat.net
Veterans Affairs Canada – www.veterans.gc.ca
Western Front Association – www.westernfrontassociation.com
World War One Photos – www.ww1photos.com

About the Author

Brian Bates has lived in Dorchester with his wife Doreen and two daughters for 41 years. His love of social and economic history was ignited by John Haley, an inspirational schoolmaster, and his particular passion for the history of Dorchester began when he wrote a thesis on the town's 17th-century economy. For him, 'real history' is the story of the ordinary person and their communities, especially when they find themselves in extraordinary predicaments. Brian gives talks on 17th-century Dorchester, and the effects of the Great War on the town, including one of its greatest secrets, the WW1 POW camp. His previous publications have included a transcription of the diary of William Whiteway, a 17th-century Dorchester merchant, and three military biographies. The author's royalties from this book will be donated to the charities Sense and Sightsavers.

Brian with his assistant researchers grandsons Jacob and George.

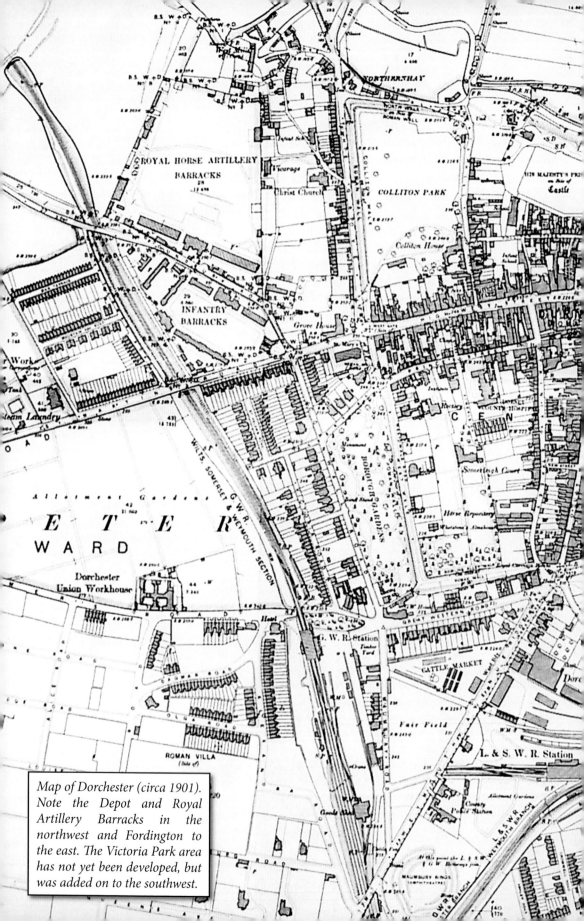

Map of Dorchester (circa 1901). Note the Depot and Royal Artillery Barracks in the northwest and Fordington to the east. The Victoria Park area has not yet been developed, but was added on to the southwest.

Index

Publisher's Note: this index has been condensed and therefore not all military units are necessarily listed or specified in full.

Other Roving Press Titles

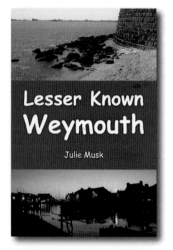

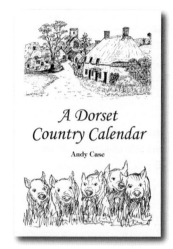

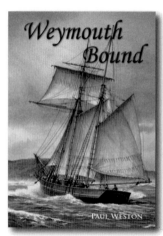

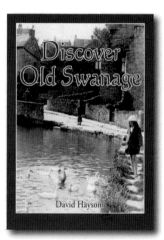

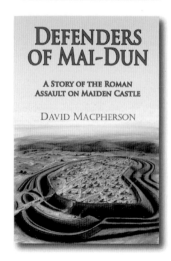

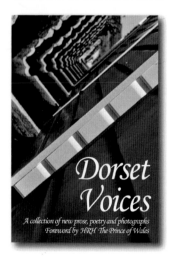

If you like exploring, you'll love our books